Economic Damages
in Intellectual Property

Economic Damages
in Intellectual Property

A Hands-on Guide to Litigation

EDITED BY DANIEL SLOTTJE

WILEY

John Wiley & Sons, Inc.

For general information on our other products and services, or technical support,
please contact our Customer Care Department within the United States at 800-762-2974,
outside the United States at 317-572-3993 or fax 317-572-4002.

Wiley also publishes its books in a variety of electronic formats. Some content that
appears in print may not be available in electronic books.

For more information about Wiley products, visit our Web site at http://www.wiley.com.

Library of Congress Cataloging-in-Publication Data:

ISBN-10: 0-471-79341-8 (cloth)
ISBN-13: 978-0-471-79341-0 (cloth)

Printed in the United States of America

10 9 8 7 6 5 4 3 2 1

This book is dedicated to my brother, Jason, with love.

Contents

About the Authors

Marc E. Ackerman

Marc E. Ackerman is a trial and appellate litigator who concentrates on intellectual property and commercial disputes. He is a partner at White & Case LLP in New York. Mr. Ackerman has handled a broad array of intellectual property disputes, including matters involving trademark, copyright, unfair competition, trade dress, trade secrets, rights of privacy/publicity, libel, and First Amendment. He regularly advises and litigates on behalf of clients in the media, sports and financial services industries, among others. Mr. Ackerman received his B.A. from Yale University, cum laude (1989) and his J.D., from New York University School of Law, cum laude (1992).

Ashok Ayyar

Ashok Ayyar graduated from Rice University with a B.A. in mathematical economic analysis. He currently works at the U.S. International Trade Commission, Office of Economics, where he analyzes cases of dumping and intellectual property infringement by imported goods.

Robert Basmann

Robert Basmann is a professor of economics at Binghamton University and Emeritus professor of economics at Texas A&M University. Professor Basmann was one of the pioneers in the development of modern econometrics with his path-breaking work on the estimation of simultaneous equation systems and finite sample distribution theory. Professor Basmann also was one of the first economists to introduce experimental economics into mainstream economic thought and did much of the original work on variable consumer preferences. His papers have appeared in *Econometrica* (numerous times), the *Journal of Econometrics,* the *Journal of the American Statistical Association,* and many others. He has directed dozens of dissertations and is a Fellow of the Econometric Society as well.

Jack B. Blumenfeld

Jack B. Blumenfeld is a partner at Morris Nichols. For the last 25 years, he has specialized in intellectual property litigation and other matters relating to patents, trade secrets, trademarks, and copyrights.

Michael Buchanan

Mike Buchanan is a Managing Director in FTI Consulting, Inc.'s Forensic practice in Dallas, Texas, where he provides economic and statistical analysis to clients involved in litigation, arbitration, mediation and other contexts where parties are engaged in complex business disputes. He specializes in providing advisory and expert witness services to clients involved in litigation matters and other matters involving economic analysis.

Felix Chan, Ph.D.

Felix Chan is Senior Lecturer in Economics and Finance at the Curtin University of Technology. He was previously an Australian Research Council Postdoctoral Fellow after receiving his Ph.D. degree with Distinction from the University of Western Australia in 2005. Dr. Chan has co-authored a number of articles in leading international journals in financial econometrics, risk management, tourism research, and intellectual property, including *Journal of Econometrics, Journal of Applied Econometrics, Scientometrics,* and *Environmental Modelling and Software.* He has co-authored a number of published articles modelling the trends and volatility in patents registered in the United States.

Michaelyn Corbett, Ph.D.

Michaelyn Corbett is a managing economist at LECG. She has extensive experience in economic analysis related to antitrust matters in litigation, especially in the healthcare industry, and intellectual property issues. Dr. Corbett received her Ph.D. in economics from the University of Illinois.

Scott W. Cragun

Scott W. Cragun is a manager in FTI Consulting, Inc.'s Forensic and Litigation Consulting practice in Salt Lake City, Utah. Mr. Cragun has over seven years of experience in financial and litigation consulting. His areas of expertise are damages analysis including lost profit, reasonable royalty, and other quantitative analysis involving intellectual property. He has also advised on unfair competition breach of contract and business interruption issues and conducted royalty audits. Mr. Cragun holds a B.S. in communication from the University of Utah and an M.B.A. from Brigham Young University.

Jesse David, Ph.D.

Jesse David is a vice president in NERA's Antitrust and Intellectual Property practices. At NERA, Dr. David provides consulting and expert testimony for clients with emphasis in the areas of competition analysis and damages estimation in patent infringement cases, antitrust matters, and other business disputes. Dr. David also conducts valuation analyses for intangible assets in the context of due diligence, insurance purchases, and litigation risk assessments. He has researched recent trends in patent litigation and the effects of litigation on patent value. Dr. David has written and spoken frequently on issues related to intellectual property, the calculations of economic damages, and other topics. Dr. David received his B.A. from Brandeis University and his Ph.D. from the Economics Department at Stanford University. Dr. David's graduate research focused on modeling markets for publicly provided services and associated aspects related to taxation and policy.

Stephen E. Dell

Stephen E. Dell is a manager in FTI Consulting, Inc.'s Forensic and Litigation Consulting practice in Houston, Texas. He is experienced in both financial and litigation consulting, primarily assisting clients with complex intellectual property damage analyses. Mr. Dell has experience in the entire litigation process, including discovery, complex damages/ financial analysis, report writing, and licensing. Mr. Dell holds a B.A. degree in Economics (emphasis in Finance) from the University of Texas at Austin.

Jeffrey A. Dubin, Ph.D.

Jeffrey A. Dubin is currently professor of economics at the California Institute of Technology, where he has been a faculty member since 1982. Dr. Dubin earned his undergraduate degree in economics with highest honors and great distinction from the University of California, Berkeley, and received a Ph.D. in economics from the Massachusetts Institute of Technology. Dr. Dubin's research focuses on microeconomic modeling with particular emphasis in applied econometrics. He is the author of numerous publications, including *Consumer Durable Choice and the Demand for Electricity*; *Studies in Consumer Demand— Econometric Methods Applied to Market Data*; *Empirical Studies in Applied Economics*; and *The California Energy Crisis: What, Why, and What's Next*. Dr. Dubin is also co-founding member and director of statistical and economic analysis at Pacific Economics Group in Pasadena.

Christopher Gerardi

Christopher Gerardi is a senior managing director in FTI's Forensic practice in New York. Mr. Gerardi has over 15 years of experience assisting companies and plaintiffs' and defendants' counsel with complex economic, financial, and accounting and litigation issues. He specializes in applied economic analysis and damage analyses as they relate to intellectual property, securities, business interruption, and commercial litigation matters. He has worked on numerous matters before U.S. federal and state courts as well as the International Chamber of Commerce, AAA, and other international forums and has provided expert witness testimony in commercial disputes. Prior to its acquisition by FTI, Mr. Gerardi was a partner in KPMG's Forensic Services practice, where he served as a member of the National Intellectual Property Leadership team and as the Northeast area leader for the intellectual property practice. Prior to joining KPMG, he was with Pricewaterhouse-Coopers' Financial Advisory Services division.

Mary B. Graham

Mary B. Graham is a partner at Morris Nichols, where she has litigated patent and other intellectual property matters for more than 20 years. Ms. Graham is a member of the District of Delaware Intellectual Property Advisory Committee and serves on the Delaware State Board of Education.

Lance E. Gunderson

Lance E. Gunderson is a senior managing director in FTI Consulting, Inc.'s Forensic and Litigation Consulting practice in Houston, Texas. He is experienced not only in financial and litigation consulting involving intellectual property damages but also other business consulting outside of litigation. He has testified numerous times in both state and federal court primarily regarding damages related to IP. Mr. Gunderson holds a B.S. degree in Business Administration (Finance emphasis) from Brigham Young University and an M.B.A. from Texas A&M University. He is an Accredited Valuation Analyst and a member of the Licensing Executives Society and the National Association of Certified Valuation Analysts.

Dawn Hall

Dawn Hall is a director in the Forensic and Litigation Consulting in FTI's New York Office. In that capacity, Ms. Hall provides dispute advisory and financial consulting services to attorneys and corporate clients. Her experience includes various business disputes across many industries. The focus of her over eight years of experience has been in assisting clients with complex financial, accounting, and damages matters in intellectual property disputes. Prior to its acquisition by FTI, Ms. Hall was a manager in KPMG's Forensic Services practice focusing primarily on intellectual property disputes. Prior to joining KPMG, she was with Arthur Andersen's Dispute and Advisory Services practice.

Blake Inglish

Blake Inglish, a director in FTI Consulting's Los Angeles office, has consulted on over 150 matters involving accounting, economic, financial, and valuation issues. He has spent over 10 years assisting businesses, government entities, and law firms in analyzing profits, costs, cash flows, market trends, valuations, relevant regulations and laws, and other necessary data. Mr. Inglish has experience testifying as an expert witness and has consulted attorneys across a wide variety of venues. These venues have included state and federal courts as well as matters decided by various panels such as the International Trade Commission (ITC) and the International Chamber of Commerce (ICC).

Esfandiar Maasoumi, Ph.D.

Esfandiar (Essie) Maasoumi is the Robert H. and Nancy Dedman Professor of Economics and adjunct professor of statistics at Southern Methodist University, Dallas, Texas. He is author and coauthor of more than 100 articles, reviews, and books, including special issues of *Journal of Econometrics* and *Econometric Reviews*. He has written theoretical and empirical papers in both economics and econometrics, and consults on law and economics issues. He received his B.S. (1972), M.S. (1973), and Ph.D. (1977) degrees from the London School of Economics. He is the editor of *Econometric Reviews* and on the board of the North American Free Trade Association. He is ranked thirty-seventh in the world in the Econometricians' Hall of Fame.

Michael McAleer, Ph.D.

Michael McAleer is Professor of Economics (Econometrics) at the University of Western Australia, Adjunct Professor in the Faculty of Science at the Australian National University,

Adjunct Professor in the Department of Economics and the Department of Mathematics and Statistics at the University of Canterbury, New Zealand, and Adjunct Professor at Ling Tung University, Taiwan. He has published more than 400 journal articles, chapters of books, monographs, edited books and edited special issues of journals in econometrics, financial econometrics, statistics, empirical finance, risk analysis and management, environmental modelling, tourism research, and intellectual property. He is an elected Fellow of the Academy of the Social Sciences in Australia and the International Environmental Modelling and Software Society.

Matthew G. Mercurio, Ph.D.
Matthew G. Mercurio is a director in the San Francisco office of FTI Consulting, Inc. Dr. Mercurio specializes in applying microeconomic analysis and rigorous econometrics to policymaking, regulatory issues, and public and private litigation. His particular areas of expertise include computation of economic damages in competitive practices, patent/intellectual property, and price-fixing litigation, the use of empirical methods in market definition, survey design, sampling, and survey analysis techniques. Dr. Mercurio has provided expert advice to legal counsel, businesses, trade associations, and government agencies. He has developed econometric models for survey analysis, competitive analysis, damage estimates, and cost modeling. Dr. Mercurio received his Ph.D. in economics from Princeton University in 1996. He also holds an M.A. in Economics from Princeton and a B.A. in economics in mathematics from Boston University.

Daniel Millimet, Ph.D.
Daniel Millimet is an associate professor of economics at Southern Methodist University. He received his Ph.D. in economics from Brown University in 1999 and his B.A. in economics from the University of Michigan in 1994. His research is primarily in the area of applied microeconometrics, with topics spanning environmental economics, labor economics, development economics, and international trade. He teaches courses in labor economics at the undergraduate, master's, and Ph.D. level and econometrics at the Ph.D. level.

Clarke B. Nelson
Clarke B. Nelson is a director in the FTI Forensic and Litigation Consulting practice and is based in Salt Lake City, Utah. Mr. Nelson specializes in damages and other quantitative analyses involving intellectual property disputes, including issues related to patents, trademarks, trade secrets, and license/royalty agreements as well as other general damages calculations. Mr. Nelson received a B.S. in accounting from Brigham Young University and an M.B.A. from the Wharton School, University of Pennsylvania, and is a Certified Public Accountant (licensed in Utah and Colorado).

Michael Nieswiadomy, Ph.D.
Michael Nieswiadomy, professor of economics at the University of North Texas, received his B.A. from the University of Dallas (1979) and his Ph.D. in economics from Texas A&M

University (1983). He has published in numerous prestigious journals. He has been a consultant to the U.S. President's Council of Environmental Quality, the Texas Natural Resources Conservation Commission, the Texas General Land Office, and the Harris-Galveston Coastal Subsidence District. He is a past president of the Dallas Economists' Club. His research expertise is in the areas of environmental and natural resource economics, labor and human resource economics, and econometrics, and he has received over $100,000 in research grants.

Daren M. Orzechowski

Daren Orzechowski is an intellectual property attorney with White & Case LLP in New York. Mr. Orzechowski represents clients in various industries, including electronics, entertainment, media, publishing, sports, and software. In addition to assisting clients in complex licensing transactions as well as intellectual property acquisitions and transfers, he represents clients in litigations involving issues of trademark, patent, copyright, trade secret, unfair competition, and libel law. Mr. Orzechowski received his B.A. from Tufts University (1996) and his J.D., cum laude, from Fordham University School of Law (1999).

Donald F. Parsons

The Honorable Donald F. Parsons was appointed to the Delaware Court of Chancery on October 22, 2003. Prior to his appointment, Vice Chancellor Parsons was a partner at Morris, Nichols, Arsht & Tunnell in Wilmington, Delaware, where he specialized in patent and other intellectual property litigation for 24 years.

Chase Perry

Chase Perry is a director in the FTI Forensic and Litigation Consulting practice and is based in Dallas, Texas. Mr. Perry has significant experience in providing financial and economic analysis related to the calculation of damages in disputes, particularly those involving intellectual property. He has been designated as an expert witness, filed expert reports, and given expert deposition testimony on damages issues.

Leslie A. Polizoti

Leslie A. Polizoti is an associate in the intellectual property group at Morris Nichols, where her practice focuses on patent litigation. In 2002 Ms. Polizoti served as an extern for the Honorable Randy J. Holland, Associate Justice of the Delaware Supreme Court.

Mohan Rao, Ph.D.

Mohan Rao is a director with LECG, an international economics and business consulting firm. He specializes in intellectual property, antitrust economics, and economic analysis in complex commercial disputes. His IP expertise includes valuation, business strategy, and the interplay between IP and antitrust issues. Dr. Rao is an author of the chapter on econometric analysis in the *Litigation Services Handbook,* a leading reference for economic and financial experts. He also teaches courses on valuing intellectual property at the Licensing Executives Society. Prior to LECG, Dr. Rao was a vice president with Charles

River Associates and a professor at UCLA. He has a B.S. in engineering from the University of Michigan, a predoctoral fellowship from Harvard University, and a Ph.D. from the University of Colorado.

Robin C. Sickles, Ph.D.

Robin C. Sickles is professor of economics and professor of statistics at Rice University. He received his B.S. in economics from the Georgia Institute of Technology in 1972 and his Ph.D. in economics from the University of North Carolina at Chapel in 1976. He is a member of the American Economics Association and the Econometric Society, is a fellow of the *Handbook of Economics* and the *Journal of Econometrics*, and is cited in *Who's Who in Economics, Who's Who in America, Who's Who in World*, and *Who's Who in Social Sciences Higher Education*. He has authored or coauthored more than 90 articles and papers and two books. He has held or holds senior editorial positions with the *Journal of Applied Econometrics, Communications in Statistics: Theory and Methods, Southern Economic Journal, Journal of Business and Economics Statistics, Journal of Econometrics, and Empirical Economics*. He is editor-in-chief of the *Journal of Productivity Analysis* and a director in the Houston office of LECG, LLC.

Daniel Slottje, Ph.D.

Daniel Slottje has provided consulting services to clients in various industries. He has significant experience in litigation consulting, including economic damages and statistical issues. In addition to advising counsel, he has provided testimony in these matters as well as in others. Dr. Slottje is a professor of economics at Southern Methodist University in Dallas, Texas, and a senior managing director with FTI Consulting. He has published more than 120 articles and written books on many economic issues.

Marion B. Stewart, Ph.D.

Marion B. Stewart is a senior vice president at NERA and chaired NERA's intellectual property practice between 1996 and 2006. His interest in the economics of intellectual property began with his doctoral dissertation on industrial research and development and has ranged from fundamental economic research on "preemptive innovation" to practical calculation of the value of patents and trademarks. His analysis of large-firm research and development rivalry, published in the *Quarterly Journal of Economics,* was a seminal investigation of the impact of mandatory licensing and other profit-sharing mechanisms on the rate of innovation. At NERA, his IP practice has focused on the valuation of patents and trademarks, consideration of the commercial success of patented inventions, and the calculation of economic damages resulting from alleged infringement. He has investigated the importance of IP in numerous industries.

Ryan Sullivan, Ph.D.

Ryan Sullivan is the chief economist of Quant Economics, Inc., and is an expert in economics, finance, and statistics. Dr. Sullivan applies his skills in three areas: litigation consulting, business consulting, and financial markets. On the litigation front, he provides expert economic analysis for disputes involving intellectual property and technology, antitrust and unfair competition, financial markets and services, and other commercial litigation. For businesses, Dr. Sullivan assists companies in licensing technology and valuing assets. In the financial markets arena, he develops and applies statistical models for active investors. Dr. Sullivan earned his B.A., M.A., and Ph.D. in economics from the University of California, San Diego. Dr. Sullivan is committed to research and analysis that consistently produces reliable results.

David Teece, Ph.D.

David Teece is an applied industrial organization economist who has studied and consulted on issues on technological change, technology transfer, and intellectual property for over two decades. He is the Mitsubishi Bank Professor at the Haas School of Business at University of California, Berkeley, where he also directs the Institute of Management, Innovation and Organization. He is also chairman of LECG, a publicly traded expert services firm. Professor Teece has a Ph.D. in economics from the University of Pennsylvania and has held teaching and research positions at Stanford University and Oxford University. He has authored over 150 books and articles including "When is Virtual Virtuous? Organizing for Innovation" (with Hank Chesbrough), "Profiting from Technological Innovation," and *Managing Intellectual Capital.*

Vincent A. Thomas

Vincent A. Thomas is a senior managing director in FTI's Forensic practice in Chicago and serves on FTI's National Intellectual Property Leadership team. He has over 15 years of experience assisting companies and plaintiffs' and defendants' counsel with complex economic, financial, accounting, and valuation issues and specializes in matters involving intellectual property including patent, copyright, trade secret, and trademark. He has conducted several complex studies of damages and on several occasions has provided expert testimony in U.S. federal and state courts as well as at arbitration. Prior to its acquisition by FTI, Mr. Thomas was a partner in KPMG's Forensic Services practice, where he served as a member of the National Intellectual Property Leadership team. Mr. Thomas has also served in corporate financial and management positions, including director and chief financial officer.

Introduction

This book is a "hands-on" guide to how economists, accountants, and financial analysts, interacting with attorneys and their clients, quantify damages in litigation matters involving intellectual property (IP) matters. In this arena of pure applied microeconomics, statistics and econometrics are playing an ever-increasing role. Patent activity in the United States has grown at remarkable levels in the past 20 years (as can be seen in Chapter 2). Concurrent with the filing of new patents has been an attendant increase in the level of IP litigation. In an effort to promote greater uniformity in certain areas of federal jurisdiction and to relieve the pressure on the dockets of the Supreme Court and the courts of appeals for the regional circuits, Congress in 1982 established the U.S. Court of Appeals for the Federal Circuit. This court assumed the jurisdiction of the U.S. Court of Customs and Patent Appeals and the appellate jurisdiction of the U.S. Court of Claims. As a result, a relatively new field of expertise has arisen, that of the IP economic damages expert. Damages expertise has become the purview of economists, accountants, financial analysts, and attorneys alike. This book presents an overview of how individuals in this field, working alone or as members of a multidisciplinary team, evaluate and ultimately quantify economic damages in various types of IP matters. The book should be of interest to anyone interested in this burgeoning field, both from an academic and/or career path perspective. In addition, attorneys will find this book useful; they are the end users of this talent pool, as they need experts to quantify damages in their cases. In addition, many attorneys are serving as damages experts themselves, so the book might be particularly useful to them. The contributors to this book are a diverse group of intellectual property professionals including attorneys, economics professors, certified public accounts, and others who consider themselves to be experts on economics damages or to be damages professionals.

It is very important to note that all of the opinions in this book represent the views of the particular author or team of coauthors who rendered those opinions. A fundamental pillar of academic freedom is that each individual scholar must by necessity have the right to express his or her views in an unfettered and uncensored way. As the editor of this book,

I do not necessarily agree with any or all of the views of all the contributors; likewise, they may well not agree with any or all of my views on the appropriate way to quantify damages in any particular IP matter. It is left to the reader to evaluate the various methods for damages quantification and to determine which method(s) are most sound for the problem at hand. Concurrently, the views expressed by the individual contributors do not necessarily reflect those of the organizations for which they work, or for other individuals affiliated with the same organization. The discussions in many of the chapters are of a general nature and frequently are for illustrative purposes only. They are not intended to address the specific circumstances of any individual or entity. Each case is different and should be evaluated in light of its own facts. In specific circumstances, the services of a professional should be sought. In the chapters by my coauthors and me, the views and opinions are solely ours and do not reflect any opinions of FTI Consulting, Inc. or its clients as to the proper measure of damages.

Chapter 1, by Chase Perry, Elizabeth Whitaker, and me, discusses the evolution of case law pertaining to the calculation of economic damages in patent infringement matters in the United States. This chapter is not intended as a representation of giving legal opinions. The cases are presented from the perspective of damages expert, not as a legal opinion or treatise. Studying how court decisions have evolved in the context of the analysis of economic damages in disputes over patents reveals that economic theory, although sometimes applied imprecisely, has come to be of paramount importance in the valuation of IP and the calculation of economic damages.

In **Chapter 2,** Felix Chan and Michael McAleer describe graphically and empirically trends and patterns in the level and growth of patent activity in the United States over time, with additional statistical information on worldwide patent activity. The purpose of registering patents in the United States (and elsewhere) is to protect the intellectual property of the innovators and rightful owners. Although this book is primarily concerned with the quantification of economic damages in IP matters, it is important to understand U.S. trends in patent activity over time to be able to discern the patenting "basis" from whence innovation arises and for which protection requirements may increase over time, fueling the causal nexus for litigation over time.

Chapter 3, by intellectual property attorneys Marc Ackerman and Daren Orzechowski, presents trademark law as it pertains to economic damages. The chapter educates the reader on the history and purpose of American trademark law, the current law of trademarks in the United States as it relates to infringement and damages, and the legal bases for calculating trademark infringement damages. The authors discuss the origins of trademark law and the dual benefit that it provides to trademark owners as well as consumers. This background serves to increase the reader's understanding of how goodwill is captured in trademarks and the scope of trademark rights. It also provides an overview of some of the basic terminology that may be encountered in analyzing trademarks, including a discussion of the varying levels of strength, and corresponding value, that a mark may possess. Finally, the authors provide an overview of the federal law regarding trademark infringement and the economic recovery to which a successful litigant may be entitled.

Chapter 4, by Donald Parsons, Jack Blumenfeld, Mary Graham, and Leslie Polizoti, presents an interesting discussion on how litigants may select a venue in patent disputes and how some courts have become magnets for attracting patent litigation. The authors focus on Delaware, which seems to be heavily involved in patent litigation. This venue is interesting because it does not appear to favor litigants of either persuasion in its trial outcomes yet attracts a lot of patent litigation. The authors offer several interesting hypotheses on why Delaware has attracted so many patent cases.

Chapter 5, by Chase Perry, Clarke Nelson, and Elizabeth Whitaker, presents some interesting discussions on how experts may disagree about particular aspects of a damages methodology or about the underlying assumptions of the economics damages quantification process in determining reasonable economic damages.

Chapter 6, by Vincent A. Thomas, Christopher Gerardi, and Dawn Hall, discusses the fact that, in patent litigation, the guiding principle in computing damages is that of "adequately compensating" the patent owner for the infringement. Such adequate compensation can be measured in different ways, one of which being the profits that a patent holder has lost as a result of the infringer's presence in the marketplace. The authors identify certain measures of profits lost by the infringer, provide an explanation of the methodology behind such measures including case examples, and comment on factors one should consider when claiming such measures

Chapter 7, by Robert Basmann, Michael Buchanan, Esfandiar Massoumi, and me, notes that in many lost profit cases, the *Panduit* factors are invoked. A proper analysis requires the practitioner to adhere to the well-known economic principles embodied in the law of demand. Although "the law of demand" is easy enough to understand, some of the exceptions and dynamics that arise in its use, as well as the conceptual disputes, are not as generally well understood. It is important to have a strong grounding in the basic concepts of demand and supply in order to fully understand how to model and quantify damages in lost profit matters.

Chapter 8, by Ryan Sullivan, discusses the notion that in real-world markets, prices and quantities are jointly determined. However, in patent litigation, Dr. Sullivan argues this fundamental economic principle is often ignored. He uses a hypothetical patent infringement suit in the ice cream industry to demonstrate what he refers to as a "holistic approach" to patent damages analysis. His approach argues that patent infringement can have an effect on prices, quantities, and other economic factors, such as product substitution. His analysis illustrates what he considers appropriate methods for implementing a holistic approach that addresses these factors and the impact they have on profits.

Chapter 9, by Jesse David and Marion Stewart, addresses the situation that arises when a party accused of infringing a patent contends that the asserted patent is invalid because of obviousness. The authors note that to help evaluate that issue, courts may consider whether the patented invention is a "commercial success." Determining whether an invention has, or has not, been a commercial success is primarily an economic exercise and can be tested, and economists increasingly assist courts in evaluating this issue. This chapter discusses these economic tests and considers them alongside another test suggested by economic principles, namely, whether the patented invention has earned or can be expected to earn a positive net return on invested capital after accounting for all the relevant costs associated with developing and commercializing the product. The authors, both economists, analyze the commercial success standard in the context of two recent cases in which they applied these principles.

Chapter 10, also by Vincent Thomas, Christopher Gerardi, and Dawn Hall, presents a thorough discussion of how one quantifies or determines a reasonable royalty in a patent infringement matter, including a complete discussion of the well-known *Georgia-Pacific* case.

Chapter 11, by Lance Gunderson, Stephen Dell, and Scott Cragun, explores how a party seeking reasonable royalty damages may use various techniques as support for a contended reasonable royalty. One of the methods to support a reasonable royalty analysis, the analytical approach, is a way to value the benefit or excess profits of the patented feature(s) of a product relative to a normal rate of return or the profit generated by a prior product or what is common in a given industry or company profits. Determining whether the facts support the use of the analytical approach is critical; otherwise other methods may be more appropriate. The authors argue that case law is not entirely clear on the approach and that it may be applied inappropriately. They discuss the traditional elements of the analytical approach that lead to its application in determining a reasonable royalty and also analyze a recent case in which this approach was used in context of a reasonable royalty calculation.

Chapter 12, by Jeffrey Dubin, explores the situation when intangible technology assets have value arising from proprietary knowledge, processes, or methods that provide competitive advantages through product differentiation or favorable cost structures. The purpose of the chapter is to calculate a royalty rate for a technology intangible asset using economic analysis of quasi-comparables. The method calculates what consumers would be willing to pay for a patented feature embodied in a consumer good. Analyzing products, with and without the patented feature, allows quasi-comparability even in situations where true comparable sales do not exist. The author demonstrates that market information can establish an upper bound to the royalty and profit rate attributable to a technology intangible. Finally, Professor Dubin applies this model to a computer CPU upgrade technology used in the early 1990s.

Chapter 13, by Esfandiar Maasoumi and Matthew Mercurio, explains that while the use of statistics (particularly survey methods) in copyright and trademark matters continues to grow, statistics has seen far less use in patent cases. However, elementary statistics can be a powerful tool in investigation of patent liability. Of course, as in other fields where applied statistics are used, statistics are just as often misused. The authors' analysis illustrates how statistics can be used as well as some pitfalls and potential misuses of statistics in conceptualizing the "similarity" of two products, and possible solutions.

Chapter 14, by Daniel Millimet, Michael Nieswiadomy, and me, describes the general logic of hypothesis testing and illustrates how this tool and others from the field of statistics can be used to determine the impact of an important explanatory variable in an actual copyright infringement case. The field of econometrics is essentially a branch of applied statistics, but one being practiced by individuals who are also trained economists. We demonstrate that rigorous econometric techniques can play an important role in intellectual property rights cases to assist the judge or jury in determining the level, if any, of damages to award.

Chapter 15, by Blake Inglish, discusses the fact that in a time of increasing reliance on intellectual property, trademarks have become a key component in the successful strategy of many businesses. Trademark applications filed with the United States Patent and Trademark Office (USPTO) have nearly doubled in the past 10 years. A basic understanding of trademarks as well as relevant damages considerations can be of tremendous benefit to companies that rely on these forms of IP to identify their products or services as well as to the firms that assist them in resolving trademark disputes.

Chapter 16, also by Jeffrey Dubin, looks at one approach to splitting the profits between owners and users of a trademark, the 25 percent rule. This rule of thumb states that typically one-quarter to one-third of the profit should be apportioned to the licensor for the use of the trademarked product. Professor Dubin suggests that regardless of the validity of the rule, it is commonly cited and applied in the licensing community. The chapter develops an econometric estimate of the trademark fraction based on an economic analysis of trademark value. Trademark fractions determined for five products using econometric demand analysis show considerable variation and are generally much larger than the 25 percent rule would suggest.

Chapter 17, by Robin Sickles and Ashok Ayyar, presents a case study of a matter, *AAA v. BBB,* handled by the first author, in which trade secret information was allegedly misappropriated. Reviewing the case record brought to light problems that existed in the preparation of damages claims. By flagging these issues in practicum, the study outlined and explored in this chapter should serve as a guide to the trade secrets aspect of intellectual property damages claims. The authors begin with what they believe is a strategy and method for building a sound damages model and then annotate their findings.

Finally, **Chapter 18,** by Michealyn Corbett, Mohan Rao, and David Teece, presents a broad overview of what a trademark is and how to quantify damages in a matter involving trademarks. These authors, all economists, present a different perspective on trademark damages from the one presented in Chapter 15 by Blake Inglish, who is a CPA. This chapter outlines how a trademark is a distinctive word, phrase, name, or symbol that is used in commerce to indicate the source of a good or service and to distinguish it from the goods or services of others. Like patents, trademarks can constitute a significant portion of a firm's asset value; therefore, they need to be strategically developed and protected. This chapter provides a primer on trademarks and trademark valuation. The authors also discuss their take on the economic principles of licensing and describe some of the commonly used approaches to trademark valuation, particularly in the context of licensing trademarks.

January 25, 2006

DANIEL SLOTTJE
Dallas, Texas

Economic Damages
in Intellectual Property

PART ONE

IP Law on Economic Damages

CHAPTER 1

U.S. Case Law and Economic Damages in Patent Litigation

CHASE PERRY
FTI Consulting, Inc.

DANIEL SLOTTJE
SMU and FTI Consulting, Inc.

ELIZABETH WHITAKER
Bracewell & Giuliani LLP

This chapter discusses significant case law pertaining to the calculation of economic damages in patent infringement matters in the United States. Understanding how court decisions have evolved in the context of the analysis of economic damages in disputes over patents reveals that economic theory, although sometimes applied imprecisely, has come to be of paramount importance in the valuation of intellectual property and the calculation of economic damages.

INTRODUCTION

This chapter traces the development of case law in the United States as it pertains to the quantification of economic damages in litigation matters involving patent disputes. Patent law is a distinct and (relatively speaking) quite complex branch of the body of case law in the United States. As this case law has evolved for patent infringement, damages remedies have also evolved. Use of economic theory in quantifying the "economic damage" from patent infringement has been widely used (and sometimes misused). This chapter surveys the legal developments of this branch of U.S. case law and briefly shows how economic concepts have shaped what is accepted in quantifying damages. This chapter is intended as a brief introduction to these cases for several reasons. First, this book is not a legal treatise; it is an introduction to damages issues and quantification methodologies, which rely on the law to shape how damages are quantified. Second, several of the most significant legal cases (e.g., *Panduit* and *Georgia-Pacific*) are discussed in much more detail in various chapters of this book but must of course be mentioned here. Thus, the primary purpose of this chapter is to provide the practitioner with a relatively straightforward guide to understanding these key legal cases (and their damages ramifications); the interested reader is strongly urged to read the case law to get a deeper understanding of the legal and economics of the cited matters.

The foundation of the body of case law regarding patent infringement damages is, of course, the U.S. patent statutes, now contained in Title 35 of the United States Code. There have been four major iterations of the U.S. statutes dealing with patent laws. The damages provisions from these statutes follow.

Patent Act of 1790, Ch. 7, 1 Stat. 109-112, Sec. 4 (April 10, 1790):

> And be it further enacted, That if any person or persons shall devise, make, construct, use, employ, or vend within these United States, any art, manufacture, engine, machine or device, or any invention or improvement upon, or in any art, manufacture, engine, machine or device, the sole and exclusive right of which shall be so as aforesaid granted by patent to any person or persons, by virtue and in pursuance of this act, without the consent of the patentee or patentees, their executors, administrators or assigns, first had and obtained in writing, every person so offending, shall forfeit and pay to the said patentee or patentees, his, her or their executors, administrators or assigns such damages as shall be assessed by a jury, and moreover shall forfeit to the person aggrieved, the thing or things so devised, made, constructed, used, employed or vended, contrary to the true intent of this act, which may be recovered in an action on the case founded on this act.

Patent Act of 1836, Ch. 357, 5 Stat. 117, Sec. 14 (July 4, 1836):

> And be it further enacted, That whenever, in any action for damages for making, using, or selling the thing whereof the exclusive right is secured by any patent heretofore granted, or by any patent which may hereafter be granted, a verdict shall be rendered for the plaintiff in such action, it shall be in the power of the court to render judgment for any sum above the amount found by such verdict as the actual damages sustained by the plaintiff, not exceeding three times the amount hereof, according to the circumstances of the case, with costs; and such damages may be recovered by action on the case in any court of competent jurisdiction, to be brought in the name or names of the person or persons interested, whether as patentees, assignees, or as grantees of the exclusive right within and throughout a specified part of the United States.

Patent Act of 1870, Ch. 230, 16 Stat. 198-217, Sec. 55 (July 8, 1870):

> And be if further enacted, That all actions, suits, controversies, and cases arising under the patent laws of the United States shall be originally cognizable, as well in equity as at law, by the circuit courts of the United States, or any district court having the powers and jurisdiction of a circuit court, or by the supreme court of the District

of Columbia, or of any Territory; and the court shall have power, upon bill in equity filed by any party aggrieved, to grant injunctions according to the course and principles of courts of equity, to prevent the violation of any right secured by patent, on such terms as the court may deem reasonable; and upon a decree being rendered in any such case for an infringement, the claimant [complainant] shall be entitled to recover, in addition to the profits to be accounted for by the defendant, the damages the complainant has sustained thereby, and the court shall assess the same or cause the same to be assessed under its direction, and the court shall have the same powers to increase the same in its discretion that are given by this act to increase the damages found by verdicts in actions upon the case; but all actions shall be brought during the term for which the letters-patent shall be granted or extended, or within six years after the expiration thereof.

Patent Act of 1952, Ch. 950, 66 Stat. 792, Sec. 283 to 286 (July 19, 1952) (codified as 35 U.S.C. Sec. 283 to 286):

The several courts having jurisdiction of cases under this title may grant injunctions in accordance with the principles of equity to prevent the violation of any right secured by patent, on such terms as the court deems reasonable. Upon finding for the claimant the court shall award the claimant damages adequate to compensate for the infringement, but in no event less than a reasonable royalty for the use made of the invention by the infringer, together with interest and costs as fixed by the court. When the damages are not found by a jury, the court shall assess them. In either event the court may increase the damages up to three times the amount found or assessed. Increased damages under this paragraph shall not apply to provisional rights under section 154 (d) of this title. The court may receive expert testimony as an aid to the determination of damages or of what royalty would be reasonable under the circumstances. The court in exceptional cases may award reasonable attorney fees to the prevailing party. Except as otherwise provided by law, no recovery shall be had for any infringement committed more than six years prior to the filing of the complaint or counterclaim for infringement in the action. In the case of claims against the United States Government for use of a patented invention, the period before bringing suit, up to six years, between the date of receipt of a written claim for compensation by the department or agency of the Government having authority to settle such claim, and the date of mailing by the Government of a notice to the claimant that his claim has been denied shall not be counted as part of the period referred to in the preceding paragraph.

Each statute in succession has sought to canonize the existing state of the case law of the day. The theories of recovery have evolved:

1790 Act: Damages plus forfeiture of infringing articles →

1836 Act: Damages up to three times that found by a jury plus costs →

1870 Act: Injunction, infringer's profits, damages up to three times that found by a jury →

1952 Act: Injunction, damages adequate to compensate, but no less than a reasonable royalty up to three times that found by the court or a jury, reasonable attorneys' fees, all limited to six years prior to filing suit.

Although the 1952 Patent Act omitted language providing for recovery of the infringer's profit, Congress otherwise intended the statute to be broad. The United States Court of Appeals for the Federal Circuit, which maintains jurisdiction for patent appeals, was established in 1982. This was supposed to ensure uniformity and predictability in the case law involving all aspects of patent law but has perhaps only succeeded in the area of damages.

The patent statute has been defined, modified, trimmed, and sometimes extended through the case law. We now discuss these changes as they have evolved in law and impacted the quantification of economic damages, focusing on four main areas of interest: lost profits, price erosion, the entire market value rule, and the law as it pertains to the economic determination of a reasonable royalty.

LOST PROFITS

Tektronix, Inc. v. United States, 552 F.2d 343 (Ct. Cl. 1977)

Although this is an eminent domain case, it sheds some light on what is meant by "profit." The court deducted (in the context of a reasonable royalty determination using the analytical method, to be discussed in the "Reasonable Royalty" section of this chapter and in Chapter 11) actual and allocated costs, including direct and indirect costs such as variable manufacturing cost, fixed burden, marketing and administrative costs.

Panduit Corp. v. Stahlin Brothers Fibre Works, Inc., 575 F.2d 1152 (6th Cir. 1978)

This case is considered to be the bedrock or guidepost of rulings on lost profit damages. The court established a four-prong basis for the awarding of lost profits in a patent infringement case. That is, the court held that a plaintiff seeking lost profits damages must prove demand for its patented product, the absence of acceptable noninfringing substitutes, sufficient manufacturing and marketing capability to exploit the demand, and the amount of the profit lost. Both the weight given to each of the four factors and the proof requirements for each of the factors have changed over time. A more complete discussion of these issues is given in Chapter 6.

Hanson v. Alpine Valley Ski Area, Inc., 718 F.2d 1075 (Fed. Cir. 1983)

This case makes it clear that "damages adequate to compensate" in the patent statute means lost profits if they are able to be determined.

Paper Converting Machine Company v. Magna-Graphics Corporation, 745 F.2d 11 (Fed. Cir. 1984)

This case confirms that lost profits awards are made on the basis of incremental profit, which excludes fixed costs from the analysis.

Kori Corp. v. Wilco Marsh Buggies & Draglines, Inc., 761 F.2d 649 (Fed. Cir. 1985)

In this case the court found the use of lost profits for compensation appropriate because Kori would have sold or rented the machines built by Wilco were it not for Wilco's infringement. Wilco argued that there were noninfringing substitutes available, but the court concluded that Wilco directly competed with Kori and that, from a buyer's perspective, the only acceptable substitute for the patented Kori machines was the infringing Wilco machines. Further, although the patent statue had been amended to omit language providing for recovery of the infringer's profit, this does not mean that the fact of the infringer's profits cannot be considered in the process of estimating plaintiff's damages.

State Industries, Inc. v. Mor-Flo Industries, Inc., 883 F.2d 1573 (Fed. Cir. 1989)

This case directly amends the *Panduit* case discussed earlier by allowing for the recovery of lost profits damages even if more than two parties (a duopoly) operated and competed in a market. So under *Panduit* factor two, even if noninfringing substitutes or alternatives are available, by parsing the market based on market share, lost profits can still be awarded.

BIC Leisure Products, Inc. v. Windsurfing Int'l, Inc., 1 F.3d 1214 (Fed. Cir. 1993)

This case also served as a refinement of the *Panduit* test. *Panduit* factor 1, "demand for the patented product," was clarified to mean demand in a particular market with respect to price and income elasticities of demand. While the patent holder and alleged infringer both made and sold wind surfing equipment, the court found that one produced the machines for the low end of the market (meaning it sold its machines at relatively lower prices) and one company marketed and sold its machines for the high end of the market (it sold it machines at higher prices). The court ruled that if the patent owner competes in a different market segment from the infringer, it is unlikely that the patent owner has lost any sales or profits due to the infringement.

King Instruments Corp. v. Perego, 65 F.3d 941 (Fed. Cir. 1995)

The court ruled that a patentee may recover lost profits for infringement even where the patentee has never made, used, or sold a device embodying the infringed patent. The court awarded lost profits to a patentee for lost sales of a device that was not covered by the patent at issue in the suit. This decision was important because it suggested that when calculating "but for" (what sales would have been, "but for" the infringement) lost profits in a patent infringement case, the patent holder is not required actually to make the product with the patented features, just a product that competes with the infringing product. This decision was extended in *Rite-Hite,* discussed later in the section entitled "Entire Market Value Rule."

Grain Processing Corp. v. Am. Maize-Products Co., 185 F.3d 1341 (Fed. Cir. 1999)

This case deals with the question of availability, more specifically the question of patent infringement involving a product that may or may not have an available substitute currently on the market. This case expanded the doctrine of *Panduit* factor 2 regarding the availability of noninfringing substitutes. This case expanded the scope of the "but for" rule to include actions that both the patent holder and the infringer *could* have taken "but for" the infringement. In this instance, the infringer used the existence of a noninfringing alternative that was not on the market, but was available to be used, to defeat the lost profits claim.

Crystal Semiconductor Corp. v. Tritec Microelectronics, Int'l, Inc., 246 F.3d 1336 (Fed. Cir. 2001)

In tackling competing versions of the product(s) at issue, regarding calculations of the market shares of the parties, the court stated: "To show 'but for' causation and entitlement to lost profits, a patentee must reconstruct the market to show, hypothetically, 'likely outcomes with infringement factored out of the economic picture.'" Particular attention needs to be paid to market segments such as were considered in *BIC Leisure Products* as well as geographic differences in market share. Finally, the infringer's share must be factored out of the equation when calculating a "but for" market share for the patent owner.

PRICE EROSION

Yale Lock Manufacturing Co. v. Sargent, 117 U.S. 536 (1886)

When attempting to quantify lost profits, economic damages under the lost profits rubric should include the effects of price changes on lost profits. If the patent owner could have sold products embodying the patent for a higher price, the defendant is liable for the difference between the "but for" price and the actual price. This is what is meant by "price erosion": the market price has been lowered by the infringement.

LAM Inc. v. Johns-Manville Corp., 718 F.2d 1056 (Fed. Cir. 1983)

The case makes it clear that "but for" means the determination of a "but for" world would have occurred with reasonable probability, and the patent owner need not prove its damages to a certainty. This opened the door to many forms of econometric analysis that do not seek to "prove" the level of economic damages but instead seek to "explain" or account for, to a specified degree of statistical significance, what probable damages would be.

Brooktree Corp. v. Advanced Micro Devices, Inc., 977 F.2d 1555 (Fed. Cir. 1992)

The Federal Circuit upheld an award of lost profits based on price erosion because of evidence presented by Brooktree that it was forced to reduce its prices when AMD *announced* its chips at lower prices. Therefore, "but for" the infringement, Brooktree would have continued to sell its chips at its established prices. This is another minor expansion of the "but for" rule to compensate a patent owner for prospective, defensive price erosion.

Crystal Semiconductor Corp. v. Tritec Microelectronics, Int'l, Inc., 246 F.3d 1336 (Fed. Cir. 2001)

In addition to its treatment of lost profits concepts discussed in the "Lost Profits" section, the *Crystal Semiconductor* case also made clear that in calculating economic damages under a price erosion theory, the damages expert should be careful of the "law of demand" and its implications, as discussed in Chapter 7. An award of lost profits using a higher "but for" price than the actual price at which the infringer sold accused products will normally imply that fewer "but for" units were sold.

ENTIRE MARKET VALUE RULE

Paper Converting Machine Company v. Magna-Graphics Corporation, 745 F.2d 11 (Fed. Cir. 1984)

In addition to the preceding discussion regarding lost profits, this case defined the concept of recovery of damages under an "entire market value rule." This rule allows for the recovery of damages based on the value of an entire apparatus containing several features, when the feature patented constitutes the basis for customer demand. It is the "financial and marketing dependence on the patented item under standard marketing procedures" that determines whether the nonpatented features of a product are compensable. ". . . Physical joinder or separation" is not what determines whether nonpatented items are compensable.

Rite-Hite Corp. v. Kelley Co., Inc., 56 F.3d 1538 (Fed. Cir. 1995)

The patented item or process must drive the sale of the entire product for nonpatented components to be included in the lost profits award. If this requirement is met, then one must further determine whether the components are sold together as a commercial unit, and if so, whether this is out of necessity or convenience. If the components are sold as a commercial unit out of necessity, then they should be part of the lost profits award. If only sold together out of convenience, the nonpatented components should not be part of the award.

Stryker Corp. v. Intermedics Orthopedics Inc., 96 F.3d 1409 (Fed. Cir. 1996)

This case expanded the opportunity to get lost profits. That is, the court ruled that lost profits damages are appropriate on an entire product even where the infringing item is optional for the customer and not always used, when the optional item is always sold with the product. The harm to the patent holder occurs when the infringing sale is made, not when the infringing item is used.

Fonar Corp. v. General Electric Co., 107 F.3d 1543 (Fed. Cir. 1997)

This case clarified the "entire market value rule" in that it allows for recovery of damages based on value of entire apparatus containing several features, even though only one feature is patented, when the patented feature is the basis for customer demand for the entire machine.

Tec Air v. Denso Manufacturing Michigan Inc., 192 F.3d 1353 (Fed. Cir. 1999)

This case makes it clear that customer behavior is the determining factor in an entire market value rule case. The court was swayed here by the fact that performance and price of the entire assembly were what customers cared about and that the patented method was necessary to meet a certain product specification. Moreover, when the infringer changed this specification, a customer complained.

Micro Chemical, Inc. v. Lextron, Inc. and Turnkey Computer Systems, Inc., 317 F.3d 1387 (Fed. Cir. 2003)

The court confirmed that even when circumstances do not permit the consideration of nonpatented items in the royalty base, they should be taken into account in the royalty rate determination.

REASONABLE ROYALTY

Columbia Wire Co. v. Kokomo Steel & Wire Co., 194 F. 108 (C.C.A. 1911)

This case makes it clear that the existence of noninfringing alternatives impacts the extent of damages. Because the value of a patented product is only in its superiority over the prior art, it would be a windfall to the patent owner to award damages on anything more than the added effectiveness of the infringing product over products embodying the prior art.

Aro Manufacturing Co. v. Convertible Top Replacement Co., 377 U.S. 476 (1964)

The court held that when a patent owner releases a direct infringer from liability in exchange for an amount that it would have received if it had licensed the patent, it is not entitled to anything more than nominal damages from a contributory infringer. That is, if the patent owner collected a sufficient amount to cover damages for the infringement, it cannot collect actual damages from a party liable only for contributing to the same infringement.

Georgia-Pacific Corp. v. U.S. Plywood Corp., 318 F. Supp. 1116 (S.D.N.Y. 1970)

An analysis of a reasonable royalty rate in patent litigation typically incorporates consideration of all relevant and reliable economic and qualitative factors. In *Georgia-Pacific,* the court enumerated 15 separate factors to consider when determining a reasonable royalty. This case is discussed in much more detail in Chapter 10. The factors address issues regarding comparable royalty rates, the parties, the prospective license, the technology, and the products embodying the allegedly infringing technology. These issues inform the amount of a reasonable royalty arrived at between the parties in a hypothetical negotiation that takes place just before the alleged infringement occurred.

Tektronix, Inc. v. United States, 552 F.2d 343 (Ct. Cl. 1977)

Again, although this is an eminent domain case, some of the analysis is generally applicable. The court adopted the willing-buyer/willing-seller concept and utilized what has come to be known as the "analytical approach" in reasonable royalty calculations. The analytical approach determines the excess profit the infringer was able to make through use of the patented invention and awards it to the patent owner as a reasonable royalty. See Gunderson et al. in Chapter 11 for a broader discussion.

Ellipse Corp. v. Ford Motor Co., 461 F. Supp. 1354 (N.D. Ill. 1978)

The court explained the hypothetical negotiation in this way: "A willing buyer for a patent license must make a decision as to the maximum he can pay as a royalty for the patented item and still be better off than choosing an available alternative. Similarly, the willing seller must make a decision as to the minimum royalty he can accept from a prospective buyer and still be better off than choosing an alternative course of action."

TWM Manufacturing Co., Inc. v. Dura Corp., 789 F.2d 895 (Fed Cir. 1986)

The court found that the reasonable royalty computation was within the discretion of the court, even though it did not separately evaluate each of the *Georgia-Pacific* factors. The special master instead used the "analytical approach" based on *Georgia-Pacific* and *Tektronix* to estimate the incremental profit margin the infringer made from using the patented invention. Also, the court noted that the presence of a competing product does not necessarily amount to an acceptable substitute—the substitute must have "all beneficial characteristics of the patented device."

Fromson v. Western Litho Plate & Supply Co., 853 F.2d 1568 (Fed. Cir. 1988)

This case cautions courts about the limitations of a reasonable royalty based on a hypothetical negotiation between a willing buyer and willing seller. Specifically, there is a danger that this framework is an incentive to large corporations to infringe at will, to the detriment of individual inventors who can only ask at trial for the reasonable royalty that it should have received in the first place. Courts should ensure that the resulting award is truly "adequate to compensate" and "reasonable" rather than engaging in rigid and dogmatic calculation exercises.

Slimfold Mfg. Co., Inc. v. Kinkead Industries, Inc., 932 F.2d 1453 (Fed. Cir. 1991)

The case recognizes that damages can be broader than a reasonable royalty, as they were not the only damages which the trial court awarded. The District Court also awarded all profits that Kinkead realized in the form of manufacturing cost savings.

Mahurkar v. C.R. Bard, Inc., 79 F.3d 1572 (Fed. Cir. 1996)

This case makes it clear that there is no basis for the concept of "royalty for the infringer" (sometimes known as a litigation kicker) merely because of the infringement or because of litigation expenses. To account for concerns over the infringement itself, the patent statute sets forth statutory requirements for awards of enhanced damages. To account for concerns over litigation expenses, the patent statute sets forth provisions for the award of attorney's fees. These awards require clear and convincing proof of willfulness and exceptionality.

Maxwell v. J. Baker, Inc., 86 F.3d 1098 (Fed. Cir. 1996)

This case further explains *Mahurkar* by holding that additional damages, if necessary to adequately compensate the patent holder, can be awarded in addition to a reasonable royalty. Examples of situations where such additional compensation would be warranted are when the infringer's activities have caused the patent owner's licensing program to suffer and when the patent owner had a strong policy of not licensing its patents.

Minco, Inc. v. Combustion Engineering Inc., 95 F.3d 1109 (Fed. Cir. 1996)

The court stated, "Because fashioning an adequate damages award depends on the unique economic circumstances of each case, the trial court has discretion to make important subsidiary determinations in the damages trial, such as choosing a methodology to calculate damages." The case involved a reasonable royalty award based on the sale of processed material produced by the patented machine.

Grain Processing Corp. v. Am. Maize-Products Co., 185 F.3d 1341 (Fed. Cir. 1999)

In addition to the lost profits implications discussed above, this case also offers insight into what makes a royalty a reasonable one. The court noted that ". . . the district court supported its royalty amount with sound economic data and with actual, observed behavior in the market. Though both parties maintained at trial that they would not have agreed to a license including 3 percent royalties at the time of infringement, the appropriateness of the rate is perhaps reflected in the decision of the parties to forego an appeal on this issue." Thus, it is not what the parties might want, but what they would actually negotiate, that matters.

Conclusion

It is evident from the preceding discussion of the case law in the United States regarding patent infringement damages that economic analysis has become integral to the outcomes formulated by the courts and that the determination of economic damages in patent infringement cases has been a process that will continue to evolve over time.

References

Aro Manufacturing Co. v. Convertible Top Replacement Co., 377 U.S. 476 (1964).

BIC Leisure Products, Inc. v. Windsurfing Int'l, Inc., 1 F.3d 1214 (Fed. Cir. 1993).

Brooktree Corp. v. Advanced Micro Devices, Inc., 977 F.2d 1555 (Fed. Cir. 1992).

Columbia Wire Co. v. Kokomo Steel & Wire Co., 194 F. 108 (C.C.A. 1911).

Crystal Semiconductor Corp. v. Tritec Microelectronics, Int'l, Inc., 246 F.3d 1336 (Fed. Cir. 2001).

Ellipse Corp. v. Ford Motor Co., 461 F. Supp. 1354 (N.D. Ill. 1978).

Fonar Corp. v. General Electric Co., 107 F.3d 1543 (Fed. Cir. 1997).

Fromson v. Western Litho Plate & Supply Co., 853 F.2d 1568 (Fed. Cir. 1988).

Georgia-Pacific Corp. v. U.S. Plywood Corp., 318 F. Supp. 1116 (S.D.N.Y. 1970).

Grain Processing Corp. v. Am. Maize-Products Co., 185 F.3d 1341 (Fed. Cir. 1999).

Hanson v. Alpine Valley Ski Area, Inc., 718 F.2d 1075 (Fed. Cir. 1983).

King Instruments Corp v. Perego, 65 F.3d 941 (Fed. Cir. 1995).

Kori Corp. v. Wilco Marsh Buggies & Draglines, Inc., 761 F.2d 649 (Fed. Cir. 1985).

LAM Inc. v. Johns-Manville Corp., 718 F.2d 1056 (Fed. Cir. 1983).

Mahurkar v. C.R. Bard, Inc., 79 F.3d 1572 (Fed. Cir. 1996).

Maxwell v. J. Baker, Inc., 86 F.3d 1098 (Fed. Cir. 1996).

Micro Chemical, Inc. v. Lextron, Inc. and Turnkey Computer Systems, Inc., 317 F.3d 1387 (Fed. Cir. 2003).

Minco, Inc. v. Combustion Engineering Inc., 95 F.3d 1109 (Fed. Cir. 1996).

Panduit Corp. v. Stahlin Brothers Fibre Works, Inc., 575 F.2d 1152 (6th Cir. 1978).

Paper Converting Machine Company v. Magna-Graphics Corporation, 745 F.2d 11 (Fed. Cir. 1984).

Rite-Hite Corp. v. Kelley Co., Inc., 56 F.3d 1538 (Fed. Cir. 1995).

Slimfold Mfg. Co., Inc. v. Kinkead Industries, Inc., 932 F.2d 1453 (Fed. Cir. 1991).

State Industries, Inc. v. Mor-Flo Industries, Inc., 883 F.2d 1573 (Fed. Cir. 1989).

Stryker Corp. v. Intermedics Orthopedics Inc., 96 F.3d 1409 (Fed. Cir. 1996).

Tec Air v. Denso Manufacturing Michigan Inc., 192 F.3d 1353 (Fed. Cir. 1999).

Tektronix, Inc. v. United States, 552 F.2d 343 (Ct. Cl. 1977).

TWM Manufacturing Co., Inc. v. Dura Corp., 789 F.2d 895 (Fed Cir. 1986).

Yale Lock Manufacturing Co. v. Sargent, 117 U.S. 536 (1886).

CHAPTER 2

Trends in U.S. Patent Activity[1]

FELIX CHAN
School of Economics and Finance
Curtin University of Technology

MICHAEL MCALEER
School of Economics and Commerce
University of Western Australia

The chapter discusses trends and patterns in the level and growth of patent activity in the United States over time, with additional statistical information on worldwide patent activity. The purpose of registering patents in the United States (and elsewhere) is to protect the intellectual property of the innovators and rightful owners. Although this book is primarily concerned with the quantification of economic damages in intellectual property matters, it is important to understand the trends in patent activity over time in the United States to be able to discern the patenting "basis" from whence innovation arises and for which protection requirements may increase over time, fueling the causal nexus for litigation over time.

INTRODUCTION

This chapter describes the trends and summary statistics of patent activity in the United States and in other countries over the past 40 years. While lawyers focus on legal ramifications of the U.S. patent system, economists have long been concerned about issues related to economic damages that stem from licensing and protecting intellectual property (IP), specifically with respect to how changes in IP protection and licensing behavior may lead to more innovation and to issues in understanding and quantifying technological change. A key aspect of economic growth is differential inventiveness in the production function. A patent is an intellectual (industrial) property that confers to its owner or holder monopoly rights to a product or process over a stipulated period of time. Applications are granted on the basis of innovation and nonobviousness. The United States Patent and Trademark Office (USPTO) has been collecting data on patent applications and patents granted since 1790. As the USPTO Web site notes, for over 200 years the basic role of the Patent and Trademark Office (PTO) has remained the same: to promote the progress of science and the useful arts by securing for limited times to inventors the exclusive right to their respective inventions (Article 1, Section 8 of the United States Constitution; cf. www.uspto.gov). They further note that the PTO is a noncommercial federal entity and one of 14 bureaus in the Department of Commerce (DOC). To understand the magnitude of the USPTO, its official Web site reveals that the office occupies a combined total of over 1,400,000 square feet in numerous buildings in Arlington, Virginia. The office employs over 5,000 full-time equivalent (FTE) staff to support its major functions: the examination and issuance of patents and the examination and registration of trademarks. Finally, the Web site notes:

> PTO programs are conducted under the following principal statutory authorities:
> - 15 U.S.C. 1051–1127 contains provisions of the Trademark Act of 1946 that govern the administration of the trademark registration system of the Patent and trademark Office.
> - 15 U.S.C. 1511 states that the Patent and Trademark Office is under the jurisdiction and supervision of the Department of Commerce.
> - 35 U.S.C. contains basic authorities for administration of patent laws, derived from the Act of July 19, 1952, and subsequent enactment. Revenues from fees are available, to the extent provided for in appropriations acts, to the Commissioner to carry out the activities of the Office. The Patent and Trademark Office is authorized to charge international fees for activities undertaken pursuant to the Patent Cooperation Treaty. Deployment of automated search systems of the Office to the public is authorized.
> - 44 U.S.C. 1337–1338 contains authority to print patents, trademarks, and other matters relating to the business of the Office.

These laws and statutes have served as the basis for the regulation of IP in the United States. for many years. In order to understand how damages should be quantified in patent cases, it is useful to understand the trends in some of the patent statistics, such as the patent shares and patent growth rates.

The use of patent statistics in empirical research is not without its risks, suffering from classification problems and incompatibility issues with the Standard Industrial Classification (SIC) that was widely used in practice up until recently. More important, patent statistics are intrinsic variables in technical and economic significance (Griliches 1990). Despite these problems, patent statistics are plentiful and objective. Patents are, by definition, related to inventiveness, and they have been long considered a reasonable measure of innovation (Hall, Griliches, and Hausman 1986).

An extensive literature exists on the use of patent statistics in economic research. (See Griliches 1990 for a useful review.) These range from the use of patent renewal data to determine the stock market returns of firms, to the valuation of patent rights held by firms in Europe (Pakes and Simpson, 1989). Lanjouw and Lerner (1997) explore the optimality of patent structures and the effects of litigation on innovative activity. McAleer, Chan, and Marinova (2002) investigate the time series properties of patent activity from the perspective of modeling the volatility inherent in monthly patent shares and develop an Innovation Strengths Model for purposes of international comparisons. This chapter presents patent statistics for the United States over time and describes the trends in this behavior over time, with additional discussion on worldwide activities. U.S.

DATA

For over two centuries, the United States has firmly adopted the patents system as a mechanism for protection of intellectual property and stimulation of innovative activities. According to Goel (1999), the patents system is supported by government as a tool to correct market imperfections, thereby allowing imitating firms to benefit from costly technologies developed elsewhere. The system assures appropriateness of returns to inventors[2] and benefits society by making the revealed information public knowledge after the expiry of the patent.[3]

Patent laws were introduced in the United States in the 1780s. The U.S. patents system has steadily attracted international companies and individuals interested in developing technologies and establishing trade links. In absolute numbers, the USPTO receives by far the largest number of foreign applications (Archibugi 1992). Not surprisingly, around 40 percent of all patents in the United States are granted to residents and companies of 12 foreign countries (Griliches 1990; Goel 1999).

There are, however, large variations between firms and countries in terms of what costs they can afford (i.e., patenting fees) to protect their inventions or to purchase patents rights originating elsewhere. As reported in McAleer et al. (2002), the foreign country with the largest number of U.S. patents is Japan, followed distantly by Germany and then France. Of these 12 countries, the country with the highest patent intensity (or patents per capita) is Switzerland, followed by Japan, Sweden, and Germany.[4] France and Italy have numerous patents but relatively low patent intensities, whereas Switzerland and Sweden have relatively few patents but high patent intensities.

The sample period selected for the empirical analysis covers all granted patents with dates of lodged applications between 1964 and 2003 (inclusive), with the data extracted on December 21, 2005. Patent data have been obtained from the official Internet Web page of the USPTO (www.uspto.gov/web/offices/ac/ido/oeip/taf/h_at.htm). The date of lodgement of granted applications for the time series is used instead of the date of issue of patents to avoid organizational delays associated with the complicated process of issuing a patent (which includes procedures such as examination, expert review, and appeals). Consequently, the data on patents by date of application represent more accurately the process of commercial protection for intellectual property and innovative outcomes from research and development.

Data prior to 1963 are not readily available. Previous studies have indicated that, during the 1980s and 1990s, the number of patents by foreign countries in the United States surged at an unprecedented rate.[5] The USPTO updates the information on patents granted every two weeks. However, the time from application to the granting of a patent can be very long. In 1997, the USPTO estimated that it takes 22.9 months on average between a patent application being lodged and a decision (issue or rejection) being made, and it could take more than 10 years in some cases (Chan, Marinova, and McAleer 2005).

Trends in U.S. Patent Activity

Exhibits 2.1 and 2.2 contain the total number of patents registered in the United States and the number of patents registered in the United States by U.S residents and/or companies over the last 40 years, respectively. In order to avoid confusion, the term "U.S. Patents" is used to describe patents registered in the United States by U.S. residents and/or companies, while the term "total U.S. Patents" is used to describe the total number of patents registered in the United States.

As shown, the trends in U.S. patents correlate closely with those of total U.S. patents. However, U.S. patents exhibits a downward trend in the late 1970s whereas the total U.S. patents remains mostly stable for the same period. Both statistics share a dramatic increase from the mid-1980s to the mid-1990s. Although there appears to have been a dramatic decrease in the number of patents after 1998 for both patent activity variables, this trend could well be misleading due to the fact that the process of granting patents has been delayed as the USPTO has been inundated with patent applications over the past few years. Therefore, it is likely that once the PTO makes resource adjustments, the number of approved applications in future years will likely increase significantly.

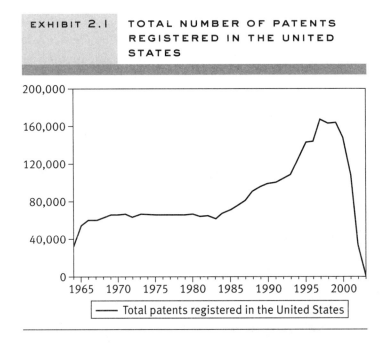

EXHIBIT 2.1 TOTAL NUMBER OF PATENTS REGISTERED IN THE UNITED STATES

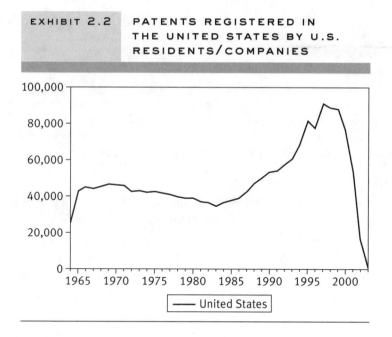

EXHIBIT 2.2   PATENTS REGISTERED IN
THE UNITED STATES BY U.S.
RESIDENTS/COMPANIES

Exhibit 2.3 presents the summary statistics for U.S. patents and total U.S. patents. In the past 40 years, 57 percent of total U.S. patents were registered by U.S. residents and/or companies on average. Given the United States is one of the world's largest economic markets, these figures seem to reflect in part the United States' domination with respect to technological innovation for the last four decades.

In order to examine some of the dynamics of the U.S. patents and total U.S. patents variables, Exhibit 2.4 contains the mean and standard deviations of U.S. patents and total U.S. patents by decade. Interestingly, the average number of U.S. patents appears to be stable in the 1960s and 1970s but increases dramatically in the 1990s. This could perhaps be due in part to the rapid development in computing, telecommunication, and information technology industries. In terms of the average total U.S. patents per year, there appears to be a steady increase from the 1960s to the late 1980s. However, there is a 56 percent increase

EXHIBIT 2.3   SUMMARY STATISTICS
OF U.S. PATENTS AND TOTAL
U.S. PATENTS

	U.S. Patents	Total U.S. Patents
Mean	48430.65	83515.98
Median	43508.50	66426.00
Maximum	91000.00	167798.0
Minimum	572.0000	1064.000
Standard Deviation	18772.37	37592.23
Skewness	0.501528	0.722609
Kurtosis	3.758594	3.208726

EXHIBIT 2.4   MEANS AND STANDARD DEVIATIONS OF U.S. PATENTS
                AND TOTAL U.S. PATENTS BY DECADE

	1964–1969		1970–1979		1980–1989		1990–1999		2000–2003	
	U.S. Patents	Total U.S. Patents	U.S. Patents	Total U.S. Patents	U.S. Patents	Total U.S. Patents	U.S. Patents	Total U.S. Patents	U.S. Patents	Total U.S. Patents
Mean	41290.17	55969	42209.9	65764.4	39967.6	73843.9	71998.5	131859.9	36931.25	72535.75
Standard Deviation	8387.971	12204.27	2229.793	876.9424	5104.492	11807.15	15029.77	28108.64	34578.8	67090.39

in the average number of total U.S. patents from the 1980s to the 1990s, which is about the same percentage increase in U.S. patents over the same time frame.

The 1970s seem to be the least volatile period in terms of patents registration for both U.S. patents and total U.S. patents, as the standard deviations are at their lowest levels during this period (relative to the other decades under scrutiny) in both cases. As shown in Exhibit 2.4, the standard deviations seem to be changing over time in both cases and the changes do not necessary follow the changes in the mean level of patent registrations. Recently, the dynamic of the "conditional" variance has been investigated by using more sophisticated statistical techniques.[6]

TRENDS IN PATENT SHARES

In this chapter, the "patent share" of a country is defined to be the ratio between the number of patent registered in the United States from the country at time t and the total U.S. patents at the same time, that is

$$PS_{it} = \frac{P_{it}}{T_t} \times 100,$$

where

P_{it} denotes the number of patent registered in the U.S. from country i, at time t

T_t denotes the total U.S. patents at time t

Patent share provides important information about the level of research activities and outputs from a particular country. It also provides indication on the strength and capability of technological innovations from a particular country relative to the rest of the World (McAleer, Chan, and Marinova 2002).

Exhibit 2.5 contains the U.S. patent share from 1963 to 2003. Although there is an upward trend in U.S. patents, the U.S. patent share is decreasing over time, as shown in Exhibit 2.3. From the late 1960s to mid-1980s, the patent share is decreasing in a consistent manner, indicating an increase in technological capability and innovations in foreign countries. However, the U.S. patent share seems to have increased from the mid-1980s to the mid-1990s. Despite the downward trend in the U.S. patent share, more than 50 percent of total U.S. patents are still registered by U.S. residents and/or companies, with the exception of 2001, when the U.S. patent share is 49.56 percent.

EXHIBIT 2.5   U.S. PATENT SHARE,
1963 TO 2003

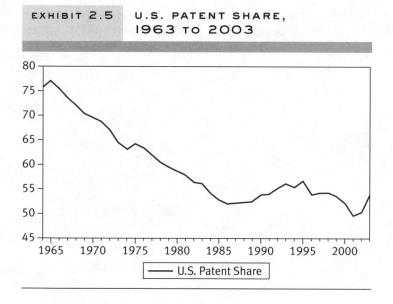

Exhibit 2.6 contains the means and standard deviations of U.S. patent share by decade. Although the average U.S. patent share is 59.55 percent for the 40-year period, the average U.S. patent share decreased consistently from 74 percent in the 1960s to 54.65 percent in the 1990s. Interestingly, the standard deviation of the U.S. patent share is also decreasing over time, from 2.48 in the 1960s to 1.07 in the 1990s with the average of 7.94 for the whole period.

In order to examine the cause of the decline in the U.S. patent share, the patent shares of four foreign countries—Canada, Japan, Korea, and Taiwan—are presented in Exhibit 2.7.

As shown in these graphs, the patent shares of all four countries (relative to the United States) increase over time. Japan has less than a 2 percent patent share in the 1960s but increases consistently for 20 years. By the end of 1990s the Japanese patent share reaches 22.81 percent. In fact, the average Japanese patent share in the 1990s is 21.076 percent, which implies that in that decade, almost 75 percent of total U.S. patents consist of U.S. patents and Japanese patents. Although the Canadian patent share is increasing steadily over time, it occupies no more than 2.5 percent of the total U.S. patents. The patent shares of the two Southeast Asian countries, however, are increasing in an explosive manner from

EXHIBIT 2.6   MEANS AND STANDARD DEVIATIONS OF U.S. PATENT
SHARE BY DECADE

Years	1964–2003	1964–1969	1970–1979	1980–1989	1990–1999	2000–2003
Mean	59.552%	74.044%	64.188%	54.391%	54.645%	51.395%
Standard Deviation	7.942	2.481	3.368	2.534	1.070	1.894

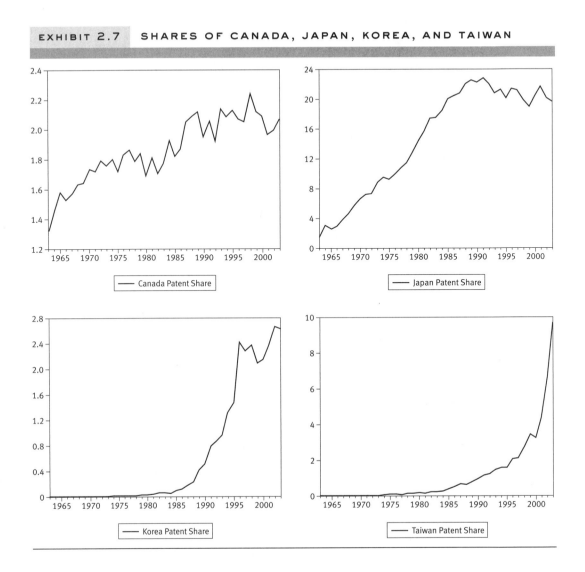

EXHIBIT 2.7   SHARES OF CANADA, JAPAN, KOREA, AND TAIWAN

the mid-1980s. In fact, Korea has virtually zero patent share prior to 1980, and its patent share reaches almost 2.5 percent in the mid-1990s. Similarly for Taiwan, which has virtually zero patent share in the 1970s; its patent share reaches almost 10 percent in 2003.

TRENDS IN THE U.S. PATENT GROWTH RATE

The patent growth rate of a country is defined as the percentage change in the number of patents registered in the United States from that country. That is,

$$G_t = \frac{P_{it} - P_{it-1}}{P_{it-1}} \times 100$$

where P_{it} is the number of patent registered in the United States from country i, at time t

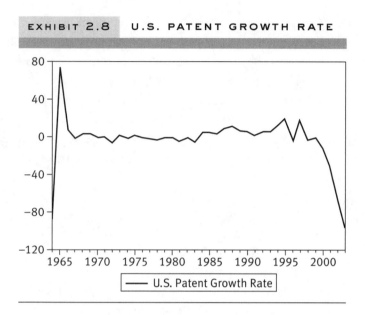

EXHIBIT 2.8   U.S. PATENT GROWTH RATE

The growth rate in the number of registered patents from a particular country provides information regarding the trends and momentum of research activities and technological innovations. A country with a high growth rate in registered patents indicates high potential capability in technological innovations as well as stable economic and social environment in which innovation can be realized into practical inventions.

Exhibit 2.8 contains the U.S. patent growth rate. Interestingly, there seems to be a negative growth in the early 1960s, then the number of U.S. patents increases, which leads to a dramatic rise in the U.S. patent growth rate. Despite the rapid movement in the early period, the U.S. patent growth rate is stable at around 2.45 percent from 1966 to 1998. This positive average growth rate is consistent with the upward trend in the number of U.S. patents for the same period. However, the average growth rate of total U.S. patents is 3.50 patents for the same period, indicating that the number of U.S. patents is growing at a slower rate than the total number of patents registered in the United States, which leads to the decrease in patent share.

Exhibit 2.9 contains the means and standard deviations of U.S. patent and total U.S. patent growth rate by decade. The number of U.S. patents is growing at a slower rate than the

EXHIBIT 2.9   MEANS AND STANDARD DEVIATIONS OF U.S. PATENT AND TOTAL U.S. PATENT GROWTH RATE BY DECADE

	1964–1969		1970–1979		1980–1989		1990–1999		2000–2003	
	U.S. Patents	Total U.S. Patents	U.S. Patents	Total U.S. Patents	U.S. Patents	Total U.S. Patents	U.S. Patents	Total U.S. Patents	U.S. Patents	Total U.S. Patents
Mean	−0.774	0.426	−1.708	−0.003	2.718	4.004	6.008	5.710	−51.972	−50.660
Standard Deviation	51.124	50.237	2.185	2.197	5.645	5.428	8.268	7.207	37.818	39.477

number of total U.S. patents until the 1990s, as shown in Exhibit 2.9. Although there appears to be substantial negative growth in the 2000s, this is not reliable because the process of granting patents can be time consuming. Therefore, the growth rate for this period is expected to rise in the future for both U.S. patents and total U.S. patents.

Interestingly, the volatility in the growth rates seem to be increasing for both U.S. patents and total U.S. patents from the 1970s to the 1990s, as the standard deviations are increasing over time. This could be a result of increasing research activities, which lead to higher uncertainty in the number of future patents depending on the outcome of the research.

CONCLUSION

This chapter provided some background information about the U.S. Patent and Trademark Office and presented some basic statistical analysis on several patent statistics, namely the number of patents registered in the U.S. by U.S. residents and/or companies, the U.S. patent share, and the U.S. patent growth rate. Overall, there is an upward trend in the number of U.S. patents, especially in the 1990s. This is consistent with the positive U.S. patent growth rate. However, the U.S. growth rate is lower than the total U.S. patent growth rate (i.e., the growth rate of the total number of patents registered in the United States). This is consistent with the decline in the U.S. patent share. Examining patent shares of Canada, Japan, Korea, and Taiwan revealed that Japanese patent shares increase steadily for most of the 1980s and 1990s. Japan is the country with the second highest number of patents registered in the United States for the last 40 years.

NOTES

1. The authors wish to thank Dora Marinova and Daniel Slottje for helpful discussions and to acknowledge the financial support of the Australian Research Council.
2. A patent in the United States confers to the inventor a 20-year monopoly over the technical idea(s) covered. However, a large number of patented inventions can remain dormant without ever reaching the innovation stage (Oi 1995).
3. Being an invention of the neoclassical economic model, the patents system also incorporates a number of deficiencies. For example, it has been used to establish monopoly positions in industries, such as aluminum or shoe manufacturing (Mansfield 1993). Patent fees can also be highly prohibitive, which can discriminate against potential applicants. The patents system cannot accommodate a number of ethical and economic issues newly emerging from the scientific and technological advances in the fields of biotechnology, pharmaceutical or information technologies. Scotchmer (1991, p. 40) describes the patents system as "a very blunt instrument trying to solve a very delicate problem."
4. The small economies of Liechtenstein and Monaco have higher patent intensities than that of Switzerland (Marinova 2001) but are not included in the analysis as their total patent numbers are very small.
5. *See, e.g.,* Patel and Pavitt 1995; Arundel and Kabla 1998; Kortum and Lerner 1999.
6. *See* McAleer, Chan, and Marinova 2002.

REFERENCES

Archibugi, D. "Patenting as an Indicator of Technological Innovation: A Review," *Science and Public Policy* 19, no. 6 (1992): 357–368.

Arundel, A., and I. Kabla. "What Percentage of Innovations Are Patented? Empirical Estimates from European Firms," *Research Policy* 27, no. 2 (1998): 127–141.

Chan, F., D. Marinova, and M. McAleer. "Rolling Regressions and Conditional Correlations of Foreign Patents in the USA," *Environmental Modelling and Software* 20, no. 11 (2005): 1413–1422.

Goel, R. K. *Economic Models of Technological Change: Theory and Application* (Westport, CT: Quorum Books, 1999), p. 131.

Griliches, Z. "Patent Statistics as Economic Indicator: A Survey," *Journal of Economic Literature* 28, no. 4 (1990): 1661–1707.

Hall, B. H., Z. Griliches, and J. Hausman. "Patents and R&D: Is There a Lag?" *International Economic Review* 27, no. 2 (1986): 265–283.

Kortum, S., and J. Lerner (1999). "What Is behind the Recent Surge in Patenting?" *Research Policy* 28, no. 1 (1999): 1–22.

Mansfield, E. "Unauthorised Use of Intellectual Property: Effects on Investment, Technology Transfer, and Innovation," in M. B. Wallerstein, M. E. Mogee, and R. A. Schoen (eds.), *Global Dimensions of Intellectual Property Rights in Science and Technology* (National Academy Press, Washington, D.C., 1993), pp. 107–145; also in E. Mansfield, *Innovation, Technology and the Economy: The Selected Essays of Edwin Mansfield,* Vol. II (Aldershot, UK: Edward Elgar, 1995), pp. 281–319.

Marinova, D. "Eastern European Patenting Activities in the USA," *Technovation* 21, no. 9(2001): 571–584.

McAleer, M., F. Chan, and D. Marinova. "An Econometric Analysis of Asymmetric Volatility: Theory and Application to Patents," paper presented to the Australasian meeting of the Econometric Society, Brisbane, Australia, July 2002.

Oi, W. Y. "On the Uncertain Returns to Inventive Activity," in S. Dowrick (ed.), *Economic Approaches to Innovation* (Aldershot, UK: Edward Elgar, 1995), pp. 54–75.

Patel, P., and K. Pavitt. "Divergence in Technological Development among Countries and Firms," in J. Hagedoorn (ed.), *Technical Change and the World Economy: Convergence and Divergence in Technology Strategies* (Aldershot, UK: Edward Elgar, 1995), pp. 147–181.

Scotchmer, S. "Standing on the Shoulders of Giants: Cumulative Research and the Patent Law," *Journal of Economic Perspectives* 5, no. 1(1991): 29–41.

United States Patent and Trademark Office. *Trilateral Statistical Report* (1997). www.uspto.gov/web/offices/dcom/olia/trilat/tsr97/index.htm#contents, accessed August 18, 2002.

3

Trademark Infringement and the Legal Bases for the Recovery of Economic Damages[1]

Marc E. Ackerman
White & Case LLP

Daren M. Orzechowski
White & Case LLP

The aim of this chapter is to educate the reader on the history and purpose of American trademark law and the current law of trademarks in the United States as it relates to infringement and damages, and how one may calculate trademark infringement damages as part of a litigation remedy or analysis. We discuss the origins of trademark law and the dual benefit that it provides to trademark owners as well as consumers. This background will further the reader's understanding of how goodwill is captured in trademarks and the scope of trademark rights. It will also provide an overview of some of the basic terminology that may be encountered in analyzing trademarks, including a discussion of the varying levels of strength, and corresponding value, that a mark may possess.

INTRODUCTION

Image and reputation in any context can be extraordinarily valuable assets. In the business context, these assets are embodied in trademarks. Trademarks are distinctive marks of authenticity through which the goods or services[2] of a party are offered to the marketplace so as to distinguish them from the goods and services of others, whether competitors or otherwise.[3] Trademarks are the law's recognition of the psychological function of symbols.[4] Although trademarks may vary substantially and come in different forms such as names, symbols, brands or logos, they all serve the fundamental purpose of acting as source identifiers. Thus, in addition to being valuable assets to trademark owners, trademarks provide a benefit to consumers by allowing them to find products and identify their manufacturers with greater ease.[5]

Justice Frankfurter astutely summarized the function of trademarks and the rights of trademark owners in *Mishawaka Rubber & Woolen Mfg. Co. v. S.S. Kresge Co.*:

> A trade-mark is a merchandising short-cut which induces a purchaser to select what he wants. The owner of a mark exploits this human propensity by making every effort to impregnate the atmosphere of the market with the drawing power of a congenial symbol. Whatever the means employed, the aim is the same—to convey through the mark, in the minds of potential customers, the desirability of the commodity upon which it appears. Once this is attained, the trade-mark owner has something of value. If another poaches upon the commercial magnetism of the symbol he has created, the owner can obtain legal redress.[6]

When a trademark is misused or infringed, consumers are misled and the trademark owner is injured. A litigant that establishes that its trademark rights have been infringed may recover damages in addition to obtaining various forms of injunctive relief.[7] Although these are textbook propositions, the ways in which damages are calculated by the judiciary, litigants and juries are varied, complex, and constantly evolving.

In this chapter, we provide an overview of the federal law regarding trademark infringement and the economic recovery to which a successful litigant may be entitled.

Origins of Trademark Law

Trademark law can be traced back to a time before the founding of the United States. The earliest use of marks related to the branding of cattle and other animals.[8] This is supported by ancient paintings found in Egypt and southwestern Europe that depict cattle with brands or in the process of being branded.[9] As civilization evolved, a basic common law trademark scheme developed whereby artisans and craftsmen would place a seal or logo on their products so as to identify the goods as coming from a recognized source.[10] In time this practice developed into the use of marks to represent certain families or the property of certain individuals.[11]

Eventually, governments found that marks could be used as a form of consumer protection from goods of low quality. In 1266, England enacted a compulsory marking law that forced bakers to mark their loaves of bread, so that if the weight of the bread was misstated, the goods could be traced back to the baker.[12] The teachings of a scholar named Bartolus de Saxoferre noted as early as the fourteenth century that trademarks serve a dual role in that they provide a benefit to the craftsman, but they also protect the public in that the mark allows for the identification of the source of goods.[13]

The first reported case recognizing trademark rights, *Southern v. How*,[14] arose in England in 1659. In *Southern*, a goldsmith was accused of providing counterfeit jewelry to the plaintiff who in turn sold it to the King of Barbary. The king recognized the inauthentic nature of the goods and demanded restitution from the plaintiff, who in turn sought damages from the defendant. While the defendant prevailed in *Southern* because the court reasoned that the jewelry at issue had value, just not the value that the plaintiff thought it possessed, the case is notable for its recognition of trademark rights. After determining that the plaintiff lacked a cause of action, the court entered into a discussion of how an action would lie in the case of a misleading use of marks in connection with the goods at issue. As an example, a cause of action would exist if the maker of poor-quality clothing intentionally used the mark of a clothier who produced high-quality goods and enjoyed a great reputation in the marketplace. This was in contrast to the facts in *Southern* where the plaintiff got exactly what he bargained for but incorrectly valued the jewelry at issue.

The law of trademarks continued to grow in England. Like other bodies of American law, the law of trademarks was borrowed from English law at the time of colonization.[15] New York was at the forefront of early trademark law as it was the home to both the first reported American trademark law decision[16] and the first formal trademark legislation in the United States.[17]

In *Snowden v. Noah,* the New York Court of Chancery dealt with a dispute between two rival publications, the *National Advocate* and the *New York National Advocate.*[18] Decided in 1825, *Snowden* involved defendants who sold a newspaper business and its assets to the plaintiff Snowden and then, after the sale, began to publish a newspaper with a similar name at the same address as the competing business that had been sold to the plaintiff. Further compounding the problem, the defendants and their *New York National Advocate* targeted the same subscribers as the plaintiff's *National Advocate.* Snowden filed suit and on his motion for an injunction, the court noted that the names of the publications were "nearly the same," yet determined that the question of whether the defendants' actions were "a fair competition or a fraudulent interference" was a "question wholly uncertain."[19] The court believed the dispute was nothing more than an open competition for the goodwill of the patrons of the original *National Advocate,* but felt the questions regarding defendants' conduct should be decided by a jury. As result, the court denied the motion for an injunction, but indicated that the matter should proceed to trial.

Following the decision in *Snowden,* New York passed the nation's first trademark statute.[20] The legislation, entitled "An Act to Punish and Prevent Frauds in the Use of False Stamps and Labels," was enacted on May 14, 1845 and provided that:

> Every person who shall knowingly and willfully forge or counterfeit, or cause or procure to be forged or counterfeited, upon any goods, wares or merchandize [sic], the private stamps or labels of any mechanic or manufacturer, with intent to defraud the purchasers, or manufacturers of any goods, wares or merchandize [sic] whatsoever, upon conviction thereof, shall be punished by imprisonment in a county jail for a term not exceeding six months.[21]

Similarly, it was a crime to knowingly sell goods with forged or counterfeit stamps or labels.[22] Although the knowledge requirement of the act was undoubtedly a substantial burden to plaintiffs, the legislation is important because it recognizes the need for the protection of both consumers and the providers of goods from imposters offering goods of lesser or dangerous qualities.

Common law trademark rights continued to develop in all of the states. Even today, common law rights continue to exist in addition to various state trademark registration systems.[23] Modern trademark law, however, is driven substantially and most critically by federal trademark law.

Development of Federal Trademark Law

Although trademark cases in the United States were heard early in the nineteenth century, it was not until 1870 that Congress enacted any federal trademark legislation.[24] Passed on July 8, 1870, and entitled "An Act to Revise, Consolidate, and Amend the Statutes Relating to Patents and Copyrights," the legislation provided for a system whereby a party could register and enforce its trademarks.[25] The initial legislation was eventually held unconstitutional on the grounds that Congress had exceeded the limits of its constitutional power to regulate interstate and foreign commerce.[26] The Supreme Court in *In re Trade-Mark Cases* held that Congress's ability to regulate trademarks could not be found under Article 1, Section 8, Clause 8 of the Constitution because that clause pertained only to copyrights and patents.[27] The aforementioned clause empowers Congress "to promote the progress of science and useful arts, by securing for limited times to authors and inventors the exclusive right to their respective writings or discoveries."[28] Trademarks, unlike copyrights and patents, do not fall under that provision as they do not directly promote the "progress of science" or the "useful arts."[29]

Instead, Congress derives the power to regulate trademarks from the "Commerce Clause" of the Constitution, which states that Congress may pass laws "to regulate commerce with foreign nations, and among the several states, and with the Indian tribes."[30] The fatal flaw of the initial trademark legislation was that it sought to regulate intrastate as well as interstate commerce.[31] Intrastate commerce is an area reserved to the states under the Constitution and is the reason state trademark systems still exist today.[32]

Congress cured the aforementioned defect by passing new legislation in 1881 that limited the scope of the federal trademark law to regulation of trade with foreign nations and Indian tribes.[33] The legislation oddly omitted interstate commerce.[34] Subsequent federal legislation, beginning in 1905, was passed in attempts to bring the law squarely within the scope of the Commerce Clause and the holding of *In Re Trade-Mark Cases,* and to provide some uniformity in the decisions of the courts.[35] Beginning in the 1930s, in response to the complaints about problems in the federal trademark law, efforts were made to pass new, comprehensive trademark legislation. As stated in the Senate Committee's report for the new legislation:

> The purpose of this bill is to place all matters relating to trademarks in one statute and to eliminate judicial obscurity, to simplify registration and to make it stronger and

more liberal, to dispense with mere technical prohibitions and arbitrary provisions, to make procedure simple and relief against infringement prompt and effective.[36]

Eventually a new comprehensive trademark law, the Lanham Act, was passed in 1946.[37] As amended, the Lanham Act provides the basis for federal trademark law today.

The Lanham Act provides for a system of national registration of trademarks, provided the marks meet certain requirements and are actually used in interstate commerce.[38] Although it is possible to apply for a federal trademark registration based on an "intent to use" the mark, no trademark registration will be upheld absent actual use of the mark in interstate or foreign commerce, which is the basis for the exercise of federal authority.[39] Use of a trademark in commerce promotes goodwill, which is a valuable asset. The recognition of that goodwill is valuable to consumers who in turn reduce their product search efforts and costs and can easily identify and acquire certain goods and services.[40]

Under the Lanham Act, a trademark owner, of either a registered or unregistered trademark used in interstate or foreign commerce, may sue a party that infringes its mark.[41] As discussed later in greater detail, a successful party may obtain an injunction to stop the infringing use and may also collect certain damages from the infringer.

DIFFERENT CATEGORIES OF TRADEMARKS

The strength of a trademark is determined by its tendency to uniquely identify the source of a product.[42] Such tendencies are strongest where the mark is distinctive, either by its inherent characteristics or as a result of acquired distinctiveness, which is referred to in trademark law as "secondary meaning."[43] Secondary meaning has generally been referred to as "association nothing more" and is essentially "a mental recognition in buyers' and potential buyers' minds that products connected with the symbol or device emanate from or are associated with the same source."[44] Establishing secondary meaning often requires proof through use of a consumer survey that polls the recognition of the mark in relation to the goods of the trademark holder.[45]

Four (sometimes listed as five) general categories of trademarks have been recognized by courts and commentators. Such categorization of a mark based on its distinctiveness reflects its strength in the market and arguably affects its corresponding value. Judge Friendly in *Abercrombie & Fitch Co. v. Hunting World, Inc.* identified four general categories for marks "[a]rrayed in an ascending order which roughly reflects their eligibility to trademark status and the degree of protection accorded, these classes are (1) generic, (2) descriptive, (3) suggestive, and (4) arbitrary or fanciful."[46] These categories, generally referred to as the "spectrum of distinctiveness,"[47] are used as guidelines for determining as a matter of law whether a term is even eligible for protection as a trademark and if so, whether the trademark owner is required to provide evidence of secondary meaning prior to obtaining trademark rights.[48] The spectrum of distinctiveness as detailed by Judge Friendly has been adopted by many federal courts throughout the United States, including the Supreme Court.[49]

Generic marks are those marks that simply identify the actual product or service being offered and are in no way distinctive.[50] For example, no party selling bath soap could exclusively claim rights to the term "soap" as a mark. Judge Friendly described these types of marks as referring to the "genus of which the particular product is the species."[51] In fact, it would be unfair to grant one party exclusive rights in such terms because competitors would potentially be prohibited from even naming the products they were endeavoring to sell.[52] As a result, even if a generic mark arguably obtains some secondary meaning it can never serve as a trademark.[53] A generic mark is not eligible for registration with the United States Patent and Trademark Office ("USPTO").[54]

Descriptive marks consist of words that identify the qualities of the product or service.[55] An example of a descriptive mark would be "Yellow Pages" as used with telephone books. Such a mark describes the color of the book and its pages, but the generic product itself is referred to as a "telephone book." A descriptive mark by itself is not inherently distinctive and as a result, is not automatically afforded trademark protection.[56] However, if the mark acquires secondary meaning, it is eligible for trademark protection.[57] Once secondary meaning for a descriptive mark is demonstrated, the mark may be registered with the USPTO.[58]

Suggestive marks are those that, while not directly descriptive of the product or service, suggest qualities of the products or services that require the use of "imagination, thought and perception to reach a conclusion as to the nature of the goods."[59] This is in contrast to a descriptive mark, which "conveys an immediate idea of the ingredients, qualities or characteristics of the goods."[60] An example of a suggestive mark would be "Roach Motel" for insect traps.[61] The line between descriptive and suggestive marks is very close and at times confusing.[62] Indeed, Judge Learned Hand once stated that "[i]t is quite impossible to get any rule out of the cases beyond this: That the validity of the mark ends where suggestion ends and description begins."[63] The distinction is important though because if a mark is determined to be suggestive, it will be afforded trademark protection even in the absence of secondary meaning.[64] This can be a very important advantage in litigation and in applying to register a trademark with the USPTO.

Sometimes referred to as two separate categories, arbitrary or fanciful marks are the most distinctive marks and command the highest level of trademark protection.[65] Both are distinctive in that the terms they incorporate are totally unrelated to the product.[66] They differ in that arbitrary marks utilize existing terms and arbitrarily apply them to an unrelated product whereas a fanciful or coined mark consists of newly invented terms.[67] An example of an arbitrary mark is the use of the term "apple" when used with respect to computers. The mark "Kodak" is a fanciful mark as it was not a term existing in the English language prior to being coined by the Eastman Kodak Company for use in connection with cameras, film, and related products.[68]

As Judge Friendly himself noted, the "lines of demarcation are not always bright."[69] This is because in one circumstance a term used as a mark could have one meaning that differs drastically from the meaning that it has with respect to a different product. Using the "apple" example just mentioned, the term "apple" when used with respect to computers is arbitrary, while if used to describe fruit would likely be generic as it would be needed by other apple producers to describe their competing apple products. Another example is the term "ivory." When used as a brand for the popular soap, the term is an arbitrary mark commanding a very high level of trademark protection. When used as a mark for products made from the tusks of elephants, the term is likely descriptive or generic and subject to little or no trademark protection.

The strength of a mark, while not dispositive on the issue of damages, merits strong consideration in evaluating damages. It may be of particular use in determining whether the trademark owner has suffered actual damages based on a diminution of the strength of the mark and whether the strength of the mark was such that the trademark owner would reasonably have expected to obtain the sales it lost due to the sales of the infringing goods.

LAW OF TRADEMARK INFRINGEMENT

The unauthorized use of another's trademark or a confusingly similar mark will give rise to a claim of trademark infringement. As explained by one court:

> [A trademark owner's] mark is his authentic seal; by it he vouches for the goods which bear it; it carries his name for good or ill. If another uses it, he borrows the owner's reputation, whose quality no longer lies within his own control. This is an injury, even though the borrower does not tarnish it, or divert any sales by its use; for a reputation, like a face, is the symbol of its possessor and creator, and another can use it only as a mask. And so it has come to be recognized that, unless the borrower's use is so foreign to the owner's as to insure against any identification of the two, it is unlawful.[70]

The owner of a federally registered trademark may have a cause of action for trademark infringement pursuant to Section 32 of the Lanham Act, which is codified at 15 U.S.C. § 1114(1), which states:

> Any person who shall, without the consent of the registrant—
>
> (a) use in commerce any reproduction, counterfeit, copy, or colorable imitation of a registered mark in connection with the sale, offering for sale, distribution, or advertising of any goods or services on or in connection with which such use is likely to cause confusion, or to cause mistake, or to deceive; or
>
> (b) reproduce, counterfeit, copy, or colorably imitate a registered mark and apply such reproduction, counterfeit, copy, or colorable imitation to labels, signs, prints, packages, wrappers, receptacles or advertisements intended to be used in commerce upon or in connection with the sale, offering for sale, distribution, or advertising of goods or services on or in connection with which such use is likely to cause confusion, or to cause mistake, or to deceive;
>
> shall be liable in a civil action by the registrant for the remedies hereinafter provided.[71]

Not all trademarks, however, are registered with the USPTO. Parties who have actually used a mark in commerce may still have rights at common law such that they may sue for trademark infringement.[72] Such claims are governed by Section 43(a) of the Lanham Act, 15 U.S.C. § 1125(a), which, as amended, provides for actions covering such claims as false advertising, trade libel, and product disparagement in addition to common law trademark infringement, all under the heading of unfair competition:[73]

> Any person who, on or in connection with any goods or services, or any container for goods, uses in commerce any word, term, name, symbol, or device, or any combination thereof, or any false designation of origin, false or misleading description of fact, or false or misleading representation of fact, which—
>
> (a) is likely to cause confusion, or to cause mistake, or to deceive as to the affiliation, connection, or association of such person with another person, or as to the origin, sponsorship, or approval of his or her goods, services, or commercial activities by another person, or
>
> (b) in commercial advertising or promotion, misrepresents the nature, characteristics, qualities, or geographic origin of his or her or another person's goods, services, or commercial activities,
>
> shall be liable in a civil action by any person who believes that he or she is or is likely to be damaged by such act.[74]

The two cited statutes set forth the framework for deciding trademark infringement matters under federal law. The only differentiating factor is the registration status of a mark. Today, one general standard determines whether trademark infringement has occurred. To succeed on a claim of federal trademark infringement, a trademark holder must demonstrate that (1) its mark is entitled to protection, and (2) the alleged infringer's use of the mark on its products is likely to cause consumer confusion as to the origin or sponsorship of the goods or services.[75] While it may vary slightly with respect to certain state law claims, for the most part state unfair competition and trademark infringement claims are decided using the aforementioned legal standard.[76]

In terms of establishing the first prong of the infringement test, a party with a registration is at a substantial advantage. A certificate of registration from the USPTO is prima facie evidence that a trademark is registered and valid, the registrant owns the mark, and the registrant has the exclusive right to use the mark in commerce.[77] An infringer could counterclaim, seeking cancellation of the trademark registration and the related rights on a number of grounds.[78] Registrations, however, are presumed valid; therefore, a challenge to a trademark registration requires the challenger to rebut this presumption by a preponderance of the evidence.[79] As a result, having a registration will not automatically establish that the trademark at issue is entitled to protection, but it does have the effect of shifting the burden of proof on the matter to the alleged infringer.[80]

If the plaintiff is pursuing a Section 43(a) claim of unfair competition based on common law trademark infringement, then it must prove that its mark is distinctive, and thus entitled to protection.[81] This is done using the spectrum of distinctiveness enumerated in the

Abercrombie case.[82] If the mark at issue is inherently distinctive, that is, arbitrary or fanciful, the process and arguments will be straightforward. But if the mark is descriptive, the plaintiff will have to establish secondary meaning, which can be an expensive process.[83] An infringer may also challenge that the mark is generic, raising the threat that the plaintiff will lose all rights in the mark.[84] Assuming the mark at issue is deemed distinctive, the analysis then proceeds to an examination of the plaintiff's mark and that of the alleged infringer.

The second prong requires the trademark owner to demonstrate a likelihood of consumer confusion.[85] Confusion under the Lanham Act occurs where the public is likely to believe that "the mark's owner sponsored or otherwise approved of the use of the trademark."[86] This analysis is customarily performed using a series of factors, and many courts follow the list set forth by the United States Court of Appeals for the Second Circuit in the influential decision of *Polaroid Corp. v. Polarad Elecs. Corp.*[87] The factors that are weighed include: (1) the strength of the plaintiff's mark; (2) the similarity of the parties' marks; (3) the proximity of the parties' products or services; (4) the likelihood that the senior user will "bridge the gap"; (5) evidence of actual confusion; (6) the defendant's intent in selecting the mark; (7) the quality of defendant's products or services; and (8) the sophistication of the consumers.[88] Variations of these factors have been adopted, and in some cases renamed, by the other Circuit Courts of Appeals.[89] These factors are not exclusive, and each must be evaluated under the facts of the case.[90] Each factor, however, is evaluated in the context of how it bears on the ultimate question of likelihood of confusion.[91]

Strength of the Mark

The strength of the mark factor focuses on the distinctiveness of the trademark, or in other words, "[its] tendency to identify the goods sold under the mark as emanating from a particular . . . source."[92] There are two aspects to a trademark's strength: inherent distinctiveness and acquired distinctiveness.[93] These relate to consideration of the *Abercrombie* factors discussed earlier and whether the mark requires and has established secondary meaning.[94]

In analyzing whether a mark has acquired distinctiveness in the marketplace, a court will look to see whether "prominent use of the mark in commerce has resulted in a high degree of consumer recognition."[95] If a mark has been "long, prominently and notoriously used in commerce" consumers are more apt to recognize it.[96] A mark has acquired distinctiveness when it "comes to identify not only the goods, but the source of those goods, even though the relevant consuming public might not know the name of the producer."[97] The more distinctive the mark, the greater its strength will be under this factor.

Similarity between Defendant's and Plaintiff's Marks

The similarity between the parties' marks is assessed by "[c]onsidering 'the general impression created by the marks, taking into account all factors that potential purchasers will likely perceive and remember.'"[98] Courts give greater weight to the important or dominant parts of a mark because those parts make the greatest impression on consumers.[99] Conversely, in comparing two marks, the generic or descriptive elements are ignored, or given little weight.[100]

Whether the Products Compete in the Marketplace

This factor is relatively self-explanatory. "Products which directly compete in the marketplace clearly warrant a finding of the highest degree of competitive proximity."[101] If the products are competitive with each other, it is more likely that there will be confusion.[102] A competitor whose product is alleged to be infringing will be more likely to be found to have infringed intentionally, as it will have difficulty claiming it was unaware of the competitor's protected branding.

Likelihood That the Trademark Owner Will "Bridge the Gap"

This factor recognizes "the senior user's interest in preserving avenues of expansion and entering into related fields."[103] This factor considers whether the trademark owner is likely to expand the scope of its goods and services into an area that is logically related. For example, if the trademark owner sells computers, it is conceivable that it might expand its market into selling computer parts and accessories. To the extent the infringer is operating in that market, this factor favors the trademark owner, even if it does not yet operate there. If the infringer's market or goods and services are dramatically different from those of the trademark owner, it is less likely that the trademark owner would "bridge the gap" into the infringer's market and therefore the likelihood of confusion is theoretically less.[104]

Evidence of Actual Consumer Confusion

Evidence of actual consumer confusion strongly tips the analysis in favor of a finding of trademark infringement.[105] Given that the standard for finding infringement is a likelihood of confusion, the value of such evidence is self-evident. Any proof that consumers, for example, requested a certain product by brand name and were instead provided with an infringing product or that the consumer purchased an infringing product only to learn later that it did not get the real thing will substantially support a trademark owner's claims of infringement. Although such evidence is extremely useful, it must be noted that "it is black letter law that actual confusion need not be shown to prevail under the Lanham Act."[106]

Defendant's Intent in Selecting Its Trademark

Similar to proof of actual consumer confusion, evidence of an infringer's intentional selection of an infringing mark is strong evidence of confusion. In fact, demonstration of an infringer's intent to copy creates a presumption of confusion.[107] Additionally, knowledge of a competitor's mark prior to the adoption of the infringing mark may signal bad faith.[108] If the infringer knew of the plaintiff's trademark prior to the adoption of its own mark and/or intentionally selected a mark that was highly similar to the trademark owner's brand or logo, infringement is more likely to be found.

Quality of the Defendant's Goods or Services

The quality of the defendant's goods or services may be relevant in different ways. If the products are close or equal in quality, this may raise the likelihood of confusion.[109] However, if the quality of defendant's goods or services is substantially lower, there is a risk that confusion will injure plaintiff's reputation.[110] The quality factor presumes that if the infringing goods are of a dramatically poorer quality, then the infringer likely intentionally adopted a confusingly similar trademark in the hopes of free-riding on and misappropriating the goodwill embodied in the trademark of the plaintiff.[111] The law seeks to protect the consumer from goods of poor or dangerous quality and at the same time protect a trademark owner who is recognized in the marketplace as a provider of quality goods. The Second Circuit Court of Appeals has held that the quality of an accused infringer's product may be relevant to the trademark infringement inquiry in that an inferior product may debase or tarnish the senior user's reputation because people may think that the products come from the same source.[112] Other Courts of Appeals have agreed with this reasoning.[113]

Sophistication of the Consumers

This factor acknowledges that the more sophisticated consumers are, the less likely they are to be misled by similar marks.[114] Where a product solicits a "general clientele," however, there is no reason to expect that a high level of sophistication will protect them from confusion.[115] Thus, where a product is targeted both to discriminating and casual buyers, a court must consider the likelihood of confusion on the part of the relatively unknowledgeable buyers as well as of the former group.[116] This factor also takes into account the degree of care and attention the relevant universe of consumers takes in selecting the product or service at issue.[117] Where a "purchase" takes only a few seconds to consummate, courts have found the likelihood of consumer confusion to be greater.[118]

Balancing each of these factors, the trier of fact, either judge or jury, will determine if infringement has occurred. If the defendant is found to have committed trademark infringement, the case then proceeds to a determination of the damages to which the trademark owner is entitled.

REMEDIES AND ECONOMIC RECOVERY FOR TRADEMARK INFRINGEMENT

There are various remedies available to redress trademark infringement. Traditionally under the Lanham Act, a trademark holder's primary remedy will be that of equitable relief.[119] The Lanham Act authorizes the federal courts to "grant injunctions, according to the principles of equity, and upon such terms as the court may deem reasonable, to prevent" further infringement and harm to the trademark owner.[120] The entry of a preliminary injunction or temporary restraining order at the outset of a litigation requires various proofs, one of which is typically a showing that irreparable harm will be suffered by the trademark owner in the absence of an injunction.[121] That irreparable harm requirement is typically satisfied once the trademark owner establishes a "likelihood of confusion."[122] This is because consumer confusion causes the trademark owner to lose control over its reputation which is symbolized by its trademark.[123]

This "likelihood of confusion" standard in the injunction context is the same standard discussed in the preceding section with respect to the underlying trademark infringement claim. Therefore, one would reasonably assume that by prevailing on such a claim, a party would in turn automatically be able to recover damages. Such is not the case. In order to obtain a damages recovery, a plaintiff will be required to show evidence of actual confusion, instead of just a likelihood of confusion.[124] This is ordinarily done by showing that specific consumers were literally confused or by demonstrating that the infringer set out with a calculated plan of infringement, in which case actual confusion will be assumed.[125]

To calculate trademark infringement damages and other monetary recovery to which a successful plaintiff may be entitled, a few component theories, which are described later, should be considered. In each case, certain data should be collected prior to engaging in expert witness discovery or advancing to trial. Those items include, but are not always limited to, the gross revenue from the sales of the infringer's products or services, the number of units of infringing goods or services sold, the time period over which the infringement occurred, the trademark owner's profit margins on its products or services with which the infringing goods or services compete, and any quantifiable losses that the trademark owner may have suffered as a result of the infringement. Such data will ordinarily be considered regardless of the specific theory of recovery that is selected.

Determining the Relevant Damages Period

The first step in assessing damages is to understand the time period at issue. Generally, this period will begin when infringement began through the time of trial or entry of judgment.[126] In calculating the relevant damages period, one should also determine whether there has been any limitation placed on the relevant time period, such as restrictions imposed by statutes of limitations or any court ordered limitations. Without first properly determining the relevant damages period, it is impossible to accurately calculate damages.

Although the Lanham Act does not itself contain a statute of limitations, at least one court has borrowed from an analogous state law and held that a presumption of laches, a common equitable defense in trademark litigation that bars claims based on the passage of time, applies to a Lanham Act claim that is not asserted within six years.[127] As a result, borrowing statutes of limitation periods from equitable defenses under state law may be something the practitioner should consider or be aware of depending on the jurisdiction of the lawsuit. Assuming a trademark infringement claim is not barred all together under a statute of limitations type defense, such a defense may serve to limit the period in which the plaintiff is claiming infringement, and correspondingly damages. This is often the case where the infringement began several years ago but is continuing into the present time.[128] In such circumstances, an infringement claim may be viable, but the damages will only be recoverable back to the time during which the legal limitation applies.[129]

One limiting legal requirement that often arises in the calculation of damages is the notice requirement. Under the Lanham Act, the owner of a registered trademark may not recover any "profits" or "damages" unless it has given notice of its registration by marking its products or by providing actual notice of infringement to the infringer.[130] Constructive notice by the registrant is provided in a variety of ways, but is typically done with the familiar "®."[131] Registration of a trademark provides "constructive notice"; however, such constructive notice applies only to ownership of the mark and not notice of an entitlement to damages.[132] In the absence of proper marking, the trademark owner will ordinarily fulfill the notice requirement by sending a cease and desist letter.[133] The filing of a complaint alleging trademark infringement, although arguably late in the game, will also constitute actual notice. If infringement is believed to have occurred, some written documentation providing specific notice of the alleged infringement should be sent to the accused in order to establish the date of actual notice and the beginning of the damages period.

Another limitation on the damages period is the knowledge requirement of Section 32(1)(b). Under that section, when the claim of infringement is based on conduct that involves the act of actually reproducing, copying, or colorably imitating a registered mark, as opposed to actually using that infringing reproduction or imitation in commerce, knowledge that such imitation or copy will later be used in commerce is required before damages may be recovered. Specifically, the statute states that "the registrant shall not be entitled to recover profits or damages unless the acts have been committed with knowledge that such imitation is intended to be used to cause confusion, or to cause mistake, or to deceive."[134] The purpose here is to protect people such as printers who may manufacture packaging or advertising at the request of a third party without any knowledge of the potential infringement.[135]

Because these limitations may have dramatic effects on the amounts that can be considered for recovery, the appropriate time period must be determined prior to embarking on discovery in litigation.

Once the damages period has been set, certain information should be obtained and, if necessary and not already available, calculated. The litigants can and should determine how many units of the infringer's products or services were sold as well as the gross revenue that is attributable to such sales activity. The accused infringer should also determine whether it has any quantifiable expenses that can reduce the potential damages that the trademark owner will claim. Similarly, an analysis of the trademark owner's own sales should be conducted to see what the profit margins were on the trademark owner's sales and whether the trademark owner arguably suffered some other form of quantifiable injury during the relevant time period. For example, the trademark owner may have suffered a loss in sales or been forced to lower its prices as a result of the infringement.[136] The trademark owner may have also been forced to expend resources to combat consumer confusion caused by the infringer. This is often referred to as "corrective advertising."[137] Taking these pieces of important information, the next step is to consider the theories of recovery that are available.

Theories of Recovery under the Lanham Act

Although there are multiple theories for the recovery of damages under federal law for trademark infringement, they all find their basis in the same statute. Section 35(a) of the Lanham Act provides:

> When a violation of any right of the registrant of a mark registered in the Patent and Trademark Office, a violation under section 43(a), (c), or (d) [§1125(a), (c), or (d)], or a willful violation under section 43(c), shall have been established in any civil action arising under this Act, the plaintiff shall be entitled, subject to the provisions of sections 29 and 32 [§§1111, 1114] of this Act, and the subject to the principles of equity, to recover (1) defendant's profits, (2) any damages sustained by the plaintiff, and (3) the costs of the action.[138]

Three general categories of recovery can be taken from the statute, namely (1) the infringer's profits, (2) damages sustained by the trademark owner, and (3) the costs of the action. In addition, a federal court may enter judgment for any amount up to three times the amount found to be the trademark owner's actual damage (i.e., treble damages).[139] Conversely, the court may also decrease an award based on notions of equity after considering the totality of the circumstances.[140]

Recovery Based on the Infringer's Profits   Under earlier American trademark law, a successful plaintiff could recover the infringer's profits only if the plaintiff and defendant were in competition with each other.[141] The rationale was that if the parties were not competing, the infringer's profits would have no nexus to the harm suffered by the trademark owner and therefore the infringer's profits would not properly measure damages.[142]

The broader, modern view on awarding the infringer's profits expands these policy considerations and focuses more on preventing the infringer from profiting from the infringement. Three theories are now generally asserted as justification for awarding the infringer's profits to the prevailing trademark owner: (1) such award is a measure of the damage the plaintiff has suffered, (2) an award of the infringer's profits assumes that the infringer has been unjustly enriched and seeks to take away the benefit the infringer received, and (3) an award of the infringer's profits serves as a deterrent against future infringement.[143] This is not to say that a court will not consider whether the parties are competitors.[144] It simply reflects a recognition by the courts that even where the parties are not in competition, the infringer should not be allowed to profit from its unlawful conduct.[145] It also bears mentioning that, in accordance with these policy considerations, even if the trademark owner cannot establish that it suffered actual damage, it may still recover the infringer's profits.[146]

The law is very straightforward on how to calculate an award based on the infringer's profits. Section 35 of the Lanham Act states "[i]n assessing profits the plaintiff shall be required to prove defendant's sales only; defendant must prove all elements of cost or deduction claimed."[147] Essentially, the prevailing plaintiff need only demonstrate the infringer's gross revenues that have some nexus to the infringement.[148] It is then the infringer's heavy burden to establish any expenses or elements of cost that should be rightfully deducted in determining the profits.[149]

In calculating the infringer's profits, the trademark owner will presumably cast as wide a net as possible. All revenues that arguably bear some nexus to the infringement or the use of the marks that have been infringed should be totaled.[150] The trademark owner is not entitled to claim damages on revenue that is not attributable to the use of the infringing mark.[151] However, the burden of removing certain amounts from the damages pot rests with the infringer as the law imposes a presumption that all goods and services sold using the infringing mark were due to the selling power of the mark that was infringed.[152] Any doubts as to whether certain gross revenue should be included in the damages calculation are resolved against the infringer, in favor of the victorious trademark owner.[153] The Supreme Court, recognizing the infringer's evidentiary burden, held that as between the trademark owner and the infringer, any windfall in recovery that may result should be given to the trademark owner.[154]

Once the gross revenue figures have been calculated, the next battle between the parties will be as to what expenses the infringer can claim.[155] Various items are often sought as deductible expenses, such as income tax,[156] cost of good sold,[157] and operating expenses.[158] If the infringer seeks to claim expenses that relate to its entire business or to a product line that differs from the infringing product line, then an allocation must be made to capture only those expenses that relate to the infringing good or services.[159] Again this burden will fall to the infringer.[160] Ordinary accounting and economic principles should apply, and allocations as to revenue should similarly be applied to expenses.

Recovery Based on Damages Suffered by the Trademark Owner The statutory language provides that a prevailing plaintiff may recover its damages sustained as a result of the infringement. These damages may come in many forms, and there are a few different theories of measuring actual damages. Among the theories that have been employed are lost profits, reasonable royalty, and costs of corrective advertising.

The successful plaintiff seeking its actual damages will not have to show actual deceptive intent or willfulness in order to recover its actual damages.[161] Courts will, however, ordinarily require the plaintiff to show evidence of actual consumer confusion before an award of actual damages for trademark infringement will be granted.[162] That being said, several courts will imply that actual confusion has occurred where evidence of the infringer's deceptive intent is offered.[163]

We now turn our attention to an analysis of each individual theory of measuring damages suffered as a consequence of infringement.

Lost Profits   A lost profits analysis is a very common way of establishing actual damages, and perhaps the most traditional from an economic prospective. Lost profits may be calculated in a number of ways. For example, the profit margin per unit of the trademark owner's goods could be calculated and then applied to the total number of infringing units sold by the defendant.[164]

In theory, one could also look to the sales of infringing goods that were made by the defendant, but that approach is not without its complications.[165] In addition to the legal issues and burdens that may arise, there are economic concerns. For example, the profit margins between defendant's and plaintiff's product may differ drastically as the quality of knock-off goods is often intentionally lower and such goods are intentionally priced lower to undercut the trademark owner's market. Additionally, in the absence of a two-player market, causation for the loss in unit sales may be difficult to establish with any reasonable certainty. There may have been other third-party or market factors that contributed to the decline in sales as well. Of course, the burden of establishing these other influences will fall on the infringer.[166]

The Fifth Circuit has accepted an alternative approach for calculating lost profits where a defendant has committed the acts of infringement in a territorial market into which plaintiff may, but has yet to, expand. This method is known as the "head start" theory of damages. In *Taco Cabana v. Two Pesos,* later appealed to the Supreme Court on a separate issue, the court held that that the loss incurred by plaintiff as a result of the infringer's use of the trade dress within plaintiff's potential markets for expansion was compensable.[167] This eliminates the need for proof of actual confusion and diverted sales to measure damages in situations where the infringer has acted first, cultivating a consumer association with plaintiff's trade dress before plaintiff has had an opportunity to enter that market.[168] In *Taco Cabana,* the court estimated lost profits to be $4.4 million based on defendant establishing restaurants which infringed plaintiff's trade dress in "one of the most affluent Mexican food markets in the country."[169]

As is clear from the preceding discussion, several economic theories may be used to calculate lost profits. The facts of each particular case will dictate the most reliable approach as business and industry practices may vary. In the end, one must have several reliable data points from which to calculate amounts that were lost by the plaintiff as well as a related and credible theory as to the causation of the damages flowing from the infringement.

Reasonable Royalty   An award of a reasonable royalty—where the court makes a hypothetical determination of a reasonable amount the defendant would have paid the plaintiff to license use of the mark—is a viable, but rarely used, method of compensating an injured trademark holder.[170]

Typically, a reasonable royalty is employed in trademark litigations where the parties have previously shown a willingness to enter into a license agreement.[171] This most commonly arises when the parties had a prior licensing relationship that expired and the defendant continued to use the mark.[172] This may also arise where the defendant made an offer to license the plaintiff's mark, but an agreement was never consummated.[173]

Some courts have stated that the imposition of a royalty award is disfavored in cases where the plaintiff had previously been unwilling to license its mark.[174] In addition, a royalty award is not appropriate where the defendant has not fully used everything a license would normally provide.[175] In essence, a reasonable royalty should bear a "rational relationship to the rights appropriated."[176] A court may not, under any circumstances, impose a compulsory license allowing the infringer to continue a previously unauthorized use of a mark for a fixed rate.[177]

Even if there is no evidence probative of the parties' intent regarding licensing, exigent circumstances may still justify the use of a reasonable royalty. For example, the parties in the landmark case of *Sands, Taylor & Woods Co. v. The Quaker Oats Co.* had no prior licensing relationship, but that did not prevent an award of the largest reasonable royalty judgment in the United States.[178] In *Sands,* the plaintiff, a small, Vermont-based company, owned the trademark "THIRST-AID," which it used and licensed for various beverage products. The defendant, producer of the drink Gatorade, launched a nationally televised advertising campaign intended to educate the public about the benefits of drinking Gatorade. The slogan used for the campaign was "Gatorade is Thirst Aid for that Deep Down Body Thirst."[179] The plaintiff filed suit for reverse confusion,[180] and the district court initially awarded 10 percent of defendant's pretax profits as damages for the infringement. On appeal, the Seventh Circuit held that the district court should have made a more precise determination, but permitted the court to take into account the need for deterrence in calculating damages. In addition, the court held that awarding a percentage of defendant's profits "bears no relationship" to the infringement and "[a] reasonable royalty," perhaps similar to the royalty a third party paid to plaintiff to license the mark, "would more accurately reflect both the extent of [defendant's] unjust enrichment and the interest of [plaintiff] that has been infringed."[181]

On remand, the district court used a reasonable royalty (1 percent of defendant's sales for the first year and .5 percent thereafter) to calculate the damages and also doubled the award pursuant to 15 U.S.C. 1117(a). The Seventh Circuit remanded again for more precision in the royalty computation, requiring that particular care be taken to make certain the trademark owner had not been undercompensated. In addition, the court held that judicial enhancement of a reasonable royalty award is permissible, although not to punish, and provided two justifications: (1) to ensure deterrence so that payment of a royalty does not simply become a cost of doing business as an infringer; and (2) the difficulty of computing a royalty for a hypothetical transaction.[182]

Reasonable royalty is a viable theory, although not often available absent appropriate facts. Because there is a great deal of debate as to how a hypothetical negotiation between the parties would occur, a reasonable royalty theory will ordinarily be subject to greater scrutiny than other theories.

Corrective Advertising   The owner of an infringed trademark may need to counteract the deleterious effect of public confusion on its profits and commercial goodwill with rebuttal advertising. The amount expended in disseminating these "corrective advertisements" is recoverable as compensatory damages in a trademark infringement action.[183] Courts will award the amount actually incurred by the aggrieved party in correcting the mistaken public perception.[184] The Eighth Circuit has held that the computation should take into account only money spent by the defendant on items "designed to reach out and affect the public mind," and thus intracompany items, such as office forms and memo pads, should not be included.[185] Moreover, the Sixth Circuit has held that the plaintiff need not demonstrate actual confusion or actual damage; rather, to recover "damage control" damages, plaintiff must prove a violation of the Lanham Act and that (1) there was a likelihood of confusion or damage to sales, profits or goodwill; (2) plaintiff's "damage control" expenditures were caused by the violation; and (3) plaintiff's expenses were reasonable under the circumstances and proportionate to the damage that was likely to occur.[186] Damages to cover remedial advertising may actually exceed the cost of the infringing advertising campaign, as demonstrated in a Ninth Circuit case where the plaintiff spent, and was consequently awarded, more than twice the cost of the infringing advertisements.[187]

A trademark owner may also obtain prospective damages for post-judgment corrective advertising necessary to repair public confusion. In the influential decision *Big O Tire Dealer, Inc. v. Goodyear Tire and Rubber Co.,* the Tenth Circuit, relying on Federal Trade Commission regulations concerning deceptive advertising, held that a plaintiff may recover 25 percent of the amount defendant spent on the infringing advertising campaign to cover the future cost of corrective advertising.[188] The court also justified granting prospective damages based on the plaintiff's lack of resources to undertake a corrective advertising campaign prior to litigation.[189] Some subsequent cases require the plaintiff to prove financial hardship in order to receive damages for future corrective advertising.[190] The Ninth Circuit, however, rejected such a requirement, stating that it could "see no reason to so limit the availability of essentially compensatory damages."[191]

Attorneys' Fees and Court Costs   Attorneys' fees may be an available remedy in a trademark case under Section 35 of the Lanham Act. In 1975, Congress amended Section 35 to include: "The court in exceptional cases may award reasonable attorney fees to the prevailing party."[192] The terseness of the provision and the lack of any statutory guidance has yielded a "rainbow of standards" for determining what constitutes an "exceptional case."[193] The Senate Committee on the Judiciary stated that exceptional cases includes "acts of infringement [which] can be characterized as 'malicious,' 'fraudulent,' 'deliberate' or willful.'"[194] Some Circuit Courts of Appeals hold that the standard should differ depending on whether the plaintiff or defendant is the prevailing party (Fourth, Sixth, Tenth, and Eleventh Circuits),[195] while others apply a single standard (Second, Third, and Ninth Circuits).[196]

Prevailing plaintiffs succeed in recovering attorneys' fees with "some regularity."[197] A plaintiff has not "prevailed" if the defendant has merely consented to a settlement.[198] Generally, courts will look to "the totality of the circumstances, rather than a particular item alone," in determining whether granting attorneys' fees is warranted,[199] and typically, intentional, deliberate, or willful infringement is deemed sufficient.[200] The conduct must exceed, in terms of culpability, mere negligence.[201]

To satisfy Section 35, many courts use the phraseology "bad faith" and require the plaintiff prove that defendant intended to infringe the plaintiff's mark by trading on the plaintiff's commercial goodwill and reputation.[202] In the Second Circuit, for example, a showing of fraud or bad faith is required for the case to be exceptional.[203] Similarly, the Tenth Circuit requires that "some degree of bad faith fuel[] the infringement at issue" and defined the term by observing that "bad faith endows the defendant's conduct with not only the knowledge that the act is wrongful but also the commitment to proceed anyway."[204] Other circuits, however, do not require proof of bad faith; thus harm to the plaintiff through deliberate conduct may be sufficient. The First Circuit has explicitly rejected bad faith as a prerequisite, holding that "willful conduct may be sufficient when the trial court takes into account all the facts and equities of the case."[205] The Ninth Circuit takes the view that while bad faith "may provide evidence that the case is exceptional, other exceptional circumstances may warrant a fee award."[206]

Often courts state that willful or deliberate infringement renders a case exceptional. Such conduct consists of "more than the accidental encroachment of another's rights. It involves an intent to infringe or a deliberate disregard of a mark holder's rights."[207] The requisite willfulness has been found where a defendant agreed not to use a mark but continued to anyway,[208] or where a defendant has intentionally misled the public.[209] However, where the defendant knowingly created a similar trade dress, but made conscious, yet unavailing, efforts to make it sufficiently dissimilar to avoid liability, the court held that the infringement could not be willful.[210]

Receipt of a cease and desist letter and subsequent refusal to comply will not alone constitute willful infringement,[211] but additional factors, such as receipt of two letters and failure to consult counsel, may be sufficient to justify awarding attorneys' fees.[212] In addition, failure to follow counsel's advice to conduct a trademark search, along with continued use of a mark after suit was filed and a trademark search was conducted, constituted willful infringement and made at least one case exceptional.[213] It bears mentioning that reliance on advice of counsel alone will not aid a defendant unless such reliance is reasonable.[214]

Section 35 does not preclude defendants from being awarded attorneys' fees. The legislative history confirms Congress's intent to make attorneys' fees available to defendants to "provide protection against unfounded suits brought by trademark owners for harassment and the like."[215] Courts applying a different standard to prevailing defendants than prevailing plaintiffs hold that the defendant need not prove bad faith.[216] Instead, the defendant needs to prove "something less than bad faith"[217]; that the plaintiff's actions were oppressive[218] or that plaintiff's case was "groundless, unreasonable, vexatious, or pursued in bad faith."[219] The courts harmonizing the standards for prevailing plaintiffs and defendants apply the same "bad faith" test discussed above for prevailing plaintiffs.[220]

Standards for determining when to award attorneys' fees to a prevailing defendant differ considerably among the Circuit Courts of Appeals.[221] However, where a plaintiff's claims are obviously without merit, the defendant will likely receive attorneys' fees.[222] A court that follows the "bad faith" standard may not grant attorneys' fees where a meritless claim has been brought in good faith.[223] Most courts will award attorneys' fees if plaintiff has filed suit as a form of economic coercion or intimidation.[224]

Once the court has decided that a case is exceptional, and thus an award of attorneys' fees is warranted, it must then calculate a "reasonable" fee. The Supreme Court has advocated the use of a "lodestar" analysis for any case involving the granting of fees to a "prevailing party."[225] The lodestar figure is calculated by multiplying the reasonable number of hours spent on the case by a reasonable hourly rate.[226] Some courts consider trademark to be a difficult and specialized field requiring particular expertise and thus meriting a higher hourly billing rate.[227] The court should set a rate based on "competent, trustworthy evidence of the market" proffered by the parties.[228] It should not substitute the hourly rate based solely on its "own familiarity with the relevant rates in [the] community."[229] The party seeking the fees bears the burden of proving the number of hours spent on the case and a reasonable hourly rate.[230] The court should then eliminate the hours "not reasonably expended," excessive, redundant or unnecessary.[231]

Once the lodestar figure is determined, courts may, and do, adjust this figure in different ways. For example, the Ninth Circuit uses a lodestar-plus formulation in which twelve factors are considered in adjusting the figure:

1. The time and labor required
2. The novelty and difficulty of the questions
3. The skill requisite to perform the legal services properly
4. The preclusion of other employment due to acceptance of the case
5. The customary fee
6. The contingent or fixed nature of the fee
7. The limitations imposed by the client or the case
8. The amount involved and the results obtained
9. The experience, reputation, and ability of the attorneys
10. The undesirability of the case
11. The nature of the professional relationship with the client
12. Awards in similar cases[232]

The Supreme Court has held that there is a "strong presumption" against adjusting the lodestar figure.[233] While permissible, any adjustment must be supported by specific evidence and detailed findings.[234]

The prevailing party in a multi-claim case may only receive attorneys' fees for work related to the Lanham Act claims.[235] If work overlaps between the exceptional claims qualifying for fees and the nonrecoverable claims, the court should reduce the total fee by the percentage which represents the non-Lanham Act claims.[236] The Ninth Circuit has admonished lower courts that "the impossibility of making an exact apportionment does not relieve the district court of its duty to make some attempt to adjust the fee award in an effort to reflect an apportionment. In other words, apportionment or an attempt at apportionment is required unless the court finds the claims are so inextricably intertwined that even an estimated adjustment would be meaningless."[237]

Courts have held that the decision of whether to award attorneys' fees and the calculation of the actual monetary amount using the guidelines just stated are committed to the judge's discretion.[238] Most courts require the prevailing party prove that a case is exceptional with clear and convincing evidence, which makes the recovery of attorneys' fees more challenging.[239]

A prevailing plaintiff may also obtain court costs under Section 35(a). Specifically, the provision provides that once liability has been established in a trademark suit, "the plaintiff shall be entitled, . . . subject to the principles of equity, to recover . . . (3) the costs of the action."[240] The expenses that the plaintiff may permissibly tax to the defendant are delineated in the Federal Judicial Code.[241] In contrast to attorneys' fees, which are awarded only in exceptional cases, the district court is limited only by principles of equity, and thus costs are typically granted to the prevailing party.[242]

Statutory Damages in Counterfeiting Cases

Congress enacted the Anticounterfeiting Consumer Protection Act in 1996, which permits the plaintiff, at any time prior to final judgment, to elect to recover statutory damages in lieu of actual damages and profits where the defendant has used a counterfeit trademark.[243] Often counterfeiters will not maintain records of their illicit activities, making actual damages difficult to calculate and prove.[244] Under the aforementioned legislation, a plaintiff is entitled to an award of "not less than $500 or more than $100,000 per counterfeit mark per type of goods or services sold, offered for sale, or distributed, as the court considers just."[245] In addition, if the court finds that the use of the counterfeit mark was willful, the court may award statutory damages of up to $1 million.[246]

The statute intentionally provides little guidance for calculating the precise amount, leaving the court with broad discretion to craft a damages amount as it "considers just."[247] There is little precedent interpreting this fairly new provision, so precedent under a similar provision in copyright law is instructive.[248] In the copyright context, the Second Circuit has held that relevant factors include use of any available figures, including the expenses saved and the profits collected by the infringer, and the revenues lost by the plaintiff.[249] The defendant's culpability, conduct during the proceeding, and the necessity of deterrence may also be considered.[250] One district court calculated statutory damages in the amount of $900,000 for a defendant's use of the Nike logo and "swoosh" design on various articles of clothing and shoes.[251]

Judicial Modification of Damages Award

Once the court has determined the amount of actual damages to which the plaintiff is entitled using the preceding theories, the Lanham Act empowers it to adjust that award where appropriate. Section 35(a) permits the court substantial discretion to modify the amount of profits being awarded if the amount constitutes either insufficient or excessive compensation. The court may also multiply the damages award up to treble damages. Additionally, the court may grant prejudgment interest when appropriate.

Treble Damages, Enhancement, Reduction   Courts cannot award punitive damages for claims under the Lanham Act, even if the offending conduct is willful.[252] Instead, courts can enhance or reduce a damages award pursuant to Section 35(a).[253] This section gives the court discretion to either increase the amount of actual damages up to treble damages,[254] or increase or decrease the award of profits if the amount is "either inadequate or excessive."[255] The analysis for increasing "damages" is distinct from a modification of defendant's "profits."[256] A court cannot simply treble an award of profits; it may only "award the amount proved, subject only to an adjustment, up or down, where the recovery would be otherwise unjust."[257]

Section 35 further states that enhancement of an award "shall constitute compensation and not a penalty."[258] The intended purpose of this language is uncertain. The Fifth Circuit has acknowledged the apparent contradiction in increasing actual damages as a means of compensation and held that damages should be enhanced when speculative or difficult to calculate and the imprecision results from defendant's conduct.[259] Alternatively, many courts and scholars interpret the provision as permitting courts to increase damage awards to deter malicious or willful conduct provided there is still some compensatory aspect to the award.[260] Accordingly, where the plaintiff has not proven any actual damages, exemplary damages cannot be awarded.[261]

Judicial enhancement of a monetary award is most often granted where defendant used a counterfeit mark or was a knowing and intentional infringer.[262] In fact, Section 35(b) *requires* treble damages, absent any extenuating circumstances, where a defendant intentionally used a counterfeit mark.[263] Lost profits and market distortion resulting from defendant's infringement may also be appropriate grounds for enhancing compensatory damages as they cannot be precisely calculated.[264] Additionally, undeserved "intangible benefits" gained at plaintiff's expense, such as attracting additional customers and avoiding the expenditure of resources, may justify increasing damages.[265]

Interest   Section 35(a) does not explicitly provide for the award of prejudgment interest in an infringement suit.[266] However, district courts do have discretion to award prejudgment interest pursuant to this section.[267] Circuit Courts of Appeals have crafted varying standards on the availability of interest. For example, in the Second Circuit, "such an award is within the discretion of the trial court and is normally reserved for 'exceptional' cases."[268] The Tenth Circuit has a more liberal standard, recognizing that prejudgment interest may be most warranted where a violation is "intentional, and indeed outrageous," but the Lanham Act creates a "preference, if not a presumption, for prejudgment interest."[269] The Seventh Circuit goes the furthest, stating that "prejudgment interest should be presumptively available to victims of federal law violations" to avoid both incomplete compensation for the plaintiff and to discourage a defendant's delay.[270]

In most cases, a plaintiff and its economic experts should seek prejudgment interest. The interest represents actual damage that the plaintiff has suffered by being deprived of such funds during the period of infringement.

CONCLUSION

This chapter sets forth the framework for damages awards in trademark cases, and the relative burdens of proof. This information, of course, is merely the starting point. With these standards in mind, the practitioner must appropriately tailor discovery and trial strategy toward the end goal of compensation (for the plaintiff) or avoidance of damages (for the defendant). As is clear, there is considerable flexibility in the standards applied, so that expert analysis and testimony likely will play a pivotal role. Early identification of damages issues and early retention of experts are of critical importance. Similarly, the practitioner must retain the flexibility to adapt damages theories to the particular facts of the case.

NOTES

1. The authors would like to thank Adam Turkel, an associate at White & Case LLP, for his assistance in the preparation of this chapter.
2. Although there are both trademarks and service marks, for the purposes of this chapter, they shall both be referred to collectively as trademarks for ease of presentation. Generally, trademarks are an indicator of source for products and tangible goods, while service marks relate to services made available by an identifiable provider. *See* 15 U.S.C. § 1127 (2005) (defining trademark and service mark); *Chance v. Pac-Tel Teletrac Inc.,* 242 F.3d 1151, 1156 (9th Cir. 2001) (observing that "the only difference between a trademark and a service mark is that a trademark identifies goods while a service mark identifies services").
3. *See* 15 U.S.C. § 1127 (2005); *In re Trade-Mark Cases,* 100 U.S. 82, 87 (1879); *New Kids on the Block v. News Am. Publ'g, Inc.,* 971 F.2d 302, 305–06 (9th Cir. 1992); *Blue Bell, Inc. v. Farah Mfg. Co., Inc.,* 508 F.2d 1260, 1264 (5th Cir. 1975); Black's Law Dictionary 1493 (6th ed. 1990).
4. *Mishawaka Rubber & Woolen Mfg. Co. v. S.S. Kresge Co.,* 316 U.S. 203, 205 (1942).
5. J. Thomas McCarthy, McCarthy on Trademarks and Unfair Competition § 3:2 (4th ed. 2005) [*hereinafter* "McCarthy"].
6. *Mishawaka Rubber & Woolen Mfg. Co.,* 316 U.S. at 205.
7. *See, e.g.,* 15 U.S.C. § 1114 (2005).
8. *Trademark Timeline,* 82 Trademark Rep. 1022 (1992).
9. *See id.* at 1022–23 (1992); McCarthy, *supra* note 5, § 5:1.
10. McCarthy, *supra* note 5, § 5:1.
11. *See Trademark Timeline, supra* note 8, at 1023.
12. *Id.*
13. *Id.* at 1024.
14. *Southern v. How,* 79 Eng. Rep. 1243, 2 Popham 144 (1618).

15. *See Trademark Timeline, supra* note 8, at 1023–25; McCarthy, *supra* note 5, § 5:2.

16. *Snowden v. Noah,* Hopk. Ch. 347 (N.Y. Ch. 347).

17. Act of May 18, 1845, 279 Stat. 304, entitled "An Act to Punish and Prevent Frauds in the Use of False Stamps and Labels."

18. *Snowden,* Hopk. Ch. at 351.

19. *Id.* at 352–53.

20. Act of May 18, 1845, 279 Stat. 304, §§ 1–3.

21. *Id.* at § 1.

22. *Id.* at § 2.

23. *See* Jerome Gilson et al., Trademark Protection and Practice § 1.04 (2005); *see, e.g., Watec Co., Ltd. v. Genwac Inc.,* 403 F.3d 645 (9th Cir. 2005).

24. Act of July 8, 1870, 16 Stat. at L 198, §§ 77–84.

25. *Id.*

26. *In re Trade-Mark Cases,* 100 U.S. 82 (1879).

27. *Id.* at 94.

28. U.S. Const. art. 1, § 8, cl. 8.

29. *In re Trade-Mark Cases,* 100 U.S. at 94.

30. U.S. Const. art. 1, § 8, cl. 3.

31. *In re Trade-Mark Cases,* 100 U.S. at 96–97.

32. *Id.*

33. Act of Mar. 3, 1881, 21 Stat. 502.

34. *Id.*

35. McCarthy, *supra* note 5, § 5:3.

36. S. Res. No. 1333, 79th Cong., 2d Sess. (1946), U.S.C.C.A.N. 1274.

37. The Lanham Act is currently codified as 15 U.S.C. §§ 1051–1141 (2005). For information on its legislative history, *see* S. Res. No. 1333, 79th Cong., 2d Sess. (1946), U.S.C.C.A.N. 1274.

38. 15 U.S.C. § 1051(a) (2005).

39. 15 U.S.C. § 1051(b)–(d) (2005).

40. *Mishawaka Rubber & Woolen Mfg. Co. v. S.S. Kresge Co.,* 316 U.S. 203 (1942).

41. 15 U.S.C. §§ 1114, 1125 (2005).

42. *See Star Indus., Inc. v. Bacardi & Co. Ltd.,* 412 F.3d 373, 384 (2d Cir. 2005).

43. *See Two Pesos, Inc. v. Taco Cabana, Inc.,* 505 U.S. 763, 769 (1992) (describing the manner in which an otherwise unprotectable mark may become protectable through the acquisition of secondary meaning).

44. *Levi Strauss & Co. v. Blue Bell, Inc.,* 632 F.2d 817, 820 (9th Cir. 1980); *see also Safeway Stores, Inc. v. Safeway Props., Inc.,* 307 F.2d 495, 499 (2d Cir. 1962) ("If because of association with a particular product or firm over a period of time a word has come to stand in the minds of the public as a name or identification for that product or firm, the word is said to have acquired a secondary meaning.").

45. *See Vision Sports, Inc. v. Melville Corp.*, 888 F.2d 609, 615 (9th Cir. 1989) (opining that "[a]n expert survey . . . can provide the most persuasive evidence of secondary meaning").

46. *Abercrombie & Fitch Co. v. Hunting World, Inc.*, 537 F.2d 4, 9 (2d Cir. 1976).

47. *See* McCarthy, *supra* note 5, § 11:2.

48. *See Star Indus., Inc. v. Bacardi & Co. Ltd.*, 412 F.3d 373, 384 (2d Cir. 2005) ("Determination of strength therefore begins with inquiry as to whether the mark has the inherent distinctiveness that would entitle it to protection in the absence of secondary meaning").

49. *See, e.g., Two Pesos, Inc. v. Taco Cabana, Inc.*, 505 U.S. 763, 768 (1992); *Star Indus., Inc.*, 412 F.3d at 384–85; *Interstellar Starship Servs., Ltd. v. EPIX, Inc.*, 304 F.3d 936, 943 n.6 (9th Cir 2002); *CAE, Inc. v. Clean Air Eng'g, Inc.*, 267 F.3d 660, 684 (7th Cir. 2001); *Ashley Furniture Indus., Inc. v. Sangiacomo N.A. Ltd.*, 187 F.3d 363, 369 (4th Cir. 1999); *Union Nat'l Bank of Texas, Laredo, Texas v. Union Nat'l Bank of Texas, Austin, Texas*, 909 F.2d 839, 844 (5th Cir. 1990).

50. *Two Pesos, Inc.*, 505 U.S. at 768 (Friendly, J.) ("In contrast, generic marks—those that 'refe[r] to the genus of which the particular product is a species,' . . . are not registrable as trademarks.").

51. *Abercrombie & Fitch Co.*, 537 F.2d at 9.

52. *Id.*

53. *Star Indus., Inc.*, 412 F.3d at 385; *TCPIP Holding Co. v. Haar Commc'ns, Inc.*, 244 F.3d 88, 93 (2d Cir. 2001).

54. 15 U.S.C. § 1052(f) (2005).

55. *In re MBNA Am. Bank, N.A.*, 340 F.3d 1328, 1332 (Fed. Cir. 2003).

56. *Two Pesos, Inc. v. Taco Cabana, Inc.*, 505 U.S. 763, 769 (1992) ("Marks which are merely descriptive of a product are not inherently distinctive. When used to describe a product, they do not inherently identify a particular source, and hence cannot be protected.").

57. *Id.* ("However, descriptive marks may acquire the distinctiveness which will allow them to be protected. . . . This acquired distinctiveness is generally called 'secondary meaning.'").

58. 15 U.S.C. § 1052(f) (2005).

59. *Time, Inc v. Petersen Publ'g Co.*, 173 F.3d 113, 118 (2d Cir. 1999) (quoting *Stix Prods., Inc. v. United Merchs. & Mfrs., Inc.*, 295 F. Supp. 479, 488 (S.D.N.Y. 1968)).

60. *Stix Prods., Inc. v. United Merchs. & Mfrs., Inc.*, 295 F. Supp. 479, 488 (S.D.N.Y. 1968).

61. *Am. Home Prods. Corp. v. Johnson Chem. Co.*, 589 F.2d 103 (2d Cir. 1978) (finding ROACH MOTEL was suggestive for an insect trap). For other examples, *see Wal-Mart Stores, Inc. v. Samara Bros.*, 529 U.S. 205, 210 (2000) (providing TIDE as an example of a suggestive mark); *Madison Ave. Caviarteria, Inc. v. Caviaria.com*, No. 04 Civ. 00493 RO, 2004 WL 744481, at *2 (S.D.N.Y. Apr. 7, 2004) (finding CAVIARTERIA suggestive of a gourmet boutique and restaurant); *Stern's Miracle-Gro Prods., Inc. v. Shark Prods., Inc.*, 823 F. Supp. 1077, 1084 (S.D.N.Y. 1993) (finding MIRACLE-GRO suggestive of plant food).

62. *Compare Anheuser-Busch, Inc. v. Stroh Brewery Co.*, 750 F.2d 631, 640–43 (8th Cir. 1984) (term "L.A." is determined to be suggestive of low-alcohol beer), *with G. Heileman Brewing Co. v. Anheuser-Busch, Inc.*, 873 F.2d 985, 994–98 (7th Cir. 1989) (term "L.A." is determined to be descriptive of low-alcohol beer).

63. *Franklin Knitting Mills, Inc. v. Fashionit Sweater Mills, Inc.*, 297 F. 247, 248 (2d Cir. 1923).

64. *Abercrombie & Fitch Co. v. Hunting World, Inc.*, 537 F.2d 4, 11 (2d Cir. 1976); *Patsy's Brand, Inc. v. I.O.B. Realty, Inc.*, 317 F.3d 209, 217 (2d Cir. 2003) (even in the absence of secondary meaning, suggestive words, when stylized, may serve as strong marks).

65. *See Star Indus., Inc. v. Bacardi & Co. Ltd.*, 412 F.3d 373, 385 (2d Cir. 2005). Courts routinely state that arbitrary and fanciful marks are necessarily strong marks, and this is usually the case. However, even if an arbitrary mark suggests or describes nothing about a particular product, if it is in very common use in the same or a different marketplace, the mark may then be considered weak. *See* McCarthy, *supra* note 5, § 11:14.

66. *See Star Indus., Inc.*, 412 F.3d at 385 ("Arbitrary or fanciful marks are ones that do not communicate any information about the product either directly or by suggestion."); *Abercrombie & Fitch Co.*, 537 F.2d at 9–11.

67. *Interstellar Starship Servs., Ltd. v. EPIX, Inc.*, 304 F.3d 936, 943 n.6 (9th Cir 2002) ("'Fanciful' trademarks are nondictionary words (e.g., EXXON or KODAK); 'arbitrary' trademarks are common words used in uncommon or unexpected ways (e.g. AMAZON for an on-line bookstore).").

68. *See* George Eastman, http://www.kodak.com/global/en/corp/historyOfKodak/eastman-TheMan.jhtml?pq-path=2217/2687/2689 (last visited Dec. 13, 2005) ("The word 'Kodak' was first registered as a trademark in 1888. There has been some fanciful speculation, from time to time, on how the name was originated. But the plain truth is that Eastman invented it out of thin air.").

69. *Abercrombie & Fitch Co.*, 537 F.2d at 9.

70. *Yale Elec. Corp. v. Robertson*, 26 F.2d 972, 974 (2d Cir. 1928).

71. 15 U.S.C. § 1114(1) (2005).

72. *See, e.g., Two Pesos, Inc. v. Taco Cabana, Inc.*, 505 U.S. 763, 768 (1992) ("[I]t is common ground that § 43(a) protects qualifying unregistered trademarks."); *Genesee Brewing Co., Inc. v. Stroh Brewing Co.*, 124 F.3d 137, 142 (2d Cir. 1997) (section 43(a) provides protection to unregistered marks); *Metro Publ'g, Ltd. v. San Jose Mercury News*, 987 F.2d 637, 640 (9th Cir. 1993) ("It is not necessary that a trademark be registered in order for it to qualify for protection under the Lanham Act.").

73. Trademark Remedy Clarification Act, Pub. L. 102-542, § 3(b), 106 Stat. 3567 (1992); Trademark Law Revision of 1988, Pub. L. 100-667, § 132, 102 Stat. 3935 (1988). The reader will note that the Lanham Act deals with other claims in addition to trademark infringement. For example, additional claims under the Lanham Act include the false advertising and product disparagement claims under Section 43(a) that were previously referenced as well as trademark dilution (15 U.S.C. § 1125(c) (2005)) and claims against the registration and use of certain Internet domain names in bad faith (15 U.S.C. § 1125(d) (2005)). These claims and related theories are not the focal point of this discussion and so any discussion herein of infringement or damages theories that may apply to such claims is merely incidental.

74. 15 U.S.C. § 1125(a)(1) (2005).

75. *Lamparello v. Falwell*, 420 F.3d 309, 313 (4th Cir. 2005); *Surfvivor Media, Inc. v. Survivor Prods.*, 406 F.3d 625, 630 (9th Cir. 2005); *Virgin Enters. Ltd. v. Nawab*, 335 F.3d 141, 146 (2d Cir. 2003); *Ty, Inc. v. Jones Group, Inc.*, 237 F.3d 891, 897 (7th Cir. 2001); *Morningside Group Ltd. v. Morningside Capital Group LLC*, 182 F.3d 133, 137 (2d Cir. 1999).

76. *See Surfvivor Media, Inc.,* 406 F.3d at 635 (Hawaii state infringement claims apply the same standard as Lanham Act claims); *Scott Fetzer Co. v. House of Vacuums, Inc.,* 381 F.3d 477, 483 (5th Cir. 2004) (same standard under Texas law); *Kregos v. Associated Press,* 795 F. Supp. 1325, 1336 (S.D.N.Y. 1992), *aff'd,* 3 F.3d 656 (2d Cir. 1993), *cert. denied,* 510 U.S. 1112 (1994) (Sections 43(a) and 32(1) draw on the same legal tests); *Bio-Technology Gen. Corp. v. Genentech, Inc.,* 886 F. Supp. 377, 384 (S.D.N.Y. 1995) (same); *Safeway Stores, Inc. v. Safeway Props., Inc.,* 307 F.2d 495, 497 n.1 (2d Cir. 1962) (test under New York common law is same as that used under federal law).

77. 15 U.S.C. § 1057(b) (2005); *see also Lane Capital Mgmt., Inc. v. Lane Capital Mgmt., Inc.,* 192 F.3d 337, 345 (2d Cir. 1999).

78. Grounds for cancellation include that the registered mark has become the generic name for all or a portion of the goods or services for which it was registered, is functional, has been abandoned, its registration was obtained fraudulently or contrary to registration provisions in the Lanham Act, if the registered mark is being used by, or with the permission of the registrant so as to misrepresent the source of the goods or services associated with the mark, or that there is a likelihood of confusion between a previously used mark and the registered mark. 15 U.S.C. § 1064 (2005).

79. *See W. Florida Seafood, Inc. v. Jet Rests., Inc.,* 31 F.3d 1122, 1125 (Fed. Cir. 1994) ("Thus, a presumption of validity attaches to a service mark registration, and the party seeking cancellation must rebut this presumption by a preponderance of the evidence."). In addition, after being registered for five years, a registered trademark will be deemed incontestable. *See* 15 U.S.C. § 1065 (2005); *see also Lois Sportswear, U.S.A., Inc. v. Levi Strauss & Co.,* 799 F. 2d 867, 871 (2d Cir. 1986) ("[T]he mark is registered and incontestable. This, of course, entitles the mark to significant protection."). Furthermore, "[r]egistration by the PTO without proof of secondary meaning creates the presumption that the mark is more than merely descriptive, and, thus, that the mark is inherently distinctive." *Lane Capital Mgmt., Inc.,* 192 F.3d at 345.

80. *See Cent. Mfg. Co. v. Casablanca Indus., Inc.,* 87 Fed. Appx. 156, 159 (Fed. Cir. 2003); *Glover v. Ampak, Inc.,* 74 F.3d 57, 59 (4th Cir. 1996) (holding that the party seeking cancellation of a mark must prove it is merited by a preponderance of the evidence).

81. Section 2 of the Lanham Act, 15 U.S.C. § 1052 (2005), requires that a trademark be at least distinctive for protection.

82. *Abercrombie & Fitch Co. v. Hunting World, Inc.,* 537 F.2d 4, 9 (2d Cir. 1976).

83. *See supra* Section entitled "The Different Categories of Trademarks."

84. *See Park N' Fly, Inc. v. Dollar Park and Fly, Inc.,* 469 U.S. 189, 193–94 (1985).

85. The Lanham Act prohibits registration or use of a trademark if it is likely to cause confusion. 15 U.S.C. §§ 1114(1), 1025 (2005); *Arrow Fastener Co., Inc. v. Stanley Works,* 59 F.3d 284, 400 (2d Cir. 1995).

86. *Lois Sportswear, U.S.A., Inc. v. Levi Strauss & Co.,* 799 F.2d 867, 872 (2d Cir. 1986) (quoting *Dallas Cowboys Cheerleaders, Inc. v. Pussycat Cinema, Ltd.,* 604 F.2d 200, 205 (2d Cir. 1979)).

87. *Polaroid Corp. v. Polarad Elecs. Corp.,* 287 F.2d 492, 495 (2d Cir. 1961), *cert. denied,* 368 U.S. 820 (1961).

88. *Id.*

89. *See AMF Inc. v. Sleekcraft Boats*, 599 F.2d 341, 348–49 (9th Cir. 1979) (adopting the Second Circuit's list of factors); *Scott Paper Co. v. Scott's Liquid Gold, Inc.*, 589 F.2d 1225, 1229 (3d Cir. 1978) (relying on Second Circuit precedent in delineating list of factors for likelihood of confusion analysis); *Helene Curtis Indus., Inc. v. Church & Dwight Co., Inc.*, 560 F.2d 1325, 1330 (7th Cir. 1977) (citing Second Circuit precedent for likelihood of confusion factors).

90. *See Banff, Ltd. v. Federated Dep't Stores, Inc.*, 841 F.2d 486, 490 (2d Cir. 1988).

91. *See Lois Sportswear, U.S.A., Inc.*, 799 F.2d at 872.

92. *Hasbro, Inc. v. Lanard Toys, Ltd.*, 858 F.2d 70, 76 (2d Cir. 1988) (quoting *McGregor-Doniger, Inc. v. Drizzle Inc.*, 599 F.2d 1126, 1131 (2d Cir. 1979)); *see also Surfvivor Media, Inc. v. Survivor Prods.*, 406 F.3d 625, 631 (9th Cir. 2005); *Patsy's Brand, Inc. v. I.O.B. Realty, Inc.*, 317 F.3d 209, 217 (2d Cir. 2003).

93. *See Virgin Enters. Ltd. v. Nawab*, 335 F.3d 141, 147 (2d Cir. 2003).

94. *See supra* Section entitled "The Different Categories of Trademarks."

95. *Virgin Enters. Ltd.*, 335 F.3d at 147; *Versa Prods., Inc. v. Bifold Co.*, 50 F.3d 189, 203 (3d Cir. 1995) ("A strong trademark is . . . one that carries widespread, immediate recognition that one producer [even if unknown] is associated with the mark, and so with the product. If a second comer adopts a mark substantially identical to a strong mark, there is a correspondingly high likelihood that consumers will mistakenly associate the newcomer's product with the owner of the strong mark.").

96. *Virgin Enters. Ltd.*, 335 F.3d at 148; *see also Lois Sportswear, U.S.A., Inc.*, 631 F. Supp. at 741 (evidence of widespread advertising and promotion, longtime continuous use of the mark, and sales figures relevant to the commercial strength of the mark).

97. *Frank Brunckhorst Co. v. Heileman Brewing Co., Inc.*, 875 F. Supp. 966, 977–78 (E.D.N.Y. 1994) (quoting *Centaur Commc'ns Ltd. v. A/S/M Commc'ns, Inc.*, 830 F.2d 1217, 1226 (2d Cir. 1987)) (internal quotations omitted).

98. *Morningside Group Ltd. v. Morningside Capital Group, LLC*, 182 F.3d 133, 140 (2d Cir. 1999) (quoting *Lang v. Ret. Living Publ'g Co.*, 949 F.2d 576, 581 (2d Cir. 1991)); *see also Surfvivor Media, Inc. v. Survivor Prods.*, 406 F.3d 625, 633 (9th Cir. 2005).

99. *See Morningside Group Ltd.*, 182 F.3d at 140; *Versace v. Versace*, No. 01 Civ. 9645 (PKL) (THK), 2003 WL 22023946, at *10 (S.D.N.Y. Aug. 27, 2003) ("Versace" was dominant feature of parties' marks); *Guinness United Distillers & Vintners B.V. v. Anheuser Busch, Inc.*, No. 02 Civ. 0861 (LMM), 2002 WL 1543817, at *3 (S.D.N.Y. July 12, 2002) (finding "Red Label" was the dominant feature of both "Johnnie Walker Red Label" and "Red Label from Budweiser" marks); McCarthy, *supra* note 5, § 23:44 ("If the 'dominant' portion of both marks is the same, then confusion may be likely, notwithstanding peripheral differences.").

100. *See Morningside Group Ltd.*, 182 F.3d at 140 (comparing "The Morningside Group Limited" and "Morningside Capital Group, LLC" and finding "Capital" in defendant's mark "does not serve any differentiating role"); McCarthy, *supra* note 5, § 23:49.

101. *Hasbro, Inc. v. Lanard Toys, Ltd.*, 858 F.2d 70, 77 (2d Cir. 1988); *see also Morningside Group Ltd.*, 182 F.3d at 140 (noting that when parties provide "essentially the same service to the same customer base, their services 'are related and proximate'"); *Banff, Ltd. v. Federated Dep't Stores, Inc.*, 841 F.2d 486, 492 (2d Cir. 1988) ("To establish likelihood of confusion, competing goods require less proof under the *Polaroid* factors than noncompetitive items.").

102. *See A & H Sportswear, Inc. v. Victoria's Secret Stores,* 237 F.3d 198, 207 (3d Cir. 2000) (holding that, while a court "need not look beyond the marks when goods are directly competing and the marks virtually identical," a lower court should, but is not required to, look at the other factors).

103. *Morningside Group Ltd.,* 182 F.3d at 141 (quoting *Hormel Foods Corp. v. Jim Hensen Prods., Inc.* 73 F.3d 497, 504 (2d Cir. 1996)); *see also Hasbro,* 858 F.2d at 78 (noting this factor assesses whether "the senior user of the mark will bridge the gap by entering the market in which the junior user operates").

104. *Surfvivor Media, Inc. v. Survivor Prods.,* 406 F.3d 625, 634 (9th Cir. 2005) (lack of evidence that trademark owner intended to expand its business into infringer's market militated against a finding of likelihood of confusion).

105. *GoTo.com, Inc. v. Walt Disney Co.,* 202 F.3d 1199, 1208 (9th Cir. 2000) (citing *AMF Inc. v. Sleekcraft Boats,* 599 F.2d 341, 352 (9th Cir. 1979)).

106. *Lois Sportswear, U.S.A., Inc. v. Levi Strauss & Co.,* 799 F.2d 867, 875 (2d Cir. 1986).

107. *See Mobil Oil Corp. v. Pegasus Petroleum Corp.,* 818 F.2d 254, 258 (2d Cir. 1987); *Perfect Fit Indus., Inc. v. Acme Quilting Co., Inc.,* 618 F.2d 950, 954 (2d Cir. 1980); *see also Samara Bros., Inc. v. Wal-Mart Stores, Inc.,* 165 F.3d 120, 127 (2d Cir. 1998), *rev'd on other grounds,* 529 U.S. 205 (2000) ("Intentionally deceptive conduct thus serves as a proxy for actual consumer confusion, raising a rebuttable legal presumption that the actor's intent to confuse will be successful."). A second comer who intended to create a confusing similarity of appearance "will be presumed to have succeeded." *Perfect Fit,* 618 F.2d at 954; *see also Mobil Oil Corp.,* 818 F.2d at 258.

108. *See Mobil Oil Corp.,* 818 F.2d at 259. Where a senior user's mark is commercially very strong, a court may infer that the junior user knew of its existence. *Id.* (upholding district court's inference of defendant's bad faith where plaintiff's mark was commercially strong); *see also Stern's Miracle-Gro Prods., Inc. v. Shark Prods., Inc.,* 823 F. Supp. 1077, 1084 (S.D.N.Y. 1993) (inferring knowledge of Plaintiff's commercially strong MIRACLE-GRO plant food when Defendant adopted MIRACLE GRO for its hair care products); McCarthy, *supra* note 5, § 23:115 ("Where we can perceive freedom of choice with full knowledge of a senior user's mark, we can readily read into defendant's choice of a confusingly similar mark the intent to get a free ride upon the reputation of a well-known mark.").

109. *See Morningside Group Ltd. v. Morningside Capital Group, LLC,* 182 F.3d 133, 142 (2d Cir. 1999); *Star Indus., Inc. v. Bacardi & Co. Ltd.,* 412 F.3d 373, 384 (2d Cir. 2005).

110. *Id. See also The Sports Auth., Inc. v. Prime Hospitality Corp.,* 89 F.3d 955, 965 (2d Cir. 1996) ("This factor is primarily concerned with whether the senior user's reputation could be jeopardized by virtue of the fact that the junior user's product is of inferior quality.").

111. *See Sara Lee Corp. v. Kayser-Roth Corp.,* 81 F.3d 455, 467 (4th Cir. 1996) ("Consideration of the quality of the defendant's product is most appropriate in situations involving the production of cheap copies or knockoffs of a competitor's trademark-protected goods. If a defendant markets a product under a mark similar to that affixed by a competitor to a commodity of like nature but superior manufacture, that the defendant's product is markedly inferior is likely to be highly probative of its reliance on the similarity of the two marks to generate undeserved sales.").

112. *See Nikon, Inc. v. Ikon Corp.*, 987 F.2d 91, 95 (2d Cir. 1993); *see Guinness United Distillers & Vintners B.V. v. Anheuser Busch, Inc.*, No. 02 Civ. 0861 (LMM), 2002 WL 1543817, at *5 (S.D.N.Y. July 12, 2002). A senior user is entitled to protect "the good reputation associated with his mark from the possibility of being tarnished by inferior merchandise." *See Scarves by Vera, Inc. v. Todo Imps. Ltd., Inc.*, 544 F.2d 1167, 1172 (2d Cir. 1976).

113. *See, e.g., Sweetarts v. Sunline, Inc.*, 380 F.2d 923, 927 (8th Cir. 1967) ("Plaintiff has the right to make and keep its own reputation without entrusting it to others over whom it cannot exercise any control. Some may treat it tenderly, nurture and enhance it, while others during the course of time may tarnish or degrade it; and the public is confused and suffers along with the infringed.").

114. *See Stern's Miracle-Gro Prods., Inc. v. Shark Prods., Inc.*, 823 F. Supp. 1077, 1089 (S.D.N.Y. 1993).

115. *TCPIP Holding Co., Inc. v. Haar Commc'ns, Inc.*, 244 F.3d 88, 102 (2d Cir. 2001).

116. *See Omega Importing Corp. v. Petri-Kine Camera Co.*, 451 F.2d 1190, 1195 (2d Cir. 1971); McCarthy, *supra* note 5, § 23:100 (advocating this approach); *cf. Ford Motor Co. v. Summit Motor Prods., Inc.*, 930 F.2d 277, 293 (3d Cir. 1991) (holding that in mixed buyer care cases, "the standard of care to be exercised by the reasonably prudent purchaser will be equal to that of the least sophisticated consumer").

117. *See Frank Brunckhorst Co. v. Heileman Brewing Co., Inc.*, 875 F. Supp. 966, 983 (E.D.N.Y. 1994) ("[T]he Court must consider the general impression of the ordinary purchaser, buying under the normally prevalent conditions of the market and giving the attention such purchasers usually give in buying that class of goods.") (internal quotations omitted).

118. *See Playboy Enters., Inc. v. Chuckleberry Publ'g, Inc.*, 687 F.2d 563, 566 (2d Cir. 1982) (noting that a newsstand purchase only takes a few seconds to make).

119. *See* McCarthy, *supra* note 5, § 30:1 ("A prevailing plaintiff in a case of trademark infringement or false advertising is ordinarily entitled to injunctive relief of some kind.").

120. 15 U.S.C. § 1116 (2005).

121. *See AM Gen. Corp. v. DaimlerChrysler Corp.*, 311 F.3d 796, 803 (7th Cir. 2002); *Stuhlbarg Int'l Sales Co. v. John D. Brush & Co.*, 240 F.3d 832, 839–40 (9th Cir. 2001); *Warner-Lambert Co. v. Northside Dev. Corp.*, 86 F.3d 3, 6 (2d Cir. 1996).

122. *Virgin Enters. Ltd. v. Nawab*, 335 F.3d 141, 146 (2d Cir. 2003); *Ty, Inc. v. Jones Group, Inc.*, 237 F.3d 891 (7th Cir. 2001); *GoTo. Comm., Inc., v. Walt Disney Co.*, 202 F.3d 1199 (9th Cir. 2000); *Fed. Express Corp. v. Fed. Espresso, Inc.*, 201 F.3d 168 (2d Cir. 2000); *Fun-Damental Too, Ltd. v. Gemmy Indus. Corp.*, 111 F.3d 993, 999 (2d Cir. 1997); *Societe des Produits Nestle, S.A. v. Casa Helvetia, Inc.*, 982 F.2d 633 (1st Cir. 1992); *Opticians Ass'n of Am. v. Indep. Opticisions of Am.*, 920 F.2d 187 (3d Cir. 1990); *Home Box Office, Inc. v. Showtime/The Movie Channel Inc.*, 832 F.2d 1311 (2d Cir. 1987); *Hasbro, Inc. v. Lanard Toys, Ltd.*, 858 F.2d 70, 73 (2d Cir. 1988).

123. *See Church of Scientology Int'l v. Elmira Mission of the Church of Scientology*, 794 F.2d 38, 43 (2d Cir. 1986); *Power Test Petroleum Distribs., Inc. v. Calcu Gas, Inc.*, 754 F.2d 91, 95 (2d Cir. 1985).

124. *See Cashmere & Camel Hair Mfrs. Inst. v. Saks Fifth Ave.*, 284 F.3d 302, 311 & n.9 (1st Cir. 2002); *Int'l Star Class Yacht Racing Ass'n v. Tommy Hilfiger, U.S.A., Inc.*, 80 F.3d 749, 753 (2d Cir. 1996).

125. *See Boosey & Hawkes Music Publishers, Ltd. v. Walt Disney Co.*, 145 F.3d 481, 493 (2d Cir. 1998) (finding it "well settled that in order for a Lanham Act plaintiff to receive an award of *damages* the plaintiff must prove either actual consumer confusion or deception resulting from the violation, . . . or that the defendant's actions were intentionally deceptive thus giving rise to a rebuttable presumption of consumer confusion"); *Res. Developers, Inc. v Statue of Liberty-Ellis Island Found., Inc.* 926 F.2d 134, 139–40 (2d Cir. 1991); *U-Haul Int'l, Inc. v. Jartran, Inc.*, 793 F.2d 1034, 1040–41 (9th Cir. 1986).

126. *See Brunswick Corp. v. Spinit Reel Co.*, 832 F.2d 513, 526 (10th Cir. 1987) ("Trademark infringement is a continuous wrong and, as such, gives rise to a claim for relief so long as the infringement persists. [The plaintiff] is entitled to damages until the time the wrongful infringement ceased. The trial court had jurisdiction to award damages up to the date of final judgment[.]"); *Rea v. Ford Motor Co.*, 560 F.2d 554, 557 (3d Cir. 1977), *cert. denied*, 434 U.S. 923 (1977) ("[I]n general, a court has the power to award damages occurring up to the date of the ultimate judgment in the case.").

127. *See Conopco, Inc. v. Campbell Soup Co.*, 95 F.3d 187, 191–92 (2d Cir. 1996) (finding "an intimate relationship between fraud and injury under the Lanham Act," the court concluded that "[i]t is clear that section 43(a) . . . , pertaining to 'false description[s] or representation[s],' is properly analogized to New York's six year fraud statute").

128. *See generally James Burrough Ltd. v. Sign of the Beefeater, Inc.*, 572 F.2d 574 (7th Cir. 1978) (trademark infringement); *Jarrow Formulas, Inc. v. Nutrition Now, Inc.*, 304 F.3d 829 (9th Cir. 2002) (false advertising).

129. *Jarrow Formulas, Inc.*, 304 F.3d at 837 ("For many Lanham Act claims, the alleged violations are ongoing, *i.e.*, the wrongful acts occurred both within and without the limitations period. As such, the statute of limitations is conceivably only a bar to monetary relief for the period outside the statute of limitations; the plaintiff is free to pursue monetary and equitable relief for the time within the limitations period."); McCarthy, *supra* note 5, § 31.33 ("Usually, infringement is a continuing wrong, and the statute of limitations is no bar except as to damages beyond the statutory period.").

130. 15 U.S.C. § 1111 (2005).

131. *See id.* Under the statute, notice may also be given by displaying the mark with the terms "Registered in the U.S. Patent and Trademark Office" or "Reg. U.S. Pat. & Tm. Off." *Id.*

132. *Compare* 15 U.S.C. § 1072 (2005) *with* 15 U.S.C. § 1111 (2005).

133. *See* McCarthy, *supra* note 5, § 19:144 ("To constitute 'actual notice,' the usual 'cease and desist letter' or 'infringement letter' to an alleged infringer should suffice.").

134. 15 U.S.C. § 1114(1) (2005).

135. *See* McCarthy, *supra* note 5, § 30:62.

136. *See Int'l Star Class Yacht Racing Ass'n v. Tommy Hilfiger, U.S.A., Inc.*, 80 F.3d 749, 753 (2d Cir. 1996) ("[D]amages may include compensation for (1) lost sales or revenue; (2) sales at lower prices; (3) harm to market reputation; or (4) expenditures to prevent, correct, or mitigate consumer confusion."); *Heaton Distrib. Co., Inc. v. Union Tank Car Co.*, 387 F.2d 477, 486 (8th Cir. 1967) ("Damages recoverable may include all elements of injury to the business of the trademark owner proximately resulting from the infringer's wrongful acts, such as profits on lost sales, loss from reduction in the price of goods due to the infringing

competition, damage to the reputation of the trademark owner's goods or business, and expenses incurred in preventing purchasers from being deceived by the infringer's wrongful conduct.") (internal citations and quotations omitted).

137. *See generally* McCarthy, *supra* note 5, §§ 30:6 & 30:80–30:84; *see also Zazu Designs v. L'Oreal, S.A.,* 979 F.2d 499, 506 (7th Cir. 1992) ("'Corrective advertising' is a method of repair. Defendant diminishes the value of plaintiff's trademark, and advertising restores that mark to its original value.").

138. 15 U.S.C. § 1117(a) (2005) (emphasis added).

139. *Id.* ("In assessing damages the court may enter judgment, according to the circumstances of the case, for any sum above the amount found as actual damages, not exceeding three times such amount.")

140. *Id.* ("If the court shall find that the amount of recovery based on profits is either inadequate or excessive the court may in its discretion enter judgment for such sum as the court shall find to be just, according to the circumstances of the case. Such sum in either of the above circumstances shall constitute compensation and not a penalty.")

141. *See* McCarthy, *supra* note 5, § 30:64.

142. "The view of an accounting as a surrogate for plaintiff's lost profits resulted in a rule that an accounting was appropriate only in cases involving directly competing goods, since noncompeting goods could not divert sales from the plaintiff." Restatement (Third) of Unfair Competition § 37 cmt. b (1995).

143. *See George Basch Co. v. Blue Coral, Inc.,* 968 F.2d 1532, 1537–39 (2d Cir. 1992), *cert. denied,* 506 U.S. 881 (1992).

144. *See Monsanto Chem. Co. v. Perfect Fit Prods. Mfg. Co.,* 349 F.2d 389, 397 (2d Cir. 1965), *cert. denied,* 383 U.S. 942 (1966) ("We do not hold that it is irrelevant whether the parties are in direct competition; compensation for diverted trade is one important purpose which an accounting may serve. To restrict accountings to this single purpose, however fails to take account of the other purposes served by trademark law.").

145. *See id.; Maier Brewing Co. v. Fleishmann Distilling Corp.,* 390 F.2d 117, 123 (9th Cir. 1968), *cert. denied,* 391 U.S. 966 ("It would seem fairly evident that the purpose of the Lanham Act can be accomplished by making acts of deliberate infringement unprofitable. . . . In those cases where there is infringement, but no direct competition, this can be accomplished by use of an accounting of profits based on the unjust enrichment rationale. Such an approach to the granting of accountings of profits would, by removing the motive for infringements, have the effect of deterring future infringements. The courts would therefore be able to protect the intangible value of associated with trademarks and at the same time be protecting the buying public from some of the more unscrupulous members of our economic community.").

146. *See Bishop v. Equinox Int'l Corp.,* 154 F.3d 1220, 1222 (10th Cir. 1998); *Int'l Star Class Yacht Racing Ass'n v. Tommy Hilfiger, U.S.A., Inc.,* 80 F.3d 749, 753 (2d Cir. 1996).

147. 15 U.S.C. § 1117(a) (2005); *see also* Restatement (Third) of Unfair Competition § 37 cmt. g (1995) ("When an accounting of the defendant's profits is appropriate, the plaintiff is entitled to recover the net profits on the sales attributable to the wrongful conduct. The defendant bears the burden of proving any costs or expenses to be deducted from gross income in calculating net profit.").

148. *See* 15 U.S.C. § 1117(a) (2005) ("In assessing profits the plaintiff shall be required to prove defendant's sales only; defendant must prove all elements of cost or deduction claimed.").

149. *Id.; Maier Brewing Co. v. Fleischmann Distilling Corp.*, 390 F.2d 117, 124.(9th Cir. 1968) ("[B]oth the language of Section 1117 and the case law . . . indicate that the defendant has the burden of proof as to any deductions from his gross sales.").

150. *See* Restatement (Third) of Unfair Competition § 37 cmt. d (1995) ("If the wrongful conduct is a substantial factor in producing a sale, the defendant is liable for the resulting profit without diminution for other contributing factors.").

151. *See Seatrax, Inc. v. Sonbeck Int'l, Inc.*, 200 F.3d 358, 369 (5th Cir. 2000) (holding that "the plaintiff is entitled to only those profits attributable to the unlawful use of its trademark").

152. *See Mishawaka Rubber & Woolen Mfg. Co. v. S.S. Kresge Co.*, 316 U.S. 203, 204 (1942); *Lindy Pen Co. Inc. v. Bic Pen Corp.*, 982 F.2d 1400 (9th Cir. 1993).

153. *See Louis Vuitton S.A. v. Spencer Handbags Corp.*, 765 F.2d 966, 973 (2d Cir. 1985) (holding that uncertainties in damages calculation should be resolved against the party evading ascertainment of damages).

154. *See Mishawaka Rubber & Woolen Mfg. Co.*, 316 U.S. at 207.

155. 15 U.S.C. § 1117(a) (2005); *see also* Restatement (Third) of Unfair Competition § 37 cmt. g (1995) ("When an accounting of the defendant's profits is appropriate, the plaintiff is entitled to recover the net profits on sales attributable to the wrongful conduct. The defendant bears the burden of proving any costs or expenses to be deducted from gross income in calculating net profit.").

156. *See L.P. Larson, Jr., Co. v. Wm. Wrigley, Jr., Co.*, 277 U.S. 97, 99 (1928) (holding that a district court has discretion to deduct federal taxes); McCarthy, *supra* note 5, § 30:67.

157. *See Murphy Door Bed Co., Inc. v. Interior Sleep Sys., Inc.*, 874 F.2d 95, 103 (2d Cir. 1989).

158. *See W.E. Bassett Co. v. Revlon, Inc.*, 435 F.2d 656, 665 (2d Cir. 1970); *Daisy Group, Ltd. v. Newport News, Inc.*, No. 96 Civ. 2517 (MGC), 1998 WL 796473, at *2 (S.D.N.Y. Nov. 17, 1998).

159. *See Int'l Star Class Yacht Racing Ass'n v. Tommy Hilfiger U.S.A., Inc.*, 146 F.3d 66, 72 (2d Cir. 1998) (holding that trial court can take into account sales attributable to defendant's market dominance and well-established reputation); *Holiday Inns, Inc. v. Airport Holiday Corp.*, 493 F. Supp. 1025, 1027–28 (N.D. Tex. 1980), *aff'd*, 683 F.2d 931 (5th Cir. 1982).

160. *See Int'l Star Class Yacht Racing Ass'n*, 146 F.3d at 72; *Holiday Inns, Inc.*, 493 F. Supp. at 1027–28.

161. *See SecuraComm Consulting Inc. v. Securacom Inc.*, 166 F.3d 182 (3d Cir. 1999) (stating that monetary damages are appropriate regardless of the willfulness of defendant's infringement).

162. *See Int'l Star Class Yacht Racing Ass'n*, 80 F.3d at 753.

163. *See, e.g., Res. Developers, Inc. v Statue of Liberty-Ellis Island Found., Inc.*, 926 F2d 134, 139–40 (2d Cir. 1991); *U-Haul Int'l, Inc. v. Jartran, Inc.*, 793 F.2d 1034, 1040–41 (9th Cir. 1986).

164. *See Intel Corp. v. Terabyte Int'l*, 6 F.3d 614, 620–21 (9th Cir. 1993) (multiplying the number of infringing computer chips defendant sold by the per/chip profit that plaintiff lost by not selling their authentic computer chips).

165. *See Jerry's Famous Deli, Inc. v. Papanicolaou*, 383 F.3d 998, 1004 (9th Cir. 2004) (holding that use of defendant's revenues as a measure of damages is "hardly a novel proposition.").

166. *See Int'l Star Class Yacht Racing Ass'n v. Tommy Hilfiger U.S.A.*, 146 F.3d 66, 72 (2d Cir. 1998).

167. *See Taco Cabana Int'l, Inc. v. Two Pesos, Inc.*, 932 F.2d 1113, 1126–27 (5th Cir. 1991).

168. *Id.* at 1126.

169. *Id.*

170. *See A&H Sportswear, Inc. v. Victoria's Secret Stores, Inc.*, 166 F.3d 197, 208 (3d Cir. 1999) ("A royalty is a measure of damages for past infringement, often used in patent cases and in the context of trade secrets, but its use in trademark has been atypical."); *Sands, Taylor & Wood Co. v. Quaker Oats Co.*, 43 F.3d 1340 (7th Cir. 1994); *Apollo Theater Found., Inc. v. Western Int'l Syndication*, No. 02 Civ. 10037 (DLC), 2005 WL 1041141, at *13 (S.D.N.Y.); McCarthy, *supra* note 5, § 30:85.

171. *See Howard Johnson Co., Inc. v. Khimani*, 892 F.2d 1512, 1519 (11th Cir. 1990) (awarding actual damages using a reasonable royalty calculation against holdover licensee); *Boston Prof'l Hockey Ass'n v. Dallas Cap & Emblem Mfg.*, 597 F.2d 71, 76–78 (5th Cir. 1979) (calculating reasonable royalty based on offer in letter from defendant to plaintiff); *Trovan, Ltd. v. Pfizer, Inc.*, No. CV-98-00094 LGB MCX, 2000 WL 709149, at *16 (C.D. Cal.) ("[T]he Court has recognized that such damages were appropriate when the parties had shown a willingness to license the mark.").

172. *See U.S. Structures, Inc. v. J.P. Structures, Inc.*, 130 F.3d 1185, 1190–92 (6th Cir. 1997) (awarding past profits and trebled profits of defendant holdover franchisee); *Howard Johnson Co., Inc.*, 892 F.2d at 1519; McCarthy, *supra* note 5, § 30:85.

173. *See, e.g., Boston Prof'l Hockey Ass'n*, 597 F.2d at 76–78.

174. *See A&H Sportswear, Inc. v. Victoria's Secret Stores, Inc.*, 166 F.3d 197, 208 (3d Cir. 1999) ("The objections to the royalty award are well taken. . . . The court's award of a royalty for future sales put the court in the position of imposing a license neither party had requested or negotiated."); *Trovan, Ltd.*, 2000 WL 709149, *13–18 (holding that the Ninth Circuit would not recognize reasonable royalties as a measure of damages where no evidence has been proffered that a party intended to license their trademark).

175. *See Bandag, Inc. v. Al Bolster's Tire Stores, Inc.*, 750 F.2d 903, 920 (Fed. Cir. 1984) (holding that a reasonable royalty rate consisting of the amount plaintiff typically charges franchisees was inapposite since the defendant did not use everything for which a true franchisee pays).

176. *Id.*

177. *See A&H Sportswear, Inc.*, 166 F.3d at 208; McCarthy, *supra* note 5, § 30:85.

178. *Sands, Taylor & Wood v. Quaker Oats Co.*, 34 F.3d 1340 (7th Cir. 1994). Ultimately, the Seventh Circuit affirmed an award of almost $10.5 million.

179. The facts are detailed in the first 7th Circuit opinion, *Sands, Taylor & Wood v. Quaker Oats Co.*, 978 F.2d 947, 949–51 (7th Cir. 1992).

180. Reverse confusion occurs when the defendant, a much larger, higher-profile business, begins using a confusingly similar trademark to plaintiff's trademark and advertising it on a sufficiently large scale to convince the public to associate plaintiff's products, bearing the senior mark, with defendant. This is the opposite of the typical confusion case in which the misapprehension is that the senior user is the source of the junior user's goods. *See*

Banff, Ltd. v. Federated Dept. Stores, Inc., 845 F.2d 486, 490 (2nd Cir. 1988) ("Under the Lanham Act confusion is ordinarily the misimpression that the senior user . . . is the source of the junior user's . . . goods. Reverse confusion is the misimpression that the junior user is the source of the senior user's goods."); *see also Sands, Taylor & Wood v. Quaker Oats Co.,* 978 F.2d 947, 957 (7th Cir. 1992) ("Under the Lanham Act confusion is ordinarily the misimpression that the senior user . . . is the source of the junior user's . . . goods. Reverse confusion is the misimpression that the junior user is the source of the senior user's goods.").

181. *Sands, Taylor & Woods,* 978 F.2d at 962.

182. *Sands, Taylor & Woods,* 34 F.3d at 1352 n.19.

183. *See* 15 U.S.C. 1117 (2005) ("[A]ny damages sustained by plaintiff" are recoverable); *Zazu Designs v. L'Oreal, S.A.,* 979 F.2d 499, 506 (7th Cir. 1992) ("'Corrective advertising' is a method of repair. Defendant diminishes the value of plaintiff's trademark, and advertising restores that mark to its original value."); *Playtex Products, Inc. v. Procter & Gamble Co.,* No. 02 Civ. 8046(WHP), 2003 WL 21242769, at *6 (S.D.N.Y 2003).

184. *See, e.g., Otis Clapp & Son v. Filmore Vitamin Co.,* 754 F.2d 738 (7th Cir. 1985) (awarding the costs of plaintiff's "curative advertising campaign" in a case of mixed false advertising and trademark infringement); *Cuisinarts, Inc. v. Robot-Coupe Intern. Corp.,* 580 F.Supp. 634 (S.D.N.Y. 1984). There is little incentive for a plaintiff to overspend on corrective advertising, so a court will simply rely on the actual amount spent by the plaintiff in calculating damages. However, a defense of inefficient advertising has been suggested. *See* Heald, Paul, *Money Damages and Corrective Advertising: An Economic Analysis,* 55 U. Chi. L.Rev. 629, 633 (1988).

185. *West Des Moines State Bank v. Hawkeye Bancorporation,* 722 F.2d 411, 414 (8th Cir. 1983).

186. *Balance Dynamics Corp. v. Schmitt Indus., Inc.,* 204 F.3d 683, 692–93 (6th Cir. 2000).

187. *See U-Haul Intern. v. Jartran, Inc.,* 793 F.2d 1034 (9th Cir. 1986) (awarding $13.6 million even though the defendant had only spent $6 million in its original offending advertising).

188. *See Big O Tire Dealer, Inc. v. Goodyear Tire and Rubber Co.,* 561 F.2d 1365, 1375 (10th Cir. 1977).

189. *Id.*

190. *See Playtex Products, Inc. v. Procter & Gamble Co.,* 2003 WL 21242769, *8 (S.D.N.Y 2003) ("[I]n order to recover prospective corrective advertising damages, [plaintiff] must show that it was financially incapable of undertaking effective concurrent corrective advertising measures to counteract the false ads."); *Lurzer GMBH v. Am. Showcase, Inc.,* 75 F. Supp. 2d 98, 101 (S.D.N.Y. 1998), *aff'd* 201 F.3d 431 (2d Cir. 1999).

191. *Adray v. Adry-Mart, Inc.,* 76 F.3d 984, 989 (9th Cir. 1996).

192. 15 U.S.C. § 1117(a).

193. *Yankee Candle Co. v. Bridgewater Candle Co.,* 140 F. Supp. 2d 111, 120 (D. Mass. 2001).

194. Senate Rep. No. 93-1400, 93rd Cong. 2d Sess. 2 (Dec. 17, 1974), reprinted in 1974 U.S.C.C.A.N. 7132, 7133. Significantly, the federal patent statute, 35 U.S.C. § 285, contains exactly the same language and the Federal Circuit has stated that "willful infringement, inequitable conduct before the P.T.O., misconduct during litigation, vexatious or unjustified litigation, and frivolous suit" are all exceptional types of conduct justifying the

award of attorneys' fees. *Beckman Instruments, Inc. v. LKB Produkter AB,* 892 F.2d 1547, 1551 (Fed. Cir. 1989).

195. *See Eagles, Ltd. v. American Eagle Found.,* 356 F.3d 724, 728 (6th Cir. 2004) ("It is difficult to imagine how the standards . . . could be the same given that prevailing plaintiffs focus on the act of infringement while prevailing defendants point to the act of litigation."); *National Ass'n of Prof'l Baseball Leagues, Inc. v. Very Minor Leagues, Inc.,* 223 F.3d 1143, 1148 (10th Cir. 2000) ("[W]e disagree that there should be, or even could be, perfect harmony between the standard for awarding attorney fees to a prevailing plaintiff and a prevailing defendant."); *Door Systems, Inc. v. Pro-Line Door Systems, Inc.,* 126 F.3d 1028, 1031–32 (7th Cir. 1997); *Scotch Whisky Ass'n v. Majestic Drilling Co., Inc.,* 958 F.2d 594, 599 (4th Cir. 1992). Arguably, the Supreme Court's decision in *Fogerty v. Fantasy Inc.,* 510 U.S. 517 (1994), has called into question the continued viability of applying different standards for prevailing plaintiffs and defendants. *See id.* at 525 n.12, *citing Scotch Whisky Ass'n v. Majestic Distilling Co.,* 958 F.2d 594, 599 (4th Cir. 1992).

196. *See SecuraComm Consulting Inc. v. Securacom, Inc.,* 224 F.3d 273, 280 n.1 (3d Cir. 2000) (applying an "evenhanded" approach); *Stephen W. Boney, Inc. v. Boney Servs., Inc.,* 127 F.3d 821, 827 (9th Cir. 1997); *Conopco, Inc. v. Campbell Soup Co.,* 95 F.3d 187 (2d Cir. 1996).

197. McCarthy, *supra* note 5, § 30:100.

198. *See New York State Soc'y of Certified Public Accountants v. Eric Louis Assocs., Inc.,* 79 F. Supp 2d 331 (S.D.N.Y. 1999) (opining that consenting to an injunction precludes the court from closely examining the defendant's conduct and to award attorneys' fees in this context would discourage settlements).

199. *Tamko Roofing Prods., Inc. v. Ideal Roofing Co.,* 282 F.3d 23, 33 (1st Cir. 2002).

200. *See Horphag Research Ltd. v. Pellegrini,* 337 F.3d 1036 (9th Cir. 2003) (affirming attorneys' fees award since infringement was "willful and deliberate"); *Tamko Roofing Prods., Inc. v. Ideal Roofing Co.,* 282 F.3d 23, 33 (1st Cir. 2002) (holding that "willfulness" is a sufficient state of mind to justify an award); *Securacomm Consulting Inc. v. Securacom Inc.,* 224 F.3d 273 (3d Cir. 2000); (requiring "culpable conduct" by the losing party); *BASF Corp. v. Old World Trading Co.,* 41 F.3d 1081, 1099 (7th Cir. 1994) (affirming the award of attorney's fees since the defendant's "conduct was not malicious, [but] was deliberate"); *Quaker State Oil Refining Corp. v. Kooltone, Inc.,* 649 F.2d 94 (2d Cir. 1981) (opining that "deliberate and willful" satisfies Section 35).

201. *See Martin's Herend Imports, Inc. v. Diamond & Gem Trading USA Co.,* 112 F.3d 1296 (5th Cir. 1997) (denying attorneys' fees where "[p]laintiff did not demonstrate the kind of highly culpable conduct meriting an award"); *Kelley Blue Book v. Car-Smarts, Inc.,* 802 F. Supp. 278, 293 (C.D. Cal. 1992).

202. The Second, Third, Fourth, Fifth, Seventh, and Tenth Circuits all require some showing of bad faith.

203. *See Conopco, Inc. v. Campbell Soup Co.,* 95 F.3d 187, 194 (2d Cir. 1996) (2d Cir. 1996) (requiring showing of fraud or bad faith on the part of the infringer).

204. *TakeCare Corp. v. Takecare of Oklahoma, Inc.,* 889 F.2d 955, 957 (10th Cir. 1989).

205. *Tamko Roofing Prods., Inc. v. Ideal Roofing Co.,* 282 F.3d 23, 27 (1st Cir. 2002). The Eighth Circuit has similarly rejected bad faith as a requirement. *See Hartman v. Hallmark Cards, Inc.,* 833 F.2d 117, 123 (8th Cir. 1987).

206. *Stephen W. Boney, Inc. v. Boney Servs., Inc.*, 127 F.3d 821, 827 (9th Cir. 1997).

207. *SecuraComm Consulting Inc. v. Securacom Inc.*, 166 F.3d 182, 187 (3d Cir. 1999).

208. *See United Phosphorus, Ltd. v. Midland Fumigant, Inc.*, 205 F.3d 1219, 1232 (10th Cir. 2000) (granting fees where defendant violated settlement agreement which prohibited use of the mark).

209. *See Porous Media Corp. v. Pall Corp.*, 110 F.3d 1329 (8th Cir. 1997) (finding that defendant acted willfully and in bad faith by publishing false statements about its own and plaintiff's products); *Committee for Idaho's High Desert, Inc. v. Yost*, 92 F.3d 814 (9th Cir. 1996) (granting fees where defendants intentionally and knowingly adopted and used plaintiff's name to cause public confusion and impede plaintiff's agenda).

210. *See Pebble Beach Co. v. Tour 18 Ltd.*, 155 F.3d 526, 556 (5th Cir. 1998); *Roulo v. Russ Berrie & Co.*, 886 F.2d 931 (7th Cir. 1989).

211. *See SecuraComm Consulting Inc.*, 166 F.3d at 187.

212. *See New York State Soc'y of Certified Public Accountants v. Eric Louis Assocs., Inc.*, 79 F.Supp. 2d 331 (S.D.N.Y. 1999).

213. *Int'l Star Class Yacht Racing Assn v. Tommy Hilfiger, U.S.A., Inc.*, 80 F.3d 749, 754 (2d Cir. 1996). *See also Tamko Roofing Products, Inc. v. Ideal Roofing Co., Ltd.*, 282 F.3d 23 (1st Cir. 2002) (holding that defendant's instruction to its advertising agency not to do a trademark search, which is typically performed, constituted willful infringement).

214. *See TakeCare Corp. v. Takecare of Oklahoma, Inc.*, 889 F.2d 955, 957-58 (10th Cir. 1989).

215. H. R. Rep. No. 524, 93d Cong., 1st Sess. 2, 6 (1973); S. Rep. No. 93-1400, 93d Cong. 2d Sess. 2, 5 (1974).

216. *See Procter & Gamble Co. v. Amway Corp.*, 280 F.3d 519 (5th Cir. 2002) (noting that the Fourth, Seventh, Eighth, Ninth, Tenth, and D.C. Circuits have refused to follow a "symmetrical" test for prevailing plaintiffs and defendants and will evaluate the merits of the underlying suit as an independent factor); *Scotch Whisky Ass'n v. Majestic Distilling Co.*, 958 F.2d 594 (4th Cir. 1992).

217. *Stephen W. Boney Inc. v. Boney Servs. Inc.*, 127 F.3d 821 (9th Cir. 1997) (concluding that an award of fees would not be barred by the absence of bad faith); *Reader's Digest Ass'n, Inc. v. Conservative Digest, Inc.*, 821 F.2d 800, 808–09 (D.C. Cir. 1987).

218. *S. Indus., Inc. v. Centra 2000, Inc.*, 249 F.3d 625, 627 (7th Cir. 2001); *Securacomm Consulting, Inc. v. Securacom Inc.*, 224 F.3d 273, 282–83 (3d Cir. 2000) (upholding grant of fees where the litigation clearly involved an attempt to "beat a financially weaker opponent through vexatious litigation).

219. *Cairns v. Franklin Mint Co.*, 292 F.3d 1139, 1156 (9th Cir. 2002) (granting fees where plaintiff's claims were "groundless and unreasonable"); *see Waco Int'l, Inc. v. KHK Scaffolding Houston Inc.*, 278 F.3d 523, 536 (5th Cir. 2002); *Scott Fetzer Co. v. Williamson*, 101 F.3d 549, 555 (8th Cir. 1996).

220. *See, e.g., Conopco, Inc. v. Campbell Soup Co.*, 95 F.3d 187, 194 (2d Cir. 1996).

221. For an in-depth discussion of each circuit, see McCarthy, *supra* note 5, § 30:101.

222. *See, e.g., Cairns v. Franklin Mint Co.*, 292 F.3d 1139, 1156 (9th Cir. 2002) (finding that plaintiff, who was bringing false advertising claim, had no reason to believe that advertisements were false and dilution claim was based on "absurd" foundation); *National Distillers*

Products Co. v. Refreshment Brands, Inc., No. 00 Civ. 8418 (NRB), 2002 WL 1766548, at *2 (S.D.N.Y.) (concluding fees were appropriate where plaintiff filed dilution claim and its mark was "nowhere near as famous as it must be in order to support a dilution claim under either state or federal law").

223. *See Multivideo Labs, Inc. v. Intel Corp.*, No. 99 Civ. 3908 (DLC), 2000 WL 502866, at *3 (S.D.N.Y.) (denying fee award since there was no evidence of an improper purpose).

224. *See Securacomm Consulting, Inc. v. Securacom Inc.*, 224 F.3d 273, 282–83 (3d Cir. 2000); *Ale House Mgmt., Inc. v. Raleigh Ale House, Inc.*, 205 F.3d 137, 144 (4th Cir. 2000); *Universal City Studios, Inc. v. Nintendo Co.*, 797 F.2d 70 (2d Cir. 1986).

225. The lodestar calculation is based on the standard generally applicable to all cases in which fees are awarded to a "prevailing plaintiff," which is detailed in *Hensley v. Eckerhart*, 461 U.S. 424, 433 n. 7 (1983). *See also United Phosphorus, Ltd. v. Midland Fumigant, Inc.*, 205 F.3d 1219, 1233 (10th Cir. 2000) (holding that the calculation for attorneys' fees first requires the district court to calculate the "lodestar"); *U.S. Structures, Inc. v. J.P. Structures, Inc.*, 130 F.3d 1185, 1993 (6th Cir. 1997) (specifying that a district court must first calculate the lodestar amount to set an award of attorneys' fees).

226. *See Hensley*, 461 U.S. at 433 n. 7; *United Phosphorus, Ltd.*, 205 F.3d at 1233.

227. *See Clairol, Inc. v. Save-Way Indus., Inc.*, 211 U.S.P.Q. 223, 225 (S.D. Fla. 1980); McCarthy, *supra* note 5, § 30:102.

228. *United Phosphorus, Ltd.*, 205 F.3d at 1234–35.

229. *Id.*

230. *Id.* (requiring submission of "meticulous, contemporaneous time records that reveal, for each lawyer for whom fees are sought, all hours for which compensation is requested and how those hours were allotted to specific tasks").

231. *Hensley*, 461 U.S. at 433.

232. *Cairns v. Franklin Mint Co.*, 292 F.3d 1139 (9th Cir. 2002). The court should only consider the relevant factors.

233. *Pennsylvania v. Delaware Valley Citizens' Council for Clean Air*, 478 U.S. 546, 565 (1986).

234. *See id.*

235. *See Procter & Gamble Co. v. Amway Corp.*, 280 F.3d 519, 527 (5th Cir. 2002) ; *Gracie v. Gracie*, 217 F.3d 1060, 1071 (9th Cir. 2000) (remanding case so district court can apportion fees between Lanham Act and non-Lanham Act claims).

236. *See Gracie v. Gracie*, 217 F.3d 1060, 1071 (9th Cir. 2000); *United Phosphorus, Ltd. v. Midland Fumigant, Inc.*, 205 F.3d 1219 (10th Cir. 2000) ("The resulting twenty percent reduction is not on its face inadequate given the importance of the infringement cases as opposed to [plaintiff's] other claims.").

237. *Gracie*, 217 F.3d at 1071 (9th Cir. 2000).

238. *See Tamko Roofing Products, Inc. v. Ideal Roofing Co., Ltd.*, 282 F.3d 23, 61 (1st Cir. 2002); McCarthy, *supra* note 5, § 30:99.

239. *See NuPulse, Inc. v. Schlueter Co.*, 853 F.2d 545, 549 (7th Cir. 1988); *Hartman v. Hallmark Cards, Inc.*, 833 F.2d 117, 123 (8th Cir. 1987); *Rickard v. Auto Publisher, Inc.*, 735 F.2d 450, 453-58 (11th Cir. 1984); *Brunswick Corp. v. Spinit Reel Co.*, 832 F.2d 513, 528 (10th Cir. 1987); *Centaur Commc'ns, Ltd. v. A/S/M Commc'ns*, 830 F.3d 1217, 1229 (2d Cir. 1987).

240. 15 U.S.C. § 1117(a) (2005); Fed. R. Civ. P. 54(d)(1) (2005) ("Except when express provision therefore is made either in a statute of the United States or in these rules, costs other than attorneys' fees shall be allowed as of course to the prevailing party unless the court otherwise directs.").

241. 28 U.S.C. § 1920 (Taxation of Costs).

242. *See Fasa Corp. v. Playmates Toys, Inc.*, 108 F.3d 140, 144 (7th Cir. 1997) (Observing that "costs . . . are normally awarded to the prevailing party as a matter of course, unless exceptional circumstances are present or unless the case has a mixed outcome."); *Planetary Motion, Inc. v. Techsplosion, Inc.*, 261 F.3d 1188 (11th Cir. 2001) (holding that a court has wide equitable discretion to award costs); *Henegan Constr. Co. v. Heneghan Contracting Corp.*, 63 U.S.P.Q.2d 1984, 1992 (S.D.N.Y. 2002) (holding that "upon establishing a claim for trademark infringement, a plaintiff is entitled to the costs of the action.").

243. 15 U.S.C. § 1117(c) (2005); *Sara Lee Corp. v. Bags of N.Y., Inc.*, 36 F. Supp. 2d 161, 165 (S.D.N.Y. 1999) (stating that statutory damages serve as an alternative to traditional awards consisting of actual losses).

244. *See Sara Lee Corp.*, 36 F. Supp. 2d at 166.

245. 15 U.S.C. § 1117(c)(1) (2005).

246. 15 U.S.C. § 1117(c)(2) (2005).

247. *Sara Lee Corp.*, 36 F. Supp. 2d at 166.

248. *See* McCarthy, *supra* note 5, at § 30:95. The analogous provision is 17 U.S.C. § 504(c) (2005).

249. *See Fitzgerald Publ'g Co. v. Baylor Publ'g Co., et al.*, 807 F.2d 1110, 1117 (2d Cir. 1986).

250. *Id.*

251. *Nike Inc. v. Variety Wholesalers, Inc.*, 274 F. Supp. 2d 1352 1373 (S.D. Ga. 2003), *aff'd*, 107 Fed. Appx. 183 (11th Cir. 2004).

252. *See Dial One of the Mid-South, Inc. v. BellSouth Telecommunications, Inc.*, 269 F.3d 523, 527 (5th Cir. 2001); *Duncan v. Stuetzle*, 76 F.3d 1480, 1490 (9th Cir. 1996); *Getty Petroleum Corp. v. Bartco Petroleum Corp.*, 858 F.2d 103 (2d Cir. 1988); *Caesars World, Inc. v. Venus Lounge, Inc.*, 520 F.2d 269, 274 (3d Cir. 1975). Punitive damages may be available for state law claims where the defendant's conduct is particularly willful or reckless. *See, e.g., Leatherman Tool Group, Inc. v. Cooper Indus.*, 285 F.3d 1146 (9th Cir. 2002); *Getty Petroleum Corp. v. Island Transportation Corp.*, 878 F.2d 650 (2d Cir. 1989).

253. 15 U.S.C. § 1117(a) (2005).

254. *Id.; see U.S. Structures, Inc. v. J.P. Structures, Inc.*, 130 F.3d 1185, 1191–92 (6th Cir. 1997).

255. 15 U.S.C. § 1117(a) (2005).

256. *Thompson v. Haynes*, 305 F.3d 1369, 1380–81 (Fed. Cir. 2002) (affirming award of infringer's profits but reversing trebling of profits and reversing the award of damages as speculative).

257. *Id.* at 1380.

258. 15 U.S.C. § 1117(a) (2005).

259. *See Taco Cabana Int'l, Inc. v. Two Pesos, Inc.*, 932 F.2d 1113, 1126 (5th Cir. 1991).

260. *See, e.g., Gorenstein Enterp., Inc. v. Quality Care-USA, Inc.,* 874 F.2d 431 (7th Cir. 1989); *Getty Petroleum Corp. v. Bartco Petroleum Corp.,* 858 F.2d 103 (2d Cir. 1988); McCarthy, *supra* note 5, § 30:91.

261. *See SecuraComm Consulting Inc. v. Securacom Inc.,* 166 F.3d 182, 190 (3d Cir. 1999) (finding that because an award of profits was unwarranted, so too was trebling that award).

262. *See McCarthy, supra* note 5, § 30:91, 92.

263. 15 U.S.C. § 1117(b) (2005); *Babbit Elecs., Inc. v. Dynascan Corp.,* 38 F.3d 1161, 1183 (11th Cir. 1994); *Louis Vuitton S.A. v. Lee;* 875 F.2d 584, 589–90 (7th Cir. 1989).

264. *See ALPO Petfoods, Inc. v. Ralston Purina Co.,* 997 F.2d 949, 955 (D.C. Cir. 1993).

265. *New York Racing Ass'n, Inc. v. Stroup News Agency Corp.,* 920 F. Supp. 295, 301 (N.D.N.Y. 1996) (trebling an award of profits to deter defendant in the future).

266. 15 U.S.C. § 1117(a) (2005).

267. *See, e.g., R.J. Reynolds Tobacco Co. v. Premium Tobacco Stores Inc.,* 75 U.S.P.Q.2d 1206, 1208-09 (N.D. Ill. 2005) (awarding prejudgment interest for defendant's sale of "gray market" products bearing plaintiff's trademarks); *GTFM, Inc. v. Solid Clothing, Inc.,* 215 F. Supp. 2d 273, 306 (S.D.N.Y. 2002) (granting prejudgment interest due to defendant's "willful intent to profit illegally from the goodwill" of plaintiff).

268. *American Honda Motor Co., Inc. v. Two Wheel Corp.,* 918 F.2d 1060, 1064 (2d Cir. 1990).

269. *United Phosphorus, Ltd. v. Midland Fumigant, Inc.,* 205 F.3d 1219, 1236 (10th Cir. 2000).

270. *Gorenstein Enterp., Inc. v. Quality Care-USA, Inc.,* 874 F.2d 431, 436 (7th Cir. 1989).

CHAPTER 4

Explaining Venue Choice and Litigant Preferences: Solving the Delaware "Mystery"[1]

DONALD F. PARSONS JR.
Vice Chancellor, Delaware Court of Chancery

JACK B. BLUMENFELD, MARY B. GRAHAM,
AND LESLIE A. POLIZOTI
Morris, Nichols, Arsht & Tunnell LLP

Certain districts have long been top patent venues. This chapter discusses reasons that some venues attract more patent litigation than others, with particular emphasis on Delaware. Patentees continue to choose this district for several reasons relating to all aspects of their cases. The Delaware district judges have a history of receptivity to patent cases and have unparalleled experience, given the district's record of having the most patent trials, both per district and per judge. The judges set predictable case schedules within the first few months of a complaint being filed, including a trial date, which is rarely moved.

INTRODUCTION

Although Delaware has long garnered attention for its disproportionate influence in matters of corporation law and its primacy as a forum for corporate disputes, only recently has attention been focused on its prominent role in patent litigation. In fact, the federal bench in Delaware has more experience in resolving patent disputes than any other district in the nation, a fact that has lead commentators elsewhere to ask: Why Delaware?

In 2001, Professor Kimberly Moore of the George Mason University School of Law published a seminal article reporting on patent litigation in the 94 federal judicial districts around the country.[2] She focused on "forum shopping" and the reasons litigants choose to sue where they do. Professor Moore generated a "top10" list of popular patent venues and found that Delaware ranked sixth. She was surprised by Delaware's stature and was unable from her statistics to find a legitimate reason for "plaintiffs' collective enthusiasm" for Delaware: "[E]ither patent holders are selecting Delaware simply for its convenience (an unlikely answer in light of the size of the state and dearth of industry headquartered there) or patent holders are inaccurately perceiving Delaware to be more favorable to them than it is."[3] Further refinement of her statistics, however, and experience in the District of Delaware yield the mystery's solution.

Delaware's experience in patent litigation reaches back to the beginning of the last century. In the 1920s, Judge Hugh Morris—then the sole federal judge in Delaware—decided many of the country's most important patent cases. In the 1960s and 1970s, Chief Judge Caleb Wright presided over numerous patent cases (involving technologies such as the manufacture of synthetic rubber and polyurethane foam insulation, the zeolite cracking of petroleum to produce gasoline, and the manufacture of transistors), thereby helping "to establish on a national scale the reputation of the District of Delaware as a forum for the expeditious and knowledgeable resolution of patent disputes."[4] This history offers the first clue to patent plaintiffs' choice of Delaware.

Another clue comes from the predictability Delaware offers. Delaware's four district court judges now manage over 50 active patent cases each. This caseload results in a bench with extensive practical experience and a rich collection of rulings that enhance the predictability of patent law as applied in Delaware. As companies have appreciated in bringing their corporate disputes to Delaware's Court of Chancery, predictability can be as important as end results.

Procedural aspects in the Delaware district court's handling of cases are also attractive to litigants. Delaware offers a stable forum where transfer occurs only in specific circumstances. There is a great likelihood of getting to trial, and predictable case schedules are set.

The final clue comes from the fact that, at the end of the day, there is a high patentee win rate, with juries awarding some of the highest damages in the country.

This chapter relies on empirical data, complemented by the authors' experience in litigating patent suits in Delaware. The primary source of our data is the Cornell Judicial Statistics Database.[5] The Cornell Database uses data from the Administrative Office of the Courts, the government agency responsible for keeping statistics on federal litigation.[6] Other sources include the District of Delaware Pacer[7] and the U.S. Party/Case Index,[8] which are docketing systems that allow the user to obtain information such as case name, civil action number, filing date, termination date, and docket sheets.

DELAWARE'S HISTORICAL PROMINENCE IN PATENT LITIGATION

Delaware has been a popular forum for patent lawsuits for decades.[9] Before the 1989 amendments to the general venue statute, a corporate defendant could be sued where it committed allegedly infringing acts and had an established place of business, or where it

	EXHIBIT 4.1	NUMBER OF PATENT CASES FILED IN DELAWARE

Fiscal Year	Total # of Patent Cases Filed in Delaware	# of Patent Cases Filed in Delaware per Judge
1987	9	2.3
1988	13	3.3
1989	15	3.8
1990	23	5.8
1991	34	8.5
1992[a]	27	6.8
1993	29	7.3
1994	35	8.8
1995	56	14
1996	48	12
1997	65	16.3
1998	91	22.8
1999	84	21
2000	97	24.3
2001	131	32.8
2002	125	31.3
2003	122	30.5
2004	161	40.3

[a] In 1992, the Judicial Conference changed the end of the reporting period for judicial statistics from June 30 to September 30 to correspond to the federal fiscal year. Administrative Office of the United States Courts (1992). Therefore, statistics for 1992 cover a 15-month period.

was incorporated.[10] As the leading state for incorporation, Delaware often presented an attractive venue to plaintiffs in patent cases, particularly compared to a defendant's own "backyard."

Delaware retained its popularity, however, even after the 1989 venue amendment allowed plaintiffs to bring a patent suit in any judicial district where the defendant was subject to personal jurisdiction—almost anywhere in today's commercial environment.[11] Exhibit 4.1 shows Delaware's popularity, as measured by the number of patent cases filed, during fiscal years 1987 to 2004, based on data from the U.S. Party/Case Index. The number of patent cases filed in Delaware has increased steadily. In short, this district has remained a popular forum for patent litigation, resulting in significant institutional experience with patent cases.

UNMATCHED JUDICIAL EXPERIENCE

There are currently four judges and one magistrate judge on Delaware's district court: Chief Judge Sue L. Robinson; Judges Joseph J. Farnan, Gregory M. Sleet, and Kent A. Jordan; and Magistrate Judge Mary Pat Thynge. Judge Farnan has been on the bench the longest, having been sworn in on July 26, 1985. Chief Judge Robinson was a magistrate judge from February 1, 1988, until December 15, 1991, when she became a district judge. She was appointed chief judge in 2000. Judge Sleet was appointed as a district judge on September 23, 1998; and Judge Jordan, the newest member of the bench, was appointed on November 27, 2002. Judge Jordan replaced Judge Roderick R. McKelvie, who retired on June 28, 2002, after 10 years as a district judge. Magistrate Judge Mary Pat Thynge was appointed on June 17, 1992, and, in effect, filled the half-year vacancy in 2002 left by Judge McKelvie until Judge Jordan's appointment.

As noted, because of the expansive venue statute, a plaintiff generally can bring a patent case in a number of districts. The number of patent complaints filed per district, therefore, is a reflection of plaintiffs' preferences. We found that Delaware ranks fourth of the 94 districts in terms of the number of patent complaints filed since 1994, accounting for about 4.5 percent of the patent complaints. Consistent with Professor Moore's results, we also found, based on data from 1995 to 1999, that Delaware ranks seventh of the 94 judicial districts in terms of number of patent cases *terminated* (i.e., resolved).[12]

Adjusting these statistics for the number of judges in each district, however, is a better proxy for the experience that each judge develops with patent cases. Exhibit 4.2 shows that, during the last 10 years, the Delaware district judges have averaged over 23 patent complaints filed per judge, per year. The Northern District of California came in a distant second with almost 11 patent cases filed per judge, per year—less than half of Delaware's average.

The number of patent complaints filed per judgeship is derived from the U.S. Party/Case Index.[13] We determined the number of judgeships per district using the *Administrative Office of the U.S. Courts, Federal Court Management Statistics* publication for 2000.

| EXHIBIT 4.2 | NUMBER OF PATENT COMPLAINTS FILED PER JUDGESHIP PER YEAR, JANUARY 1, 1994 TO SEPTEMBER 30, 2004 |

Rank	District	# Patent Complaints Filed per Judgeship per Year
1	Delaware, D.	23.4
2	California, N.D.	10.4
3	Wisconsin, W.D.	10.1
4	Minnesota, D.	9.3
5	Utah, D.	7.1
6	California, S.D.	6.9
7/8	Illinois, N.D.	6.0
7/8	Washington, W.D.	6.0
9	Florida, M.D.	5.8
10	Massachusetts, D.	5.3

D = District; N.D. = Northern District; W.D. = Western District;
S.D. = Southern District

EXHIBIT 4.3	PATENT CASES TERMINATED WITH COURT INVOLVEMENT PER JUDGE PER YEAR, 1998 TO 2000

Rank	District	# Patent Cases Terminated per Judge per Year
1	Delaware, D.	13.3
2	Wisconsin, W.D.	8.7
3	Minnesota, D.	5.4
4	Michigan, W.D.	5.1
5	Washington, W.D.	3.9
6	California, S.D.	3.7
7	Texas, N.D.	3.4
8	Utah, D.	3.3
9	California, N.D.	3.2
10	Illinois, N.D.	3.1

D = District; W.D. = Western District; S.D. = Southern District;
N.D. = Northern District

Of all the districts, Delaware also *resolves* the most patent cases per judge. Using Cornell's Judicial Statistics Database, we analyzed the number of terminations with court involvement per district for fiscal years 1998 to 2000.[14] The top 10 districts are shown in Exhibit 4.3.

On average, Delaware district judges resolve more cases per year than any other district judges in the country. Of the top 10 districts in Exhibit 4.3, district judges in Delaware resolve, on average, three times more patent cases than judges in the bottom half of the top 10 and about one and a half times more than the judges in the second-highest ranking district.

Unquestionably, Delaware's judges can rightfully claim first place in experience with patent litigation.

PREDICTABLE CASE MANAGEMENT

Patent cases brought in Delaware have a high likelihood of staying in Delaware. The Court employs predictable case scheduling practices while, at the same time, the Court is open to new ideas for better case management.

Rare Transfer

Transfer motions in Delaware are rarely granted. This factor may be important to patentees who wish to avoid suit in the defendant's backyard, given that a likely forum for transfer is the defendant's home turf. Since 1990, only 3.8 percent of all patent cases filed in Delaware have been transferred. Of the transfer motions granted, more than half involved related litigation in another forum.

Early Scheduling Conference and Predictable Dates

The District of Delaware distinguishes itself by holding a scheduling conference early on, where all dates in the litigation—including a trial date—are set. Although the exact timing depends on the judge, scheduling conferences are usually held within three months of filing. Trial dates are set at the scheduling conference and are usually slated for 16 to 22 months after filing. Barring unforeseen circumstances or agreement of the parties, that date usually holds. Thus, unlike in many other districts where the trial date may be uncertain, far off, or subject to last-minute scheduling or deferral, litigants in Delaware have predictability about when they will get to trial.

The Delaware judges resolve patent cases quickly. Exhibit 4.4 shows the total number of patent cases pending, terminated, and filed in Delaware as of December 31 each year from 1991 to 2002.

The number of patent cases pending and terminated are data provided to us by the Delaware District Court. The number of cases filed as of December 31 is from the U.S. Party/Case Index (see Exhibit 4.5).

The Delaware judges take about 1.35 years (about 16 months), on average, to resolve a patent case. To calculate this statistic, we documented the date filed and the date closed of the patent suits filed in 1999, 2000, and 2001 in Delaware using the U.S. Party/Case Index and calculated the time from filing until closing:

Year	# Patent Cases Filed	# Patent Cases Closed	Average Time to Termination (in years)
1999	83	81	1.49
2000	97	93	1.35
2001	144	131	1.2

Because there are still cases pending for each of these years, we can expect the average time from filing to closing to rise slightly.

Professor Moore categorized Delaware as a "slow" district, which was one reason she was unable to explain "plaintiffs' collective enthusiasm" for Delaware.[15] From her data, Professor Moore concluded that the average time from filing to closing of patent cases filed from 1995 to 1999 in all jurisdictions was 1.12 years, with the quickest districts with 50 or more patent cases having average terminations of .43 to .77 years.[16] Delaware's average time of resolution for cases filed during that time was 1.68 years. The fact that Delaware has so many patent trials (see "Frequent Patent Trials" section) but takes only 8 months longer, on average, than the average time of disposition indicates that most of its patent cases (including those that reach trial) are resolved relatively quickly.

Flexible Approaches

The Delaware judges experiment with procedures to resolve patent cases efficiently and effectively, with frequent consultation with litigants about best practices. For example,

	NUMBER OF PATENT CASES IN DELAWARE PENDING, TERMINATED, AND FILED AS OF DECEMBER 31		
EXHIBIT 4.4			
Year	Pending as of 12/31	Terminated as of 12/31	Filed as of 12/31
1991	84	40	18
1992	60	31	32
1993	40	43	25
1994	48	30	37
1995	78	33	60
1996	82	48	51
1997	99	44	61
1998	134	66	99
1999	151	69	83
2000	177	72	97
2001	203	115	144
2002	188	135	117

Chief Judge Robinson and an ad hoc committee have established a default standard for discovery of electronic documents to be used in cases pending before her (and which are available for use by the other Delaware district judges) if the parties are unable to agree about procedures for electronic discovery. Judge Jordan has revitalized the District of Delaware

EXHIBIT 4.5   PATENT CASES PENDING AND TERMINATED

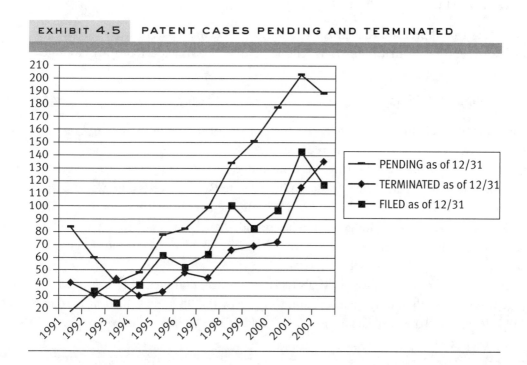

Intellectual Property Advisory Committee, consisting of experienced patent litigators from Delaware and around the country, as a means for the court to discuss efforts to continue to improve the administration of justice in intellectual property cases in Delaware.

The Court is now experimenting with the use of special masters for discovery disputes in patent cases. On September 15, 2004, the Court established a Special Master Panel for Intellectual Property cases:

> [G]iven this Court's significant docket of complex intellectual property cases and given that this Court's Magistrate Judge is routinely scheduling hearings and media-tion calendars six to eight months out, the need to appoint Special Masters to achieve these stated goals [of effective case management and prompt disposition] is clear.

When judges appoint a special master in an intellectual property case, the matter will be referred to the panel, which will assign a special master from the panel. Judge Farnan was the first to make a referral to the panel in the *St. Clair v. Canon* case, when he appointed a special master to resolve a dispute regarding St. Clair's assertion of privilege for documents sought by the defendants.[17] Chief Judge Robinson recently appointed a special master in three of her patent cases.[18]

Even before the Court's September 15 order, special masters were occasionally appointed to handle a variety of issues, such as pre-trial matters, claim construction, and discovery disputes. Notwithstanding the creation of the Special Master Panel, members of the court have emphasized that special masters will be appointed only on those few occasions where circumstances warrant their use.

FREQUENT PATENT TRIALS

Patentees can appreciate that prospects are good for their patent cases reaching trial in Delaware, and know that their trials will be handled by an experienced trial judge.

High Number of Trials

More patent trials are held in Delaware than in any other district. Since the beginning of 1997 (to September 30, 2004), there have been at least 70 patent jury trials and 38 patent bench trials in Delaware.[19] During this time, Judge Farnan has presided over 23 patent jury trials and at least 13 patent bench trials. Chief Judge Robinson has conducted 22 jury and at least 13 bench trials. Judge Sleet, since joining the bench in 1998, has held 5 jury trials and at least 2 bench trials. Judge Jordan has presided over 1 patent bench trial and 4 patent jury trials, including 1 that settled before the trial concluded. Magistrate Thynge has pre-sided over 2 jury trials and 1 bench trial.

Indicative of how many patent trials Delaware judges conduct, only 1 *district* held more patent jury trials than Judge Farnan, and only 10 of the 94 *districts* held more than Chief Judge Robinson, based on data from 1997 to 2000. Over 16 percent of patent cases in Dela-ware reach trial.

EXHIBIT 4.6	PERCENTAGE OF PATENT CASES REACHING TRIAL (BENCH AND JURY) IN DISTRICTS

	Trying At Least Ten Patent Cases During 1995–2000		
District	# Patent Trials, 1995–2000	# Patent Cases Filed, 1995–2000	% Patent Cases Actually Tried
Delaware, D.	73	451	16.2%
Wisconsin, W.D.	13	118	11.0%
Wisconsin, E.D.	13	137	9.5%
Texas, W.D.	10	115	8.7%
Oregon, D.	10	129	7.8%
Florida, M.D.	18	234	7.7%
Colorado, D.	14	188	7.4%
Virginia, E.D.	22	345	6.4%
Minnesota, D.	13	356	3.7%
Illinois, N.D.	27	740	3.6%
New York, S.D.	17	470	3.6%
Ohio, N.D.	10	282	3.5%
Texas, N.D.	11	317	3.5%
California, N.D.	28	842	3.3%
Massachusetts, D.	11	405	2.7%
California, C.D.	14	1166	1.2%

D = District; W.D. = Western District; E.D. = Eastern District; M.D. = Middle District; S.D. = Southern District; N.D. = Northern District; C.D. = Central District

The number of patent trials is based on the Cornell Judicial Statistics Database; the number of patent cases filed is from the U.S. Party/Case Index; and the percent of patent cases actually tried is the district's historical percentage, calculated by dividing the number of trials by the number of cases filed. As shown by Exhibit 4.6, Delaware has the highest percentage of patent cases reaching trial.

Infrequent Summary Judgment

Trials occur so frequently in Delaware presumably in part because summary judgment motions disposing of the entire case are rarely granted. For example, in 2003, there were 64 rulings on summary judgment motions. The vast majority (70.3 percent) were denied. Of those granted, none disposed of the entire case. Similarly, from January to September 2004, there were 47 rulings on summary judgment motions. About 60 percent were denied, and none of the motions that were granted disposed of the entire case.

In particular, the judges rarely grant summary judgment in patent bench trials. It is the practice of some of the judges not to entertain summary judgment motions or claim construction hearings prior to a patent bench trial.[20] This type of schedule virtually ensures a trial, absent settlement, which can make settlement look more attractive to a defendant, who knows it cannot easily avoid trial or delay the case by the device of an inappropriate summary judgment motion. Such scheduling orders, however, are always subject to the parties' ability to convince the court that a case could be disposed of by motion before trial.

For patent jury trials, Judges Farnan and Sleet have put in place screening procedures for summary judgment motions. Judge Farnan, for example, requires a party filing a motion for summary judgment to include a "statement certifying that no genuine issues of material fact exist with regard to the facts argued in support of the motion." In lieu of an answering brief, the party opposing the motion may file a counterstatement "certifying that genuine issues of material fact exist and setting forth the material facts the party contends are disputed." The movant then files a response to the counterstatement. If the Court decides that there are no factual disputes, the parties then submit answering and reply briefs.

Judge Sleet's procedures require submittal of short letter-briefs seeking permission to file a motion for summary judgment. Answering and reply letter-briefs are permitted. The court then holds a status conference to determine whether any of the proposed motions will be allowed. If so, briefing commences pursuant to the district's local rules. As with the prohibitions on summary judgment and claim construction in bench trials already described, these screening procedures for case-dispositive motions increase the likelihood that a case will reach trial.

High Win Rates and High Damages

One reason Professor Moore expressed an inability to explain Delaware's popularity as a patent forum was her conclusion that patentees prevailed at trial (as opposed to win rates based on pretrial disposition) only 46 percent of the time. This percentage placed Delaware ninth among her top 10 districts. She found that the highest-ranking district was the Northern District of California, at 68 percent.[21] Thus, Professor Moore concluded that Delaware is among the least favorable of her top 10 districts for patentees[22] and that "either patent holders are selecting Delaware simply for its convenience . . . or patent holders are inaccurately perceiving Delaware to be more favorable to them than it is."[23]

Professor Moore's calculation of a win rate, which comprises verdicts from both bench and jury trials, warrants careful examination. Generally, consistent with anecdotal data, the win rate for bench trials is lower than the win rate for jury trials.[24] Because patentees typically have the option to demand a jury trial, we recalculated win rate based on the number of jury verdicts where damages were awarded to the patentee. Our statistics show that Delaware is a more favorable forum for patentees who demand a jury trial than indicated by Professor Moore. Of the patent jury trials with verdicts occurring between 1997 and September 30, 2004, in which the jury was asked to award damages, 38 of 57 juries—or 67 percent—awarded damages to the patentee. Of the patent jury trials with verdicts in 2002 through September 30, 2004, about 80 percent of the juries awarded damages to the patentee.

The significance to litigants of the patentee win rate at trial may also depend on the probability that a case will reach trial in that jurisdiction, given the general view that summary judgment is a device for defendants. Thus, the probability of reaching trial should also be considered in determining how favorable a district is for patentees. A district with a lower win rate at trial (the measure used by Professor Moore) may in fact be more favorable to patentees if patent cases in that district have a higher probability of surviving summary judgment and reaching trial. Conversely, a district's apparently high win rate at trial may reflect a less patentee-friendly forum if patent cases in that district are rarely tried.[25]

In Exhibit 4.7, we used Professor Moore's win rates from 1983 to 1999 and reordered her top 10 jurisdictions based on the probability that a patentee will get to trial and win:

The probability that a patent case will get to trial is based on historical data of the number of patent cases that went to trial in the district. To determine the number of patent suits filed, we used the U.S. Party/Case Index. The number of patent trials is from the Cornell Judicial Statistics Database.

Even using Professor Moore's win rate at trial, the probability of a patentee's reaching trial and winning between 1983 and 1999 in Delaware is almost twice that of any of her top 10 patent districts. Thus, there is a far higher probability of reaching trial and winning a patent case in this district than in any of Professor Moore's top 10 patent districts.

We also extended Professor Moore's analysis by calculating the size of damages awards in patent cases, which provides another potential explanation for Delaware's popularity as a patent forum. Using the Cornell Judicial Statistics Database, we sampled the damages awarded in patent jury trials over three time periods.[26] The District of Delaware consistently ranks in the top three jurisdictions having the highest damages awarded.

We first analyzed average amounts awarded in patent jury trials between 1978 and 2000 in districts with at least 10 jury trials. Delaware ranks second to the Western District of Texas. A more recent sample of the 17 districts that held at least 10 patent jury trials between 1990 and 2000 produced the same result: Delaware is second to the Western District of

EXHIBIT 4.7	PROFESSOR MOORE'S TOP 10 DISTRICTS ORDERED BY PROBABILITY OF GETTING TO TRIAL AND WINNING

District	# Patent Cases Filed, 1/1/83–12/31/99	# Patent Trials, 1983–1999	% of Patent Cases Going to Trial	Moore's Win Rate for Bench and Jury Trials	Probability of Getting to Trial and Winning
Delaware, D.	571	116	20.3%	46%	9.3%
Virginia, E.D.	445	41	9.2%	58%	5.3%
Illinois, N.D.	1,036	87	8.4%	48%	4.0%
Minnesota, D.	553	32	5.8%	67%	3.9%
California, N.D.	1,191	67	5.6%	68%	3.8%
New York, S.D.	780	43	5.5%	63%	3.5%
California, C.D.	1,511	77	5.1%	63%	3.2%
Florida, S.D.	516	25	4.8%	63%	3.0%
New Jersey, D.	632	30	4.7%	61%	2.9%
Massachusetts, D.	657	35	5.3%	30%	1.6%

D = District; E.D. = Eastern District; N.D. = Northern District; S.D. = Southern District; C.D. = Central District

Texas for highest average amount awarded. Of Professor Moore's top 10 patent jurisdictions, Delaware has the highest average amount awarded in patent jury trials from 1995 to 1999 (the time period Professor Moore used to generate her top 10 districts).

That damages awards in Delaware, on average, are among the highest in the country may help to explain why plaintiffs file patent litigation there, particularly when one considers that patentees who sue in Delaware have the highest probability of getting to trial and winning in patent cases of any jurisdiction.

THE MEDIATION BONUS

Most patent cases in the District of Delaware are referred to Magistrate Judge Mary Pat Thynge for mediation. Indeed, the standard patent scheduling orders of Chief Judge Robinson, Judge Sleet, and Judge Jordan all contain a referral to Judge Thynge. Mediation provides an opportunity to settle a case without the full expense and risks of litigation. Mediation in Delaware with Judge Thynge has the additional benefit of mediating before someone who is sophisticated with patent matters and is well respected.

In the 10 years beginning January 1, 1993, Judge Thynge mediated 893 cases. As of January 2003, 12 of these cases were still in various stages of mediation.[27] Of 893 cases, 203 were patent matters. Of those 203 cases, 136.5 (67.2 percent) settled at or after the mediation. About 23 patent matters settled before mediation.

According to the Magistrate Judge:

> [I]t seems that it was more common for non-patent matters to settle before media-
> tion when it was first introduced in our jurisdiction. Now counsel appear to have
> more of a comfort level with our process. Local counsel's familiarity with mediation
> at that time had been limited to mediation in the state court, which due to the larger
> number of cases is more like a settlement conference with time limitations (usually
> 2–3 hours) and no follow up meetings, [telephone conferences] or emails.[28]

From January 2002 to January 9, 2003, Judge Thynge mediated 58 cases, in addition to handling former Judge McKelvie's caseload. Twenty of the 58 were patent matters, and almost all of those settled (87.5 percent). Judge Thynge also presided as trial judge, by consent of the parties, over at least three patent cases—*Genzyme v. Atrium*[29] and two trials involving *Honeywell v. Universal Avionics*[30]—and is expected to hear another case in 2007.[31]

CONCLUSION

Delaware has long been a top patent venue. Patentees continue to choose this district for several reasons relating to all aspects of their cases. The Delaware district judges have a history of receptivity to patent cases and have unparalleled experience, given the district's record of having the most patent trials, both per district and per judge. The judges set predictable case schedules within the first few months of a complaint being filed, including a trial date, which is rarely moved. Patent cases are rarely transferred except in predictable circumstances and are infrequently disposed of by summary judgment. The Delaware judges experiment with new ways to handle patent litigation more efficiently and effectively. Of Professor Moore's top 10 districts, Delaware has the highest probability of a patentee's reaching trial and winning. Moreover, patent juries in Delaware award higher damages, on average, than patent juries in most other districts in the country. Finally, patent litigants in Delaware can mediate with Magistrate Judge Thynge and take advantage of her patent litigation experience.

All of these reasons, taken together, which comport with the authors' experience, demonstrate that the reasons for patentees' choice of the District of Delaware are rational, fully understandable, and legitimate. The mystery is solved.

NOTES

1. This chapter is based on an article entitled "Solving the Mystery of Patentees' 'Collective Enthusiasm' for Delaware" by the same authors that appeared in 2004 in volume 7 of the *Delaware Law Review.* The authors would especially like to thank Magistrate Judge Mary Pat Thynge, Maria Moore and Robert Butts at the United States District Court for the District of Delaware, and Melissa Stone Myers for their assistance in providing information for this chapter.

2. Kimberly A. Moore, *Forum Shopping in Patent Cases: Does Geographic Choice Affect Innovation?* 79 N.C. L. REV. 889 (2001). The district courts in the 94 judicial districts are the exclusive trial courts for "any civil action arising under any Act of Congress relating to patents. . . ." 28 U.S.C. § 1338(a).

3. Moore, *Forum Shopping, supra* note 2, at 918.

4. *See, e.g.*, Arthur G. Connolly Sr. and Donald F. Parsons Jr., *Senior Judge Caleb M. Wright's Contributions to the Trial of Complex Patent Cases,* 7 DEL. LAWYER 6 (Mar. 1989).

5. Cornell Judicial Statistics Database, http://teddy.law.cornell.edu:8090/questata.htm (last visited November 29, 2004). This database was created by Theodore Eisenberg and Kevin M. Clermont.

6. *See generally* www.uscourts.gov/adminoff.html (last visited November 29, 2004).

7. http://pacer.ded.uscourts.gov (last visited November 29, 2004).

8. http://pacer.uspci.uscourts.gov (last visited November 29, 2004).

9. *See, e.g.,* Connolly and Parsons, *supra* note 4.

10. The patent venue statute allows suit "in the judicial district where the defendant resides or where the defendant has committed acts of infringement and has a regular and established place of business." 28 U.S.C. § 1400(b). Prior to the 1989 amendment, the Supreme Court defined "resides" narrowly, to refer only to the defendant's state of incorporation. David D. Siegel, *Venue in Patent Infringement Suits: Expanded by the New 'Residence' Definition of* 28 U.S.C.A. § 1391(c)? 1 ALB. L.J. SCI. & TECH. 271, 273 (1991).

11. Congress amended the *general* venue statute to make venue proper in any district where a corporation is subject to personal jurisdiction, and deemed that district to be the corporation's residence for purposes of the *patent* venue statute. Siegel, *Venue in Patent Infringement*

Suits, supra note 10, at 274. The Federal Circuit, in *VE Holding,* confirmed that the general venue statute's definition of "resides" is applicable to the patent venue statute. VE Holding Corp. v. Johnson Gas Appliance Co., 917 F.2d 1574, 1583 (Fed. Cir. 1990), *cert. denied,* 499 U.S. 922 (1991).

12. As noted in the introduction, Professor Moore listed the "top 10" patent districts based on number of patent cases terminated from 1995 to 1999. From greatest to least terminations, those districts are: Central District of California, Northern District of California, Northern District of Illinois, Southern District of New York, District of Massachusetts, District of Delaware, Southern District of Florida, Eastern District of Virginia, District of New Jersey, and the District of Minnesota. Professor Moore ranked Delaware sixth and the Southern District of Florida seventh. Moore, *Forum Shopping, supra* note 2, at 903. The number of terminations in these jurisdictions is almost identical, so the margins of error in Moore's data and our data easily account for the difference in rank.

13. The authors have been informed by the PACER Service Center that the district courts update statistics on PACER from time to time. Therefore, cases may have been filed in the district courts that are not reflected in these numbers. This observation is true for all of the data herein that relies on the U.S. Party/Case Index.

14. Year 2000 is the last year for which information is available on the Cornell Judicial Statistics Web site. Although it is possible to get pre-1998 data, we chose to focus on the most recent three years of data. Note that these are terminations with court involvement.

15. Moore, *Forum Shopping, supra* note 2, at 909.

16. *Id.* at 908.

17. C.A. No. 03-241-JJF (D.I. 843).

18. British Telecom. v. Qwest Comm'ns, C.A. No. 03-527-SLR (D.I. 96); British Telecom. v. Level 3 Comm'ns, C.A. No. 03-530-SLR (D.I. 161); Arnco Corp. v. British Telecom., C.A. No. 04-222-SLR (D.I. 94).

19. The bench trials include trials of equitable issues, where infringement or invalidity was tried to a jury.

20. *See, e.g.,* KAO Corp. v. Unilever U.S. Inc., C.A. No. 01-680-SLR (D.I. 65) (disallowing summary judgment motions and claim construction hearing); Original Creatine Patent Co. v. Muscletech Research & Development, Inc., C.A. No. 02-366-SLR (D.I. 29) (same); Astrazeneca AB v. Andrx Pharmaceuticals, LLC, C.A. No. 04-080-SLR (D.I. 21) (same); Merck & Co. v. Teva Pharms. USA, Inc., C.A. No. 00-035-JJF (D.I. 121) (disallowing claim construction hearing); Bayer AG v. Sony Electronics, Inc., C.A. No. 95-8-JJF (D.I. 494) (same); C.A. No. 01-294-RRM (D.I. 146), published in 209 F. Supp. 2d 348 (D. Del. 2002) (same).

21. Moore, *Forum Shopping, supra* note 2, at 917.

22. *Id.*

23. *Id.* at 918.

24. *See generally* Kimberly A. Moore, *Judges, Juries and Patent Cases—An Empirical Peek Inside the Black Box,* 99 MICH. L. REV. 365 (2000).

25. For example, suppose District X has a low 40 percent win rate at trial and a high 20 percent chance of getting to trial. The chance of a patentee getting to trial and winning is 8 percent.

Alternatively, suppose District Y has a high 60 percent win rate at trial but a low 5 percent probability of getting to trial. The chance of getting to trial and winning is 3 percent.

26. Although Administrative Office of the Courts' data is widely used, it should be understood that there are certain limitations to the data's accuracy. For example, only damages awards up to $9,999,000 are recorded, so a $200 million damage award is reported as a $10 million award. *See, e.g.,* Moore, *Judges, Juries and Patent Cases, supra* note 24, at 381.

27. As of January 2003, the Magistrate Judge had mediated 690 nonpatent matters, of which 567.5, or 82 percent, settled via mediation.

28. January 21, 2003 email from Magistrate Judge Thynge to Donald F. Parsons, Jr.

29. C.A. No. 00-958 (D.I. 213).

30. C.A. No. 02-359; C.A. No. 03-242.

31. Inline Connection v. AOL Time Warner, Inc., C.A. No. 02-272 (D.I. 23).

Commonly Debated Issues in Performing Economic Damages Analyses in Intellectual Property Matters

CHASE PERRY
FTI Consulting, Inc.

CLARKE B. NELSON
FTI Consulting, Inc.

ELIZABETH WHITAKER
Bracewell & Giuliani

This chapter discusses some commonly debated and sometimes disputed methodologies and analyses performed by experts in the calculation of economic damages in patent infringement matters in the United States. Performing an analysis of economic damages in disputes over intellectual property can be a complicated process; this chapter identifies and clarifies some of the issues that experts often contemplate in undergoing that process.

INTRODUCTION

In our capacity as experts and attorneys working on intellectual property (IP) matters, primarily patent cases, we have observed a Letterman-like list of commonly debated issues. Expert disagreement is a necessary consequence of the adversarial process of litigation. We hope that, by reading this chapter, the bases for recurring differences in thought, opinion, and methodology among experts will become clear and understandable. Before presenting the list, a basic review of the law and a few seminal cases is beneficial.

Damages under U.S. Patent Law

Section 284 of title 35, United States Code, forms the basis for damages awarded by a court for the infringement of a patent and states:

> Upon finding for the claimant the court shall award the claimant damages adequate to compensate for the infringement, but in no event less than a reasonable royalty for the use made of the invention by the infringer, together with interest and costs as fixed by the court.

An evaluation of damages in patent infringement cases should incorporate consideration of all relevant and reliable economic and qualitative factors. The basic test for lost profits is the "but for" test, which requires that the patent owner establish with a reasonable probability that it would have made the sales of the alleged infringer had the latter not allegedly infringed.

The most prevalent method for evaluating this "but for" test is set forth in *Panduit Corp. v. Stahlin Bros. Fibre Works* (1978), where the court established that a patent owner seeking lost profits damages must prove: (1) demand for its patented product, (2) the absence of acceptable noninfringing substitutes, (3) sufficient manufacturing and marketing capability to exploit the demand, and (4) the amount of the profit lost. Federal circuit cases have relaxed the second requirement (negating the condition that there must be a two-player market, e.g., *State Industries, Inc. v. Mor-Flo Industries, Inc.* (1989)) and expanded the class of products eligible for recovery of lost profits (the "entire market value" rule, e.g., *Rite-Hite v. Kelley* (1995). Other cases emphasize that an award of lost profits is appropriate only when embodying products and accused products occupy the same market segment.[1] When lost profits are unavailable to the patent owner, a reasonable royalty is the most common measure of damages. In *Georgia-Pacific Corp. v. U.S. Plywood-Champion Papers, Inc.* (1970), the court enumerated 15 factors to consider when determining a reasonable royalty. The factors address issues regarding comparable royalties, the parties, the prospective license, the technology, and the accused products.

Commonly Debated Issues in Intellectual Property Damage Calculations

Definition of the Relevant Market

An understanding of the market for the products accused of infringement is the bedrock for discussion of potential noninfringing alternatives and whether the patent owner and alleged infringer are competitors. Experts often disagree on the definition of the relevant market. Different classes of buyers have different reservation prices (what they are willing to pay for a good), different price elasticities (how responsive they are to price changes), different preferences, and different income elasticities. It is not uncommon for experts to disagree on the definition of a relevant market, particularly when submarkets exist at various levels of the broader consumer market. For example, consider an accused technology related to the formulation of nonstick cooking spray. Depending on how one viewed the product and the accused technology, one could define the relevant market to be any of all nonstick cooking sprays, store brand or off-label cooking sprays, or even any product that provides the desired effect of a nonstick cooking spray, such as Crisco and/or other, generic nonstick cooking products.

Reliance on the "Book of Wisdom"

Experts commonly disagree on how much weight to give information or data points obtained after the date of the alleged first infringement, when the hypothetical negotiation occurs. For example, it is common in a patent infringement matter for an expert to cite royalty rates that were negotiated by one of the parties after the hypothetical negotiation date in their particular matter. That is, factors 1 and 2 of the well-known *Georgia-Pacific* case go to the licensing behavior of the two parties. Factor 1 considers "[t]he royalties received by the patent holder for the licensing of the patent-in-suit, proving or tending to prove an established royalty." Factor 2 considers "[t]he rates paid by the licensee for the use of other patents comparable to the patents-in-suit." Debate over the "Book of Wisdom" can effectively be attributed to attorneys' and experts' varying interpretation of *Georgia-Pacific* Factor 15, which reads, "The amount that a licensor (such as the patentee) and a licensee (such as the infringer) would have agreed upon (at the time the infringement began) if both had been reasonably and voluntarily trying to reach an agreement. . . ."

Some experts take a hard line, saying that only information known at the time of the hypothetical negotiation can be considered. Other experts disagree and point to federal circuit decisions where the court has ruled that it cannot ignore facts and events that occurred after the alleged infringement began. For example, in *Fromson v. Western Litho Plate and Supply Co., et al,* (1988), the court expressed this view in stating:

> Like all methodologies based on a hypothetical, there will be an element of uncertainty; yet, a court is not at liberty, in conducting the methodology, to abandon entirely the statutory standard of damages "adequate to compensate" for the infringement. The royalty arrived at must be "reasonable" under all the circumstances; i.e., it must be at least a close approximation of what would be "adequate to compensate" for the "use made of the invention by the infringer."

The methodology encompasses fantasy and flexibility—fantasy because it requires a court to imagine what warring parties would have agreed to as willing negotiators; flexibility because it speaks of negotiations as of the time infringement began, yet permits and often requires a court to look to events and facts that occurred thereafter and that could not have been known to or predicted by the hypothesized negotiators." The court further expounded, "To correct uncertain prophecies in such circumstances is not to charge the offender with elements of value non-existent at the time of his offense. It is to bring out and expose to light the elements of value that were there from the beginning. . . ."

However, some experts argue that *Georgia-Pacific* Factor 15 is an overriding factor that forces the other 14 factors to be taken only in the context created at the time infringement began. However, the court in *Georgia-Pacific* stated that ". . . the Court has taken into account the modifying effect of the facts developed subsequent to 1955 and has assessed them together with all other probative evidence so far as they bear upon the reasonableness of the assumptions and expectations of the parties in their hypothetical negotiations in 1955."

Where to Begin a *Georgia-Pacific* Analysis

Some debate exists among experts over whether to apply the *Georgia-Pacific* factors to a predetermined "starting point," or whether that starting point is undetermined. For example, we have observed some experts first arrive at a starting point for the royalty determined either through use of the "25 percent" rule or based on an existing license agreement. The expert then proceeds to adjust that starting point upward or downward for each *Georgia-Pacific* factor. Other experts, in contrary, essentially start their analysis without any predetermined starting point and rely on the *Georgia-Pacific* factors to provide them with instructive data points so as to determine the reasonable royalty.

Application of the "Entire Market Value" Rule

The issue of what products or components thereof should be included in the damages calculation frequently arises in patent litigation. An influential case in this area is *Rite-Hite Corp. v. Kelly Co.* (1995). This case gives some guidelines regarding the recovery of lost profits on nonpatented items and also whether such items are to be included in a reasonable royalty base versus being considered in the determination of the royalty rate. Specifically, the court stated, "We have held that the entire market value rule permits recovery of damages based on the value of a patentee's entire apparatus containing several features when the patent-related feature is the 'basis for customer demand.' . . . The entire market value rule has typically been applied to include in the compensation base unpatented components of a device when the unpatented and patented components are physically part of the same machine. . . . The rule has been extended to allow inclusion of physically separate unpatented components normally sold with the patented components."

Generally, disagreement among experts and attorneys is not over the conceptual validity of the entire market value rule but rather its interpretation and application. Experts frequently debate the apportionment of the damages between the value of the unpatented and patented component of the accused product. Experts further disagree on inclusion or exclusion of sales of nonpatented items in their lost profits calculations and the varying bases for such inclusion or exclusion. *Georgia Pacific* factor 6 reads: "The effect of selling the patented specialty in promoting sales of other products of the licensee; the existing value of the invention to the licensor as a generator of sales of his non-patented items; and the extent of such derivative or convoyed sales." Debate also exists as to whether this factor instructs the expert to include the convoyed sales in the royalty base versus increase the actual reasonable royalty rate. We have observed both positions argued by expert witnesses.

Interpretation and Application of the "25 Percent Rule"

IP damages experts will frequently claim their estimate of a royalty rate in a patent infringement matter is consistent with the so-called "25 Percent Rule" or "rule of thumb," which suggests that 25 percent of the operating profit[2] from sales of a product should be credited to the intellectual property that enables the product. This methodology is also known as a profit split. Robert Goldscheider, an international licensing expert, first popularized the rule in 1971 and has since emphasized that the rule is to be used as a starting point that will be modified based on other relevant information (see, e.g., Goldscheider, "The Negotiation of Royalties and Other Sources of Income from Licensing," IDEA: *Journal of Law and Technology,* PTC Research Foundation of Franklin Pierce Law Center, 1995).

Other experts, however, argue there is no basis in economic theory, empirical evidence from financial economics, or in analyzing rates of returns across firms that would suggest the 25 Rule is scientifically valid as a means of determining the relative price of intellectual property. They further argue the 25 percent starting point is based mainly on Mr. Goldscheider's personal experience and does not provide any advantage over evaluating all relevant information and making an independent judgment of what royalty rate would be reasonable.

Incremental versus Gross or Operating Profits to the Patent Holder

Although many experts agree that lost profits on "but for" sales should be calculated based on the infringed company's incremental profit rate, we have observed some experts apply a gross or operating profit rate to the accused lost sales. In performing a lost profits calculation, it is not uncommon for the damages expert to estimate the gross sales of the infringer and to then apply a gross profit rate or operating profit rate to determine lost profits.

The difference between using gross, operating, and incremental profit can be broken down in this way: Gross profit will likely exclude certain costs that vary as a function of product sales but are not captured as costs of good sold. For example, marketing and advertising expended in launching a new product line is not likely to be captured in the cost of goods sold, but would not have been expended unless the product was launched. Operating profit will generally include certain costs that would have been expended regardless of whether the accused product sales occurred. An example of such operating costs is the salaries paid to company executives already in place. Incremental profit will include the costs of goods sold and any additional costs that would have been incurred by the infringed company to obtain the accused lost sales. In other words, incremental profit is the profit from the additional units of output that would have presumed to have been sold, absent the infringement. Debate over how to determine incremental profit or the marginal costs of additional units of output is also common and is discussed in the next section.

Calculating Marginal Costs

We have seen damages experts estimate what they deem to be a fixed or sunk cost versus what they consider to be a variable cost. Usually this estimate is based on interviews with and/or testimony from the key financial personnel at the infringed company. Other experts argue that the correct procedure, assuming adequate data are available, is to perform a regression (a statistical procedure) where one attempts to isolate costs that vary with the level of production. Using this methodology, the expert typically assumes that costs of sales are incremental and then performs a regression on monthly operating cost data. Provided the results are statistically significant, the total incremental cost is the cost of sales plus the incremental portion of operating cost. We have observed some experts attempt to apply this methodology when little or no monthly data was available. Experts in favor of performing a regression analysis argue that the regression distills out the incremental cost hidden in the various operating cost categories. Experts who use the former approach argue that a careful understanding and analysis of each operating cost item allows them to predict the incremental profits that would have been earned by the infringed company.

Exclusivity and Duration of the Hypothetical Licenses: Factors 3 and 7 under *Georgia-Pacific*

Factor 3 in the *Georgia-Pacific* case reads: "The nature and scope of the license, as exclusive or non-exclusive; or as restricted or non-restricted in terms of territory or with respect to whom the manufactured product may be sold." Factor 7 reads: "The duration of the patent and the term of the license." Although these factors generally do not often drive extensive analysis by experts, they still are not without disagreement. Many experts differ in their opinions on the effect of a nonexclusive license. Some argue that it results in a higher royalty and some a lower royalty. We have also observed experts claim exclusivity has no impact on royalty at all. Similarly, we have observed the same range of opinions with respect to the duration of the hypothetical license. For example, in one recent case where infringement first occurred with only approximately 18 months remaining on the life of the patent, one expert argued that the not-so-distant expiration increased the value of the patent (and thus the royalty rate), because the licensor, in theory, would want to extract as much value as possible from the product before it expires. In similar circumstances, however, we have also observed experts opine that little time remaining on the life the patent decreases the value.

Acceptability of Noninfringing Substitutes

We have often observed experts disagree over the acceptability of a potential noninfringing substitute, both from an economic and technical standpoint. In *TWM Manufacturing Co., Inc. v. Dura Corp.* (1986), the court ruled, "Mere existence of a competing device does not make that device an acceptable substitute." In *SmithKline Diagnostics v. Helena Laboratories*

(1991), the court expounded, "If purchasers are motivated to purchase because of particular features of a product available only from the patent owner and infringers, products without such features would obviously not be acceptable non-infringing substitutes. . . . On the other hand, if the realities of the market are that others would likely have captured sales made by the infringer, despite a difference in the products, it follows that the 'but for' test is not met."

Further, the Federal Circuit ruled that a noninfringing substitute need not be commercially available at the time infringement began. In *Grain Processing Corp. v. American Maize-Products Co.* (1999), the court stated, "The district court found that American Maize proved that a non-infringing substitute was available, though not on the market or for sale, during the period of infringement. The court found further that this substitute was acceptable to all purchasers of the infringing product and concluded that American Maize rebutted the inference of 'but for' causation for Grain Processing's alleged lost sales. Upholding the district court's findings and conclusions, this court affirms." Thus, experts and attorneys frequently debate whether the substitute could have been commercially available at the time infringement first began. For example, in *Micro Chemical, Inc. v. Lextron, Inc.* (2003), the Federal Circuit ruled that while a noninfringing substitute could have existed at the time of first infringement, the defendant itself didn't have the "necessary equipment, know-how, and experience" to make the noninfringing product at that time.

Also often debated is whether the implementation of new technology would be more costly than the infringed technology. In the *Grain Processing* case, the defendant was able to show that it cost only 2.3 percent more to make the noninfringing substitute than the accused product. The court, on this basis, placed a cap of 2.3 percent on the royalty.

While these debates regarding noninfringing substitutes and design around options are often predicated on assumptions and technical considerations, they are nonetheless a frequent source for disagreement in expert opinions relating to lost profits and reasonable royalty calculations.

Analytical Approach to a Royalty

The court's decision in *TWM Manufacturing v. Dura* (cited earlier) states, "The special master, citing *Georgia-Pacific* and *Tektronix,* used the so-called 'analytical approach,' in which she subtracted the infringer's usual or acceptable net profit from its anticipated net profit realized from sales of infringing devices." It is not uncommon for experts to differ in their application of the instruction given in the *TWM Manufacturing* case. For example, a key divergence we have observed relates to what kind of profitability measurement is used— profitability based on the actual dollar amounts versus profitability as measured as a percent of sales on the respective products. Exhibit 5.1 demonstrates an example.

As the exhibit shows, some experts calculate the differential based on the per-unit profitability amounts for the accused product and the "usual" product ($0.60/$2.00 = 30%). Other experts calculate the differential based on the percent of sales measurement (55% − 50% = 5%).

EXHIBIT 5.1   PROFITABILITY—DOLLAR AMOUNT VERSUS PERCENT
OF SALES

| Measurement: Actual Dollar Amounts | | | |
Average Price	Average Cost	Gross Profit	Royalty
Accused Product	$2.00	$0.90	$1.10	
Usual Product	$1.00	$0.50	$0.50	
Difference	$1.00	$0.40	$0.60	30%

| Measurement: Percent of Sales | | | |
Average Price	Average Cost	Gross Profit	Gross Profit %
Accused Product	$2.00	$0.90	$1.10	55%
Usual Product	$1.00	$0.50	$0.50	50%
Difference				5%

CONCLUSION

There are many unresolved issues in the field of damages analysis in intellectual property matters. Although the examples cited relate to patent infringement cases, the economic concepts find application in other IP cases as well. The case law has developed to embrace economic analysis in damages calculations, but these issues may well persist as qualified experts continue to respectfully disagree.

NOTES

1. For example, *BIC Leisure Products v. Windsurfing International, Inc.,* (1993); and *Crystal Semiconductor Corporation v. Tritech Microelectronics International, Inc.* (2001).

2. Even among experts who agree on using the 25 percent rule, we have observed disagreement over the level of profit to which the 25 percent is applied. Many experts believe the 25 percent should be applied to operating profit (or fully loaded profit), but some have argued that the 25 percent should be applied to incremental or net profit. We have further observed that several district courts, in their respective rulings, have differed in their understanding of gross sales, gross profit, and net profit.

REFERENCES

BIC Leisure Products v. Windsurfing International, Inc., 1 F.3d 1214 (Fed. Cir. 1993).

Crystal Semiconductor Corporation v. Tritech Microelectronics International, Inc., 246 F.3d 1336 (Fed. Cir. 2001).

Fromson v. Western Litho Plate and Supply Co., et al., 853 F.2d 1568 (Fed. Cir. 1988).

Georgia-Pacific Corp. v. U.S. Plywood-Champion Papers, Inc., 318 F. Supp. 116 (S.D.N.Y. 1970).

Robert Goldscheider. "The Negotiation of Royalties and Other Sources of Income from Licensing," IDEA: *Journal of Law and Technology*, PTC Research Foundation of Franklin Pierce Law Center, 1995.

Grain Processing Corp. v. American Maize-Products Co., 185 F.3d 1341 (Fed. Cir. 1999).

Micro Chemical, Inc. v. Lextron, Inc., 318 F.3d 1119 (Fed. Cir. 2003).

Panduit Corp. v. Stahlin Bros. Fibre Works, 575 F.2d 1152 (6th Cir. 1978).

Rite-Hite Corp. v. Kelly Co., 56 F.3d 1538 (Fed. Cir. 1995).

SmithKline Diagnostics v. Helena Laboratories, 926 F.2d 1161 (Fed. Cir. 1991).

State Industries, Inc. v. Mor-Flo Industries, Inc., 883 F.2d 1573 (Fed. Cir. 1989).

TWM Manufacturing Co., Inc. v. Dura Corp., 789 F.2d 895 (Fed. Cir. 1986).

Section 284, title 35, United States Code.

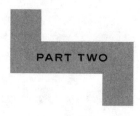

PART TWO

Economics of Patent Damages

6

Loss of Profits as a Measure of Damages in Patent Infringement Matters

VINCENT A. THOMAS
FTI Consulting, Inc.

CHRISTOPHER GERARDI
FTI Consulting, Inc.

DAWN HALL
FTI Consulting, Inc.

In patent litigation, the guiding principle in computing damages is that of "adequately compensating" the patent owner for the infringement. Such adequate compensation can be measured in different ways, one of which is the profits that a patent holder has lost as a result of the infringer's presence in the marketplace. In this chapter, we identify certain measures of profits recognized by the infringer, provide an explanation of the methodology behind such measures including case examples, and comment on factors one should consider when claiming such measures.[1]

INTRODUCTION

One potential remedy available to a patent owner that successfully proves infringement in a patent infringement matter is monetary damages, guided by Section 35 U.S.C. 284 of the United States Code (1970), which states that

> [u]pon finding for the claimant the court shall award damages adequate to compensate for the infringement, but in no event less than a reasonable royalty for the use made of the invention. . . . [t]ogether with interest and costs as fixed by the court. The court may increase the damages up to three times the amount.

It is important to recognize that although the amount of recoverable damages is a question of fact, the measure of damages on which the factual computation is based is a question of law as the appropriate measure of damages will be determined by the Court. The role of a damages expert is to prepare various analyses that address the different measures of damages to assist the trier of fact in assessing the amount of damages that will adequately compensate for the infringement.

Additionally, the *"damages adequate to compensate for the infringement"* will depend on the facts and circumstances of each matter and can be viewed differently by each party to the dispute. That said, if the patent holder's claim the profits on sales of its own products or profits on its own operations have been adversely impacted by the infringing party's presence in the marketplace, a patent holder's claim for those profits that have been lost will likely be part of what the patent owner believes will provide adequate compensation.[2] Such profits can take many different forms including but not limited to:

- *Patented products.* Profits that would have been generated on the patent owner's sales of its products that embody the patented invention that were lost as a result of the infringement.
- *Competing nonpatented products.* Profits that would have been generated on the patent owner's sales of its products that do not embody the patented invention, but that were lost as a result of the infringement because they compete with the infringing product.
- *Convoyed/"add-on" sales.* Profits that would have been generated on the patent owner's sales of its products that would have been sold in conjunction with the patented product sales that were lost as a result of the infringement.
- *Price erosion.* Profits lost as a result of price adjustments the patent holder had to make as a direct result of entry and competition from the infringer.
- *Increased costs.* Profits lost as a result of additional costs incurred by the patent owner for items such as additional advertising, selling expenses, and distribution costs that would not have been incurred had the infringer not been competing with its infringing product.

Although these claims are not exhaustive, these items have been accepted by courts, and their history does provide a framework for setting forth such claims. Therefore, this chapter focuses on these methods for claiming the profits the patent owner has lost as a result of infringement on its patent. We include descriptions of the methodology employed for such claims and discussion of the case law that supports this methodology. We also provide case examples and commentary on actual implementation of these methods.

LOST SALES OF PATENT OWNER'S PATENTED PRODUCTS

Methodology (*Panduit* Test)

Obtaining the profits the plaintiff claims to have lost to the infringer as actual damages is not automatic. The patent owner must demonstrate with reasonable probability that it would have been able to generate such lost profits had the infringement not occurred.[3] Once such reasonable probability has been established, the infringer is responsible for showing, if possible, that such an inference is not appropriate for all or a portion of the claimed profits.[4]

Although the patent owner is not necessarily precluded from using a particular method to prove entitlement to the profits it has lost as a result of the infringement, a method that has been accepted as useful in such an endeavor is the *Panduit* test.[5] This test is based on the 1978 decision, *Panduit Corp., v. Stahlin Bros. Fibre Works, Inc.,* citing a four-factor test that is useful in proving the patent holder could have generated the claimed lost profits:

1. Demand existed for the patented product during the period of infringement.
2. Acceptable noninfringing substitutes were not available to satisfy demand for the infringer's products during the damage period.
3. The patent holder had the requisite manufacturing, sales, and marketing capacity to have been able to meet the demand and supply the customers that purchased the infringing product.
4. The patent holder can compute the profit that it claims to have lost.

Panduit **Factor 1: Demand Existed for the Patented Product**   The first prong of the *Panduit* test is to establish demand for the patented product. This demand for the patented product is used to support the patent owner claim that the patented product would have been sold in lieu of the infringing product. This demand can be supported using various information, such as historical sales information, business records, consumer surveys, plans related to product launch, and industry information that demonstrates demand for the patented product. In certain cases it may be enough for the patent holder to show sales of its products and/or the infringing products as a means of proving consumer demand.[6] However, it is important to point out that the underlying purpose of this factor is to address whether the demand for the patent owner's and infringer's products is interchangeable and that the products are sufficiently similar to compete in the same market for the same customers. It is also possible that noninfringing aspects of the infringer's products drove consumer demand and actually expanded the market beyond that which the patent holder would have enjoyed but for the infringement. If the infringer is able to show that sales of its products resulted primarily from features other than the infringing aspects of its product, the patent holder may not satisfy the first prong of the *Panduit* test, thus precluding lost profits. For example, in *Slimfold Mfg. Co. v. Kinkead Indus., Inc.* (1991), *GNB Battery Tech., Inc. v. Exide Corp.* (1995), and *Grain Processing Corp. v. American Maize-Products Co.* (1999), lost profits were denied because the patent owner failed to establish that the patented feature drove consumer buying habits. As such, it may be important for the patent owner to link the patented *feature* to the commercial success of the patented product.

Panduit **Factor 2: No Acceptable Noninfringing Substitutes**   Establishing the relevant market for the patent owner's products is a critical step, regardless of the method employed to establish a reasonable probability that additional sales of the patent owner's products would have been made "but for" the infringement. Accordingly, the second prong of the *Panduit* test, showing that no acceptable noninfringing substitutes exist, often relies on a definition of the market for the patent owner's products in order to determine whether other products that did not infringe the patent would have been available to satisfy the sales of the infringing products. A relevant market may include those products with similar functional characteristics, physical attributes and/or pricing structures.[7]

Defining the relevant market can be done in several ways but what is typically useful is gaining an understanding of consumer attitudes and buying patterns, analyzing the advertising, sales and product literature, and reviewing and analyzing studies and analysis relative to the marketplace for the patent owner's product(s). In fact, in many instances the patent owner or infringer will have performed its own market analysis relative to its respective products, which can often be very useful information in defining the relevant market.

Defining the market reveals whether other noninfringing products were available to satisfy the demand for the infringing products. For example, assume hypothetically that the market within which the patent owner's product is sold has been defined to include four products: Product A—the patent owner's product, Product B—the infringer's product, and Product C and D—competitive products that have not been found to infringe.

This assessment reflects that noninfringing substitutes do exist in Products C and D, resulting in failure of the second prong of the *Panduit* test and thus impacting the patent owner's ability to claim lost profits.

		Units	Market Share
Product A	Patent Owner	40	40%
Product B	Infringer	20	20%
Product C	Competitor	20	20%
Product D	Competitor	20	20%
Total		100	100%

Market Share Approach   It used to be a requirement that the relevant market be a "two-supplier market" (e.g., the infringer and the patent holder) or that other market participants also infringed. The reality, though, is that many markets are not "two-supplier" markets and the existence of others in the marketplace does not automatically indicate that the patent holder would not have made any of the infringer's sales. As such, the Court of Appeals for the Federal Circuit modified the requirements under the second *Panduit* factor to allow for recovery of lost profits when there are alternatives and/or substitutes in the marketplace. In *State Industries v. Mor-Flo,* the Court of Appeals stated that "the presence or absence of acceptable noninfringing substitutes does not matter . . ." and instead focuses on the patent owner showing that "but for" the infringement, it would have made the claimed portion of the infringer's related sales. This decision allowed for the concept of a multisupplier market, where, once its market share is proven, the patent owner's lost sales are determined based on its share of the market in the absence of the infringer. For example, utilizing the hypothetical example depicted in the last table, the "but for" market shares can be calculated under the market share approach.

		Units Without Infringer	"But For" Market Share		Total Units		"But For" Units
Product A	Patent Owner	40	50%	×	100	=	50
Product B	Infringer	0	0%	×	100	=	0
Product C	Competitor	20	25%	×	100	=	25
Product D	Competitor	20	25%	×	100	=	25
Total		80	100%				100

As reflected in the table, the 20 infringing units from Company B are allocated among the other market players, which include Company A (the patent owner) as well as Company C and Company D. Without the infringing units, total units are 80, which results in Company A's 40 units being 50 percent of the 80 total units and Company C and Company D's 20 units are both 25 percent of the market. When these adjusted market shares are multiplied by the actual units sold of 100, the result are the units that each company would have sold "but for" the infringement. Therefore, Company A's lost unit sales are 10 units, which is the difference between its "but for" units of 50 and its actual unit sales of 40.[8]

Alternative Design   The evolution of how the courts have viewed the issue of noninfringing substitutes did not end with *State Industries v. Mor-Flo*. The decision in *Grain Processing v. American Maize,* decided in 1999, addressed the situation where a noninfringing alternative, although not commercially available in the marketplace at the time of the infringement, would likely have been available "but for" the infringement. The Court found that even if a new process is *not* developed, it is a noninfringing alternative if the necessary materials were available, technical process was known, and the defendant had necessary equipment, know-how, and experience to create the alternative. The burden of proof falls on the infringer to demonstrate the ability to implement the alternative.

Panduit **Factor 3: Manufacturing and Marketing Capacity**   As part of showing that the patent owner could have made some or all of the sales of the infringer, the patent holder must also demonstrate that it had both the marketing and manufacturing capacity to exploit demand within the relevant time frame. From a manufacturing perspective, the patent holder can satisfy this requirement by showing its production facilities and labor force that existed during the infringement period could have accommodated the additional sales the patent owner would have generated. This might entail an analysis of production levels, plans for future growth, and contemporaneously prepared manufacturing capacity utilization reports and the like as well as discussions with manufacturing personnel.

Even if the capacity did not exist during the time of the infringement, the patent owner may satisfy the manufacturing capacity requirement if it can show that it could have expanded its capacity in some fashion to accommodate the additional sales. This might include investing in additional equipment or labor or subcontracting production. Under such a scenario, an additional investment may have been necessary to increase production capacity; therefore, it is important that the patent owner also show that it possesses the appropriate financial and technical ability to make such an investment and that the lost profit calculation is adjusted accordingly. For example, the patent owner may show that it could have obtained the needed manufacturing capacity by purchasing additional equipment. To show that such a purchase could have been executed, the patent owner's financial condition should be assessed to determine whether it had the wherewithal to make such a purchase. And if such a purchase were possible, the expense associated with the purchase of the additional equipment may need to be accounted for in the patent owner's claim for profits lost.

Even though the patent holder may have had the ability to manufacture the lost sales, it also must be able to show that it would have had the necessary marketing and distribution channels to make sales of additional products manufactured. An assessment of geographic markets, intersecting customers, size of sales force, and distribution channels may be necessary to assess whether the patent owner would have been able to make some or all of the sales of the infringer. For example, such an analysis may reveal that the infringer may have made sales through a completely different distribution network or geographic territory from that of the patent holder. Although this does not necessarily preclude the patent owner from claiming that it could have made the sales of the infringer, it does burden the patent holder with showing how such sales would have been achieved. Further, if additional investment would be required to create the necessary marketing capacity, such additional expenditure may need to be reflected as a reduction to the profits a patent owner claims as damages.

Panduit Factor 4: Computing Profits Lost　　The final criterion that must be satisfied to claim profits lost as a result of the infringement is calculation of said profits. Such calculation cannot be speculative; a reasonable basis must exist. Also, the level of profits that the patent owner may recover are the *incremental* profits it would have enjoyed "but for" the infringement. Incremental profits are those profits that result from deducting only those costs that are necessary to support the additional sales that would have been generated. As such, computing incremental profits is typically divided into two components: lost sales and incremental costs.

Lost Sales　　Estimating the sales the patent owner has lost as a result of the infringement is determined in part through the market analysis necessary to satisfy the second *Panduit* factor, no noninfringing substitutes exist. As discussed, defining the market reveals whether other noninfringing products were available to satisfy the demand for the infringing products or whether the market is a "two-supplier" market. (A "two-supplier" market provides an indication, but not necessarily a certainty, that the infringer's sales may be lost sales of the patent owner.) Combining this analysis with a showing that demand for the patented feature existed and demonstrated marketing and manufacturing capacity can provide a reasonable basis for the units the patent owner would have generated "but for" the infringement.

Also, not only is the unit share the patent owner would have garnered important, but an assessment of the price level the patent owner could have sustained is also important in that it is possible that the patent owner may have been required to charge a lower average price than it typically charges in order to make the sale. For example, the infringer may have sold a large order that it discounted in order to generate the sale. Thus, in the "but for" world, the patent owner may have had to offer this discount if it wanted to generate the additional sales. Conversely, the presence of the infringer in the marketplace may have put a downward pressure on prices that may not have been present had the infringer been absent from the market. Thus, the patent owner may have been able to charge a higher price than the infringer. As such, gaining an understanding of the product's price elasticity can be an important factor to consider that may allow the patent owner to claim it would have made all or a portion of defendant's sales and/or made sales at same or higher prices. This can also be helpful in claiming price erosion on sales the patent owner actually made of its products during the infringement period. In other words, the patent owner may be able to claim that its actual sales would have been made at a higher price "but for" the infringement; thus, the difference between the price it could have charged and the price it actually charged may be claimed as additional damages. A further discussion of the patent owner's claim for price erosion is provided later in this chapter.

Incremental Costs   Once the lost sales have been established, the patent owner must deduct the incremental costs (e.g., costs the patent owner would have incurred in order to generate sales it claims to have lost). In assessing incremental costs, it is important to understand the concepts of fixed and variable costs. Variable costs are costs that tend to change as volume changes. Increase in volume result in increases in variable costs and decreases in volume result in decreases in variable costs. Fixed costs, however, are those costs that do not change relative to sales volume. These costs generally do not change as sales volume changes.

Variable costs tend to be *incremental* costs relative to lost sales; fixed costs typically are not. However, this is not always the case. Some variable costs may vary only to a certain point. For example, the commission plan for an organization may pay commissions on certain additional sales but may be capped at a certain level. Thus, sales generated above the capped level would not result in additional commissions. Moreover, some fixed costs are fixed only over a certain sales volume and then may change in a discreet manner resulting in what is commonly referred to as a step-fixed cost. For example, electricity costs for a plant may be fixed for a defined sales volume, but after running the production line for additional shifts, these costs may increase. Also, supervisor salaries are typically fixed, but the addition of the lost sales to plaintiff's existing sales volume may require the plaintiff to add another supervisor to oversee the production lines, resulting in an incremental cost in the form of a supervisor salary.

Two approaches that are prevalent in computing incremental costs are account analysis and regression analysis. An account analysis approach entails a review of financial documents and records maintained in the normal course of business, such as financial statements, ledgers, tax returns, and other financial analysis. For example, documents such as sales history and profitability reports for the product(s) in question, product line profit and loss statements (including detailed data by product, if available), activity-based management systems documents, capital budgeting documents along with discussions with management will in many cases isolate those expenses that would increase in connection with the increase in sales measured by the lost sales calculation. Also, the analysis of expense accounts can be augmented through discussions with company personnel to better understand the manner in which the patent owner classifies and accounts for its costs. This will also allow for assessment of certain hypothetical situations that will be helpful in identifying costs that are incremental. For example, company personnel may be asked hypothetical questions such as: "If your company were to add the additional sales it claims to have lost, what costs would change and how are those costs reflected in the company's financial documents? Would payroll increase? What about electricity costs? Would additional equipment be required?"

A regression analysis is a statistical technique that is utilized for the purpose of investigating and modeling the relationship between variables. To estimate incremental costs, a regression analysis may be used to determine what, if any, relationship exists between sales volume and costs. A simplistic description of how such an analysis is performed is that an independent variable (typically units sold or sales dollars) is compared to a dependent variable (the costs incurred to generate a certain level of sales). This comparison is typically made via a computer model and several periods of historical data on costs and sales volumes are utilized to produce a more meaningful result. The result of a regression analysis is an equation that can be used to estimate incremental costs at a particular sales level.

It is important to emphasize that a regression analysis is far more complicated than just described; it is usually a mistake to simply plug data into a regression program that produces an equation and apply the results without additional investigation or consideration of other factors that should be addressed to ensure that the results of the regression analysis are reasonable, appropriate, and represent the intended relationship between the dependent and independent variable(s). That said, regression analysis can be a valuable tool for estimating incremental costs if properly designed, evaluated, and supported.

Case Example

We have devised a simplistic hypothetical example to illustrate the methodology that may be employed to determine the profits the patent owner may claim as damages in a patent infringement matter. Our example involves a hypothetical patent for a special handle utilized on reusable razors. The patent owner in our example, Company A, produces and sells both the "Comfort Grip Razor" that embodies the patented technology as well as the "Regular Razor" that does not embody the technology. Other companies that sell reusable razors in our hypothetical example include Company B, Company C, and Company D. Company B produces and sells the "Sure Grip Razor" that infringes Company A's patent on its special handle, as well as the "Standard Razor" that does not infringe Company A's patent. Company C and Company D produce and sell the "Normal Razor" and "Common Razor," respectively, neither of which infringe on Company A's patent. The patented "Comfort Grip Razor" was introduced to the market in January of 2005 and the infringing "Sure Grip Razor" was introduced in March of 2005. The damage period is through December of 2005.

Through market research and information produced during the litigation, this sales information was uncovered:

Company	Razor	Quantity	Revenues	Average Sales Price
Patent Owner				
Company A	Regular	25,000,000	$122,500,000	$4.90
Company A	Comfort Grip	6,000,000	$ 30,000,000	$5.00
Infringer				
Company B	Standard	30,000,000	$146,700,000	$4.89
Company B	Sure Grip	4,000,000	$ 19,920,000	$4.98
Noninfringer				
Company C	Normal	15,000,000	$ 73,050,000	$4.87
Company D	Common	20,000,000	$ 97,200,000	$4.86
Total		**100,000,000**	**$489,370,000**	**$4.89**

Other documents and information that has been uncovered and produced includes:

- Strategic analyses and market studies both Company A and Company B have prepared relative to reusable razors
- Production reports
- Advertising materials and product brochures related to Comfort Grip and Sure Grip
- Company A's and Company B's product line profit and loss statements, balance sheets, and tax returns
- Company A's and Company B's sales by customer of all reusable razors
- Various depositions from marketing, sales, finance, and operations personnel at both Company A and Company B
- License agreements entered into by both Company A and Company B for similar technology

Both Company A and Company B have engaged a financial expert to provide an opinion of the damages Company A has suffered, if Company B is found to have infringed. Company A engaged John Expert and Company B engaged Barbara Witness.

Company A's financial expert, John Expert, employs the *Panduit* test as a basis for concluding that a reasonable probability exists that Company A would have made additional sales of its Comfort Grip razor had Company B not infringed, citing:

- *Demand existed for the patented product during the period of infringement.*

    John Expert references that Company A sold 6,000,000 Comfort Grip razors, generating revenues of $30,000,000 in 2005, as an indication of demand for the patented product. He also cites Sure Grip sales of 4,000,000 units and revenue of $19,920,000 as further support of the market's demand.

- *Acceptable noninfringing substitutes were not available.*

    Based on reviewing market analysis, strategic plans, advertising materials, product brochures, and discussions with Company A personnel, John Expert defines the market in which the Comfort Grip razor is sold as a "two-supplier" market that includes those razors that have the specialized handle feature (e.g., only Comfort Grip and Sure Grip). As such, Mr. Expert concludes that no available noninfringing substitutes were available during the infringement period.

- *Manufacturing, sales, and marketing capacity were available to make the additional sales.*

    Based on an analysis of customer sales, Mr. Expert determined that both Company A and Company B sold the Comfort Grip and Sure Grip to essentially the same retail outlets. Since Company A's salespeople and distribution system already served these accounts, Mr. Expert concluded that Company A had the requisite marketing and sales capacity to make additional sales. Also, based on discussions with Company A's production personnel and review of the manufacturing capacity report, Mr. Expert determined that Company A had available capacity in 2005 to produce 1,000,000 more units. However, it was also determined that Company A's capacity could be easily increased by 3,000,000 additional unit (for a total of 4,000,000 units) if it leased one additional piece of equipment. Mr. Expert investigated and confirmed that Company A had the financial wherewithal to lease this additional piece of equipment. As such, Mr. Expert concludes that Company A would have had the manufacturing and marketing capacity to produce 4,000,000 additional units, if necessary.

- *Computation of lost profits amounted to $7.9 million.*

    Mr. Expert calculates the profits Company A would have generated on additional sales of its Comfort Grip razor to be $7.9 million. Lost Sales of 4,000,000 units are based on Mr. Expert's definition of the market for Comfort Grip being a "two-supplier" market (that includes only Comfort Grip and Sure Grip) and Company A's ability to easily sell to all of Company B's customers that purchased the Sure Grip. Mr. Expert concludes that Company A would have been able to sell an additional 4,000,000 Comfort Grip units if Company B had not sold 4,000,000 infringing Sure Grip units. He also concludes that Company A would have sold those units at least at Comfort Grip's 2005 average unit price of $5.00 per unit. As such, lost sales are assumed to be $20,000,000 (4,000,000 units × $5.00 per unit).

Incremental costs that Mr. Expert deducts from the $20 million in lost sales are based on an analysis of Company A's Comfort Grip profit and loss statement for the 6,000,000 Comfort Grip units sold in 2005:

	Amount	Amount Per Unit
Revenue	$30,000,000	$5.00
Cost of Sales	$15,000,000	$2.50
Gross Margin	$15,000,000	$2.50
General & Administrative Expenses:		
Administrative Salaries	$ 1,500,000	$0.25
Commissions	$ 3,000,000	$0.50
Rent	$ 2,000,000	$0.33
Depreciation	$ 2,000,000	$0.33
Operating Income	$ 6,500,000	$1.08

Based on discussions with Company A personnel and analysis of amounts that comprise the listed expense items, Mr. Expert concludes that Company A would not have had to incur any additional administrative salaries, rent, or depreciation if it produced 4,000,000 additional units of the Comfort Grip razor in 2005. However, Company A would have to incur cost of sales expenses of labor and materials at $2.50 for each unit produced as well as commission expense of $.50 for each unit sold.

Additionally, expanding capacity to be able to produce 4,000,000 more units would require leasing another piece of equipment at $100,000. Therefore, incremental costs that would have been necessary to support the additional 4,000,000 Comfort Grip units Company A would have sold are:

- Cost of sales (labor and materials) of $10,000,000 ($2.50 × 4,000,000)
- Commissions of $2,000,000 ($.50 × 4,000,000)
- Equipment lease costs of $100,000

This results in incremental profits of $7.9 million summarized as:

Lost Sales	$20,000,000
Incremental Costs:	
Cost of Sales (4,000,000 units × $2.50)	$10,000,000
Commissions (4,000,000 × $.50 per unit)	$ 2,000,000
Additional equipment lease cost	$ 100,000
Incremental Profits	$ 7,900,000

Company B's financial expert is Barbara Witness, and she sees things a little differently from Mr. Expert. She also employed the *Panduit* test, but contrary to Mr. Expert, she did not give Company A a passing grade. First, based on Ms. Witness's analysis of the market, she concludes that the handle has little or no impact on a consumer's decision to buy a razor. As such, Ms. Witness concludes that Company A has not sufficiently shown demand for the patented feature. Moreover, her analysis results in a market definition that includes all reusable razors, including the Comfort Grip, Sure Grip as well as the Regular, Standard, Normal, and Common. It is her opinion that noninfringing substitutes did exist, including the Regular, Standard, Normal, and Common.

Although Ms. Witness believes Company A has failed the *Panduit* test, she does conclude that Company A would have made additional sales of its Comfort Grip razor by applying the market share approach:

	Actual 2005 Results		Reallocated 2005 Results	
	Units	Share	Units	Share
Regular	25,000,000	25.00%	26,041,667	26.04%
Comfort Grip	6,000,000	6.00%	6,250,000	6.25%
Standard	30,000,000	30.00%	31,250,000	31.25%
Sure	4,000,000	4.00%	0	0.00%
Normal	15,000,000	15.00%	15,625,000	15.63%
Common	20,000,000	20.00%	20,833,333	20.83%
Total	100,000,000	100.00%	100,000,000	100.00%

Using that market share approach, the Sure Grip is assumed not to have been in the market under the "but for" market results. As such, instead of 6 percent of the market, the Comfort Grip would have garnered 6.25 percent of the market. Multiplying a 6.25 percent market share by the total 100,000,000 million units results in "but for" Comfort Grip sales of 6,250,000. Therefore, Ms. Witness concludes that Company A would have sold an additional 250,000 (6,250,000 "but for" units less 6,000,000 actual units). Ms. Witness computes profits on those units as:

Lost Sales (250,000 units × $5.00 per unit)	$1,250,000
Incremental Costs:	
Cost of Sales (250,000 units × $2.50 per unit)	$ 625,000
Commissions (250,000 × $.50 per unit)	$ 125,000
Additional equipment lease cost	—
Incremental Profits	$ 500,000

Like Mr. Expert, Ms. Witness has assumed a selling price of $5.00 per unit as well as incremental costs of $2.50 per unit for cost of sales and $.50 per unit for commissions. However, since Company A had existing capacity of 2,000,000 units and would lease a machine only if additional units in excess of that amount, the equipment lease cost would not be an incremental expense in this scenario. Thus, she concludes that the incremental profits for 250,000 units are $500,000. Because the patent owner is entitled to "in no event less than a reasonable royalty for the use made of the invention,"[9] Ms. Witness also computed a reasonable royalty that is applied to the other 3,750,000 infringing units. Such reasonable royalty is discussed in Chapter 10.

Lost Sales of "Nonpatented" Products That Compete with Infringing Products

Methodology

A patent holder's claim for lost profits may not be limited to its products that embody the patented invention; it can also include those products not covered by the patented invention that it would have been able to generate profits "but for" the infringement. In *Rite-Hite Corp. v. Kelley Co., Inc.,* decided in 1995, the Court concluded that the patentee can receive lost profits on those sales that it would have made "but for" the alleged infringement. Those lost sales need not be products that include the patent, but rather can include those that compete with the alleged infringing product. For example, a company may have a large patent portfolio that includes a patent covering the technology embodied in a competitors' product. However, the patent owner's product may compete directly with the infringer's product although it does not necessarily utilize the patented technology in its own product. In this case, although the patent owner does not practice its own patent, it does have a product that competes with the infringer's product, and if the infringer was taken out of the market, the patent owner may have made the sale.

Case Example

An example would be to slightly adjust our hypothetical example of razors. Instead of the patent owner producing Comfort Grip, it had not yet launched its Comfort Grip and the market looked slightly different. If Sure Grip competed with Regular, it may be able to show that in the "but for" world, it would have made more sales of its Regular product even though it was not covered by the patent and would, therefore, be entitled to lost profits damages on those units. In this instance a market share approach could also be utilized based on Regular's share of the market in the absence of the infringer.

However, if the launch of the infringing Sure Grip expanded the razor blade market, that must be quantified and deducted from the calculation

Lost Sales of Convoyed ("Add-on") Products

Methodology

In addition to sales of products that are either covered or not covered by the patented invention, but which compete with the infringing product, the patent holder can claim the profits on those convoyed or "add-on" sales of items typically sold in conjunction with such products: accessories, spare parts, or related services. In patent infringement matters, the recovery of lost sales on unpatented components ordinarily sold with patented components may be awarded if the components function together in some manner to produce an end product or result.

However, the extent to which such profits are allowed may be limited to certain factors. For example, the Court decided in the *Marconi Wireless Telegraph Co.* matter in 1942 that damages for component parts used with a patented apparatus are recoverable under the entire market value rule if the patented apparatus is "of such paramount importance that it substantially created the value of the component parts." In the *Paper Converting Machine Co.* case decided in 1984, the Court clarified that under the entire market value rule, the patent owner is able to recover damages based on the value of the entire apparatus containing several features when the patented feature constitutes the basis for consumer demand. Furthermore, the Court ruled in the *Leesona Corp v. United States* case in 1979 that it is the "financial and marketing dependence on the patented item under standard marketing procedures" that determines whether the nonpatented features of a product should be included in the damages calculation.

In the *Rite-Hite* matter, the Court also ruled that the entire market rule applied only when the patented and unpatented parts of a device are physically part of the same machine or together constitute a functional unit. Under this interpretation, the Court ruled that there is no basis for extending recovery to include damages for items that are neither competitive with nor function with the patented invention or are sold solely as a marketing convenience or a business advantage. For example, a functional unit may include a patented engine component that constitutes the essential element of the engine in order to ensure proper operation, allowing the patent owner to seek damages based on the value of the engine as a whole. In contrast, a patent on the DVD player sold as part of the media package for a new car may or may not entitle the patent owner to recover damages based on the value of the car as a whole since it may be offered only as marketing tactic.

Case Example

For example, a patented razor, such as the Comfort Grip used in the earlier example, may work properly only when using the razor blades made by the same manufacturer, which can be packaged and sold with the razor and/or sold separately. The razor blades could be considered a convoyed product since they are needed in order for the razor to function as it was intended and it is reasonably foreseeable that if the infringer was removed from the market, the patent owner would have made additional razor sales and, in turn, razor blade sales.

PRICE EROSION

Methodology

Lost profits damages may also be awarded to the patent holder as a result of price erosion. Under the price erosion theory of damages, the patentee must be able to prove a reduction in its price (or, conversely, an inability to raise prices) as a direct result of the entry and competition from the infringer in the market. The plaintiff must prove that the price reduction occurred due to the defendant's presence in the market *and* must be able to determine the price that would have been charged "but for" the infringement.

In *Mahurkar Patent Litigation* (1993), the Court concluded that price erosion damages are ". . . the difference between actual . . . and potential price—the price they could have realized had there been no competition from the infringers. This is the 'price erosion' theory of damages, one with substantial support in the cases."). Simply put, price erosion can be calculated as the differential between the price the patent owner could have charged in the "but for" world and the price it charged after the infringer's unlawful entry into the market.

Evidence of price erosion may include the patentee cutting its prices in response to the announcement of the launch of the infringing product. In this instance the prices charged by the patentee and the infringer may be evaluated as well as the business plans, forecasts, and budgets. Price erosion may also result from the patentee's inability to raise its prices "but for" the infringement

Also, when assessing price erosion damages, the effect higher prices have on the quantity demanded is typically taken into account.

Case Example

Let us assume in the example given earlier that the patented "Comfort Grip Razor" was introduced to the market in January of 2005 at $6.10 per razor and the infringing "Sure Grip Razor" was introduced in March of 2005 at $5.00 per razor. Comfort Grip had to reduce its price from $6.00 to $5.00 to compete with the Sure Grip Razor, and there were numerous internal documents stating the reason for this price decrease was solely due to lower prices offered by Sure Grip. In this instance, Comfort Grip may claim it would have continued to charge the higher price of $6.10 "but for" competitive pressure exerted by Sure Grip. Therefore, Comfort Grip may seek damages based on the $1.10 price differential on razor sales for not only the lost infringing units but also on Comfort Grip sales where it reduced its price. However, it may important to perform an analysis to assess whether the consumer would have purchased the same volume of razors given the increase in price.

INCREASED COSTS/ACCELERATED MARKET ENTRY

Methodology

Typically, patent infringement damages cease after the patent term ends since the competition is allowed to lawfully utilize the previously patented feature in the marketplace. Upon expiration of the patent, the competition would ordinarily enter the market with zero market share and a big learning curve. However, in instances where the patent has been infringed, the infringer may have gained a head start on developing relationships with customers, getting its manufacturing facility up and running, building name recognition, setting up the distribution channels, and building production know-how. Therefore, a patentee may remain damaged even after the patent expires if the infringer was given a head start in the market and was able to enter the market with an established market share rather than a zero market share upon patent expiration.

The patent owner may also seek damages to recover costs it specifically incurred or the increase in certain other costs due to the unlawful actions of the infringer. Such costs may include lost volume discounts and increased marketing costs.

Case Example

In the Comfort Grip and Sure Grip razor example, infringement damages typically would cease after the patent term ends, because at that point the competition is allowed to utilize the previously patented feature in the marketplace. However, since Sure Grip infringed Comfort Grip's patent, it may have already established itself in the marketplace at the date of patent expiration. Accelerated market entry damages might be calculated since Sure Grip had an established market share rather than a zero market share on the patent expiration date.

Also, Company A may have experienced increased marketing costs for the Comfort Grip due to Sure Grip's entry into the market. In other words, if Sure Grip was not competing, then Comfort Grip might not have increased its advertising expense beyond otherwise normal levels. Therefore, this increase in advertising costs may be claimed as increased costs that resulted from the infringement.

CONCLUSION

Claiming the profits a patent owner would have made on sales of patented products hinges on a showing with reasonable certainty that the patent owner would have made such sales in the absence of the infringement. A generally accepted, but not necessarily exclusive, approach for proving such reasonable certainty is the *Panduit* test, which provides a framework from which to draw on. Even so, however, utilizing the *Panduit* test or other method is not an exact science. As we have shown, reasonable people (assuming our hypothetical Mr. Expert and Ms. Witness are reasonable) can develop differing opinions as to what would have occurred "but for" the infringement. This does not necessarily mean that one is right and the other is wrong. In the end what matters is the conclusion that is ultimately reached by the trier of fact with the aid of a financial expert. As in all damage analysis, thorough assessment and adequate and appropriate analysis of the facts will usually be a difference maker in the outcome.

NOTES

1. The discussions in this chapter are of a general nature and have been included for illustrative purposes only. They are not intended to address the specific circumstances of any individual

or entity. Each case is different, and should be evaluated in light of its own facts. In specific circumstances, the services of a professional should be sought. The views and opinions are those of the authors and do not reflect any opinions of FTI Consulting, Inc. or its clients as to the proper measure of damages.

2. After a judgment has been determined, the Court may also award the successful plaintiff pre-judgment interest, post-judgment interest, attorney's fees and enhanced damages.

3. *King Instruments Corp. v. Perego* (1995).

4. *Panduit Corp. v. Stahlin Bros. Fibre Works, Inc.* (1978).

5. *State Indus., Inc. v. Mor-Flo Indus., Inc.* (1989).

6. *BIC Leisure Products, Inc. v. Windsurfing International, Inc.* (1993).

7. *State Indus.* (1989); in *BIC Leisure Products,* decided in 1993, the court ruled that the damages computation must take into account the economic laws of supply and demand. The "but for" lost sales should be computed at an economic price and quantity that are reasonable within the relevant marketplace. The award of lost profits may not be speculative, and the patent owner must show a reasonable probability that, absent infringement, it would have made the infringer's sales.

8. Please note that Section 35 U.S.C. 284 of the United States Code (1970) states that "[u]pon finding for the claimant the court shall award damages adequate to compensate for the in-fringement, *but in no event less than a reasonable royalty* for the use made of the invention . . . " (emphasis added). Therefore, since the total infringing sales of Product B in the example are 20 units, the patent owner is entitled to at least a reasonable royalty on the other 10 units sold by the infringer. A discussion of how a reasonable royalty may be computed on these 10 units is contained in Chapter 10.

9. Section 35 U.S.C. 284 of the United States Code (1970).

REFERENCES

BIC Leisure Products, Inc. v. Windsurfing International, Inc., 1 F.3d 1214 (Fed. Cir. 1993).

GNB Battery Tech., Inc. v. Exide Corp., 886 F. Supp. 420 (D. Del. 1995).

Grain Processing Corp. v. American Maize-Products Co., 185 F.3d 1341 (Fed. Cir. 1999).

In re Mahurkar Patent Litigation, 831 F. Supp. 1354 (N.D. Illinois 1993).

King Instruments Corp. v. Perego, 65 F.3d 941, 952 (Fed. Cir. 1995).

Leesona Corp. v. United States, 599 F.2d 958, 974, 220 Ct. Cl. 234, 202 U.S.P.Q. 424, 439 (1979).

Marconi Wireless Telegraph Co. v. United States, 99 Ct. Cl. 1 (Fed. Cir. 1942).

Panduit Corp. v. Stahlin Bros. Fibre Works, Inc., 575 F.2d 1152, 1164, 197 U.S.P.Q. 726, 736 (6th Cir 1978).

Paper Converting Machine Co. v. Magna Graphics Corp., 745 F.2d 11, 21, 223 U.S.P.Q. 591, 598 (Fed. Cir. 1984).

Rite Hite Corp, et al. v. Kelley Company, Inc., 56 F.3d 1538 (Fed. Cir. 1995).

Slimfold Mfg. Co. v. Kinkead Indus., Inc., 932 F.2d 1453 (Fed. Cir. 1991).

State Industries, Inc. v. Mor-Flo Industries, Inc., 883 F.2d 1573, 12 U.S.P.Q. 2D 1026 (CAFC 1989).

United States Code, Title 35, Section 284.

CHAPTER 7

The Law of Demand and Lost Profits Analysis

ROBERT BASMANN
Binghamton University

MICHAEL BUCHANAN
FTI Consulting, Inc.

ESFANDIAR MAASOUMI
SMU

DANIEL SLOTTJE
SMU and FTI Consulting, Inc.

In many lost profit cases, the *Panduit* factors are invoked. A proper analysis requires the practitioner to adhere to the well-known economic principles embodied in the law of demand. In patent infringement litigation, some of the fundamental economic principles are often seemingly assumed away or ignored altogether. Part and parcel of understanding the demand for a product is the need to understand the market in which the product is sold and what transpires after an alleged infringement. Generally the two concepts go together; practitioners who tend to neglect the law of demand usually are not analyzing the market dynamics in which the products are sold either. We first discuss this basic principle of economic theory and present a primer on supply and demand, and then present several examples of why the law of demand *and* its market dynamics are important and the danger that arises when they are ignored.

INTRODUCTION

In a patent infringement case, it is well known that if the court finds for a plaintiff, one potential remedy is to award the plaintiff compensation for profits lost by the plaintiff, "but for" the infringement of the patent. It is also generally accepted that the appropriate way to calculate lost profits is to uncover the revenues of the alleged infringer and to then determine the percentage of those potential sales that would have been made by the patent holder "but for" the infringement and to then apply the incremental costs of the plaintiff to those sales to determine lost profits. As always, the devil is in the details. When determining what sales would have been made "but for" the infringement, it is crucial to understand fundamental economic principles of supply and demand and especially to understand the dynamics and empirical ramifications of the "law of demand." This so-called law simply states that as price of a commodity declines in a market, all else being equal, no less will be purchased. The law generally holds, but not always! Just how much more people will buy when price declines (or how much less for a price increase) depends on all the characteristics and dynamics of the market at issue in any particular matter. This chapter carefully discusses these market dynamics at a very elementary level and presents case studies to illustrate how economic principles should be taken into account when conducting lost profit analyses. Chapters 6, 8, and 9 discuss the concept of lost profits in more detail. In order to calculate these "but for" profits, a seminal case came down in 1978: the infamous *Panduit Corp. v. Stahlin Bros.* (1978). Just as certain cases have had important ramifications for the application of economics to antitrust law, the *Panduit* case was an important legal decision in applying economic principles to the determination of lost profits. In that decision, the court laid out this four-pronged test for the patent owner's entitlement to lost profits damages:

> To obtain as damages the profits on sales she would have made absent the infringement, i.e., the sales made by the infringer, a patent owner must prove: (1) demand for the patented product, (2) absence of acceptable noninfringing substitutes, (3) her manufacturing and marketing capability to exploit the demand, and (4) the amount of the profit she would have made.

This chapter focuses on the first and second *Panduit* factors with specific reference to price. That is, some expert witnesses have calculated lost profits using the general methodology just outlined, but some have essentially ignored price differentials between potential acceptable noninfringing products and applied patent holder marginal profit rates to all sales by the infringer. As noted, such a calculation ignores fundamental economic principles and assumptions underlying the so-called law of demand. This chapter discusses that concept fully and gives examples of how the concept has been used and can be misused. Fortunately, the courts are aware of the problems that arise in ignoring some aspects of these economic principles and market dynamics. One case in particular, *BIC Leisure Products, Inc. v. Windsurfing International Inc.* (1 F.3d 1993), has made it clear that ignoring some of these economic principles and market dynamics is not acceptable. The court said in the *BIC* matter that an alternative product (here a sailboard used for windsurfing) is not acceptable (as a noninfringing alternative) if the two products in question have different price ranges or are sold to different classes of consumers. Thus, a product has to be not only noninfringing from a technical perspective, but also acceptable from an economic and consumer perspective. This chapter clarifies these concepts further.

THE LAW OF DEMAND AND ITS EVOLUTION

There are essentially two closely related ways of presenting demand relations. Most of the basics of the modern theory of supply and demand were formalized by Alfred Marshall and Leon Walras, who combined ideas about supply and demand and looked at the equilibrium point where the two curves crossed. They also began looking at the effect of markets on each other. The basic theory of supply and demand is generally unchanged since the late nineteenth century. In fact, much of the advanced work has been in examining the exceptions to the model, as in considerations of oligarchy, transaction costs, switching costs, embedded bases, and issues of rationality; and have been expanded in understanding concepts like network effects in industries that enjoy significant positive externalities due to these network effects.

Marshall's theory of supply and demand departed from the ideas of economists from Adam Smith and David Ricardo through the marginalist school of thought. Although Marshall's theories are dominant in elite universities today, not everyone has followed the same departures that he and the *marginalists* proposed. For instance, one theory counter to Marshall is that price is already known for a commodity before it reaches the market, negating his idea that some abstract market is conveying price information. In this line of thought, the only thing the market communicates is whether an object is exchangeable or not (in which case it would change from an object to a commodity). This would mean that the producer creates the goods without already having customers—blindly producing, hoping that someone will buy them, that is, exchange money for the commodities.

Keynesian economics also runs somewhat counter to the theory of supply and demand. In Keynesian theory, prices can become "sticky," or resistant to change, especially in the case of price decreases (e.g., for labor). This can lead to a market failure.

SUPPLY AND DEMAND MODELS

Dozens of economics textbooks, such as Stigler (1987), Landsburg (2005), Pindyck and Rubinfeld (2005), and Baumol and Blinder (2006), discuss the elementary principles of supply and demand and present the simple graphs that are used in this chapter. To further facilitate access, much of the discussion in the first sections of this chapter follows from Wikipedia, a World Wide Web source. One of the authors of this chapter (Slottje) has taught a price theory course for years, where of course all these concepts have been discussed. For completeness, however, we refer the reader to the textbooks cited and the Wikipedia site.

The *supply and demand* model describes the dynamic nature of prices and how they vary as a result of the equilibration process between product availability at each price (supply) and the expressed preferences of those with purchasing power at each price (demand). This model could be describing the market for bread, vitamins, telecom switches, exercise equipment, railroad cars, or a nondenumerable number of other goods and services and the attendant markets in which those goods and services are bought and sold. The graph in

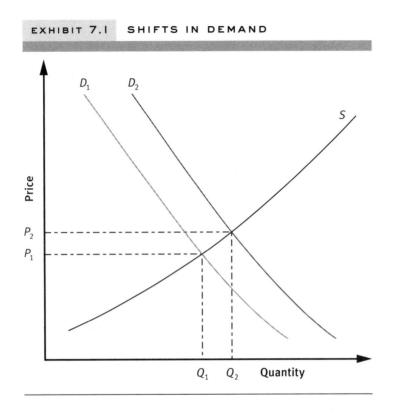

EXHIBIT 7.1 SHIFTS IN DEMAND

Exhibit 7.1 depicts an increase in demand from D_1 to D_2 along with the consequent increase in price and quantity required to reach a new market-clearing equilibrium point on the supply curve (S). The introduction of a new (perhaps allegedly infringing) technology, the enhancement of network effects, a new advertising campaign, the lowering of switching costs (again, perhaps due to infringement), or the reverse engineering of products already on the market could all cause such a movement. Any of these events could trigger a change in demand for the "generic" product depicted in the exhibit.

Shifts in supply for (say) a piece of telecommunications equipment that may be the subject of a patent infringement claim, may occur coincidentally or simultaneously or after an infringing product is introduced, and can cause movement in prices and quantities that require evaluation. A *partial equilibrium* supply and demand model attempts to describe the process for changes in the price and quantity of (say) products like a radio base station in competitive markets, without explaining, describing, and accounting for all the other factors that can be influencing the price of the base station. The model is only a first approximation for describing an *imperfectly competitive market,* as often characterizes markets with few players and innovators. The theory of demand and supply is important for understanding how a market economy operates since it provides an explanation of the mechanism by which many resource allocation decisions are made. However, unlike general equilibrium models, supply schedules in this partial equilibrium model are fixed by unexplained forces. One of those "unexplained forces" could be the infringement of someone else's intellectual property.

Assumptions and Definitions

When employing these basic generic economic models for forensic purposes and in intellectual property (IP) cases in particular, it is critical to appreciate the import of the basic assumptions, because these underlying concepts may lead to very different outcomes from case to case. For instance, the theory of supply and demand usually assumes that markets are perfectly competitive (meaning no one single seller can influence price in that market). This implies that there are so many buyers and sellers in the market that none of them has the capacity to sell in the market at a price for the good that is above marginal cost. In many real-life IP transactions, the assumption fails because some individual buyers or sellers or groups of buyers or sellers do have enough ability to influence prices. The first mover or innovator in a market (say the owner of the intellectual property, or the owner of the patents on a given machine or process) may significantly impact price in that market. Quite often more sophisticated analysis is required than some damages experts commonly perform in patent infringement cases, in order to understand the demand-supply equation of a product, especially one that is undergoing rapid technical development. However, the basic elementary economic theory may works quite well in simple situations.

Demand

A demand schedule is simply the quantity demanded at any given price. It can be represented on a graph as a line or curve by plotting the quantity demanded at each price. It can also be described mathematically by a demand equation. The main determinants of the quantity of a good demanded will be the price of the product, the person's level of income, personal preferences and characteristics, the price of "substitute" products, and the price and availability of complementary products. Interestingly, in many lost profits analyses in patent infringement cases, experts ignore these factors altogether. Ideally, the estimation of this demand relationship should be the central part of an expert's work. Quantifying elasticities (discussed later), or the empirical shape of this relationship, perhaps before and after alleged infringement occurs, is key. A new cost-effective way of producing police uniforms by a new or existing manufacturer is not likely to lead to significantly increased hiring of police and/or higher demand for police uniforms. Gas price *changes* below $2/gallon may not elicit the same *changes* in demand as changes in the $5−6/gallon range may illicit. The U.S. economy in 2006 is an excellent example of this as gas prices have broken over the $3.00 per gallon mark, with little discernible change in how consumers drive or, rather, with respect to how they have not cut back on driving. These so-called price and income elasticities are to be determined with available data.

Supply

Supply is the quantity supplied at a given price. Intellectual property is like all other "goods," in that its supply conditions generally follow the same principles. The main determinants of the quantity supplied will be the market price of the product and the *cost of producing it*. In general, supply curves are constructed from the firm's long-run (that period of time for which all inputs use can be varied) cost schedule. New product introductions, technological advances, more efficient production processes, and other economic factors may all be patented and can of course impact both the location and shape of a supply curve.

Simple Supply and Demand Curves

Economic theory conceives a series of supply and demand relationships and then adjusts for factors that produce "stickiness" between supply and demand. Analysis is then done to see what "trade-offs" are made in the "market" as interactions between sellers and buyers. Analysis takes note of the point at which the ability of sellers to sell becomes less beneficial than other opportunities. This is related to "marginal" costs — or the price to produce the last unit that can be sold profitably versus the chance of using the same effort to engage in some other activity.

The slope of the demand curve (downward to the right) indicates that a greater quantity will be demanded when the price is lower (see Exhibit 7.2). The slope of the supply curve (upward to the right) tells us that as the price goes up, producers are willing to produce more goods. The point where these curves intersect is the equilibrium point. The idea of a hypothetical negotiation where a willing seller and willing buyer arrive at a royalty rate (which is just a relative price, after all) is one example of this. At a royalty rate or price of P, producers (the patent holder) will be willing to supply Q units per period of time and buyers (the alleged infringer) will demand the same quantity. P in this example

EXHIBIT 7.2   GRAPH OF SIMPLE SUPPLY AND DEMAND CURVES

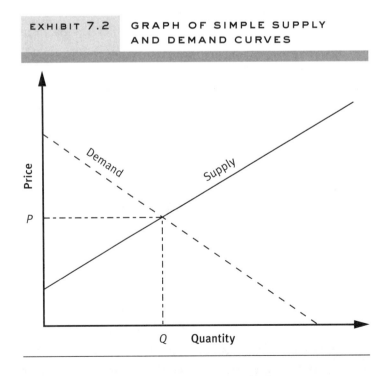

is the equilibriating price that equates supply with demand; in the context of our discussion, it is the royalty rate arrived at between a willing buyer and seller.

In the exhibits, straight lines are drawn instead of the more general curves. This is convenient and typical in economic damages analysis in IP matters looking at the simplified relationships between supply and demand. The shape of the curve, while empirically important, does not change the general relationships and the lessons of the supply and demand theory. Also, the shape of the curves far away from the equilibrium point is less likely to be important because these far areas do not affect the instant market clearing price and will not affect it unless large shifts in the supply or demand occur. So straight lines for supply and demand with the proper slope will convey most of the information the model can offer. Determining the exact shape of the curve is the domain of econometrics/statistics. The general shape of the curve, especially its slope near the equilibrium point, has an impact on how a market will adjust to changes in demand or supply. This issue is analyzed with the concept of "elasticity." The precise shape over a range and a period of alleged infringement is of central interest in IP litigation.

It should be noted that both supply and demand curves are drawn as a function of price. The two functions interact in a manner that is representative of market outcomes. In practice, any currency or commodity used to measure price is also an influence on supply and demand.

Change from the Equilibrium Point

Consider how prices and quantities not at the equilibrium point tend to move toward the equilibrium (see Exhibit 7.3). Assume that some organization (say a patent holding company or other monopolist) has the ability to set prices. If the price is set too high, such as at P_1 in the exhibit, then the quantity produced will be Q_s. The quantity demanded will be Q_d. Since the quantity demanded is less than the quantity supplied, there will be an oversupply (also called surplus or excess supply). If the price is set too low, then too little will be produced to meet demand at that price. This will cause an undersupply problem (also called a shortage).

Now assume that individual firms have the ability to alter the quantities that they supply and the price they are willing to accept, and consumers have the ability to alter the quantities that they demand and the amount they are willing to pay. Businesses and consumers will respond by adjusting their price (and quantity) levels, and eventually this will restore the quantity and the price to the equilibrium. When a damages expert is attempting to quantify how (say a "but for" world would look (i.e., without an infringer in a given market), these price and quantity adjustments can be very important.

In the case of too high a price and oversupply (seen in Exhibit 7.4), the profit–maximizing businesses will soon have too much excess inventory, so they will lower prices (from P_1 to P) to reduce this. Again, contemplate a situation where an infringing product is legally bound to exit a market; this would affect the market equilibrium as currently being discussed. Quantity supplied will be reduced from Q_s to Q and the oversupply will be

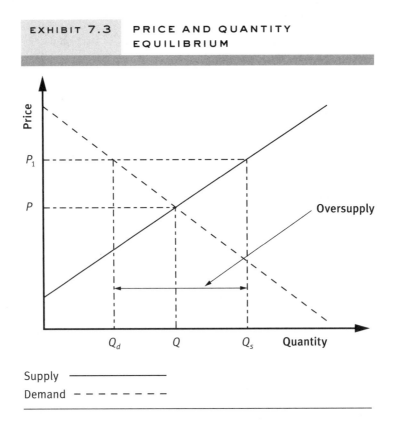

EXHIBIT 7.3   PRICE AND QUANTITY EQUILIBRIUM

eliminated. In the case of too low a price and undersupply, consumers will likely compete to obtain the good at the low price, but since more consumers would like to buy the good at the price that is too low, the profit-maximizing firm would raise the price to the highest it can, which is the equilibrium point. In each case, the actions of independent market participants cause the quantity and price to move toward the equilibrium point.

When more people want something, the quantity demanded at all prices will tend to increase. This can be referred to as an *increase in demand*. The increase in demand could also come from changing tastes due to advertising or new product introductions, where the same consumers desire more of the same good than they previously did. Increased demand can be represented on the graph as the curve being shifted right, because at each price point, a greater quantity is demanded. An example of this would be more people suddenly wanting more coffee. This will cause the demand curve to shift from the initial curve D_0 to the new curve D_1. This raises the equilibrium price from P_0 to the higher P_1. This raises the equilibrium quantity from Q_0 to the higher Q_1. In this situation, we say that there has been an *increase* in demand, which has caused an *extension* in supply.

Conversely, if the demand decreases, the opposite happens. If the demand starts at D_1 and then *decreases* to D_0, the price will decrease and the quantity supplied will decrease — a *contraction* in supply. Notice that this is purely an effect of demand changing. The quantity supplied at each price is the same as before the demand shift (at both Q_0 and Q_1). The equilibrium quantity and price are different because the demand is different.

EXHIBIT 7.4 DEMAND CURVE SHIFTS

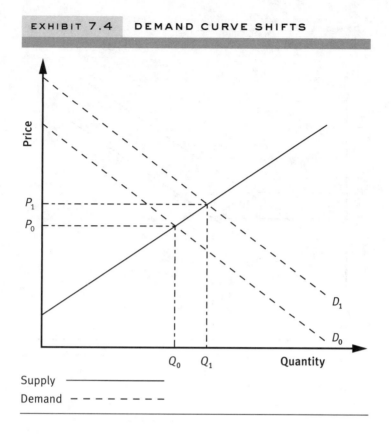

Supply Curve Shifts

When the suppliers' costs change, the supply curve will shift (see Exhibit 7.5). For example, assume that someone invents and patents a better process of growing wheat so that the amount of wheat that can be grown for a given cost will increase. Producers will be willing to supply more wheat at every price, and this shifts the supply curve S_0 to the right, to S_1—an *increase in supply*. This causes the equilibrium price to decrease from P_0 to P_1. The equilibrium quantity increases from Q_0 to Q_1 as the quantity demanded increases at the new lower prices. Notice that in the case of a supply curve shift, the price and the quantity move in opposite directions.

Conversely, if the quantity supplied decreases, the opposite happens. If the supply curve starts at S_1 and then shifts to S_0, the equilibrium price will increase and the quantity will decrease. Notice that this is purely an effect of supply changing. The quantity demanded at each price is the same as before the supply shift (at both Q_0 and Q_1). The reason that the equilibrium quantity and price are different is the *supply* is different.

Another way to view this is that the supply curve moves up and down as opposed to left and right (respectively). If the ability to produce increases as compared to a steady price, the supply shifts up (as opposed to left). If the ability to produce a given product or service decreases, the supply curve shifts down (as opposed to right). The validation or invalidation

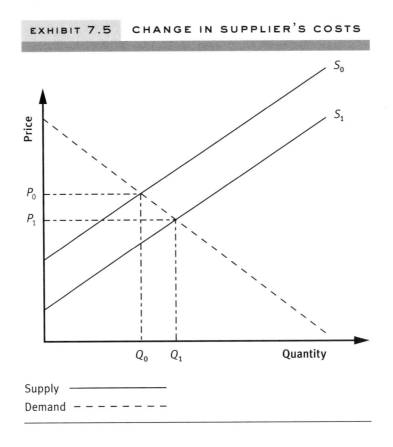

EXHIBIT 7.5   CHANGE IN SUPPLIER'S COSTS

Supply ————————
Demand – – – – – – –

of a patent (from either a court or the patent office) could cause such a shift. This is a more intuitive approach for beginners, but unfortunately it is not commonly taught.

Stigler (1987) noted that a market "clears" at the point where the entire product supplied and demanded at a given price balance. That is, the amount of a commodity available at a given price equals the amount that buyers are willing to purchase at that price. This is precisely the concept behind the idea of a hypothetical negotiation between a willing buyer of IP and a willing seller being locked in a room until they arrive at a reasonable royalty (merely an equilibrium price). It is assumed that there is a process that will result in the market reaching this point, but exactly what the process is in a real situation is an ongoing subject of research. This is why it is critical to fully understand and define the market structure in which the firms are presumed to be transacting and interacting. Markets that do not clear will react in some way: by a change in price or a change in the amount produced, or a change in the amount demanded. Graphically the situation can be represented by two curves: one showing the price-quantity combinations buyers will pay for, or the demand curve; and one showing the combinations sellers will sell for, or the supply curve. The market clears where the two are in equilibrium, that is, where the curves intersect. In general equilibrium models, all markets in all products and services clear simultaneously, and the "price" can be described entirely in terms of trade-offs with other products. Say's Law states that markets, as a whole, would always clear and thus be in balance. This idea has been a cornerstone of economic thinking for a very long time.

Similarly in a patent infringement case, the damages expert must contemplate how this market clears if an infringing product is lifted from a market or if it is prevented by (say) a court from entering a market. To understand how such an act would impact the equilibrium price in that particular market for IP, a necessary condition is that one understands the market per se. This would seem obvious, but as the case studies that follow illustrate, that is not always so.

Elasticity

An important concept in understanding supply and demand theory and in calculating lost profits is the concept of an *income or price elasticity.* In this context, the term refers to how supply and demand respond to changes in various factors such as price and income. If the Dallas Cowboys decide to increase the price of lower stadium tickets by 10%, such a price increase could have an obviously dramatic impact on whether their total revenue goes up or down, depending on how their fans react or respond to the price changes. If Company A decides to attempt to license its technology to Company B at a royalty rate that Company B considers exorbitant, it may lose sales if Company B attempts to design around the patented technology rather than take a license, whereas Company A may have taken a license if Company B had been more reasonable (from Company A's perspective). One way of defining elasticity is the percentage change in one variable divided by the percentage change in another variable (known as *arc elasticity* because it calculates the elasticity over a range of values; this can be contrasted with *point elasticity,* which uses differential calculus to determine the elasticity at a specific point). Thus elasticity is a measure of *relative or unitless* changes.

Often it is useful to know how the quantity supplied or demanded will change when the price changes. This is known as the price elasticity of demand or supply. If producers choose to increase the price of their product, how will this affect their sales revenue? It is possible that the increased price offsets the likely decrease in sales volume? If a government imposes a tax on a product, the quantity demanded will likely decrease because the effective price has been increased. The concept of price elasticity can be critically important in the context of lost profit determination in patent infringement when a damages expert is tasked with the job of quantifying lost profits on how many widgets would have been sold for (say) three times the price that they were actually sold for. The case studies show this requirement of quantifying such sales and their impact on price happens with considerable frequency.

Elasticity in relation to variables other than price can also be considered. One of the most important variables is income. This is known as the *income elasticity of demand.* For example, how much would the demand for a printer increase if average income increased by 10 percent? If it is positive, this increase in demand would be represented on a graph by a positive shift in the demand curve, because at all price levels, a greater number of printers would be demanded.

Another elasticity that is sometimes considered is the *cross elasticity of demand,* which measures the responsiveness of the quantity demanded of a good to a change in the price of another good. This elasticity is often considered when looking at the relative changes in demand when studying *complement* and *substitute* products. Complement goods are goods that are typically utilized together, where if one is consumed, usually the other is also. Substitute goods are those where one can be substituted for the other and if the price of one good rises, one may purchase less of it and instead purchase its substitute. These concepts are very important when determining *Panduit* factors 1 and 2 in a patent infringement case, for obvious reasons. We say more on this later.

Cross elasticity of demand is measured as the percentage change in demand for the first good that occurs in response to a percentage change in price of the second good. For an example with a complement good, if, in response to a 10 percent increase in the price of fuel, the quantity of new cars demanded decreased by 20 percent, the cross elasticity of demand would be -20 percent $\div$ 10 percent or, -2.

Vertical Supply Curve

It is sometimes the case that the supply curve for a good or service is vertical: That is, the quantity supplied is fixed, no matter what the market price. For example, the total amount of available land in Dallas, Texas, can be considered fixed. In this case, no matter how much

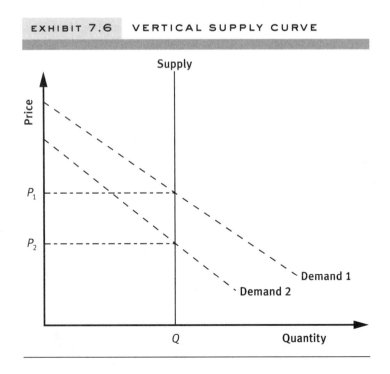

EXHIBIT 7.6   VERTICAL SUPPLY CURVE

someone would be willing to pay for a piece of land, since we do not live in the Nether-lands, extra land cannot be created. Also, even if no one wanted all the land in Dallas, it still would exist in a fixed quantity. These conditions create a vertical supply curve, giving it zero elasticity (i.e., no matter how large the change in price, the quantity supplied will not change).

Over short spans of time, vertical supply curves are more common. If a Dallas Stars hockey game is sold out, it is nearly impossible to increase the number of seats in the stadium. The supply of tickets for this hockey game is vertical. If the organizers of this event underestimated demand, then it may very well be the case that the price that they set is below the equilibrium price. In this case there will likely be people who paid the lower price who only value the ticket at that price and people who could not get tickets, even though they would be willing to pay more. If some of the people who value the tickets less sell them to people who are willing to pay more (i.e., scalp the tickets), then the effective price will rise to the equilibrium price.

Exhibit 7.6 illustrates a vertical supply curve. When the demand 1 is in effect, the price will be P_1. When demand 2 is occurring, the price will be P_2. Notice that at both values the quantity is Q. Since the supply is fixed, any shifts in demand will affect only price.

Market Structure

It is well known that when there are many buyers but a single "monopoly" supplier—say, a patent holder or trademark holder—it can influence the supply or price of a good or product. The idea of market power arises in this context. Slottje (2002) presents a series of studies by leading competition economists that discuss the notion of market power, or how market structure can influence a firm's ability to price above marginal cost. The granting of a patent is of course one example of how monopoly arises. The monopolist will adjust the price so that profit is maximized given the amount that is demanded at that price. This price will be higher than in a competitive market. A similar analysis using supply and demand can be applied when a good has a single buyer, a *monopsony,* but many sellers.

It is also well known that when there are only a few buyers or few sellers, the usual theory of supply and demand cannot be applied because both the decisions of the buyers and sellers are interdependent; compare the textbooks cited earlier and Slottje (2002). Changes in supply can affect demand and vice versa. The economic field of game theory can be brought to bear to analyze this kind of situation. Oligopoly is a similar situation in which the number of market participants or economic agents is "few" in number, and their behavior will clearly impact each of them.

The supply curve does not have to be linear. However, if the quantity supplied and price relationship is from a profit-maximizing firm, it can be proven that supply curves are not downward sloping (i.e., if the price increases, the quantity supplied will not decrease). Supply curves that are presumed to have been generated from profit-maximizing firms can be vertical, horizontal, or upward sloping. While it is possible for industry supply curves to be downward sloping, supply curves for individual firms are never downward sloping.

EXAMPLE: SUPPLY AND DEMAND IN A SIX-PERSON ECONOMY

EXAMPLE

Supply and demand can be thought of in terms of individual people interacting at a market. Suppose six people participate in this simplified economy:[1]

- Alice is willing to pay $10 for a sack of potatoes.
- Bob is willing to pay $20 for a sack of potatoes.
- Cathy is willing to pay $30 for a sack of potatoes.
- Dan is willing to sell a sack of potatoes for $5.
- Emily is willing to sell a sack of potatoes for $15.
- Fred is willing to sell a sack of potatoes for $25.

There are many possible trades that would be mutually agreeable to both people, but not all of them will happen. For example, Cathy and Fred would be interested in trading with each other for any price between $25 and $30. If the price is above $30, Cathy is not interested, since the price is too high. If the price is below $25, Fred is not interested, since the price is too low. However, at the market, Cathy will discover that there are other sellers willing to sell at well below $25, so she will not trade with Fred at all. In an efficient market, each seller will get as high a price as possible, and each buyer will get as low a price as possible.

Imagine that Cathy and Fred are bartering over the price. Fred offers $25 for a sack of potatoes. Before Cathy can agree, Emily offers a sack of potatoes for $24. Fred is not willing to sell at $24, so he drops out. At this point, Dan offers to sell for $12. Emily won't sell for that amount, so it looks like the deal might go through. At this point Bob steps in and offers $14. Now we have two people willing to pay $14 for a sack of potatoes (Cathy and Bob), but only one person (Dan) willing to sell for $14. Cathy notices this, and doesn't want to lose a good deal, so she offers Dan $16 for his potatoes. Now Emily also offers to sell for $16, so there are two buyers and two sellers at that price (note that they could have settled on any price between $15 and $20), and the bartering can stop. But what about Fred and Alice? Well, Fred and Alice are not willing to trade with each other since Alice is only willing to pay $10 and Fred will not sell for any amount under $25. Alice can't outbid Cathy or Bob to purchase from Dan so Alice will not be able to get a trade with them. Fred can't underbid Dan or Emily so he will not be able to get a trade with Cathy. In other words, a stable equilibrium has been reached.

A supply and demand graph could also be drawn from this (see Exhibit 7.7). The demand would be:

- One person is willing to pay $30 (Cathy).
- Two people are willing to pay $20 (Cathy and Bob).
- Three people are willing to pay $10 (Cathy, Bob, and Alice).

EXAMPLE

The supply would be:

- One person is willing to sell for $5 (Dan).
- Two people are willing to sell for $15 (Dan and Emily).
- Three people are willing to sell for $25 (Dan, Emily, and Fred).

Supply and demand match when the quantity traded is two sacks and the price is between $15 and $20. Whether Dan sells to Cathy, and Emily to Bob, or the other way around, and what precisely is the price agreed cannot be determined. This is the only limitation of this simple model. When considering the full assumptions of perfect competition, the price would be fully determined since there would be enough participants to determine the price. For example, if the "last trade" was between someone willing to sell at $15.50 and someone willing to pay $15.51, then the price could be determined to the penny. As more participants enter, the more likely there will be a close bracketing of the equilibrium price.

It is important to note that this example violates the assumption of perfect competition in that there are a limited number of market participants. However, this simplification shows how the equilibrium price and quantity can be determined in an easily understood situation. The results are similar when unlimited market participants and the other assumptions of perfect competition are considered.

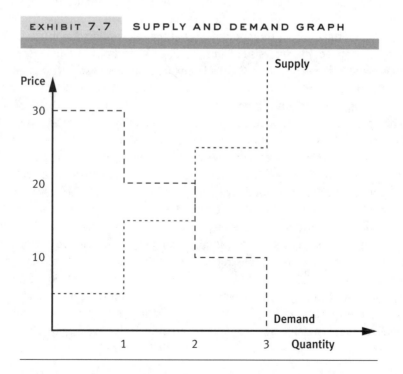

EXHIBIT 7.7   SUPPLY AND DEMAND GRAPH

CASE STUDIES

In this section we present some fictitious case studies to illustrate some of the problems that arise when experts seemingly ignore standard economic principles that determine the dynamics of a particular market under scrutiny. Elements of these fictional cases reflect real-life experiences and cases.

CASE STUDY

Case Study 1: Dance Machine

This case study involves patents relating to a dance machine. The patents at issue claimed to have the advantages of (1) low price, simple to make, and easy to use; (2) enables an individual to perform many dances; and (3) is light and easy to move. The company that makes the product FLY Up (a fictitious name) promotes itself as a leading maker of dance products. FLY Up sells the product covered by the patents in suit, the Dance Hard Always Machine (DHAM), for $2,500. Get Fit (a fictitious name) is also one of the largest manufacturers and marketers of home dance equipment worldwide. One of its products, the Brutalizer, was accused of infringing the patents at issue. The Brutalizer sells for $350. Get Fit started selling the Brutalizer in late 2000. Get Fit sold a total of 500,000 of these machines at roughly $350 per unit.

Any damages that accrue to the plaintiffs in this case arise from sales of DHAM that were lost directly to sales of the Brutalizer. In order to determine the magnitude of any such sales, an analysis of the market in which these two products are sold should have been undertaken. As a threshold matter, if the relevant market for consideration is improperly defined, the analysis of damages will be speculative and unreasonable. The fictitious plaintiff's expert (Expert A) calculated lost profits by assuming that most of the sales of the allegedly infringing product (385,000 units out of 500,000) would have been made by FLY Up, "but for" the infringement. That is, Expert A assumed that thousands of sales of a product that sold in actuality for $350 would have sold for $2,500, "but for" the infringement. This assumption is of course a textbook case of violating the law of demand. As long as there exists a downward-sloping demand curve, a price increase of seven times over the infringer's price would result in a decline (likely to be precipitous) in the quantity of units demanded, everything else being equal. The only way this outcome would not result would be if the demand for the machines was completely price inelastic (meaning consumers do not respond at all to a price change) and the demand curve was vertical (as was discussed earlier) and not negatively sloped. Expert A should have at least contemplated the construction of a statistical model to calculate the elasticity of demand (see Chapter 14) and determined the price elasticity of demand to see by how much a change in price would impact the quantity demanded of the dance machines. The discussion in this chapter should make clear that determinants of demand and supply need to be accounted for before merely asserting that two products with potentially different price and income elasticities, which might be purchased by different classes of buyers, would have a cross elasticity of demand between them of zero. Market research would have suggested that some of the important considerations for any consumer in the market for home dance equipment are price, quality of construction, variety of possible dances, and ability to deliver promised results. However, the weight afforded to each of these considerations depends crucially on the type of consumer making the purchase with respect to the factors just discussed. It would have also been apparent from a careful assessment of the market dynamics for home dance services that there are several distinct segments within the market for home dance equipment, each with distinct distribution methods and ranges of price elasticities. This is precisely the type of case the *BIC* decision was meant to address. Merely assuming away the law of demand will only result in unreasonable and speculative damages numbers.

CASE STUDY

Case Study 2: Computer Printer Component

In this case study, the patents relate to the design and functionality of the Boris Company's (fictitious name) computer printer component. In general, a utility patent is issued for the invention of a new and useful process, machine, manufacture, or composition of matter, or a new and useful improvement thereof. It generally permits its owner to exclude others from making, using, or selling the invention for a period of up to 20 years from the date of patent application filing. Design patents protect the ornamental and cosmetic aspects of products but not their function. The disclosure and description of the invention in a design application is entirely in the drawing and not in the words. The single claim in a design patent is for "the appearance of a _____ [whatever the product is usually called] as shown in the drawing."

Once again in this matter, the fictitious expert on damages (Expert B) for Boris assumed that all of the sales of the alleged infringer, Tank (a fictitious name), would have been made by Boris, "but for" the infringement. Here the printer component sold by Boris (for its own printer) was $39. A replacement component sold by Tank was $9. Here Expert B assumed that 20,000 printer components that were sold by Tank for $9 would have been sold by Boris for $39, "but for" the infringement. The market for the printers is presumed in our hypothetical example to be fiercely competitive. In the worldwide consumer market, four manufacturers are assumed to account for the majority of printer sales: Print It Now, Best Print, Hot-Cold (H-C), and Boris. Further assume that a common business model for printer components sold by the OEM (original equipment manufacturer) involves selling the actual printer at or even below cost while dramatically marking up the price of the

(continues)

(proprietary and/or patented) printer components. The most important considerations for any consumer in the market for a printer are price and print quality. However, the weight afforded to each of these considerations depends crucially on the type of user making the purchase. Different types of users can be reasonably classified based on their priorities with regard to printing needs:

What types of output will the consumer primarily print (e.g., charts, letters, presentations, photos, kids' homework, greeting cards)?

How much does the consumer wish to spend, in terms of both up-front costs and ongoing costs for replacement ink and paper?

This again suggests that users will have different price and income elasticities. Let us assume that it becomes apparent from a careful assessment of the imaginary market laid out in this case study for printer components and consumables in general, and the Boris products in particular, that there are at least two distinct market segments within the market for printer components, each with different ranges of price and income elasticities. The first segment we can call the "branded or premium-choice" segment, those customers whose concern about the quality and longevity of their prints (particularly color photographs) dictate the choice of printer component replacements, despite the fact that these components sell at up to four times the cost of the nonbranded versions. The second segment we refer to as "thrifty" users, those who are very cost-conscious and will spare no effort in finding the cheapest method of printing. The existence of these two market segments should bear crucially on the issue of what damages might accrue to the plaintiffs in this matter. As in the last example, Expert B did not analyze the market or even attempt to estimate what the price elasticity of demand was for the products in question. It is once again merely speculative and unreasonable to assume that the law of demand does not hold and that the demand for printer components is completely inelastic, meaning they exhibit a completely vertical demand curve. Expert B should have analyzed the market dynamics for the printer components carefully and formally estimated the price and income elasticity of demand for them to see how responsive consumers truly are to changes in price.

Case Study 3: Floor Lighting

As one final example, we look at the floor lighting market. Suppose the imaginary subject litigation involved a patent covering a floor lighting mechanism and its ability to light a room. The patent was owned by Easy Light (a fictitious name) that makes lights and sells them in Big Tool Home Improvement stores. Big Tools main competitor, Wrenches 'R' US, sells Cool Lights, which are alleged to infringe the patent. Neither chain sells the lights that are sold by its competitor. Once again the fictitious opposing expert (Expert C) for Easy Light assumed that "but for" the infringement, all of the sales of Cool Light in Wrenches 'R' U.S. stores would have been made by Easy Lights in Big Tool stores. Once again, a demand elasticity of zero was assumed, here by Expert C. Easy Light sells for $99 while Cool Light sells for $29. Here again, Expert C simply ignored the law of demand. The opposing expert did not analyze the market dynamics here and did not discuss the fact that there are many other brands of floor lights on the market as well. A well-known case, State Industries, Inc. v. Mor-Flo Industries, Inc., discusses how to partition sales in a lost profit analysis when there are more than two players in the relevant market. In this example it is assumed that some brands are sold by Big Tool and some brands are sold by Wrenches 'R' Us. Floor lights are also sold in specialty stores, in major retailers, and so on. The only reasonable conclusion to be drawn in evaluating Expert C's lost profit analysis would be that it is speculative, and it is devoid of any meaningful economic analysis and is not reasonable. Ignoring the law of demand dooms any calculation of economic damages in a patent infringement matter in which you are attempting to quantify lost profits.

CONCLUSION

This chapter has illustrated the importance of understanding elementary economic principles when performing a *Panduit* analysis in calculating lost profits in patent infringement matters. The chapter discussed the concepts of supply and demand in a very simple but detailed way in order to help lawyers, accountants, and decision makers grasp why these elementary concepts must be taken into account when analyzing a lost profits claim. Some expert witnesses ignore the law of demand and other economic fundamentals in performing lost profit analyses, as some of our fictitious experts did here. Market dynamics will likely vary from case to case, as will specific market characteristics that introduce nuances in estimating damages. The economic damages expert should always be cognizant of how these issues impact the particular market he or she is analyzing.

NOTE

1. This example is from Wikipedia Contributors, "Supply and Demand," Wikipedia, the Free Encyclopedia, http://en.wikipedia.org//index.php?title = supplyanddemand. The Wikipedia site also references Landsburg (2005).

REFERENCES

Baumol, W. and A. Blinder. *Microeconomics,* 10th ed. New York: Thomson-Southwestern, 2006.

BIC Leisure Products, Inc. v. Windsurfing International Inc., 1 F.3d 1993.

Landsburg, S. *Price Theory,* 6th ed. New York: Thomson, Southwestern, 2005.

Panduit Corp. v. Stahlin Bros. Fibre Works, Inc., 575 F.2d 1152, 1164, 197 U.S.P.Q. 726, 736 (6th Cir. 1978).

Pindyck, R. and D. Rubinfeld. *Microeconomics,* 6th ed. New York: Pearson-Prentice Hall, 2005.

State Industries, Inc. v. Mor-Flo Industries, Inc., 883 F.2d 1573, 12 U.S.P.Q. 2d 1026 (CAFC 1989).

Slottje, D. *Measuring Market Power,* Amsterdam: Elsevier, 2002.

Stigler, G. *The Theory of Price,* 4th ed. New York: Macmillan, 1987.

CHAPTER 8

A Holistic Approach to Patent Damages Analysis

RYAN SULLIVAN[1]
Quant Economics, Inc.

In real-world markets, prices and quantities are jointly determined. However, in patent litigation, this fundamental economic principle is often ignored. We use a hypothetical patent infringement suit in the ice cream industry to demonstrate a holistic approach to patent damages analysis. This approach recognizes that patent infringement can have an effect on prices, quantities, and other economic factors, such as product substitution. Our analysis illustrates appropriate methods for implementing a holistic approach that addresses these factors and the impact they have on profits.

INTRODUCTION

Patent law states that if the court finds for a plaintiff in a patent infringement matter, it should seek to award monetary relief that would fully compensate the plaintiff for damages resulting from the infringement.[2] This is commonly known as the "make-whole" standard. In cases where the plaintiff claims to have suffered a reduction in sales of its product due to the infringement, the make-whole standard prescribes a calculation of lost profits. In such an analysis, damages are equal to the difference between the patent owner's actual profits and the profits that the patentee would have earned "but for" the infringement ("but for" profits).

Beginning with the landmark appeals court decision in *Panduit Corp. v. Stahlin Bros.* (*Panduit*) in 1978, courts have, over the years, progressed in the direction of applying economic principles to the determination of lost profits. In that decision, the court laid out a four-pronged test for the patent owner's entitlement to lost profits damages:

> To obtain as damages the profits on sales he would have made absent the infringement, i.e., the sales made by the infringer, a patent owner must prove: (1) demand

for the patented product, (2) absence of acceptable noninfringing substitutes, (3) his manufacturing and marketing capability to exploit the demand, and (4) the amount of the profit he would have made.

The requirement that noninfringing substitutes must be absent for a damage award to stand is a narrow one, and does not make economic sense in the majority of competitive situations. In most markets, there are likely to be products that consumers view as viable substitutes even if only to a small degree. Furthermore, the decision implies that when the cited conditions are met, the appropriate damages are the infringer's sales. However, this does not typically reflect market reality, and would apply in an unrealistic setting where the patent owner would have made all the infringer's sales in the infringer's absence, thereby ignoring the effects of infringement on price and quantity.

The *State Industries v. Mor-Flo* decision (*Mor-Flo*) in 1989 was the first step toward a market-based analysis of lost profits.[3] In *Mor-Flo,* the court established the market share rule for the determination of lost sales. The market share rule is based on the notion that the patentee's ability to capture sales is accurately reflected in its market share.

The *Mor-Flo* ruling, however, overlooked several economic issues, one of which is the effect infringement can have on prices. Price erosion claims, which are now common in patent infringement litigation, are based on the idea that sales of the infringing product often cause the patentee to lower prices on its competing products. A simple reattribution of infringing sales among the remaining market players does not account for price changes and the resulting effects on quantity sold. Courts first appropriately confronted the issue of price erosion in 1993 when Judge Easterbrook offered his opinion in *In re Mahurkar Patent Litigation (Mahurkar)* stating that the calculation of "but for" profits involves a study of the impact of price changes on quantity sold, an exercise in fundamental economics. Claims of price erosion should offer an analysis of the impact that prices have on quantity demanded. This principle was stated by the circuit court, in the *Crystal-Tritech* decision in 2001, when it affirmed that an increase in the patentee's price would decrease its quantity sales.

Courts have also come to recognize that if a patent holder suffered a loss of profits on sales of products other than the patented product as a result of the infringement, a damage award should account for such lost profits. In 1995, the Federal Circuit, in *Rite-Hite v. Kelley,* affirmed a district court award of lost profits on sales of products that, while not incorporating the patent in question, suffered a reduction in sales directly due to the infringement. Similarly, courts have also sometimes awarded damages to account for increased costs, especially increased advertising and promotional expenses incurred by the patentee due to infringement.[4]

The underlying theme in the evolution of court decisions on lost profits is that the computation of "but for" profits involves a determination of several components including prices, quantities, and costs. In real-world markets, these components interact with each other and are often determined jointly by market forces. While courts are becoming increasingly aware of this issue, lost profits often are still calculated in a piecemeal manner. For instance, if price erosion is claimed, many times it is calculated separately from lost sales. However, as affirmed in the preceding decisions, accompanying price erosion will be a corresponding decrease in sales quantity. The higher price that would have occurred "but for" infringement would result in fewer sales. Moreover, the quantity changes may have an impact on per-unit costs. Similarly, the impact on a producer's related, unpatented products often are accounted for separately, even though the producer is likely to jointly maximize total profits from all of its products.

Economists recognize that a true determination of "but for" profits involves a reconstruction of market conditions as they would be absent infringement. Such a determination involves a unified or holistic approach that determines the impact of infringement on prices, quantities, and costs. In this chapter we discuss such a unified approach using a hypothetical patent litigation involving lost profits analysis. The analysis that we present embodies a holistic approach to damages by means of a simulation of market conditions.[5] The market simulation method provides a way to determine jointly the effect of infringement on market prices and quantities.

We discuss the advantages of the unified approach relative to the market share methods previously used in courts and other methods that provide improvements over the market share rule. To that end, we present three damage analyses. The first analysis is based on the market share rule applied in the *Mor-Flo* ruling. The second analysis is an improvement over the simple market share rule and is proposed in Epstein (2003). We refer to this approach as the Epstein method. The Epstein method considers the impact of price erosion by incorporating price and quantity effects into a single step. The third analysis we present, the market simulation method, determines the extent of price erosion within the model. We show that, given the availability of data and other resources, this method can be the preferred approach to estimating lost profits damages.

To discuss the different approaches to damages, we devise a hypothetical patent infringement suit in a product and geographic market of our selection. Ice cream, one of life's simple pleasures, is chosen as the product market and provides data for our numerical example. One benefit of the ice cream market is the availability of data on prices and quantities sold in different regions of the United States over a sufficient period of time.

The ice cream market provides a rich illustration of patent damages analysis because it is a market of differentiated products. The market offers products with a wide range of quality and price. There is considerable competition at the brand level with products competing on price as well as product characteristics. Firms spend a fair amount on advertising and promotion in order to achieve brand differentiation and loyalty.[6] To capture the nuances of competition in such a market, it is useful to have an analytical method with the capability to go beyond a simple diversion of quantity sales. Before discussing the different patent damage methodologies, we provide an overview of the ice cream market.[7]

ICE CREAM INDUSTRY

Market Overview

Ice cream, one of the most popular categories of products sold in supermarkets, is purchased by more than 90 percent of households in the United States.[8] In the general category of ice cream, there is a distinction between regular ice cream, frozen yogurt, reduced-fat ice cream, and nonfat ice cream, with regular ice cream accounting for more than 65 percent of total sales in 2002.[9] The ice cream categories, along with nondairy products such as sorbets and water ices, are often grouped together in the category of frozen dessert products. Not only is ice cream categorized by different levels of fat content, but there are also hundreds of flavors of ice cream from which to choose.

In 2002, 10.97 billion pints (1.37 billion gallons) of regular, low-fat, and nonfat ice cream were produced in the United States.[10] According to the International Dairy Foods Association (IDFA), about 39 percent of ice cream produced in the United States is sold in supermarkets.[11] Supermarket sales of regular, low-fat, and nonfat ice cream combined were $4.2 billion in 2001.[12] More than three-quarters of ice cream sold in supermarkets is sold in half-gallon containers. Ice cream brands are divided into the premium and the super-premium categories with the premium brands selling in half-gallon packages and the super-premium in smaller packages.[13] There is less product differentiation among the different premium brands, which are less expensive than the super-premium brands. Super-premium brands also tend to have significantly higher profit margins on average.[14]

The national ice cream market is an oligopoly where the largest vendors include a few national producers, such as Good Humor/Breyers (owned by Unilever), Dreyer's Grand Ice Cream, Nestlé Foods, Inc., and ConAgra Foods, Inc.; a few large regional vendors, such as Turkey Hill Dairy (northeastern United States), Blue Bell Creameries, Inc. (southern United States); and HP Hood Inc. and Friendly Ice Cream Corporation (both northeastern United States); and private-label brands. Private-label ice cream brands are marketed by the major grocery chains (e.g., Kroger and Safeway), and are made either by third-party manufacturers or by the chains themselves.[15] These brands tend to be more commoditized and have lower profit margins than their competitors.[16] Collectively, private-label vendors account for more than 35 percent of the volume of ice cream sold in U.S. supermarkets and more than 25 percent of U.S. ice cream revenues (see Infringement Illustration section below).

Data Description

We obtained weekly scanner data on supermarket sales of packaged ice cream from Information Resources, Inc. (IRI). The IRI data are taken from stores that report sales in excess of $2 million per year. The data, which are for the year 1999, are taken from 49 unique supermarket chains and represent 29 regions of the United States as defined by IRI. We used data only from IRI regions that had at least three supermarket chains with stores meeting the annual sales criteria.

The data contain weekly observations of quantity sold and revenue by stock keeping unit (SKU), with a SKU representing a single combination of brand and flavor. The largest vendors sell multiple brands, and within each brand there are scores of flavors. For instance, according to the IRI data, Dreyer's Grand markets 9 brands and 114 flavors of ice cream. Its leading brand, Dreyer's/Edy's Grand, has 45 distinct flavors. We determined, for the

EXHIBIT 8.1 NATIONAL MARKET SHARES OF LEADING ICE CREAM BRANDS

Brand	Vendor	Quantity Share[a]	Revenue Share
Private Label	Private Label	38.0%	26.8%
Breyers	Good Humor/Breyers	14.8%	15.6%
Dreyer's/Edy's Grand	Dreyer's Grand Ice Cream	9.1%	9.9%
Blue Bell	Blue Bell Creameries Inc	5.6%	6.7%
Turkey Hill	Turkey Hill Dairy	4.3%	3.7%
Healthy Choice	ConAgra Inc	2.4%	2.8%
Hood	H P Hood Inc	2.3%	1.7%
Friendly	Friendly Ice Cream Corp	2.1%	1.8%
Dreyer's/Edy's Grand Light	Dreyer's Grand Ice Cream	2.0%	2.3%
All other	All other	19.4%	28.8%
Total		**100.0%**	**100.0%**

[a] In all exhibits, entries may not always add up exactly to totals due to rounding error. The national market shares actually refer to the sum of the 29 regions that we considered and do not account for all of the United States.

purposes of our analysis, that an appropriate level of product categorization is the brand level. Individual flavors are numerous, with the top five flavor-vendor combinations accounting for 22 percent of the market quantity and the remaining 1,437 flavor-vendor combinations all with shares below 2 percent. The market shares of the leading brands in the regions covered by the IRI data are seen in Exhibit 8.1.

The IRI data also show the segmentation of the ice cream market into the premium and super-premium markets. The super-premium brands have higher calorie and fat content than the premium brands and tend to be priced over $2.00 per pint, as seen in Exhibit 8.2.[17]

The geographic market for ice cream based on consumer substitution options is localized. Since the geographic granularity of the data is no finer than the regional level, we opted to select one of the 29 regions as our hypothetical market. To facilitate this choice, we assume that infringement is the result of a violation of a regional restriction by a licensee of the patent. Henceforth, we use the fictional name of Springfield for the region from which we use data for the illustrative patent infringement analysis.

Infringement Illustration

In our patent infringement example we use real market data but change the names of the firms and brands. We include, in our analysis, all premium brands of ice cream sold in Springfield recorded in the IRI data.[18] There are three leading brands in the ice cream market in Springfield: the Sam's Creek brand, the Holy Cow brand from Cow-Town's Ice Cream, and the Cool Cream brand sold by Cool Cats, Inc. Together these three leading brands account for more than 58 percent of the quantity sold in the market. They are followed by a category of brands known as private-label brands, which together account for almost 9 percent of market quantity. There are 40 other brands, each with a small share

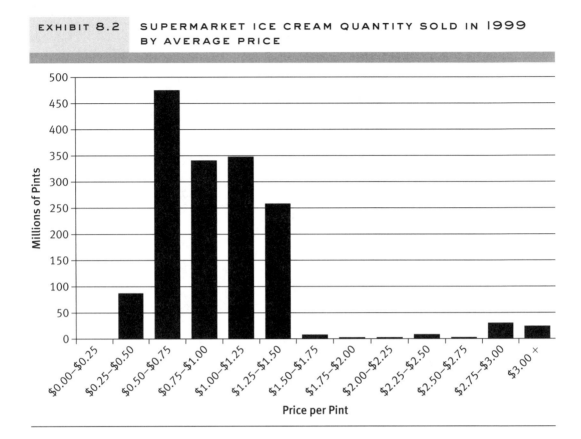

EXHIBIT 8.2   SUPERMARKET ICE CREAM QUANTITY SOLD IN 1999 BY AVERAGE PRICE

of the market, that combine for a third of the market quantity. These brands include Bliss and Good Times. For ease of illustration we have chosen to combine all brands with quantity shares below 2 percent. As seen in Exhibit 8.3, this leaves us with eight top brands (in terms of quantity sold) in Springfield and a ninth catchall brand called "Other."[19]

EXHIBIT 8.3   SPRINGFIELD ICE CREAM MARKET

Product	Quantity (Pints)	Quantity Share	Average Price (Per Pint)	Actual Revenues	Revenue Shares
Sam's Creek	26,361,271	21.6%	$0.77	$ 20,372,747	20.0%
Holy Cow (patentee)	26,101,540	21.4%	$0.92	$ 24,018,796	23.6%
Cool Cream (infringer)	18,741,177	15.4%	$0.89	$ 16,735,832	16.5%
Private label	10,741,490	8.8%	$0.60	$ 6,444,614	6.3%
Bliss	8,209,604	6.7%	$0.79	$ 6,522,017	6.4%
Good Times	5,958,714	4.9%	$0.65	$ 3,888,881	3.8%
Premium Homemade	2,884,087	2.4%	$0.95	$ 2,740,163	2.7%
Delicious Light	2,608,594	2.1%	$1.01	$ 2,643,771	2.6%
Other	20,371,091	16.7%	$0.90	$ 18,292,853	18.0%
Total	**121,977,568**	**100.0%**	**$0.83**	**$101,659,674**	**100.0%**

We assume that Cow-Town's Ice Cream owns a method patent on the production of the Holy Cow brand of ice cream and that Cool Cats, Inc. had obtained a license from Cow-Town's Ice Cream to use the patented method in the manufacturing of its Cool Cream brand. The license allowed Cool Cats, Inc. to sell the Cool Cream ice cream brand in certain regions of the United States, not including Springfield. However, subsequent to the unlicensed sale of Cool Cream brand ice cream in Springfield, Cow-Town's Ice Cream filed a patent infringement suit against Cool Cats, Inc. claiming damages from such sales. Cool Cats, Inc. also sells two other brands in Springfield supermarkets, Premium Home-made and Delicious Light.

For purposes of this example, we assume that the infringing period is the calendar year of 1999. Cow-Town's Ice Cream is claiming lost sales and price erosion as a result of the infringement. The infringing brand, Cool Cream, captured over 15 percent of the market quantity and sold at an average price of $0.89 per pint compared to $0.92 per pint for the patented product. As seen in Exhibit 8.3, the weighted average price of ice cream in Springfield is $0.83 per pint.

An analysis of lost profits often should consider the impact of infringement on both supply and demand. The entry of the infringing product may increase competitive pressure, reducing prices and taking away sales from other products. However, it is also possible that increased promotional spending due to the entry of the infringer may have a positive effect on demand. Changes in quantity sold and produced may also have an impact on the average cost of production of the firms involved as economies of scale and scope come into play. An analysis of damages should consider the infringer's alternatives, which, in this case, include its two other products. In the next sections, we discuss three damage methods and apply them to the example at hand. We compare and contrast different methodologies with the aim of arriving at a unified approach to damage analysis that is rigorous, accurate, and accounts for the multifaceted effects of infringement.

MARKET SHARE RULE

Methodology

The market share rule is based on the simple idea that in the absence of the infringing product, sales of the patented product would be divided among the remaining products in the marketplace according to their market shares. Consumers of the infringing product are diverted to other products considered to be "in the market," and the diversion ratios correspond to the market shares.

The assumption that the infringer's sales would be divided among the remaining participants on the basis of their existing market shares relies on the notion that consumer preferences exhibit the independence of irrelevant alternatives (IIA) property. This property states that the ratio of the probabilities of choosing any two alternatives from a choice set is independent of the attributes or the availability of a third alternative.[20] Hence, it follows that the market share of the patentee "but for" infringement is equal to its share of market quantity with infringement, divided by one minus the infringer's market share.[21]

The first step in applying the market share rule is to determine which products are reasonable substitutes for the infringing product and, hence, in the market, and which products are not. This exercise, known as market definition, is often an influencing force on the damage calculation as well as an issue that is often contested during litigation. If a market is defined too narrowly (i.e., relatively few products are deemed to be substitutes for the patented product), then the patent holder has a relatively large "but for" market share and can consequently claim relatively large lost profits damages. A very broadly defined market that includes sales of a greater number of products results in a relatively low figure for lost profits.

An approach that can be used to define the market is outlined in the Horizontal Merger Guidelines jointly issued by the Department of Justice (DoJ) and the Federal Trade Commission (FTC).[22] The Merger Guidelines state:

> Absent price discrimination, the Agency will delineate the product market to be a product or group of products such that a hypothetical profit-maximizing firm that was the only present and future seller of those products ("monopolist") likely would impose at least a "small but significant and non-transitory" increase in price.[23]

The approach starts with one product and expands outward adding products until the above condition is satisfied.[24] A hypothetical monopolist that controls the included set of products is likely to raise price only if it increases profit. Naturally, the monopolist's profits increase only if the negative impact of customers substituting to other products is outweighed by the positive impact of the increased price.

Application to Ice Cream Industry

In this section we apply the simple market share rule to our hypothetical ice cream patent infringement litigation and discuss the results. We include all the products listed in Exhibit 8.3 in the relevant product market. Applying the market share rule to recover quantity shares "but for" infringement gives the results listed in Exhibit 8.4.

The *Mor-Flo* market share analysis does not directly address changes in the prices of products sold by the patentee or any other producer. Exhibit 8.5 shows the calculation of the patentee's lost profits based on a constant 15 percent price-cost (incremental) margin.[25]

In the market share analysis, total quantity sold in the market remains unchanged from the actual to the "but for" infringement scenario. The total quantity sold is simply divided among all participants except for the infringer.[26]

Discussion

The market share rule has several limitations, some of which have been discussed already. The most notable limitation is that this approach has little to say about the impact of infringement on prices. This omission often makes the approach vulnerable to criticism in litigation circumstances because the entry of a new competitor or product in a market

EXHIBIT 8.4 "BUT FOR" SHARES FROM MARKET SHARE RULE

Product	Actual Quantity Shares	"But For" Quantity Shares
Sam's Creek	21.6%	25.5%
Holy Cow (patentee)	21.4%	25.3%
Cool Cream (infringer)	15.4%	0.0%
Private label	8.8%	10.4%
Bliss	6.7%	8.0%
Good Times	4.9%	5.8%
Premium Homemade	2.4%	2.8%
Delicious Light	2.1%	2.5%
Other	16.7%	19.7%
Total	100.0%	100.0%

often increases competition, putting downward pressure on prices. There may, however, be countervailing effects on prices resulting from items such as cost changes and market segmentation. Certainly, patent infringement does not always lead to a decrease in prices.

The second potential drawback of this approach is its reliance on a strict definition of the market, which requires the inclusion of some products and the exclusion of others. Due to its impact on damages, as well as the imprecise nature of methods used in implementation, market definition can become the focus of the dispute on damages in patent cases. In the absence of evidence on substitution patterns, market definition can sometimes become a source for genuine controversy, especially in the case of complex differentiated products. Indeed, product substitution is often a matter of degrees rather than an absolute all-or-nothing. For instance, consider an off-the-shelf semiconductor device that is sold to computer manufacturers as a component in their downstream products. Now consider a supplier that sells a device that is functionally almost identical to the previous one but is customized to the needs of each computer manufacturer in the same market. Should this supplier's product be included in the same market? What if some computer manufacturers buy the customized product because they have a long-standing relationship with the supplier from whom they also buy other products? What if the customized version is 20 percent more expensive than the off-the-shelf version? Making unqualified

EXHIBIT 8.5 MARKET SHARE RULE ANALYSIS OF LOST PROFITS

Product	Actual Profits (a) = 15% × actual revenues	"But For" Quantity (b) = market quantity × "but for" share	"But For" Price (c)	"But For" Revenues (d) = (b) × (c)	"But For" Profits (e) = (d) × 15%	Lost Profits (f) = (e) − (a)
Holy Cow	$3,602,819	30,840,264	$0.92	$28,379,399	$4,256,910	$654,090

decisions about which products are to be included and which are not reduces flexibility of the model.

The third primary drawback of the market share rule is that it assumes the infringer's share of sales will be distributed among the remaining suppliers according to their market share. However, other items can impact this distribution, including the price of each supplier's product. Moreover, the market share rule assumes that the total size of the market remains fixed, whereas infringement may have an impact on market size.

Last but not least, the market share rule does not explicitly account for the competitive process of markets. Firms are decision makers that actively set prices or quantities in order to maximize profits. The decisions of firms are influenced by the decisions of their competitors, and the path to market equilibrium is dynamic and interactive. The market share rule typically does not model this competitive reality. These oversights can potentially make it more difficult to defend results from this method in the face of more rigorous economic thinking.

PRICE EROSION

Methodology

Entry in an oligopolistic market typically results in lower prices and higher market quantity.[27] An infringer's entry typically lowers the price that the patentee can charge for its product simply by virtue of increased competition. A consequence of this price erosion is an increase in the market quantity. In this section we examine the Epstein method, which calculates the patentee's "but for" profits jointly accounting for lost sales, price erosion, and resulting quantity accretion.[28] Generally, this is an improvement over the market share rule, which has little to say about price changes and the consequent effects on quantity sold.

In the Epstein method, market shares are based on revenues (rather than units) and "but for" shares are calculated similar to the market share rule analysis. Just like the market share rule, the Epstein method assumes that the patentee's share of the "but for" market is equal to its actual share divided by the total share of all firms except the infringer.[29] The Epstein method also requires market definition in order to identify the competitors selling infringing as well as any noninfringing alternatives. This method takes as inputs the degree of price erosion faced by the patent holder on its product and the market elasticity of demand.

The Epstein method implicitly assumes there is a single market price (P) and the quantity sold in the market (Q) responds to changes in the market price in accordance with the market elasticity of demand. To calculate "but for" profits of the patentee, the Epstein method looks at "but for" market revenues, "but for" market share of the patentee, and "but for" margins earned by the patentee.

Based on the extent of price erosion (δ), where $\delta = \Delta P/P$, and the market elasticity of demand (ε) (both of which are determined outside the model), one can determine the effect on market quantity of a change in market price:

$$REV_{butfor} = REV^M \cdot (1 + \delta(1 + \varepsilon)),$$

where REV^M is actual market revenue and REV^{butfor} is the market revenue "but for" the infringement.

If S_p and S_i are the market shares of the patented and the infringing products respectively, then the "but for" share of the patentee is given by:

$$S_p^{butfor} = \frac{S_p}{1 - S_i}.$$

The model assumes that the patentee's marginal cost of production (C) remains the same whether the infringing product is sold or not. Due to the change in the patentee's price (P), the incremental margin (μ) also changes (see Appendix A):

$$\mu^{butfor} = \frac{\mu + \delta}{1 + \delta}.$$

The patentee's "but for" profits are given by this equation:

$$\Pi^{butfor} = REV^{butfor} \cdot S_p^{butfor} \cdot \mu^{butfor}.$$

Rearranging the last equations yields:

$$\Pi^{butfor} = REV^M \cdot (1 + \delta(1 + \varepsilon)) \cdot \frac{S_p}{1 - S_I} \cdot \left[1 - \frac{(1 - \mu)}{(1 + \delta)}\right],$$

which provides an expression for "but for" profits based on market revenue, the amount of price erosion, the market elasticity of demand, the market shares of the patentee and infringer, and the incremental margin.

Application to Ice Cream Industry

To apply the Epstein method, we need to make assumptions regarding the amount of price erosion (δ) and the market elasticity of demand (ε). To get a better sense of the method, we apply it to a range of estimates of δ ($\delta = 0.37\%, \delta = 2\%, \delta = 5\%$).[30] We assume the elasticity of demand to be 1.5.[31] The market price, P, is the weighted average price of products in the market, and is equal to $0.83 per pint in this case. Exhibit 8.6 displays actual and "but for" revenue shares for the Epstein method, while Exhibit 8.7 provides full results for the Epstein method when elasticity equals 1.5.

Discussion

While the Epstein method provides a way to account for price erosion, it does not offer a way to determine price erosion within the model jointly with quantity.[32] It takes the extent of price erosion as an input to the formula for lost profits. As a result, a method is needed for determining the extent of price erosion (δ). Epstein (2003) discusses a few methods of determining price erosion.[33] While these methods do not determine price and quantity jointly as a result of competitive profit maximization by firms, they provide an improvement over the simple market share rule in this regard. Note that the Epstein

EXHIBIT 8.6   ACTUAL AND "BUT FOR"
                REVENUE SHARES

Product	Actual Revenue Share	"But For" Revenue Share
Sam's Creek	20.0%	24.0%
Holy Cow (patentee)	23.6%	28.3%
Cool Cream (infringer)	16.5%	0.0%
Private label	6.3%	7.6%
Bliss	6.4%	7.7%
Good Times	3.8%	4.6%
Premium Homemade	2.7%	3.2%
Delicious Light	2.6%	3.1%
Other	18.0%	21.5%
Total	100.0%	100.0%

method with $\delta = 0$ is essentially identical to the market share rule with market shares based on revenues (not units sold).

The Epstein method assumes that there is a single market price that is charged by all suppliers and that all producers in the market face the same price erosion effect. These assumptions can be unrealistic to the extent that the products are differentiated and prices differ from one product to the next.

The Epstein method also takes the elasticity of demand as an input and assumes that it is constant regardless of the presence of the infringer in the market. While this assumption is not problematic within a narrow range of market quantities and prices, infringement can have a substantial impact on market quantity. A method that allows for changes in the aggregate elasticity of demand as market quantity and price change may be more realistic.

As with the market share rule, the Epstein method also faces the difficulties that come along with the requirement of a strict market definition. The damage analyst specifies which products are in the market and which are not, and the model does not directly account for substitution by consumers to excluded products.

Finally, the Epstein method does not provide a unified approach that jointly determines prices and quantities in a "but for" infringement competitive equilibrium. The method does not directly model the decision-making process of competitors.

EXHIBIT 8.7   EPSTEIN METHOD RESULTS ($\varepsilon = 1.5$)

Price Erosion (δ)	Actual Market Revenue	"But For" Market Revenue	Patentee's "But For" Revenues	"But For" Margin	"But For" Profits	Actual Profits	Lost Profits
0.37%	$101,659,674	$101,472,203	$28,699,128	15.3%	$4,394,509	$3,602,819	$ 791,690
2.00%	$101,659,674	$100,643,077	$28,464,628	16.7%	$4,744,105	$3,602,819	$1,141,285
5.00%	$101,659,674	$ 99,118,182	$28,033,346	19.1%	$5,339,685	$3,602,819	$1,736,865

MARKET SIMULATION

Methodology

Overview A limitation of both the market share rule and the Epstein method is their use of a strict market definition and delineation of products and players that are in the market. However, it can be the case that products that fall outside the boundaries of a narrowly defined market compete, to some degree, with the products within those boundaries. In markets where patented technology plays an important role and differentiated products are substitutes, there can exist competition at the margin. In an analysis that strictly defines the market, a product that is excluded from the market is essentially assigned a zero market share and deemed irrelevant to the analysis of competition.

The market simulation approach was first used to deal with this and other problems in the context of predicting the competitive effects of mergers and acquisitions. Market simulation can reduce the need for an all-or-nothing approach of market definition. The DoJ and FTC routinely use market simulation tools to predict postmerger prices in their efforts to determine whether a merger will reduce competition.

As has been discussed in recent applied economic literature, the market simulation method is ripe for application to the analysis of lost profits arising from patent infringement.[34] Generally speaking, similar to using observations from the lower-price premerger equilibrium to predict the higher-price postmerger equilibrium, market simulation for patent infringement uses observations from the lower-price with-infringement equilibrium to predict the higher-price "but for" infringement equilibrium. That is, in mergers, market simulation is used to determine the effects of combining two competitors, which removes competition from the market. In patent infringement, market simulation is used to determine the effects of removing a competitor from the marketplace, which also removes competition from the market.

The market simulation approach employs a few key assumptions in order to model competitive behavior. First, the method assumes that firms compete on the basis of price (Bertrand competition) in an oligopolistic setting. Bertrand competition is a widely applicable competitive paradigm, and it results in a set of equilibrium prices such that no firm can increase its profits by changing its price, given the prices of its competitors. Second, the method assumes that marginal costs of production are constant, which is typically a reasonable assumption within a certain range of quantity sold. Notably, however, the simulation framework allows for marginal costs to be changed externally in the "but for" infringement scenario. Finally, an assumption about the demand system or the shape of the demand curves is required. We base our analysis on Werden, Froeb, and Langenfeld (2000), which employs the logit or discrete choice model, commonly referred to as the antitrust logit model (ALM).[35] Werden and Froeb present a comprehensive discussion of ALM in several papers.[36] Although there are several market simulation methods with corresponding assumptions on the structure of demand, the ALM is sufficiently rich to provide an enlightening discussion on damage analysis in patent infringement matters.[37]

The market simulation method proceeds in three steps. In the first step, a set of inputs are obtained. The second step involves a calibration of the demand system. Calibration establishes the parameters of the demand system under the assumption that observed prices and quantities are a consequence of profit maximization by competing firms. The calibration step also provides information to determine the marginal costs of the producers. In the third step, the parameters obtained from the calibration are used in the simulation of the market equilibrium "but for" infringement (or postmerger).

The issue of market definition is addressed by assuming that in addition to the products specifically considered as being "in" the market, there is also a set of potential substitutes that are not individually considered. This set is combined as a single "outside" product that is assumed to have a constant price. The presence of an outside product relaxes the strict market definition used in the market share rule. Furthermore, the simulation method provides a way to model the competitive process and jointly determine prices and quantities.

We assume a logit or discrete choice demand system, where consumers select one alternative from among a set of possible choices. Specifically, there are a total of $n + 1$ products. Products 1 through n are the "inside" products and product $n + 1$ is the "outside" product. Each customer buys one unit of one (inside or outside) product.

The utility for consumer i purchasing product j is given by

$$U_{ij} = \alpha_j - \beta p_j + e_{ij},$$

where the price of product $j = p_j$ and the price of the outside product is normalized so that $p_{n+1} = 0$. The coefficient, α_j, controls for average quality differences (common across consumers), and β is the price coefficient (common across products and consumers). The error terms e_{ij} are independently and identically distributed as extreme values.

The choice probability for individual product j takes the form:

$$\pi_j = \frac{\exp(\alpha_j - \beta p_j)}{\sum\limits_{k=1}^{n+1} \exp(\alpha_k - \beta p_k)}.$$

In order to normalize with respect to the outside product, $\alpha_{n+1} = 0$, and as a result:

$$\exp(\alpha_{n+1} - \beta p_{n+1}) = \exp(0 - \beta_0) = 1$$

The marginal cost of production, c_i, is assumed to be constant for each product i.

Inputs   The model takes these variables as its inputs:

Prices observed during the infringement period: $p = \{p_1,\ldots,p_n\}$

Observed market shares ("inside shares") of inside products, $s = \{s_1,\ldots,s_n\}$, where

$$\sum_{j=1}^{n} s_j = 1$$

Margin for product one is:

$$m_1 = \frac{p_1 - c_1}{p_1},$$

which could be the patented product, the infringing product, or any other for which such information is available

The degree of substitutability between inside products and the outside product is described by an aggregate elasticity parameter, which is the elasticity of demand, ε, for the inside products.

The higher the aggregate elasticity, the higher is the probability that a consumer will select the outside product when faced with a price increase in the weighted average price of the inside products. A narrowly defined market (e.g., the market for running shoes with air bubbles in their soles) is likely to have an outside product with a high share. The outside product would include all choices not included on the inside, such as running shoes without air bubble soles, tennis shoes, basketball shoes, and others that are substitutes to a lesser extent. Often one should include close substitutes on the "inside," leaving only lesser substitutes in the outside product.

Notably, the data requirements for market simulation are modest. In addition to data required for the market share rule, only cost data for one product and an aggregate demand elasticity are necessary.

Calibration   The choice probability π_j is the share of good j as a percent of the entire market including the outside product. The relationship between the inside share s_j and π_j is:

$$\pi_j = s_j \left(1 - \pi_{n+1}\right).$$

Premerger profit maximization for product j results in this following first-order condition:

$$\frac{\partial[(p_j - c_j)\pi_j]}{\partial p_j} = 0.$$

Using input values, the model can be solved for its parameters, β and π_{n+1} (see Appendix B).

Once the calibration of the model is complete, the parameter values can be used to recover the marginal costs c_j for all products j:

$$p_j - c_j = \frac{1}{\beta(1 - \pi_j)}.$$

Simulation   The next step is a market simulation to solve the first-order conditions in the world "but for" infringement and predict the resulting prices and shares. The first-order conditions are given by:

$$p_j^{butfor} - c_j = \frac{1}{\beta(1 - \pi_j(p^{butfor}))}, \quad j = 1,\ldots,n.$$

There are n such equations (one for each product), and the system of equations is solved by performing a search for the equilibrium "but for" prices and shares. The parameters from the calibration are used in this simulation, and the only difference from the infringement equilibrium is the absence of the infringer.

Market shares for the inside products can be recovered from the implied choice probabilities:

$$s_j^{butfor} = \frac{\pi_j(p^{butfor})}{\sum_{k=1}^{n} \pi_k(p^{butfor})}.$$

The market simulation method allows for substitution to the outside product. As prices increase in the "but for" world, it can be expected that the share of the outside product will increase relative to the set of inside products. In determining lost profits, a principal advantage of the market simulation method over the market share approach and the Epstein method is that it allows for the simultaneous determination of price and quantity in the "but for" infringement equilibrium. Unlike the market share rule, which does not incorporate price effects, and the Epstein method, which requires the extent of price erosion be determined outside the model, market simulation jointly predicts the prices and quantities that would result in the absence of infringement.

Application to Ice Cream Industry

In the Springfield ice cream market, we include the top eight ice cream brands, which account for over 80 percent of the quantity sold during 1999, in the inside market. The remaining premium ice cream brands are included in the inside market as "Other." The weighted average price, $\bar{p}$, of the inside products is $0.83 per pint, as seen in Exhibit 8.3. We use a 15 percent margin for the patented brand, Holy Cow, and assume an aggregate elasticity of 1.5 for the inside products. The calibration results in an outside share, $\pi_{n+1} = 20.62\%$ and a price coefficient, $\beta = -8.73$. Exhibit 8.8 provides the results of market calibration.

The assumption of a catchall outside product enables the analyst to consider a finite number of products that are close substitutes as being within the market. As a result of the outside product, it is not necessary to assume that the sum of quantities sold by the inside firms must remain the same with and without infringement. The outside share can be used to calculate the total market quantity, including both inside products and outside products, which equals 153,668,655 units. Interestingly, in going from the actual to the "but for" market, the total quantity sold is constant. In the simple market share rule analysis already discussed, the total quantity that is held constant is the sum of quantities of only the inside products. This restriction reduces the flexibility of that model relative to the market simulation model. In the market simulation model, the share of the outside product changes relative to the inside products as one goes from the actual market to the "but for" market.

EXHIBIT 8.8   RESULTS OF MARKET CALIBRATION

Product	Quantity (Pints)	Inside Shares (S_i)	Choice Probabilities (π_i)
Sam's Creek	26,361,271	21.6%	17.2%
Holy Cow (patentee)	26,101,540	21.4%	17.0%
Cool Cream (infringer)	18,741,177	15.4%	12.2%
Private label	10,741,490	8.8%	7.0%
Bliss	8,209,604	6.7%	5.3%
Good Times	5,958,714	4.9%	3.9%
Premium Homemade	2,884,087	2.4%	1.9%
Delicious Light	2,608,594	2.1%	1.7%
Other	20,371,091	16.7%	13.3%
Total	121,977,568	100.0%	79.4%

Market simulation, by allowing the share of the outside product to change, allows for the aggregate elasticity of demand for the inside products to change as one goes from the actual to the "but for" equilibrium. This flexibility can allow market simulation to better represent market reality than the Epstein method, which maintains an assumption of constant elasticity.

The simulation of the "but for" market results in a "but for" outside share (π_{n+1}) of 23.7 percent, a new aggregate elasticity, $\varepsilon = 1.71$, and a new set of choice probabilities (π_i) and prices for the inside products seen in Exhibit 8.9.

In our example, the market simulation model determines that prices of the Holy Cow patented product would have been 0.37 percent higher "but for" infringement.[38] Due to the slightly higher "but for" price of the patented Holy Cow product, the margin on it increases from 15.0 percent to 15.3 percent. The model results in "but for" profits of $4,124,164 and lost profits of $521,644.[39]

EXHIBIT 8.9   MARKET SIMULATION RESULTS

Product	Actual Choice Probabilities (π_i)	"But For" Choice Probabilities (π_i)	Actual Price	"But For" Price
Sam's Creek	17.2%	19.2%	$0.77	$0.78
Holy Cow (patentee)	17.0%	19.0%	$0.92	$0.92
Cool Cream (infringer)	12.2%	0.0%	$0.89	$0.00
Private label	7.0%	8.0%	$0.60	$0.60
Bliss	5.3%	6.1%	$0.79	$0.80
Good Times	3.9%	4.4%	$0.65	$0.65
Premium Homemade	1.9%	2.5%	$0.95	$0.93
Delicious Light	1.7%	2.2%	$1.01	$1.00
Other	13.3%	14.9%	$0.90	$0.90
Total	79.4%	76.3%	$0.83	$0.83

Discussion

This application of market simulation is a leap ahead of past methods of lost profits analysis. It goes toward a holistic approach that allows for the joint determination of "but for" prices and quantities, and models the competitive process directly rather than simply making predictions of market outcomes. The simulation method also overcomes the problems that accompany assumptions of constant elasticity and market definition in the traditional sense. Furthermore, despite its advancements, the data requirements of the method are not excessively greater than other methods.

While the market simulation method is a step in the direction of a more unified approach, the method does have shortcomings. First, it is only as good as the demand system assumed in its implementation. It is possible that the logit demand system may not appropriately reflect market reality. The logit demand model possesses the independence of irrelevant alternatives (IIA) property of the market share rule as well as the problems associated with that property. The property implies that when the price of one product is increased, its sales are diverted among other products in proportion to the relative shares of those products. However, in some situations, certain products are closer substitutes than others and consumer-switching patterns are not exactly in line with relative market shares. Nested logit models, which allow for certain products to be closer to each other than others by allowing for subgroups within the market, offer an alternative to the IIA restriction.[40] Nested logit models can provide additional insight into markets that are segmented either by price or simply as a result of consumer preferences.

ALM assumes that marginal costs do not vary over the range of quantity considered. If, however, the patent owner and other suppliers are expected to produce substantially different quantities in the "but for" infringement world, then it is possible that marginal costs would change. As discussed, the model does allow for marginal costs to change when the simulation is performed. Thus, evidence from other sources on "but for" marginal costs can be incorporated in the market simulation.

The simulation model is set up such that the aggregate market elasticity with infringement is determined outside the model. The aggregate elasticity determines the share of the outside product relative to the inside products. This elasticity can either be estimated from data using econometric techniques (if sufficient data are available) or with appropriate research.

CONCLUSION

As seen in Exhibit 8.10, lost profits damages can vary significantly depending on the approach used.[41] The highest lost profits estimate comes from the Epstein method and the lowest from the market simulation method. The market simulation method results in lower damages than the market share rule when the aggregate elasticity is high enough for the outside share to be fairly sizeable.[42] The Epstein method results in higher damages than the market share rule because of the higher margin resulting from the analysis of price erosion. Note that the relative magnitude of damages estimated by each method is specific

EXHIBIT 8.10 COMPARISON OF RESULTS FROM THREE APPROACHES

Method	Lost Profits Damages	Damages as a Percent of Patentee's Actual Profits
Market share rule	$654,043	18.2%
Epstein method ($\delta = 0.37\%$)	$791,690	22.0%
Market simulation (ALM)	$521,644	14.5%

to the application. In some instances the simulation model will result in the lowest damage estimates, while in other instances it will result in higher damage estimates. Such relative magnitudes depend on the facts of the matter.

See Exhibit 8.11 for a comparison of the predicted "but for" market shares of the "inside" products under the three different models.

The Epstein method quantity shares are the same as revenue shares because in that model we assume a single market price for all products in the market. It is also interesting that in the market simulation method, the prices of Cool Cat's two noninfringing brands, Premium Homemade and Delicous Light, actually decrease in the "but for" infringement world (see Exhibit 8.9). The intuitive reason for this price drop is that as the firm goes from maximizing profit by choosing prices of three differentiated products to just two, it loses some of its market positioning. The Epstein method will not capture such effects due to its assumption of a single market price for all competing products.

EXHIBIT 8.11 QUANTITY SHARES FROM THREE DAMAGE ESTIMATION METHODS

Product	Actual "Inside" Shares of Quantity			"But For" "Inside" Shares of Quantity		
	Market Share Rule	Epstein Method	Market Simulation	Market Share Rule	Epstein Method	Market Simulation
Sam's Creek	21.6%	20.0%	21.6%	25.5%	24.0%	25.1%
Holy Cow (patentee)	21.4%	23.6%	21.4%	25.3%	28.3%	24.9%
Cool Cream (infringer)	15.4%	16.5%	15.4%	0.0%	0.0%	0.0%
Private label	8.8%	6.3%	8.8%	10.4%	7.6%	10.4%
Bliss	6.7%	6.4%	6.7%	8.0%	7.7%	8.0%
Good Times	4.9%	3.8%	4.9%	5.8%	4.6%	5.8%
Premium Homemade	2.4%	2.7%	2.4%	2.8%	3.2%	3.3%
Delicious Light	2.1%	2.6%	2.1%	2.5%	3.1%	2.9%
Other	16.7%	18.0%	16.7%	19.7%	21.5%	19.6%
Total	100.0%	100.0%	100.0%	100.0%	100.0%	100.0%

As courts advance toward the use of better economics in patent damages analysis, methods such as market simulation have become appropriate. Such methods are already the standard in merger and antitrust analysis in courts and have gained wide acceptance within the economic community. The market simulation method is often a better representation of market reality than an outcome-based approach such as the market share rule and, if implemented appropriately, may provide more accurate damage estimates in a litigation setting. However, like the other approaches discussed, the simulation approach is not perfect. For example, market simulation requires additional data beyond that required for the market share rule. As the benefits of a unified approach to patent damages become more widely recognized, we will likely see continuing refinements to the market simulation approach.

APPENDIXES

A. Epstein Method for Price Adjustment

Assume that the change in REV^M (total market revenue), corresponding to a δ percent increase in price (P) (where $\delta = \frac{\Delta P}{P}$), is ΔREV.

Then,

$$\Delta REV = \frac{\partial REV}{\partial P} \cdot \Delta P.$$

Since $REV^M = PQ$,

$$\frac{\partial REV^M}{\partial P} = Q(1 + \varepsilon).$$

Substituting yields the change in revenue,

$$\Delta REV = Q(1 + \varepsilon) \cdot \Delta P$$

$$\frac{\Delta REV}{REV^M} = \frac{Q(1 + \varepsilon)}{PQ} \cdot \delta P.$$

The "but for" margin is defined as

$$\mu^{butfor} = \frac{P(1 + \delta) - C}{P(1 + \delta)}.$$

Substituting the marginal cost $C = P(1 - \mu)$, yields

$$\mu^{butfor} = \frac{\mu + \delta}{1 + \delta}.$$

B. Antitrust Logit Model (ALM)

Taking the derivatives of

$$\pi_i = \frac{\exp(\alpha_i - \beta p_i)}{\Sigma_j \exp(\alpha_j - \beta p_j)},$$

it can be shown that

$$\frac{\partial \pi_j}{\partial p_j} = -\beta \pi_j (1 - \pi_j), \text{ and}$$

$$\frac{\partial \pi_i}{\partial p_j} = \beta \pi_i \pi_j.$$

Consequently,

$$\varepsilon_{ii} = -\beta p_i (1 - \pi_i), \text{ and}$$

$$\varepsilon_{ij} = \beta p_j \pi_j.$$

Premerger profit maximization for product j results in this first-order condition:

$$\frac{\partial [(p_j - c_j) \pi_j]}{\partial p_j} = 0.$$

The first-order condition gives us this equality in equilibrium:

$$p_j - c_j = \frac{1}{\beta (1 - \pi_j)}.$$

For the product whose margin is an input to the model, this gives us

$$p_1 - c_1 = \frac{1}{\beta (1 - s_1 + s_1 \pi_{n+1})}. \tag{1}$$

Generalizing from the own-price elasticity ε_{ii}, the aggregate elasticity, ε, of the inside products is

$$\varepsilon = -\beta \bar{p} \left(1 - \sum_{j=1}^{N} \pi_j\right),$$

where $\bar{p}$ is the weighted average price of the inside products.
This can be written as

$$\varepsilon = -\beta \bar{p} (\pi_{n+1}). \tag{2}$$

Using equations (1) and (2), we solve for the two parameters, β and π_{n+1}

$$\beta = \frac{\bar{p} - \varepsilon s_1 (p_1 - c_1)}{\bar{p} (1 - s_1)(p_1 - c_1)}$$

$$\pi_{n+1} = \frac{\varepsilon (1 - s_1)(p_1 - c_1)}{p - \varepsilon s_1 (p_1 - c_1)}.$$

Substituting input values in the two equations completes the calibration.

NOTES

1. I kindly thank Bates White, LLC for their support of this chapter, which was developed while I was a principal of Bates White, LLC. I would like to thank Sushrut Jain for substantial

contributions to this chapter. Additionally, Jeffrey Brown, Ph.D. and Oana Tocoian provided valuable assistance. All errors are mine.

2. 35 U.S. Code Section 284.

3. *State Industries, Inc. v. Mor-Flo Industries, Inc.* (1989)

4. *See Scripto-Tokai v. Gillette Co.* (1992).

5. This method is discussed in several papers, including a few by economists Gregory J. Werden and Luke M. Froeb. The analysis is based directly on the model presented in Werden, Froeb, and Langenfeld (2000).

6. For instance, one ice cream manufacturer describes its position in a 10-K filing: "The company's marketing strategy is based upon management's belief that a significant number of people prefer a quality product and quality image in ice cream just as they do in other product categories. A quality image is communicated in many ways—taste, packaging, flavor selection, price and often through advertising and promotion. If consistency in the product's quality and image are strictly maintained, a brand can develop a clearly defined and loyal consumer following. It is the company's goal to develop such a consumer following in each major market in which it does business."

7. Since the purpose of this chapter is to explore the relative merits of different analytical methods in the context of a reasonably behaved oligopolistic market, we will not discuss the background and idiosyncrasies of the ice cream market at great length.

8. *IRI Marketing Factbook* (1993).

9. International Dairy Foods Association (2003).

10. *See id.* Frozen desserts as a whole sold about 12.1 billion pints (1.5 billion gallons) in 2002, according to the IDFA's *Dairy Facts.*

11. Of the 11.0 billion pints of ice cream manufactured in 2001, 4.3 billion pints of ice cream was sold in supermarkets in 2001.

12. *See* IDFA's *Dairy Facts* (2003). The average price per pint of packaged ice cream sold in U.S. supermarkets was $0.98.

13. Some industry analysts also mention a third category consisting of the cheapest brands referred to as the "economy," "regular," or "lower-priced" products. *See* Chang (2001).

14. Lazar and Crea (2001), pp. 5, 15.

15. Kroger's private-label brand, Turkey Hill, is listed separately in the data, but other private-label brands are captured in the catchall category of "Private Label."

16. Lazar and Crea (2001), p. 27.

17. *Also see* Chang (2001), pp. 3, 21.

18. We define premium brands as brands with an average price below $2.00 per pint. We recognize that the boundary between premium and super-premium ice cream is perhaps less well defined in the industry, but this is a reasonable definition. *See* Exhibit 8.2. The difficulty with having to draw a line to define the market in this way also highlights a challenge with market definition, as we will discuss in later sections.

19. We note that the use of a catchall "Other" category to combine all the smaller products inflates the collective market power of the participants in that category. However, for the purposes of this chapter, it is reasonable.

20. McFadden, Talvittie, and associates (1977).

21. Suppose the patentee has a 40 percent market share and the infringer has a 20 percent market share. The sum of all market shares excluding the infringer would equal 80 percent. That is, the total market share of 100 percent less the infringer's market share of 20 percent equals 80 percent. Thus, the patentee's "but for" market share would be 40 percent divided by 80 percent, which equals 50 percent. The market share apportionment method implies that the patentee's market share would have been 50 percent in the absence of infringement.

22. U.S. Department of Justice and Federal Trade Commission, *Horizontal Merger Guidelines* (1992 revised), hereinafter referred to as *Merger Guidelines*. *See* Culbertson and Weinstein (1988). Culbertson and Weinstein were among the economists who suggested the use of the *Merger Guidelines* for market definition in patent cases.

23. *Merger Guidelines,* Section 1.1.

24. In a patent damages case, the starting point could be either the infringing or the patented product.

25. We use a constant 15 percent price-cost (incremental) margin for the sake of illustration. Actual profit margins in the ice cream industry may differ.

26. It is important to note that in our application of the market share rule, we used quantity sold, not dollar revenues, to measure market shares. Since a market participant's "but for" quantity is multiplied by the participant's unchanging price to calculate "but for" revenues, there may be a change in total market revenues due to the differences in prices among participants.

27. As noted previously, competitive entry can have other, countervailing effects on price.

28. The Epstein method is discussed in detail in Epstein (2003).

29. *Id.* at 7.

30. We choose 0.37 percent as one of the price erosion levels because the market simulation model to be discussed predicts $\delta = 0.37\%$. Using the same δ allows us to perform a comparison of damage calculations between the two approaches.

31. We expect the demand for ice cream to be elastic, and we use $\varepsilon = 1.5$ as a reasonable value. While the damage numbers resulting from our models change as elasticities change, our conclusions about the models and their relative merits do not.

32. Epstein (2003) does provide a method for determining price erosion under the assumption of the almost ideal demand system (AIDS). While this method provides a benchmark for price erosion, it still determines price erosion separately from the determination of "but for" quantity.

33. The methods for determining the extent of price erosion discussed in Epstein (2003) include the use of anecdotal information on prices, the use of past information on prices to predict future prices, the use of prices from a benchmark market, and the almost ideal demand system. *See* Epstein (2003), pp. 23–31.

34. *See, e.g.,* Werden et al. (2000).

35. The logit model of consumer demand exhibits the independence of irrelevant alternatives property.

36. In addition to Werden et al. (2000), *also see* Werden and Froeb (1994, 1996).

37. Alternative demand systems include isoelastic, linear, and AIDS.

38. The price of the Holy Cow brand is predicted to be \$0.9236 per pint, which is 0.37 percent higher than the with-infringement price of \$0.9202 per pint.

39. "But for" profits are the product of "but for" margins, "but for" prices, "but for" choice probabilities (all from Exhibit 8.8), and total market quantity of 153,668,655 pints.

40. *See* Jayarathne and Shapiro (2000).

41. For purposes of comparison, we use the Epstein damage amount corresponding to the price erosion of 0.37 percent. However, as seen in Exhibit 8.7, damages (as a percent of actual profits) vary substantially as the price erosion assumption in the Epstein method is changed. Damages are 31.7 percent of actual profits for $\delta = 2\%$ and 48.2 percent for $\delta = 5\%$.

42. An assumption of aggregate elasticity $\varepsilon = 1$ results in damages equal to 16.3 percent of actual profits as opposed to the 14.5% for $\varepsilon = 1.5$ in Exhibit 8.10. For an aggregate elasticity $\varepsilon = 0.5$, we get damages equal to 18.1 percent of actual profits, which is almost identical to the results from the market share rule seen in the exhibit.

REFERENCES

Chang, Victoria (under supervision of Jennifer Chatman and Glenn Carroll). "Dreyer's Grand Ice Cream (A): A Stanford GSB Case Study," OB-35 (A), Graduate School of Business, Stanford University, October 2001.

Crystal Semiconductor Corp. v. Tritech Microelectronics Int'l, Inc., 246 F.3d 1336, 1359, 57 U.S.P.Q. 2d (BNA) 1953, 1966 (Fed. Cir. 2001).

Culbertson, John, and Roy Weinstein. "Product Substitutes and the Calculation of Patent Damages," *Journal of the Patent and Trademark Office Society* 70 (1988).

Dreyer's Grand Ice Cream, Inc., 2000 10-K.

Epstein, Roy J. "The Market Share Rule with Price Erosion: Patent Infringement Lost Profits Damages after *Crystal,*" *AIPLA Quarterly Journal* 31, no. 1 (2003).

In re Mahurkar Double Lumen Hemodialysis Catheter Patent Litigation, 831 F. Supp. 1354, 28 U.S.P.Q.2d (BNA) 1801 (N.D. Ill. 1993), *aff'd,* 71 F.3d 1573, 37 U.S.P.Q.2d (BNA) 1138 (Fed. Cir. 1995).

International Dairy Foods Association (IDFA), *Dairy Facts,* 2003 edition.

IRI Marketing Factbook (1993).

Jayarathne, Jith, and Carl Shapiro. "Simulating Partial Asset Divestitures to 'Fix' Mergers," *International Journal of the Economics of Business* 7, no. 2 (2000).

Lazar, Andrew, and Robert Crea. "Dreyer's Grand Ice Cream: Initiation of Coverage," Lehman Brothers Global Equity Research, May 31, 2001.

McFadden Daniel, Antie Talvittie, and associates. *Demand Model Estimation and Validation,* Urban Travel Demand Forecasting Project Phase 1 Final Report Series, Volume V, University of California, Berkeley, 1977.

Nevo, Aviv. "A Practitioner's Guide to Estimation of Random-Coefficients Logit Models of Demand," *Journal of Economics and Management Strategy* 9, no. 4 (2000).

Panduit Corp. v. Stahlin Bros. Fibre Works, Inc., 575 F.2d 1152, 1164, 197 U.S.P.Q. 726, 736 (6th Cir. 1978).

Scripto-Tokai v. Gillette Co., 788 F. Supp. 439, 444 (C.D. Cal. 1992).

State Industries, Inc. v. Mor-Flo Industries, Inc., 883 F.2d 1573, 12 U.S.P.Q. 2D 1026 (CAFC 1989).

United States Code, Title 35, Section 284.

U.S. Department of Justice and Federal Trade Commission, *Horizontal Merger Guidelines,* (revised), 1992.

Werden, Gregory J., and Luke M. Froeb. "The Effects of Mergers in Differentiated Products Industries: Logit Demand and Merger Policy," *Journal of Law, Economics and Organization* 10, no. 2 (1994).

Werden, Gregory J., and Luke M. Froeb. "Simulation as an Alternative to Structural Merger Policy in Differentiated Products Industries." In Malcolm Coate and Andrew Kleit, eds., *The Economics of the Antitrust Process* (New York: Topics in Regulatory Economics and Policy Series, Kluwer, 1996).

Werden, Gregory J., Luke M. Froeb, and James Langenfeld. "Lost Profits from Patent Infringement: The Simulation Approach," *International Journal of the Economics of Business* 7, no. 2 (2000).

Werden, Gregory J., Luke M. Froeb, and James Langenfeld. "Lost Profits from Patent Infringement: The Simulation Approach," *International Journal of the Economics of Business* 7, no. 2 (2000).

CHAPTER 9

Commercial Success: Economic Principles Applied to Patent Litigation[1]

JESSE DAVID
NERA Economic Consulting

MARION B. STEWART
NERA Economic Consulting

A party accused of infringing a patent may contend that the asserted patent is invalid because of obviousness. To help evaluate that issue, courts may consider whether the patented invention is a "commercial success." Determining whether an invention has, or has not, been a commercial success is primarily an economic exercise, and economists increasingly assist courts in evaluating this issue. Case law indicates that courts have traditionally (1) looked at such factors as increasing revenues, gain in market share, and public acclaim in an attempt to determine whether a product has been a commercial success and (2) considered whether the patent holder has established a "nexus" between the claimed invention and the product's commercial success. In this chapter we discuss these tests and consider them alongside another test suggested by economic principles, namely, whether the patented invention has earned or can be expected to earn a positive net return on invested capital after accounting for all the relevant costs associated with developing and commercializing the product. We analyze the commercial success standard in the context of two recent cases in which we applied these principles.

INTRODUCTION

A party accused of infringing a patent may contend that the asserted patent is invalid because of obviousness. That contention may be rebutted by a showing that the patented invention is a "commercial success"—one of several "secondary considerations" that courts look to for identifying the differences between the patented invention and the prior art. These secondary considerations—known as objective indicia of nonobviousness—also include such factors as copying, long felt but unsolved need, failure of others, and licensing.[2]

Determining whether an invention has, or has not, been a commercial success is primarily an economic exercise, and economists increasingly assist courts in evaluating this issue. Case law indicates that courts have traditionally looked for such characteristics as increasing revenues, gain in share in an appropriately defined market, and public acclaim in an attempt to determine whether a product has been a commercial success. Courts have also considered whether the patent holder has established a "nexus" between the claimed invention and the product's commercial success—that is, whether the commercial success, if evident, is due to the patented feature as opposed to some other characteristic of the product or mode of selling employed by the manufacturer.

From an economic perspective, commercial success could in principle be defined by a single criterion: Does the patented invention earn a positive net return (risk-adjusted) on invested capital after accounting for all relevant costs associated with developing and commercializing the patent as well as any alternatives available to the patent holder? Patents exist to protect the human and financial investment used to develop new products, services, or processes. This investment, however, is beneficial, from a social perspective, only if consumers are willing to purchase an embodiment of the invention at such a price as to fully compensate the inventor for all costs incurred in bringing the product to market.[3] Put simply, patents are not needed to protect inventors from making poor investment decisions.

The courts' use of the previously mentioned factors is not necessarily in conflict with this definition, and many—perhaps most—previous decisions made by courts are likely to have been consistent with it. Given the limitations on available data, it is entirely reasonable that an analysis of commercial success should consider and place significant weight on the traditional measures such as market share or revenue growth. However, under certain circumstances, rapid sales growth and gains in market share will not *necessarily* reflect a profitable underlying invention. Moreover, calculating the proper measure of profitability can be a complicated task and should be considered in an appropriate context—for example, relative to an appropriate benchmark or alternative. Consequently, it is our opinion that courts should look more deeply into the economic characteristics of the product before arriving at a determination of the commercial success of the patent.

In this chapter we consider whether the tests traditionally used by the courts are consistent with the criterion suggested by economic principles. We then analyze the commercial success standard in the context of two recent cases in which we applied these principles.

SUMMARY OF THE CASE LAW

In *Graham v. John Deere Co.* (1966), the seminal case identifying commercial success as a relevant "secondary consideration" in a determination of patent validity, the U.S. Supreme Court cited a *University of Pennsylvania Law Review* article that focused on the consumer perspective for evaluating the commercial success of a patent. The article stated that "[t]he operative facts . . . are the actions of buyers rather than those of producers."[4] Case law since *Graham* has generally followed this position. For example, in *Demaco* (1988), the court stated:

> The rationale for giving weight to the so-called "secondary considerations" is that they provide objective evidence of how the patented device is viewed in the marketplace, by those directly interested in the product.[5]

Based on this approach, courts appear to have turned to a few standard measures of consumers' demand for the patented product, such as total unit sales or revenues. Although not universally, the courts have generally recognized that this information must be placed in a "meaningful context" and consequently have noted that the sales must represent a significant and/or growing share of that product in some "market." This also follows the University of Pennsylvania article, which stated that "[t]he basic measure of commercial success should be the proportion of the total market for the product that the patentee has obtained."[6] Subsequent decisions have reinforced the standard that sales figures must at least be considered in light of the size of the overall market, although the method for identifying the appropriate "market" has not generally been specified.[7]

However, achieving a significant volume of sales or even a large market share does not necessarily indicate that the inventor should view a patent as a success. For example, sales may be driven by characteristics other than the patented invention, such as other patented features, nonpatented characteristics, and brand name. For some products, market share may also be affected by advertising. (The basic formulas for Coke and Pepsi have not changed in decades, yet market shares appear to be affected by changing marketing strategies on the part of the two companies.) As an extreme example, increasing sales and market share of a product could also be generated by simply lowering price, a tactic sometimes employed by companies seeking to create customer awareness early in the product life cycle. The United States Patent and Trade Mark Office's *Manual of Patent Examining Procedure* identifies this "nexus" between the success of the product and the patent itself as a key component of a nonobviousness claim:

> An applicant who is asserting commercial success to support its contention of nonobviousness bears the burden of proof of establishing a nexus between the claimed invention and evidence of commercial success.[8]

Courts have recognized some of these possibilities and have generally required a showing that any commercial success be directly linked to demand for the patented feature rather than any other factors.

Consequently, for any data on sales or market share to be relevant, one must be able to demonstrate that whatever demand for the product exists, it is due, at least in part, to the patent, not some other features or actions by the seller.[9] A simple thought experiment can shed light on the concept of a "nexus": Suppose the patented invention were made unavailable and removed from the product. Could the seller attain the same level of commercial success? Or from an economic perspective: What is the difference in net profits that would accrue to the patent holder if the patented invention were removed from the product?

Despite courts' tendency to view commercial success from only the consumers' perspective, a few decisions have recognized profitability as a factor that might be considered along with other objective economic evidence. For example, in *Cable* (1985), the court stated:

> Without further economic evidence, for example, it would be improper to infer that the reported sales represent a substantial share of any definable market or whether the profitability per unit is anything out of the ordinary in the industry involved.

Discussions of profitability or other "supply-side" considerations have been included in assessments of commercial success in only a few other cases.[10] As these cases properly point out, ultimately an inventor's success should be judged by the returns to his investment *relative* to that inventor's next-best alternatives.

Economic Criteria

In the first edition of his ground-breaking book *Economic Analysis of Law,* the distinguished jurist Richard Posner discussed the *normative*—that is, prescriptive—and *positive*—that is, descriptive—roles of economics in the law:

> Economics turns out to be a powerful tool of normative analysis of law and legal institutions—a source of criticism and reform. . . . The normative role of economic analysis in the law is fairly obvious. The positive role—that of explaining the rules and outcomes in the legal system as they are—is less obvious, but not less important. As we shall see, many areas of the law, especially the great common law fields of property, torts, and contracts, bear the stamp of economic reasoning. Few legal opinions, to be sure, contain explicit references to economic concepts and few judges have a substantial background in economics. But the true grounds of decision are often concealed rather than illuminated by the characteristic rhetoric of judicial opinions.[11]

As described, we suggest that there is a straightforward normative role for economics in determining commercial success: A patented invention should be considered a commercial success if it can be shown to have earned, or reasonably be expected to earn, a positive net return on invested capital after accounting for all relevant costs associated with development and commercialization as well as any alternatives available to the patent holder and the amount of risk borne by the patent holder. Although courts would do well, in our view, to adopt more explicit economic reasoning along these lines in their analysis of commercial success issues, our reading of the relevant cases suggests that a substantial amount of economic analysis has already found its way into judicial opinions regarding commercial success.

Under certain circumstances, it appears that economic analysis could provide a definitive answer to the general question, Has a patented invention been a commercial success? For example, suppose that:

1. A start-up company, founded solely to exploit a single patented invention, incurred costs (in present value terms) of $1 million to develop a single salable product.

2. Over its entire life cycle—now completed—sales of that product generated net profits of $2 million (again, in present value terms).

3. There is no doubt that the product characteristics and/or other factors that led consumers to purchase the product were all due to the invention.

The first assumption allows us to say with certainly that it cost precisely $1 million to develop a product embodying the patented invention, since we assume away any difficulties that would be caused by the need to associate "common costs" in, say, a central research and development (R&D) facility with the development of a particular invention. The second assumption eliminates the difficulty of evaluating the potential profits still to be earned by a product currently on the market. The third assumption assures that the nexus between patented invention and sales success has been established. Assuming that an appropriate interest rate has been used to "discount" (or appreciate) the investment and the resultant profits, a $2 million return on a $1 million investment would surely count as a commercially successful venture from the perspective of the producer. Since (by assumption) the patented invention is what made that return possible, then the patented invention should be deemed a commercial success.

In our experience, however, the issues that need to be addressed are always more complicated than this stylized example, so it is hardly a surprise that—as far as we know—no reported case has reached a decision regarding the commercial success of a patented invention simply by comparing the cost of developing and selling the patented product with profits earned on that product. Our own research has made clear that even large, technology-oriented companies have difficulty associating early-stage R&D costs with what ultimately became a commercially viable product, inevitably leading to some uncertainty regarding the total cost of bringing a patented invention to market.[12] In addition, determining profitability for a single product sold by a multiproduct company can be further complicated if the growth in that product's sales comes at least partly at the expense of profits elsewhere in the company or, alternatively, if sales of the patented product generate additional profits for the company by drawing consumers to other products. Another complication arises from the fact that most patent disputes involve products currently or not yet on the market, not products whose life cycles have ended, adding further uncertainty regarding the profits that will ultimately be generated.[13] And finally, while there are certainly instances in which there is no doubt that the patented invention has created the performance characteristics that were responsible for the product's success, our studies have also revealed contrary examples in which it was clear that a patent played little, if any, role in generating product sales. Given the data imperfections that frequently make a "direct" measure of commercial success impractical,[14] it is therefore not surprising that courts have tended to focus on "indirect" evidence, such as growth in market share. As Judge Posner suggested, however, many of the courts' decisions on commercial success nevertheless "bear the stamp of economic reasoning."

For example, economic reasoning makes clear that pharmaceutical companies would not invest in research on a particular class of drugs, such as antibiotics, unless they believed that on an expected-value basis that research would be profitable. If companies' expectations are rational, then a bundle of "average" marketed antibiotics will generate enough profits over their life cycles to yield an acceptable return on the companies' R&D investments. A drug that clearly does much better than average is very likely, therefore, to be a commercial success.[15]

How would we know that a drug is much better than average? A large (i.e., much above-average) market share would be a likely indicator, and rapid growth in market share—particularly if the product is not too far into its life cycle—would also likely be relevant, since the expected present value of a product's profit stream will be greater, the sooner those profits are earned.[16] The courts' reliance on market share data and growth in market share, as described in the previous section, appears to be sensible in light of the likely imperfections in the data that would have shed a more direct light on the issue of a product's commercial success.

Despite the fact that, for the most part, courts' general approach to determining commercial success has been consistent with these economic concepts, it appears that some decisions would have benefited from more—or at least more explicit—economic analysis. For example, in the *Neupak* (2002) case, the Appeals Court found:

> Because the record shows that between 1995 and 2000 Neupak's patented mobile filling carts enjoyed a significant increase in sales and constituted an increasing share of Neupak's business, the district court did not clearly err in concluding that Neupak demonstrated a nexus between commercial success and the 233 patent.

In this case, not only did the courts (both District and Appeals) apparently fail to put Neupak's sales into any "meaningful context," there appears to be a possibility that the product embodying the patented invention became successful at the expense of other Neupak products. It is likely that a relatively simple analysis of the company's financial records could provide a definitive answer to that question.

In another case, *Huang* (1996), the U.S. Court of Appeals upheld a finding by the Board of Patent Appeals and Interferences that the pending claims made by Huang for a patent covering a particular kind of tennis racket grip were obvious, in part through a finding that Huang had not presented sufficient evidence of commercial success. In this case, the patent holder had cited several factors that he claimed were indicators of commercial success, including: (1) sales of over 1 million units for use on both new and resold rackets; and (2) the fact that since Huang began selling the claimed grip, sales of his company's prior grips had decreased by about 50 percent. In this case, a relatively basic review of the economics of the claimed product by the patent holder would likely have provided a sounder basis for his claim. For example, from a review of the product and patent descriptions, it appears that development costs were likely quite low—the patent claimed a change in the ratio of the thickness of the various materials used in the grip. If this was the case, then net profitability could have been reliably estimated for both the patented version of the product and the older version that it replaced. Assuming that Huang's sales of the new grip were not a result of discounting relative to the preexisting product and that manufacturing costs for the two products were similar, then a determination of commercial success could

be made based on an evaluation of the increased revenues generated by the patented product relative to an appropriate benchmark (e.g., Huang's revenues prior to introduction of
the new product or to revenues of competitors in the industry).

Two Case Studies

We were asked to evaluate and testify on commercial success issues in two recent cases.
These cases illustrate how traditional measures may be insufficient to prove commercial
success and how, if properly applied, economic analysis can provide the complete picture.

In the first case, we were asked to carry out research and testify on behalf of an accused
infringer who was challenging the validity of a patent allegedly covering a particular type
of packaged snack product. Despite rapid growth in sales of the product embodying the
patented invention (approximately $30 million in revenues during the first year rising to
about $110 million by the fourth year) and attainment of a substantial share of any rea-
sonably defined market, we identified several key facts that nonetheless indicated that the
patent may not have been a commercial success.

First, although revenues were increasing rapidly, the trend in profits was not so prom-
ising. As shown in Exhibit 9.1, the company experienced a cumulative net operating loss
of approximately $10 million to $15 million during the first five years of the product's
life cycle. Moreover, the trend through the last two years was downward—offering no
indication that profits would be forthcoming in the near future. Furthermore, our analysis found that sales of the product were coming, in part, from customers who were switching from other snack products manufactured by the same company. We estimated that an
additional $13 million in profits had been lost due to "cannibalization" of other product
lines. These data indicated to us that although the product apparently had been deemed
a "success" in the marketplace by consumers, it did not appear to be a "commercial success"
from the perspective of the patent holder.

A second major concern related to the issue of the putative "nexus" between the revenues earned by the company and the patented invention. In this case, a competitor had
entered the market one year after the patent holder with a product—acknowledged to be
noninfringing and apparently not protected by any other patent or critical trade secret—
that provided virtually the same benefits to the consumer as the disputed product, including such characteristics as ease of preparation, portion control, and shape of the package
(important for product placement on the store shelf). Moreover, as shown in Exhibit 9.2,
this product experienced a path of revenue growth almost identical to the product at issue.
The patent holder claimed that the product embodying the patented invention was *one way*
to achieve the benefits cited by customers. However, despite the dramatic growth in revenues, in our opinion the performance of this alternative product demonstrated that *causation* had not been established. Based on information we reviewed, it appeared that rapid
growth in revenues and market share for products of this type were not dependent on the
patented invention. Finally, we pointed out that the patent holder had a very well known
brand name and had used innovative techniques to introduce and market the product at

EXHIBIT 9.1   SNACK PRODUCT PATENT HOLDER PROFITABILITY, ANNUAL AND CUMULATIVE

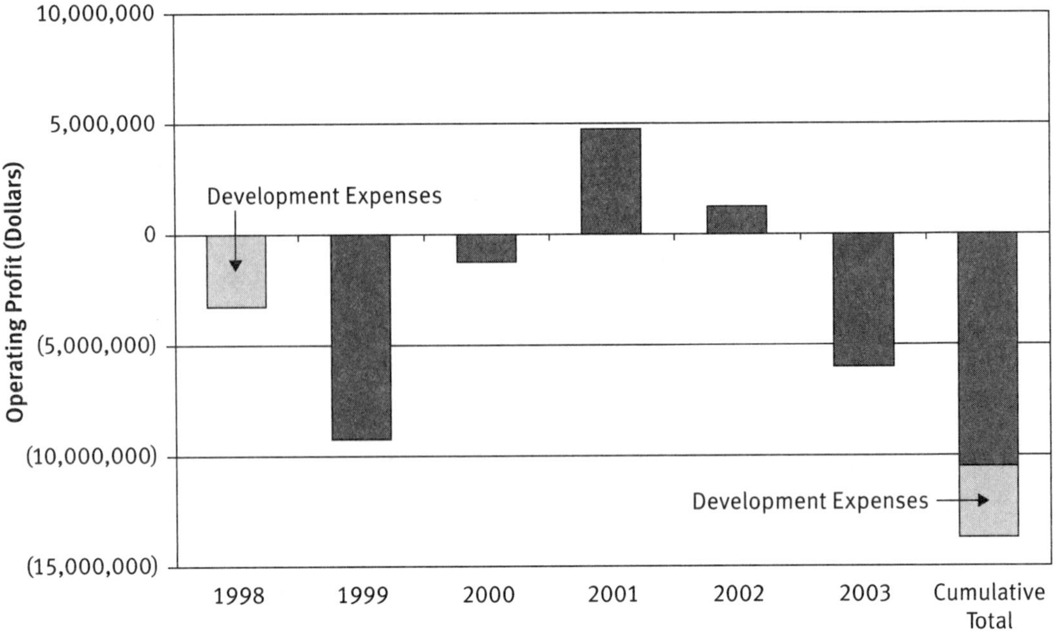

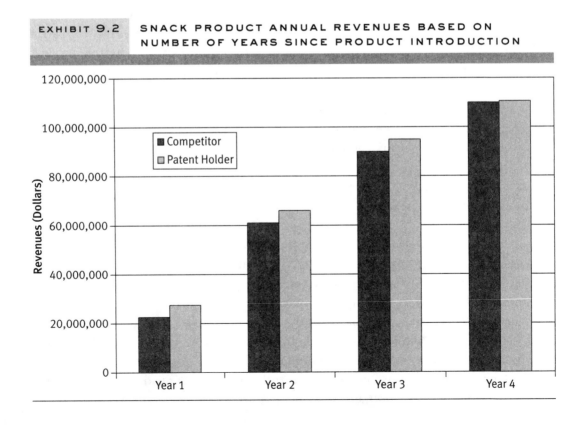

EXHIBIT 9.2   SNACK PRODUCT ANNUAL REVENUES BASED ON NUMBER OF YEARS SINCE PRODUCT INTRODUCTION

issue. These factors further weakened the link between the patented invention and any success (at least in terms of gross revenues) that the product had in the marketplace.

The facts were very different in another patent dispute in which we testified for the patent holder regarding the commercial success of an anti-infective drug. First, there did not appear to be much dispute about the nexus between the patented invention and the product's efficacy, since—as one might expect with pharmaceutical products—the patent disclosed the drug itself and its methods of use. Second, although the accused infringer contended that the product's success was due to advertising and promotion, that argument was weakened by (1) physicians' testimony and other evidence that, while promotional activities may well lead physicians to try a new product, repeated prescribing for patients is likely only if the product performs well; and (2) our analysis, which showed that the product at issue had the second-lowest ratio of promotional spending to sales of all major anti-infective products introduced in the past decade.

"Traditional" metrics, such as growth in market share, also pointed to the product's commercial success, as did a direct comparison of profits and R&D expenditures. Exhibit 9.3, for example, shows that after just four years on the market, the product ranked fourth among all oral tablet antibiotics, a market that included well over 200 products.

Although competition among antibiotics spans several classes of drugs, each class has a unique mechanism of action and therefore represents a distinct market segment that should be examined as part of an evaluation of the commercial success of a patented invention. As Exhibit 9.3 also shows, sales of the patented product grew faster than any other competing antibiotic. Exhibit 9.4 shows that, within drugs of the same class, the market leader began losing share as soon as the patented product was introduced. The product's rapid acceptance as the treatment of choice for dangerous infections such as hospital-acquired pneumonia demonstrated both the product's commercial success and the importance of its performance characteristics (since no amount of advertising or promotion would be likely to influence the use of a product in life-threatening situations). The huge sales of the product were even more impressive in light of the long odds against success in the pharmaceutical industry[17] and a history of failed attempts to develop safe and effective anti-infective drugs, leaving no doubt in our minds that the product and the patented invention were commercial successes.

CONCLUSION

Based on our understanding of the purpose of patent protection and our interpretation of precedents, it is our opinion that commercial success should be evaluated on the basis of the economic contribution of a patented invention to an inventor's financial well-being. Thus, from the perspective of economics, a key indicator of commercial success ought to be the profits generated by the patented invention, relative to an appropriate benchmark or alternative. When available, financial data on these factors should be considered in an evaluation of commercial success. Courts' historic use of factors such as revenue growth and large market share are likely to be consistent with this standard in most cases, if applied correctly.

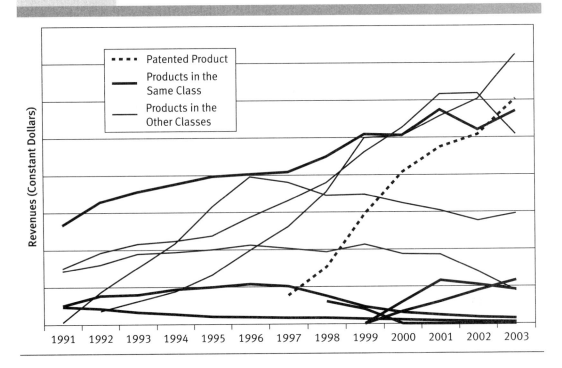

EXHIBIT 9.3   REVENUES FOR BEST-SELLING COMPETING BRANDS IN THE ORAL TABLET ANTIBIOTIC MARKET

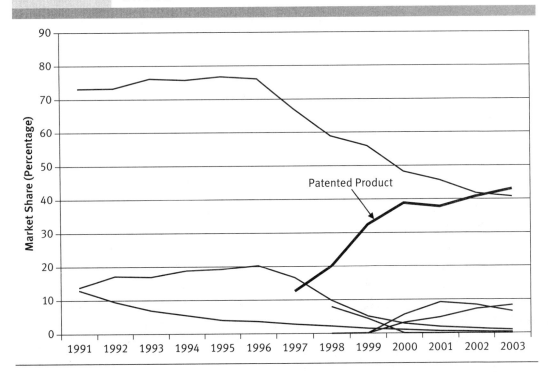

EXHIBIT 9.4   SHARES OF REVENUE FOR A CLASS OF ANTIBIOTIC DRUGS

NOTES

1. This chapter was previously published in *Economic Approaches to Intellectual Property Policy, Litigation, and Management,* ed. Gregory K. Leonard and Lauren J. Stiroh (New York: National Economic Research Associates, 2005).

2. *In re Denis Rouffet, Yannick Tanguy and Frederic Berthault* (1998). It is our understanding that courts may consider all of these indicia in an assessment of a patent's validity. For the purposes of our discussion, we consider only those factors that should weigh in a determination of commercial success, not whether, or the extent to which those factors could support a finding of validity or invalidity.

3. One could imagine that, for reasons of public policy, a patented invention related to health-care could be sold at an "artificially" low price, or even given away, but such a strategy would not reduce the true value of the invention.

4. *Graham v. John Deere Co.* (1966) and Robbins (1963–1964).

5. *Demaco Corp. v. F. Von Langsdorff Licensing Ltd.* (1988).

6. Robbins (1963–1964).

7. For example, see *Ecolochem, Inc. v. Southern California Edison Company* (2000); *Cable Electric Products, Inc. v. Genmark, Inc.* (1985); and *Hybritech Inc. v. Monoclonal Antibodies, Inc.* (1986). An exception where a decision considered sales explicitly outside the context of the size of the overall market is *Neupak, Inc., v. Ideal Manufacturing and Sales Corp.* (2002). In *J.T. Eaton & Co. v. Atlantic Paste & Glue Co.* (1997), the court similarly found that a large number of units sold *did* represent evidence of commercial success, without any showing of a share in a well-defined market.

8. United States Patent and Trademark Office (2003). *See also Demaco* (1988).

9. Although the courts have consistently recognized that the issue of a "nexus" is critical in a determination of commercial success, in many cases they have found that the existence of a significant advertising budget does not in itself rebut the presumption that the commercial success of the product at issue must be due to the patented invention. For example, see *Merck & Co. v. Danbury Pharmacal, Inc.* (1988) and *Hybritech* (1986).

10. For example, see *Miles Laboratories, Inc. v. Shandon Inc.* (1992), and *In re Ben Huang* (1996).

11. Posner (1972).

12. Even if detailed product-specific R&D cost data were not available, however, one might be able to make a reasonable evaluation of commercial success by comparing a product's profits to the average cost of developing and commercializing broadly similar products.

13. Sometimes, however, as with a "blockbuster" prescription drug that has performance features clearly due to the patent at issue, the sales and profits generated during the first few years of the product's life will be sufficiently large to leave little doubt about the patent's commercial success even if uncertainties remain regarding the precise magnitude of early-stage R&D costs.

14. A further complication relates to the possibility that infringement by a competitor may affect the profitability of a patent holder's product and therefore its apparent commercial success. In order for an analysis of profitability to be of use in assessing commercial success, one should account for the actions of the infringer. Moreover, assessing only the infringer's

profitability, rather than the patent holder's, may not provide an appropriate measure of commercial success. Such a problem could arise if, for example, the infringer had a different cost structure or sold to a different group of customers than the patent holder.

15. Note, however, that the inverse is not necessarily true. For example, in a highly profitable industry, a "below-average" product may still be a commercial success.

16. The discounted net present value (NPV) of a product that generates $10 per year in profits over the next three years will be greater than the NPV of a product that generates $5 next year, $10 the second year, and $15 the third year, even though both products will generate $30 in (undiscounted) profits.

17. Recent studies estimate that only one out of every 5,000 potential drug compounds synthesized during applied research ends up being marketed. *See* Gambardella (1995); and "PhRMA Industry Profile 2003." Only 3 of every 10 approved drugs have sales revenue that exceed the average after-tax development costs of a new drug product. *See* Pharmaceutical Research and Manufacturers of America (2004).

REFERENCES

Cable Electric Products, Inc. v. Genmark, Inc., 770 F.2d 1015, 226 U.S.P.Q. 881 (Fed. Cir. 1985).

Demaco Corp. v. F. Von Langsdorff Licensing Ltd., 851 F.2d 1387, 7 U.S.P.Q. 2d 1222 (Fed. Cir. 1988).

Ecolochem, Inc. v. Southern California Edison Company, 227 F.3d 1361 (Fed. Cir. 2000).

Gambardella, Alfonso. *Science and Innovation: The U.S. Pharmaceutical Industry during the 1980s* (Cambridge, MA: Cambridge University Press, 1995), p. 20.

Graham v. John Deere Co., 383 U.S. 1 (1966).

Hybritech Inc. v. Monoclonal Antibodies, Inc., 802 F.2d 1367 231 U.S.P.Q. 81 (Fed. Cir. 1986).

In re Ben Huang, 100 F.3d 135 40 U.S.P.Q. 2d 1685 (Fed. Cir. 1996).

In re Denis Rouffet, Yannick Tanguy and Frederic Berthault, 149 F.3d 1350 47 U.S.P.Q. 2d 1453 (Fed. Cir. 1998).

J.T. Eaton & Co. v. Atlantic Paste & Glue Co., 106 F.3d 1563, 41 U.S.P.Q. 2d 1641 (Fed. Cir. 1997).

Merck & Co. v. Danbury Pharmacal, Inc., 694 F. Supp. 1, 21 (D. Del. 1988).

Miles Laboratories, Inc. v. Shandon Inc., 1992 WL 503432 (W.D. Pa.).

Neupak, Inc., v. Ideal Manufacturing and Sales Corp., 41 Fed. Appx. 435; 2002 U.S. App. LEXIS 13843 (Fed. Cir. 2002).

Pharmaceutical Research and Manufacturers of America, "The Lengthy and Costly Challenge of Drug Development," in *Leading the Way in the Search for Cures,* available at: www.phrma. org/publications/publications/brochure/leading/index2.cfm (accessed July 6, 2004).

Pharmaceutical Research and Manufacturers of America, *Pharmaceutical Industry Profile* 2003 (Washington, DC: PhRMA, March 2004), pp. 2–6.

Posner, Richard A. *Economic Analysis of Law* (Boston: Little, Brown, 1972), p. 6.

Robbins, Richard L. "Subtests of 'Nonobviousness,'" *University of Pennsylvania Law Review* 112 (1963–1964): 1175.

United States Patent and Trademark Office, *Manual of Patent Examining Procedure,* February 2003 Revision, § 716.03.

CHAPTER 10

Reasonable Royalty as a Measure of Damages in Patent Infringement Matters

VINCENT A. THOMAS
FTI Consulting, Inc.

CHRISTOPHER GERARDI
FTI Consulting, Inc.

DAWN HALL
FTI Consulting, Inc.

In patent litigation, the guiding principle in computing damages is that of "adequately compensating" the patent owner for the infringement. Such adequate compensation can be measured in several ways, but at a minimum it is a reasonable royalty for the infringer's use of the patent owner's technology. In this chapter, we provide an explanation of what a reasonable royalty is, generally accepted methodologies for computing a reasonable royalty, and factors a damages expert should consider in analyzing reasonable royalty damages.[1]

INTRODUCTION

One potential remedy available to a patent owner that successfully proves infringement in a patent infringement matter is monetary damages, which are guided by Section 35 U.S.C. 284 of the United States Code (1970), which states that

> [u]pon finding for the claimant the court shall award damages adequate to compensate for the infringement, *but in no event less than a reasonable royalty for the use made of the invention.* . . . [t]ogether with interest and costs as fixed by the court. The court may increase the damages up to three times the amount. [Emphasis added.]

As with lost profits, it is important to recognize that although the amount of recoverable damages is a question of fact, the measure of damages upon which the factual computation is based is a question of law, as the appropriate measure of damages will be determined by the Court. The role of a damages expert is to prepare various analyses that address the different measures of damages to assist the trier of fact in assessing the amount of damages that will adequately compensate for the infringement.

That said, it is common for a damages expert to set forth an opinion of a reasonable royalty as a measure for the trier of fact to consider in light of the fact that a reasonable royalty is the minimum at which the patent owner is to be compensated. Therefore, this chapter focuses on methods for computing a reasonable royalty. We include descriptions of methodologies employed to compute a reasonable royalty, including a discussion of the case law that supports such methodologies. We also provide a case example and commentary on actual implementation of these methods.

What Is a "Reasonable" Royalty?

License Agreement

A license is an agreement between two or more parties providing permission of the user (e.g., licensee) the right to use the property of the owner (e.g., licensor). The universal element among license agreements in general is that they are profit-sharing arrangements. The licensee can minimize costs and risks by not incurring the time and expense necessary to develop the contributions of the licensor. The licensor also can enjoy economic benefits while at the same time possibly reducing its risk because the licensee is providing complementary assets that the licensor does not have to invest in or develop to achieve such benefits.

Royalty

The royalty is the component of the license agreement that is the *mechanism* by which this negotiated sharing of the expected benefits is transacted. It can take several forms, such as percentage of profits earned or selling price (which can also include convoyed profits or sales generated from the intellectual property), a fixed amount per unit, or a lump sum or minimum payments regardless of the use of the technology. It also can take the form of payments in equity or agreements for other transactions between the parties (i.e., purchasing of additional products for use in the manufacturing process). Typically the licensee must be comfortable with the information it must disclose to compute the royalty payments and the licensor must also be comfortable that it can verify the accuracy of the data. What matters is that the two parties agree to an approach that works for both.

"Reasonable" Royalty

A "reasonable" royalty is a hypothetical royalty that would adequately compensate the patent owner for the use of its patented technology by the infringer. In general, a reasonable royalty is the amount that a willing licensor and willing licensee would agree on. However, the point at which a willing licensor and willing licensee would agree is oftentimes a disputed matter between the parties.

METHODS FOR DETERMINING A REASONABLE ROYALTY RATE

Established Royalty

Several approaches are widely used and have been accepted by the Courts for determining what constitutes a reasonable royalty rate. The Courts accept these approaches assuming they are relevant to the immediate case, are not speculative, and are properly supported by facts and thorough research, properly applied.

One such approach is relying on an established royalty as being the hypothetical reasonable royalty that the patent owner is at a minimum entitled to if infringement is found. In *Hanson v. Alpine Valley Ski Area, Inc.* (1983), the Court concluded that a reasonable royalty " . . . may be based upon an established royalty, if there is one, or if not upon a hypothetical royalty resulting from arm's length negotiations between a willing licensor and a willing licensee." Whether an established royalty exists for the use of the technology at issue depends on the facts and circumstances of each matter. However, as with any method employed, such a conclusion must be adequately supported.

Hypothetical Negotiation (*Georgia-Pacific* Factors)

In addition to any established royalty rate, which is but one factor in determining a reasonable royalty rate, several other approaches are used and are commonly analyzed in the context of a hypothetical negotiation.

Under a hypothetical negotiation, the Court determines what royalty a willing patentee licenser and willing licensee would have arrived at if they had negotiated a license. The hypothetical negotiation takes place on the date that defendant's infringement began.[2] Additionally, for purposes of the hypothetical negotiation, the plaintiff's patents are deemed valid and enforceable and will be infringed by the defendant if the parties do not negotiate a license.[3] The Court must also assume, for purposes of the hypothetical negotiation, that all parties would have known all relevant information.[4] Additionally, in conducting the hypothetical negotiation, the Court, under certain circumstances, may be permitted to look to events and facts that occurred after the infringement began.[5]

Georgia-Pacific Corp. v. United States Plywood Corp., decided in 1970, provides the trier of fact with a list of 15 considerations relevant to the determination of the amount of a reasonable royalty. The fifteenth factor describes a hypothetical negotiation, where the negotiators would consider a variety of factors including the other 14 factors. The factors include such elements as existing relevant licenses; profits of the licensee; the commercial past performance of the invention in terms of public acceptance and price; the market to be tapped; and any other economic factors that a reasonably prudent businessperson would take into consideration under similar circumstances.

The specific *Georgia-Pacific* factors are:

1. The royalties received by the patentee for the licensing of the patents in suit, proving or tending to prove an established royalty. The rates paid by the licensee for the use of other patents comparable to the patents in suit.

2. The nature and scope of the license, as exclusive or nonexclusive; or as restricted or nonrestricted in terms of territory or with respect to whom the manufactured product may be sold.

3. The licensor's established policy and marketing program to maintain his patent monopoly by not licensing others to use the invention or by granting licenses under special conditions designed to preserve that monopoly.

4. The commercial relationship between the licensor and the licensee, such as whether they are competitors in the same territory in the same line of business; or whether they are inventor and promoter.

5. The effect of selling the patented specialty in promoting sales of other products of the licensee; the existing value of the invention to the licensor as a generator of sales of the nonpatented items; and the extent of such derivative or convoyed sales.

6. The duration of the patent and the term of the license.

7. The established profitability of the product made under the patents; its commercial success; and its current popularity.

8. The utility and advantages of the patented property over the old modes or devices, if any, that had been used for working out similar results.

9. The nature of the patented invention; the character of the commercial embodiment of it as owned and produced by the licensor; and the benefits to those who have used the invention.

10. The extent to which the infringer has made use of the invention; and any evidence probative of the value of that use.

11. The portion of the profit or of the selling price that may be customary in the particular business or in comparable businesses to allow for the use of the invention or analogous inventions.

12. The portion of the realizable profit that should be credited to the invention as distinguished from nonpatented elements, the manufacturing process, business risks, or significant features or improvements added by the infringer.

13. The opinion testimony of qualified experts.

14. The amount that a licensor (such as the patentee) and a licensee (such as the infringer) would have agreed on (at the time the infringement began) if both had been reasonably and voluntarily trying to reach an agreement; that is, the amount that a prudent licensee—who desired, as a business proposition, to obtain a license to manufacture and sell a particular article embodying the patented invention—would have been willing to pay as a royalty and yet be able to make a reasonable

profit and which amount would have been acceptable by a prudent patentee who was willing to grant a license.

Analytical Approach

Another approach that has been accepted by the Courts is the analytical approach. In determining a reasonable royalty rate, the analytical approach may be used as an indicator of the economic value of the technology at issue. The analytical approach subtracts a baseline profit from the profit to be realized from sales of infringing products. That profit differential may be utilized to estimate the value of the patented technology.[6]

For example, assume that an infringer's profit margin on a product that claimed to be infringing is 50 percent and that the profit margin on the same product whose only difference was that it did not embody the patented technology is 30 percent. Subtracting the noninfringing profit margin of 30 percent from the 50 percent profit margin on the infringing product, results in a 20 percent margin differential. Under the analytical approach, all or a portion of this profit differential may be considered to determine a reasonable royalty for the use of the patented technology.[7]

Cost Savings

Not only are the profits from the sale of products embodying the patented technology a consideration for determining a reasonable royalty, the cost savings the infringer may have experienced from using the patented technology may also be used as a benchmark. This method looks at the amount of savings enjoyed by a licensee by using the patented technology and assumes that a willing licensee would not pay any more than this cost savings for a license to the technology. As with the analytical approach, all or a portion of this profit differential may be considered to determine a reasonable royalty for the use of the patented technology.[8]

Alternative Design/Noninfringing Alternatives

Prudent licensors and licensees typically take into consideration the economic costs to implement noninfringing alternatives to the patented technology. The economic costs to implement these alternatives may be a consideration in determining an appropriate reasonable royalty. In fact, the decision in *Grain Processing v. American Maize,* decided in 1999, addressed the situation where a noninfringing alternative, although not commercially available in the marketplace at the time of the infringement, would likely have been available "but for" the infringement. The Court found that even if a new process is *not* developed, it is a noninfringing alternative if the necessary materials were available, technical process was known, and the defendant had necessary equipment, know-how, and experience to create the alternative. The Court concluded that the plaintiff was not entitled to lost profits because a noninfringing alternative effectively existed and therefore awarded the plaintiff a small royalty in light of these factors.

CASE EXAMPLE

Background Information

As discussed in Chapter 6, we have devised a simplistic hypothetical example to illustrate the methodology that may be employed to determine the reasonable royalty the patent owner may claim as damages in a patent infringement matter. Our example involves a hypothetical patent for a special handle utilized on reusable razors. The patent owner in our example, Company A, produces and sells both the "Comfort Grip Razor" that embodies the patented technology as well as the "Regular Razor" that does not embody the technology. Other companies that sell reusable razors in our hypothetical example include Company B, Company C, and Company D. Company B produces and sells the "Sure Grip Razor" that infringes Company A's patent on its special handle as well as the " Standard Razor" that does not infringe Company A's patent. Company C and Company D produce and sell the "Normal Razor" and "Common Razor," respectively, neither of which infringes on Company A's patent. The patented "Comfort Grip Razor" was introduced to the market in January 2005, and the infringing "Sure Grip Razor" was introduced in March 2005. The damage period is through December 2005. Through market research and information produced during the litigation, this sales information was uncovered for 2005:

Company	Razor	Quantity	Revenues	Average Sales Price
Company A	Comfort Grip	25,000,000	$122,500,000	$4.90
Company A	Regular	6,000,000	$ 30,000,000	$5.00
Company B	Sure Grip	30,000,000	$146,700,000	$4.89
Company B	Standard	4,000,000	$ 19,920,000	$4.98
Company C	Normal	15,000,000	$ 73,050,000	$4.87
Company D	Common	20,000,000	$ 97,200,000	$4.86
Total		100,000,000	$489,370,000	$4.89

Other documents and information that have been uncovered and produced include:

- Strategic analyses and market studies both Company A and Company B have prepared relative to reusable razors

- Production reports

- Advertising materials and product brochures related to Comfort Grip and Sure Grip

- Company A's and Company B's product line profit and loss statements, balance sheets and tax returns

- Company A's and Company B's sales by customers of all reusable razors

- Various depositions from marketing, sales, finance and operations personnel at both Company A and Company B

- Arm's-length license agreements for comparable technology.

Both Company A and Company B have engaged a financial expert to provide an opinion of damages Company A may be entitled to if Company B is found to have infringed. Company A's financial expert, John Expert, concluded that Company A lost profits on the sales of its Comfort Grip razor it would have sold if Company B had not infringed with its Sure Grip razor. He further concludes that all 4,000,000 units of the Sure Grip sold by Company B would have instead been Company A's Comfort Grip "but for" the infringement and that the incremental profits Company A would have generated on those Comfort Grip sales would have been $7.9 million.[9] Mr. Expert concludes that damages are $7.9 million.

Company B's financial expert, Barbara Witness, sees things a little differently and concludes that, at most, Company A would only have sold an additional 250,000 units of its Comfort Grip had the Sure Grip not been sold in the marketplace. She concludes that the incremental profits on those 250,000 units would have been $500,000. However, Ms. Witness's work is not done because, as stated, under Section 35 U.S.C. 284 of the United States Code (1970), the court shall award damages adequate to compensate for the infringement, *but in no event less than a reasonable royalty for the use made of the invention . . ."* (emphasis added). For the other 3,750,000 units of the Sure Grip that were sold, Company A would be entitled to at a minimum a reasonable royalty for use of the patented technology.

Barbara Witness Calculation

In performing the *Georgia-Pacific* analysis, Ms. Witness acknowledged the commercial relationship between Company A and Company B as well as the razors impact on sales of nonpatented products (e.g., razor blades) and the established profitability of the infringing razors. Ms. Witness also reviewed a number of different licenses that Company A granted around the time of the hypothetical negotiation covering razor technology as well as other licenses granted by other organizations licensing razor technology. The royalty rates for these agreements ranged from $.10 to $.20 per razor. She also reviewed Company A's policy on licensing its technology, which suggests a willingness to license technology. As such, in light of Ms. Witness's investigation and analysis, she concludes that a reasonable royalty that Company B should pay is a rate of $.15 per razor. Therefore, Ms. Witness's opinion of royalties due is $600,000 ($.15 × 4,000,000 units); and her opinion of total damages due is $1.1 million ($500,000 of profits lost plus $600,000 of reasonable royalty).

John Expert Calculation

Even though Mr. Expert has concluded that Company A is entitled to the profits it would have generated if it had sold all 4,000,000 infringing units, it is typical for a damages expert to provide an opinion of what a reasonable royalty would be to assist the trier of fact in the case on the appropriate reasonable royalty appropriate for some or all of the infringing units. As such, Mr. Expert has performed his own analysis and reached his own conclusions as to an appropriate reasonable royalty.

Mr. Expert reviewed the same agreements Ms. Witness reviewed, but instead concluded that they were not relevant in the determination of an appropriate royalty in this case. It was his opinion that the technology at issue was more valuable and important than the technology covered in the license agreements produced. Therefore, in evaluating the *Georgia-Pacific* factors, Mr. Expert placed more weight on other factors. Additionally, Mr. Expert also employed the analytical approach and analyzed the profitability of the Sure Grip razor in comparison to the Standard Grip noting that the that the difference between the Sure Grip and Standard Grip profit margin is 20 percent.

In light of his analysis, Mr. Expert concludes that a reasonable royalty would be 10 percent of the selling price of the Sure Grip razor, which equates to $.50 per razor, which is a rate that is $.35 higher than the rate arrived at by Ms. Witness.

CONCLUSION

Regardless of the approach used in determining a royalty rate, the mechanics of calculating reasonable royalty damages are rather straightforward. Damages are calculated by multiplying the royalty base for the relevant time period by the royalty rate to determine the reasonable royalty dollars. It is important to note that royalty rates need not always be expressed in terms of percentages and may instead represent a per-unit dollar amount, a lump sum, or an escalating royalty rate.

While the mechanics of calculating a reasonable royalty are generally straightforward, computing a reasonable royalty is not an exact science. As we have portrayed in our case example, reasonable people (assuming our hypothetical Mr. Expert and Ms. Witness are reasonable) can develop differing opinions as to what is a "reasonable" royalty. In the end, however, what matters is the conclusion that is ultimately reached by the trier of fact with the aid of a financial expert. As in all damage analysis, thorough review of the facts and circumstances, adequate and appropriate analysis of the data, and detailed support will usually differentiate the outcome.

NOTES

1. The discussion provided herein is of a general nature and have been included for illustrative purposes only. They are not intended to address the specific circumstances of any individual or entity. Each case is different, and should be evaluated in light of its own facts. In specific circumstances, the services of a professional should be sought. The views and opinions are those of the authors and do not reflect any opinions of FTI Consulting, Inc. or its clients as to the proper measure of damages.

2. *Wang Laboratories*, 993 F.2d at 870; *Hanson*, 718 F.2d at 1079; *Panduit*, 575 F.2d at 1158.

3. *TP Orthodontics, Inc. v. Professional Positioners, Inc.* (1991, 1992).

4. *Georgia-Pacific Corp. v. United States Plywood Corp.* (1970, 1971); *TP Orthodontics,* 20 U.S.P.Q. 2d at 1025 (1991, 1992).

5. *Fromson,* 853 F.2d at 1575–76 (1988).

6. E.g., *TWM Mfg. Co. v. Dura Corp.* (1986); *Hanson v. Alpine Valley Ski Area Inc.* (1983).

7. *TWM Manufacturing Co. v. Dura Corp.* (1986).

8. *Hanson v. Alpine Valley Ski Area, Inc.,* 219 USPQ 679; *Smith International, Inc. v. Hughes Tool Company,* 229 U.S.P.Q. 81; *Idacon Inc. v. Central Forest Products Inc.,* 3 U.S.P.Q. 2d 1079 (1986).

9. A more detailed description of the expert witnesses' calculations and the basis for their opinions is presented in Chapter 6.

REFERENCES

Fromson, 853 F.2d at 1575–76 (1988).

Georgia-Pacific Corp. v. United States Plywood Corp., 318 F. Supp. 1116, 1121 (S.D.N.Y. 1970), *modified and aff'd,* 446 F.2d 295 (2d Cir.), *cert. denied,* 404 U.S. 870, 30 L. Ed. 2d 114, 92 S. Ct. 105 (1971).

Hanson v. Alpine Valley Ski Area Inc., 718 F.2d 1075, 1078–82, 219 U.S.P.Q. 679, 681–85 (Fed. Cir. 1983).

Hanson v. Alpine Valley Ski Area, Inc., 718 F.2d 1075, 1078 (Fed. Cir. 1983).

Idacon Inc. v. Central Forest Products Inc., 3 U.S.P.Q. 2d 1079.

Mobil Oil Corporation, vs. Amoco Chemicals Corporation, 915 F. Supp. 1333; 1994 U.S. Dist. Lexis 20851.

TP Orthodontics, Inc. v. Professional Positioners, Inc., 1991 U.S. Dist. LEXIS 9660, 20 U.S.P.Q. 2d 1017, 1025 (E.D. Wis. 1991), *modified on other grounds,* 22 U.S.P.Q. 2d 1628 (E.D. Wis.), *aff'd,* 980 F.2d 743 [**60] (Fed. Cir. 1992).

Panduit Corp. v. Stahlin Bros. Fibre Works, Inc., 575 F.2d 1152, 1164, 197 U.S.P.Q. 726, 736, (6th Cir 1978).

Smith International, Inc. v. Hughes Tool Company, 229 U.S.P.Q. 81 (1986).

State Industries, Inc. v. Mor-Flo Industries, Inc., 883 F.2d 1573, 12 U.S.P.Q. 2d 1026 (CAFC 1989).

TP Orthodontics, Inc. v. Professional Positioners, Inc., 1991 U.S. Dist. LEXIS 9660, 20 U.S.P.Q. 2d 1017, 1025 (E.D. Wis. 1991), *modified on other grounds,* 22 U.S.P.Q. 2d 1628 (E.D. Wis.), *aff'd,* 980 F.2d 743 [**60] (Fed. Cir. 1992).

Trio Process Corp. v. L Goldstein's Sons, 612 F.2d 1353, 1359 (3d Cir. 1980), 612 F.2d at 1359.

TWM Mfg. Co. v. Dura Corp., 789 F.2d 895, 899, 229 USPQ 525, 527 (Fed. Cir.), *cert. denied,* 479 U.S. 852 (1986).

United States Code, Title 35, Section 284.

Wang Laboratories, Inc. v. Toshiba Corp., 993 F.2d 858, 870 (Fed. Cir. 1993) 993 F.2d at 870.

CHAPTER 11

The "Analytical Approach" as a Technique to Determine a Reasonable Royalty

LANCE E. GUNDERSON
FTI Consulting

STEPHEN E. DELL
FTI Consulting

SCOTT W. CRAGUN
FTI Consulting

A party seeking reasonable royalty damages may use various techniques as support for a contended reasonable royalty. One of the methods to support a reasonable royalty analysis is often called the analytical approach. The analytical approach is a way to value the benefit or excess profits of the patented feature(s) of a product relative to a "normal" profit. The profit generated by a prior product, common profit rates in a given industry or company profits can be used to support what is a "normal" profit. Determining whether the facts support the use of the analytical approach is critical; otherwise other methods may be more appropriate. Case law is not entirely clear on the approach, and there are cases in which the approach may be applied inappropriately. In this chapter we discuss the traditional elements of this specific approach that lead to its application in determining a reasonable royalty. We also analyze the use of the analytical approach in a recent case in which the approach was used in context of a reasonable royalty calculation.

INTRODUCTION

The analytical approach has been used where:

> One starts with the selling price of the infringer of the article embodying the infringing feature, and then subtracts three elements, namely the infringer's: (1) Direct and

variable costs in producing the article; (2) Fixed costs, including overhead, to produce the article; and (3) "Normal" profits to the infringer on similar products. All of the remainder is then given to the patentee, and is described to be a "reasonable royalty."[1]

Another application is:

In a hypothetical negotiation, licensee may consider its alternatives to paying the licensor a royalty on the patented product. Generally, the maximum royalty amount that licensee would be willing to pay is the excess profit licensee would expect to earn from the infringing products over the return from its [next best alternative]. The analysis of licensee's position, therefore, focuses on the determination of a "residual" profit from which licensee would be willing to pay a royalty, as follows:

Expected Profit from Infringing Product
Less: Return on Next Best Alternative
Equals: Amount Available to Pay a Royalty[2]

In an analytical approach royalty analysis, the goal is to determine the additional value of the patented technology to the licensee. The logic is that the patent holder should be compensated for the additional benefit of the patent while leaving the user of the technology with a "normal" profit in that industry to remain competitive. Generally, the expected profit or actual profit of the infringing product can be determined. A next step, selecting the appropriate "normal" profit for comparison with the expected or actual profit of the infringing product, is often a challenging task. Practitioners sometimes use the defendant's company-wide profit, profit for similar unpatented products, or even "normal" industry profit. When using a "comparable" product, the comparison should be with "similar products" or the "next best alternative." Ideally, the only difference between the infringing or patented product and the "normal" product is the patented technology or features. In other words, the operating costs (selling, general, and administrative), distribution channels, and the like are identical. Often this ideal situation is not present in a reasonable royalty analysis, which then requires the expert to make adjustments or rely on other royalty methodologies/techniques, such as the *Georgia-Pacific* analysis, cost saving analysis, cost of alternatives, or profit split as a basis for the reasonable royalty. The selection of an inappropriate alternative product to determine "normal" profit, the selection of industry/company profit rates that are not comparable, or the inclusion (exclusion) of costs unrelated to the patented products can result in a flawed or unsupportable reasonable royalty.

SUMMARY OF THE CASE LAW

Courts have considered numerous factors in determining an appropriate reasonable royalty in patent infringement litigation. A list of 15 factors regularly used and approved by the courts is set forth in the 1970 District Court opinion *Georgia-Pacific v. United States Plywood* and discussed at length elsewhere in this book. The court considered this "list of evidentiary facts relevant, in general, to the determination of the amount of a reasonable royalty for a patent license" to arrive at a reasonable royalty.

Interestingly, even though the *Georgia-Pacific* factors are used as the basis for the royalty analysis in many cases, on appeal the 2nd Circuit Court used a method not specifically addressed in one of the 15 factors in that case itself. The written decision states:

> Thus, although we affirm the other findings, we feel that despite the trial court's professed intention to do so, it did not allow GP a reasonable profit after paying the suppositious royalty. . . . Since the error was to leave GP no profit at all after payment of the suppositious reasonable royalty of $50 per thousand square feet, we must first determine what would be a reasonable profit for GP after payment of the royalty. We note that the Master found, on the basis of GP's annual reports, that GP's average net profit on sales of all products during the period of infringement was slightly over nine per cent of sales . . . It follows that GP would have been willing to pay a royalty which, after payment of its costs, would leave it nine per cent profit on sales of the licensed item. Since the trial court found that GP's "average realization" on those sales was $159.41 . . . such a profit would be $14.35 per thousand square feet in the present case. The remainder is arithmetic:

> | | |
> |---|---|
> | GP's expected profit on the item: | $50.00 per thousand square feet |
> | Less: 9% profit on sales: | − 14.35 |
> | Assumed reasonable royalty: | $35.65 |

> . . . we feel that a reasonable royalty of $35.65 per thousand square feet is a fair one on the basis of the record before us. Accordingly, we modify the lower court's award of a reasonable royalty of $50.00 per thousand square feet to $35.65 per thousand square feet. . . .

In subsequent written decisions concerning patent infringement damages, this method of determining a reasonable royalty is discussed and accepted. For example, in a 1977 opinion, *Tektronix v. The United States, et al.,* the United States Court of Claims states:

> The negotiation formula which the trial judge borrowed from Georgia-Pacific is . . . to start with the infringer's selling price, deduct its costs in order to find its gross profit,[3] then allocated to the infringer its normal profit, and end up with the residual share of the gross profit which can be assigned to the patentee as its royalty. We utilize the same formula as the beginning of our suppositious negotiation . . .

As discussed, this method of determining a reasonable royalty is commonly referred to as the analytical approach. The analytical approach was formalized by the Federal Circuit Court of Appeals in the 1986 *TWM Manufacturing Co., Inc. v. Dura Corp., et al.* decision. In that opinion it states:

> The special master . . . used the so-called "analytical approach," in which she subtracted the infringer's usual or acceptable net profit from its anticipated net profit realized from sales of infringing devices. Relying principally on a memorandum written by "Dura's top management" before the initial infringement, the special master found that Dura projected a gross profit averaging 52.7% from its infringing sales. From that figure, she subtracted overhead expenses to get an anticipated net profit in the range

of 37% to 42%. Subtracting the industry standard net profit of 6.56% to 12.5% from that anticipated net profit range, she arrived at a 30% reasonable royalty . . . Dura has cited nothing which would limit the district court's discretion in choosing the analytical approach to determine a reasonable royalty.

The Federal Circuit Court of Appeals affirmed in all respects the appealed judgment.

ECONOMIC CONSIDERATIONS

The use of the analytical approach is generally helpful in determining a reasonable royalty, but careful consideration should be taken in the selection of the "normal" profit[4] for comparison. Even if the case facts do not provide an "ideal situation," as discussed, some application of the analytical approach may still be useful in a reasonable royalty analysis. Based on the case facts available, the analytical approach may be an overriding consideration in the determination of a reasonable royalty, or it may be one of several considerations, such as the consideration of the *Georgia-Pacific* factors mentioned.

Ideally, the comparison used in the analytical approach should be between the patented product and a prior product, which helps ensure (but does not guarantee it to the extent the new product contains unpatented elements not present on the prior product or costs unrelated to the patented product) that changes in profit rate are not attributable to nonpatented business factors. The comparison can be with industry "standard"-type profits or profits for the company as a whole prior to the introduction of the patented product, but other factors aside from the technology may come into play and render the resulting differential less meaningful or even meaningless.

Certain situations with specific products are more conducive to the use of the analytical approach than others. The expert should feel comfortable that any profit premium realized is related to the patent(s) and not other differences between the normal product or profit and the patented product. For example, Round-Up™ ready corn seed has patented genes that are spliced into the corn seed that allows for the use of Round-Up™ to kill virtually all weeds but not the corn itself. The patent is the major difference between prior corn seed and the patented Round-Up™ ready corn. Much of the price premium and corresponding profit premium can be attributed directly to the patent(s). However, a myriad of differences may exist between a certain patented semiconductor and the prior-generation semiconductor including: multiple patents, know-how, trade secrets, improved manufacturing processes, additional features, and so on. The applicability of the analytical approach to the product in question should be carefully considered by the expert.

Another important consideration to analyze thoroughly is whether all additional profit derived from selling the patented product should be awarded to the patent holder. Certain situations consider the additional profit attributable to the patented invention and should therefore be awarded to the patent holder, allowing the accused infringer to keep his or her normal profit. It is important to consider all of the relevant facts surrounding each company's operations. In analyzing these data, one may find that the infringer may take on additional risks selling the accused product and should therefore be entitled to keep a greater portion of the excess profits.

CASE EXAMPLE

Background

In 2001, one of the leading game call manufacturers ("the Plaintiff") brought suit against its primary competitor ("the Defendant") alleging infringement of certain U.S. patents.[5] Game calls have been developed for many years as a way to attract game animals by replicating the various sounds and vocalizations that each animal makes. These calls serve many users including hunters, photographers, wildlife watchers, and outdoor enthusiasts. As part of the suit, Plaintiff claimed that the Defendant's in-mouth diaphragm game calls infringed two of its patents ("the patents at issue").

Traditional in-mouth diaphragm calls have been used for over half a century for both elk and turkey hunting[6] (see Exhibit 11.1). Historically, in-mouth diaphragm calls have been very difficult to use or "blow." The primary structural difference between the traditional diaphragm call and the claimed invention is the use of a "cover structure" over the latex reed which is the basis for the patents at issue. Though there are many claimed advantages of this game call, one of the most important aspects of the patented invention promoted by the Plaintiff and the Defendant was that it is easier to blow than the traditional in-mouth diaphragm calls making them easier to use for beginners and professionals.

In the mid-1990s, the Plaintiff began marketing and selling a product using the patented technology employing the cover structure (see Exhibit 11.2). In 2001, the Defendant began selling a product with a cover structure (see Exhibit 11.3).

Plaintiff's Use of the Analytical Approach

Each party retained a damages expert who offered opinion testimony through a proffered expert report, deposition, and at trial. The Plaintiff's expert opined to lost profits claiming that "but for" the infringement, the Plaintiff would have sold its patented in-mouth

EXHIBIT 11.1 TRADITIONAL GAME CALL

EXHIBIT 11.2   PLAINTIFF'S PATENTED
GAME CALL

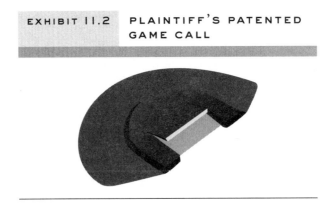

game calls in place of the Defendant's game calls. To the extent the alleged infringing sales were not awarded as lost profits, the Plaintiff's expert opined to a running royalty applied to the Defendant's game call sales.

As part of his support for his reasonable royalty calculation, the Plaintiff's damages expert testified that this game call case was well suited for the use of the analytical approach because the only difference between the accused game call and the traditional game call was the patented feature. The table demonstrates the calculation.[7]

	Average Price	Average Cost	Gross Profit
Accused Game Call	$3.67	$0.77	$2.90
Traditional Call	$2.65	$0.73	$1.92
Difference	$1.02	$0.04	$0.98

The Defendant's game call sold on average for $3.67 and cost $0.77 to manufacture, resulting in an average gross profit of $2.90 per game call. A traditional game call sold for $2.65 on average and cost $0.73 to manufacture, resulting in a gross profit of $1.92 per game call. The operating costs for both the accused and traditional calls were in all material respects the same, as were the sales and marketing costs.[8] Thus, analytically, the

EXHIBIT 11.3   DEFENDANT'S ACCUSED
GAME CALL

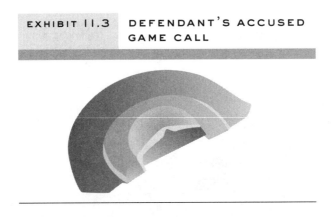

value of the technology was $0.98 per call, or almost 27 percent of the average selling price of the call. The Plaintiff's damages expert reasoned that, from an analytical standpoint, the Defendant would be willing to pay up to 27 percent as a royalty rate since a royalty of 27 percent would allow the Defendant to make the same profit it would have expected to make on its traditional game call. However, based on other evidence available in the case, including an analysis of the *Georgia-Pacific* factors, the Plaintiff's expert did not attribute 100 percent of this additional benefit to be paid as a royalty and opined to a lower royalty rate, leaving a portion of the additional profit to the Defendant.

Defendant's Use of the Analytical Approach

The Defendant's damages expert asserted lost profits were inappropriate and that a reasonable royalty was the appropriate measure of damages. The Defendant's expert opined to a two-tiered royalty based on whether the accused product was a turkey game call or an elk game call. Also referencing the analytical approach, the Defendant's expert arrived at a vastly different result. His calculation is shown in the next table.[9]

	Average Price	Average Cost	Gross Profit	Gross Profit %
Accused Game Call	$3.67	$0.77	$2.90	79%
Traditional Call	$2.65	$0.73	$1.92	72%
Difference	$1.02	$0.04	$0.98	7%

The Defendant's expert used the 7 percent difference in gross profit percentage as part of his support for his royalty rate opinion and implied that, analytically, 7 percent was the value of the patented technology at issue.

While the Defendant's expert compared the gross profit percentages of each game call, he apparently failed to consider the additional price increase of the accused product. The Defendant's expert apparently ignored the fact that due to the patented feature, the Defendant was able to sell the call at a higher price. In doing this, that is subtracting gross profit *percentages* rather than *per-unit dollars,* the Defendant's expert apparently failed to capture the essence of the analytical approach and the true economic benefit of the patented feature. The Plaintiff argued that this was a misapplication that resulted in a less meaningful result and did not capture the entire value of the patented feature.

Damages Summary

Both liability and damages were presented to the jury in a two-week trial. After short deliberations, the jury found that the Defendant's accused game call infringed the patents at issue. The jury awarded both lost profits and a reasonable royalty to the Plaintiff, with the reasonable royalty being applied to sales that the jury found not to be attributable to lost profits. In calculating the reasonable royalty damages, the jury accepted and applied the royalty rate opinion of the Plaintiff's expert.

CONCLUSION

Different experts look at the analytical approach in different ways. However, the analytical approach becomes more useful in determining a reasonable royalty when the major difference in the patented product and "next best alternative" or "comparable product" is the patented feature(s). Any additional (or lack thereof) features or business practices may cloud the true value of the patent(s), and an alternative methodology may be better suited to arrive at the appropriate reasonable royalty.

The analytical approach can supplement a traditional *Georgia-Pacific* analysis and can be an effective technique to help establish an appropriate royalty for technology. Certain pitfalls, such as the use of incomparable sales and costs and corresponding profits, can lead the expert to an inappropriate conclusion. Given the correct case facts, the analytical approach to a reasonable royalty can be quite compelling as to the determination or support of an appropriate royalty rate.

NOTES

1. Goldscheider and Maier (1989).
2. Phillips and Gerard (1990).
3. Implicit in the court's use of gross profit as a basis for the analytical approach is the assumption that SG&A costs (or costs below the gross margin line) are the same for the patented product and the product(s) with the "normal" profit. To the extent it can be shown that the SG&A costs are materially different, such differences should be accounted for to yield an accurate analytical approach result.
4. The selection of what constitutes "normal" profit can be problematic. The sales used for "normal" profit may not be comparable products and/or the costs (both gross and operating) may be different from the patented product, thus yielding an erroneous royalty rate.
5. *Primos, Inc. v. Hunter's Specialties, Inc., et al.* (Civil Action No. C01-4 MJM, U.S. Dist. Ct for the Northern District of Iowa (Cedar Rapids Division) May 10, 2001 (Amended). The authors served as consultants for the Plaintiff in this matter; of course the Defendant did not agree with the Plaintiff's perspective of the determination of damages.
6. Diaphragm calls are also used to call other animals, but their primary purpose is for elk and turkey.
7. Sales, cost, and profit information have been modified from actual information to protect confidential information from both parties.
8. The expert opined that all operating costs were the same and that this case allowed for the use of a "gross profit" comparison rather than an operating or incremental profit comparison.
9. Sales, cost, and profit information have been modified from actual information to protect confidential information from both parties.

REFERENCES

Georgia-Pacific Corporation v. United States Plywood Corporation, 318 F. Supp. 1116, 1120 (S.D.N.Y 1970).

Georgia-Pacific Corporation v. U.S. Plywood-Champion Papers Inc., 446 F.2d 295, 299 (2d Cir. 1971).

Tektronix, Inc. v. The United States, et al., 213 Ct. Cl. 257, 269 (Ct. Cl. 1977).

Goldscheider, Robert, and Gregory J. Maier. *Licensing Law Library: 1989 Licensing Law Handbook* (New York: Clark Boardman Company, 1989), pp. 82–83.

Phillips, Scott D., and Elizabeth M. Gerard. "The 'Super Royalty': Alternative Approaches to Its Determination," *Licensing Law and Business Report* (September–October 1990): 176.

Primos, Inc. v. Hunter's Specialties, Inc., et al. (Civil Action No. C01-4 MJM, U.S. Dist. Ct. for the Northern District of Iowa (Cedar Rapids Division).

TWM Manufacturing Co., Inc. v. Dura Corp. and Kidde, Inc., 789 F.2d 895, 899 (Fed. Cir. 1986).

CHAPTER 12

A Quasi-Comparable Approach to Reasonable Royalty Determination

JEFFREY A. DUBIN
Visiting Professor of Economics
University of California, Santa Barbara
Co-Founder and Partner
Pacific Economics Group, Pasadena, California

Intangible technology assets have value arising from proprietary knowledge, processes, or methods that provide competitive advantages through product differentiation or favorable cost structures. This chapter calculates a royalty rate for a technology intangible asset using economic analysis of quasi-comparables. The method calculates what consumers would be willing to pay for a patented feature embodied in a consumer good. Analyzing products, with and without the patented feature, allows quasi-comparability even in situations where true comparable sales do not exist. I demonstrate that market information can establish an upper bound to the royalty and profit rate attributable to a technology intangible. I apply this model to a computer CPU upgrade technology used in the early 1990s.

INTRODUCTION

Intangible technology assets have value arising from proprietary knowledge, processes, or methods that provide competitive advantages through product differentiation or favorable cost structures. Such assets are generally protected by trade secrets, patents, or copyrights. For instance, the owner of a technology patent may receive value from the patent in three ways:

1. The patent owner may exploit the patent itself to the legal exclusion of others.
2. The patent owner may sell all rights to the patented invention.
3. The owner may license to others.

The value of the patent depends on several factors, including its scope of application (economic, technological, and legal), its duration of application (legally limited to a fixed period of time but often constrained by noninfringing or superior substitutes), and its royalty or profit rate.

Several techniques are employed for valuing technology intangibles. In the market approach or comparables approach, sales of comparable assets establish a value. In the cost approach, the cost of reproducing the existing invention or determining its replacement cost provides a useful value especially when the technology is replaceable and not unique. Another approach (the income approach) to valuation is based on the examination of the income stream related to the invention (typically the incremental income arising from the technology intangible during its economic and legal lifetime). Valuation approaches may include calculation of cost savings from avoided royalty payments (relief from royalty) or an estimate of the royalty rate set between arm's-length licensors and licensees. In the case of patent infringement, the determination of damage due a patent holder may be based on reasonable royalties in lieu of lost profits in some circumstances. In many situations, however, a market comparable does not exist because the technology at issue cannot be isolated from the ultimate product that utilizes the technology. In this case, the profit attributable to the invention and resulting royalty rate are not easily measured.

This chapter calculates a royalty rate for a technology intangible asset using economic analysis of quasi-comparables. The method considers the price consumers are willing to pay for a patented technology intangible embodied in a consumer good. By *quasi-comparables* I mean a set of consumer products with and without the technology at issue or a single product capable of being used in distinct modes by the consumer (e.g., enabling or using a feature of the product).[1] Analyzing products with and without the patented feature (or using or not using the patented feature) allows quasi-comparability even in situations where true comparable sales do not exist. My technique is therefore similar to a "but for analysis or to the valuation of a trademark based on the value of a product to a manufacturer if forced to sell the product without its trademark.[2] I demonstrate that market information may be available to establish an upper bound on the royalty and profit rate attributable to the technology at issue. This is done outside of the hypothetical negotiation paradigm of *Panduit* and its progeny.

The patent I examine was awarded to the computer manufacturer Acer in 1991. The patent pertains to a consumer upgrade strategy. Consumer upgrades often appear in consumer goods and include memory upgrades in computers, memory upgrades in cameras, and software upgrades. By 1990, upgrading of personal computers (PCs) had become common. Consumers wanted a method to protect their investment in PCs against technological obsolescence.[3] In order to meet this need, most major manufacturers developed their own schemes for providing upgrades. In 1991, Acer applied for and received U.S. patent (5,455,927, con't of Aug. 22, 1991, "dual-socket"). Acer refers to its patents as the "Chip Up" technology. The Chip-Up technology pertains to upgrading a computer by adding a second (typically faster) control processing unit (CPU) in a socket reserved for the upgrade. A user could upgrade a computer by adding the newer CPU in the reserved socket at any time. As I discuss, using a primary socket for the main CPU and a secondary socket reserved for the upgrade implies that Acer's system is a dual-socket design. The sockets that receive the processors in Acer's design are contained on the main circuitry board (motherboard) of the computer.

The Chip-Up technology patent was designed to upgrade Intel 80386 (386) computers by a specific method. This patent would not have applied to computer upgrades using other apparently noninfringing designs (e.g., modular, daughterboard, card, cartridge, over-clocking, etc.) and would not have applied to upgrades of Intel 80486 (486) and Intel 80586 (Pentium) computers. The value of the Chip-Up technology is small due to the availability of substitutes and the limited applicable scope.

SCOPE, DURATION, AND NONINFRINGING SUBSTITUTES

Upgrading a computer might involve enlarging disk drive storage, adding random access memory (RAM) or cache memory to the motherboard, adding a math coprocessor to speed up numerical calculations, or changing the 386/387 pair to specialized chips for computer-aided design. A consumer could also upgrade a computer by over-clocking the existing CPU (running the CPU at higher clock than it was designed for). I mention these non-CPU upgrade paths because different consumers would find some upgrades more advantageous than others.[4] For instance, many applications were slowed by poor hard disk performance or insufficient disk storage space. Other applications operated slowly due to too little RAM in the computer. Some consumers did require a speed increase in their CPU. However, independent of processor speed, the preferred upgrade path for many of these consumers was a non-CPU upgrade. For example, for a great many consumers, a coprocessor to do mathematical calculations would have been the most logical upgrade. In fact, most 386 motherboards contained one or two empty sockets for coprocessors. In most cases, these coprocessors were used for arithmetic processor upgrades (adding a 387 or Weitek chip). However, in some cases, the sockets were used for other CPU upgrades.[5]

Variety of Computer Upgrade Technologies

Since the first generation of IBM PCs, it was common practice to use empty sockets for motherboard upgrades (e.g., the 8087 paired with the 8086, the 80287 paired with the 80286 and the 80387 or the Weitek paired with the 80386). Replacing existing chips with higher-speed versions or overclocking were other common upgrade paths for consumers who did not choose a full "generation skip." A *generation skip* is defined as a movement between families of CPUs, such as upgrading from a 386 to a 486. Acer's design contemplated a generation-skip upgrade.

The Acer design was not the only design to accomplish a generation-skip upgrade. Some manufacturers used a modular upgrade (a daughter-board) on which the CPU and its replacement could be interchanged in the computer (utilizing the original CPU socket for the daughter-board and hence termed a single-socket upgrade). Another upgrade solution relied on cards that plugged into the computer's bus, often using proprietary high-speed bus interfaces to maximize the computer's throughput. Other manufacturers (e.g., Acer and Atman) relied on an additional socket for the upgrade.

Acer's technique was identical to a coprocessor upgrade in that Acer left an empty socket for CPU additions to enhance performance. The 8086 system generally left one empty socket for the coprocessor. The 80286 system left one empty socket. The first 386 computers generally left two empty sockets—one for the existing 287 math coprocessor and another for the yet-to-be-released 387 math coprocessor. The preponderance of 386 systems left two empty sockets. The first empty socket was for a 387 math coprocessor while the second was left for the Weitek math coprocessor. Some dual CPU systems provided both I860 (Intel) and 80X86 (80286 and 80386) CPUs on the same motherboard, although only one processor had control at a time. In fact, there was nothing new in Acer's patent with respect to having empty sockets on the motherboard for the permanent or transitory use of a second processor.

Intel's "vacant socket" technique for upgrading 486 systems relied solidly on prior art to provide an upgrade path. Intel's upgrade method reused the existing coprocessor socket for coprocessor or CPU upgrades. By contrast, Acer's technique leaves the original CPU and coprocessor sockets and adds an additional socket reserved for the CPU upgrade. Acer's dual-socket approach was therefore only minimally different from Intel's approach. Intel's approach reused an existing empty socket whereas Acer's approach added an additional empty socket.[6] My review of the technology indicates that 486 systems were upgraded by using well-established prior art (coprocessor slots). It is for this reason that the Acer patents would not apply to any system beyond 386-based systems.

The presence of third-party upgrade solutions that were of similar quality also crowded the upgrade market. Many competitors would lead consumers to elastically demand the dual-socket motherboard design. The presence of competition would have led to lower royalty rates.

My extensive searches of *Byte* magazine and my review of articles published in other computer magazines from the 1989 to 1993 period showed few designs for upgradeable systems using the dual-socket approach. This is a very significant finding. If PC manufacturers or motherboard manufacturers used dual-socket upgrade designs and if this was an important selling feature to consumers, then I would have expected to see extensive disclosures in product advertisements of this upgrade method. On the contrary, very few manufacturers based an upgrade on the dual-socket technology, and none of the major manufacturers other than Acer adopted this technique. For new technologies, such as computer upgrades, the reputation or brand name of the manufacturer is a very important aspect of the consumer's purchase decision. Without the strong reputation or brand name of a major PC manufacturer, the dual-socket upgrade technique would in and of itself be of limited value as it would play a limited role in promoting consumer sales.

Acer Computer was the only manufacturer with any name recognition that sold dual-socket upgradeable systems. Other "brand" manufacturers of the day included EPSON,

Leading Edge, Hewlett-Packard, Toshiba, and Zenith. Available evidence suggests that their computers provided no upgrade path for their systems and instead relied on after-market (third-party) designs for customer upgrades. Of the top 20 personal computer companies in unit sales, Acer was the only company to use a dual-socket design for some of its personal computer systems. Dubin finds that 65 percent of PCs circa 1990 to 1995 provided upgrade solutions.[7] Of those that were identified as providing some upgrade path, only 2 of 23 used a dual-socket design. Furthermore, the only users of dual-socket designs appear to have been Taiwanese manufacturers. Approximately 11 percent of U.S. imports of all computer products came from Taiwan.[8] If Acer's design had been adopted by 50 percent of Taiwanese manufacturers, then only 5.5 percent of the nonbranded PC systems of the day would have used the dual-socket design.[9]

Duration Limitations

Consumers faced with rapid technological change come to expect significant price decreases in older technology as newer technology is introduced. The consequence of the rapid decline in CPU prices is that the value of the upgrade option diminishes over time. Indeed, the second-socket option in the dual-socket motherboard will have its highest value (providing an upgrade from 386 to 486 technology) when the price of 486 CPUs is also at its highest point and expected to decline the most. As the price of 486 CPUs decline, the value consumers place on a second socket system in a dual-socket motherboard CPU speeds also declines. This short interval during which consumers place a significant value for the second socket in the dual-socket system, in conjunction with the rapid decline in the 486 personal computer systems price, leads me to conclude that the time interval when dual-socket motherboards would have been desired by consumers was short. This implies that a reasonable royalty value for the design would have declined rapidly over time as the option value faded rapidly.

By 1993, 386 CPU sales and 386-based computer systems had peaked and were declining significantly. Specifically, the market for 386 computers had peaked by 1991. While sales of SX-based systems (low-end, 16-bit interface processors) continued somewhat in 1992 and 1993, 386 DX sales were exhausted by 1993. At the time, 486-based system sales were on the increase. These observations follow exactly a classical product life cycle pattern. Further, the prices for these systems and CPUs had also declined significantly. From various issues of *Byte* magazine, I observed that the 386/33 MHz CPU sold for approximately $345 in 1989. By 1990, its price had fallen to $225, to $140 by 1992, and to $90 by 1993. Price declines also occurred in 486 CPUs and systems. In May 1991, a 486/33 MHz CPU sold for $1,150. By October 1992, its price had declined by two-thirds, to approximately $360. The biggest price declines in 486 system prices and CPU prices occurred between 1991 and 1992. For instance, motherboard prices including 486/33 MHz CPUs were approximately $2,095 in May 1991. These same motherboards were sold for $849 in May 1992.

In summary, the Chip-Up method would have applied to a very limited number of 386 computer systems manufactured in Taiwan during the years 1991 through 1993. Based on the evidence of price declines in 486 CPUs, I conclude that the upgrade would have some value to consumers in 1990 and 1991, lower value in 1992, and virtually no value by 1993. Since the values consumers place on the upgrade socket determine its usefulness as a product feature and consequently determine the reasonable royalty paid by resellers, royalty values would have had a similar pattern. Moreover, the availability of noninfringing substitutes and rapidly declining 486 prices placed further limits on the economic value of the technology.

VALUE OF A CONSUMER UPGRADE OPTION

This section analyzes how consumers value an upgrade option. My model shows that consumers value the upgrade greatest when the price of the next-generation processor is also at its peak. This is also the time when the next-generation processor's price is expected to decline the most. As the next-generation processor's price declines, so does the value of the upgrade option.

The pricing model is based on a number of assumptions that reasonably describe how consumers value computer systems according to their performance. I assume in my model that the 386 processor has a speed of 1 unit. (This is a normalization that is not consequential.) Consumers can increase their computer's speed by switching to a processor in the 486 generation and receive a speed increase of γ. The system costs an amount C and the additional cost for the second socket (the upgrade solution in the dual-socket design) costs S to the consumer. Finally, today's cost of a 486 chip will be denoted by P_0, and the cost in one year (the upgrade period) is $\tilde{P}_1$. I assume that the system cost includes a 386 CPU and that the 386 has little or no residual value in one year's time. Finally, I assume that a given consumer values speed at the rate of λ per unit of speed.

Different consumers will have different values, λ, leading some to purchase a 486 today rather than waiting. Other consumers will choose to wait to get a 486 via an upgrade. The value today for a risk-neutral consumer who upgrades in one year is:

$$V_u = \lambda + \lambda(1 + \gamma) - C - S - \tilde{P}_1$$
$$= \lambda + \lambda(1 + \gamma) - C - S + \tilde{r}P_0 - P_0$$

where $\tilde{r} = (P_0 - \tilde{P}_1)/P_0$ is rate of decline in 486 prices between year 0 and year 1

The value of upgrading is equal to the value of processing in the first year, λ, plus the value of processing in the second year at higher speed, $\lambda(1 + \gamma)$, less the cost of system C, less the cost of the socket S, less the cost of the buying a new 486 chip at price $\tilde{P}_1$ in the second year. The value of buying a 486 computer system today is $V = 2\lambda(1 + \gamma) - C - P_0$. It is equal to two years of value at the higher processor speed less the system cost and less the cost of buying a 486 today. I assume that there is no extra socket cost if the consumer buys the 486 personal computer straightaway.

The maximum a consumer would pay for the option to upgrade equates these two values since if the consumer paid any more for the socket, it would be better for that consumer to upgrade immediately. Hence the price of the upgrade socket cannot exceed: $S \leq -\lambda\gamma + \tilde{r}P_0$. This implies that consumers value the upgrade most when the price today is highest and when the (expected) decline is largest. Consumers will value the socket less when the speed difference is larger because they will value the speed in the first year to a higher degree, that is, there is a greater opportunity cost of not using the faster processor. Risk-adverse consumers will value the socket less than risk-neutral consumers, given the uncertainty in the future rate of price decline. Additionally, a positive rate of time preference will make consumers prefer faster speeds today rather than next year and further lower the implicit socket value.

DETERMINING A REASONABLE ROYALTY

The inequality determined in the last section places an upper limit on the value of the upgrade option. This upper limit may be fairly broad. For instance, between 1991 and 1992, the average price decline in 486 CPUs was on the order of 70 percent. Meanwhile, a switch in processors from the 386 to 486 class at this time resulted in a nearly 250 percent increase in speed. Using an average price for 486 CPUs in 1991 of approximately $1,000, the socket would be worth as little as zero for consumers with speed valuations as high as $466 per unit speed (unit speed is taken to be speed of 386 CPU at 33 Mhz). Under my assumptions, consumers must value speed at least at $200 per unit speed if 486 computers would have had positive surplus or if an upgrade from a 386 to a 486 using the upgrade option would have had positive surplus. Using these figures, the socket could cost as much as $400 before consumers would stop upgrading altogether. This range is clearly too large to be useful. Clearly the distribution of consumer's valuation of computer speed is critical to determining the upgrade socket's value. Alternatively, auxiliary information regarding the fraction of consumers actually choosing upgrades could be used to narrow this range. Such data are not available in this case.

Instead, I establish a reasonable royalty based on quasi-comparables. Using advertisements by Atman, a manufacturer of motherboards that used a dual-socket upgrade, I analyzed the prices for motherboards in September 1992. Atman's motherboard with a 386/40 MHz CPU then sold for $200. Using *Byte* magazine, I determined that Intel 386/40 MHz CPU chips were selling for $80 to $100 at this time. At the same time, Atman offered the same motherboard with a 486/33 MHz CPU for $480. During this period, 486/33 MHz CPUs sold in the range of $340 to $380. Hence I ascertained that the Atman motherboard was worth approximately $100 to $140 (the total price less the CPU cost). This price is little different from the price that Acer sold its motherboards for in 1992. Furthermore, prices for the motherboard with 386 CPU imply a value of $100 to $120 together for the motherboard and the empty socket. Using M to represent the value of the motherboard and S to represent the value of the socket, it follows that $100 \leq M \leq $140 and $100 \leq M + S \leq$ $120, so that $0 \leq S \leq $20. Since both products are sold in market equilibrium, the socket has an implicit value between $0 and $20. I take the average value in this range of $10. Furthermore, manufacturing is not free and involves an incremental cost of $1 or more. Thus, incremental profits are no more than $9.00 for the socket at retail. Assuming a retailer or dealer markup of approximately 33 percent implies that the profit to the manufacturer is about $6.00. Of this amount, the licensee will typically receive 25 percent while the licensor will receive the remainder.[10] Hence, a patent owner might expect roughly $1.50 from the sale of each motherboard. Using the 386 motherboard price with CPU as the base for calculation of the royalty percentage, the royalty rate would be approximately 0.75 percent. This figure is in the middle of range given by Smith (1997) when applied to commercial/industrial corporate trademarks.

CONCLUSION

For technology intangibles and especially for technology embodied in final consumer products either as a feature or through a step in manufacturing, market transactions of comparable products may not exist. In such cases, the method of quasi-comparables or "but for" analysis may be used. This technique measures the value of the invention by inferring the price consumers would be willing pay for a product with or without the patented feature or the value to a consumer of a product with or without a particular patented feature enabled. Using these comparisons, it is possible to place an upper bound on the reasonable royalty or to infer its likely duration of applicability. In the case of the Chip-Up technology, I found that the patent would have limited value. The market for computer upgrades using the Chip-Up technology was limited in scope and duration, and by the presence of noninfringing substitutes. Economic analysis of related consumer products with and without the dual-socket technology implied royalty rates at the low-end of typical values for commercial corporate assets. This calculation was done outside the fiction of a hypothetical negotiation between licensor and licensee.

NOTES

1. In some cases, such products must be envisioned as hypothetical constructs since not every configuration of products is sold in the marketplace.
2. See Dubin, Chapter 4 (1998).
3. The situation is somewhat different today. Computers are fast enough for most users and sufficiently inexpensive that the entire computer is replaced rather than upgraded after a relatively short period of usage (two to three years).
4. Upgrading a PC (especially a motherboard upgrade) was never considered an easy process. For instance, *Byte* magazine (1991) noted that replacing a CPU is a "nightmare," recommending only "the most grizzled hardware veterans" attempt it. Problems with user upgrades include breaking pins on the old or new CPU, destroying a part with static discharge, BIOS incompatibilities, failure of the system to function after the upgrade, software incompatibilities, and so on. These issues made CPU upgrades a non–user-friendly task. Consequently, the market for CPU upgrades was not large even in 1990.
5. For example, the Intel CAD discussed in *PC Week* (1992).

6. An Intel senior vice president, David House, noted that "starting with the new 486SX CPU board, the coprocessor is no longer just a math coprocessor socket—it has become a universal upgrade socket." House also noted that Intel would introduce several products that fit into this socket to increase not only math performance but overall system performance as well. House said, "Some systems today have an upgrade path. Today you can insert a 487 math chip to boost math performance. Next year, you'll be given a second upgrade that will run at 40 MHz internally." *PC Week* (1992).

7. Dubin, Chapter 4 (2001).

8. U.S. Department of Commerce and EIA Research Department (1990).

9. Based on historical PC sales, the number of PCs that potentially infringed the patent would haven been less than 131,000 during the period from 1991 through 1993; see Dubin, Chapter 4, 2001).

10. Goldscheider (1980) and Goldscheider, Jarosz, and Mulhern (2002).

REFERENCES

Byte magazine 16, no. 14 (April 1, 1991): 283–286.

Dubin, Jeffrey A. *Empirical Studies in Applied Economics* (Boston: Kluwer Academic Publishers, 2001).

Dubin, Jeffrey A. *Studies in Consumer Demand—Econometric Methods Applied to Market Data* (Boston: Kluwer Academic Publishers, 1998).

Goldscheider, Robert, and James T. Marshall. "The Art of Licensing—From the Consultant's Point of View," Vol. 2, *The Law and Business of Licensing,* 1980, p. 645.

Goldscheider, Robert, John Jarosz, and Carla Mulhern. "Use of The 25 Per Cent Rule in Valuing IP," *Les Nouvelles Journal of the Licensing Executives Society* 37, no. 4 (December 2002): 123–133.

"Intel Coprocessor to Boost CAD Performance on 386 PCs," *PC Week* 9, no. 7 (February 17, 1992): 30.

Smith, Gordon. *Trademark Valuation* (New York: John Wiley & Sons, 1997).

U.S. Department of Commerce and EIA Research (1990).

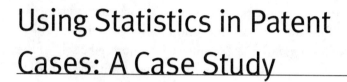

CHAPTER 13

Using Statistics in Patent Cases: A Case Study

Esfandiar Maasoumi
SMU, Dallas, TX

Matthew G. Mercurio
FTI Consulting, Inc.

While the use of statistics (particularly survey methods) in copyright and trademark matters continues to grow, statistics has seen far less use in patent cases. However, elementary statistics can be a powerful tool in investigation of patent liability. Of course, as in other fields where applied statistics are used, statistics are just as often misused. Our analysis illustrates how statistics can be used, as well as some pitfalls and potential misuses of statistics, in conceptualizing the "similarity" of two products, and possible solutions.

INTRODUCTION

The determination of whether the intellectual property owned by one party has been infringed upon by another party is usually the realm of patent lawyers and subject matter experts. One approach that has been used is to attempt to determine the degree of similarity between two products that resulted from two (or more) purportedly independent processes. There are numerous metrics and methods in mathematics and statistics for defining similarity or closeness.[1] Care must be exercised in the choice of appropriate metrics and concepts as well as in the practical execution of measurements and tests. Otherwise, nonsensical outcomes and inferences can result, camouflaged by sophisticated technology and/or presentations. The authors are aware of work on a matter that involved a more purely mathematical approach to the issues discussed in the fictitious case in this chapter, namely physical measures of "sameness."

The fictitious product at hand is croquet mallets. The plaintiff in this case alleged that the design for his mallet (which we will hereafter refer to as the Duff Mallet) had been copied by another manufacturer and was being sold under a brand name that we will here-after refer to as the Cramer Mallet.

The plaintiff's expert, Dr. M, conducted a statistical analysis of the allegedly infringing Cramer Mallet as well as a sample of other mallets and concluded that it was "exceedingly unlikely" that the two mallets in question would have appeared so similar by chance alone. The expert for the defense responded with a different statistical analysis of Dr. M's work using the same data. The basic ideas may be summarized as: Any entity may be sufficiently well "represented" by a multitude of measurements on as many distinct characteristics of that entity as possible. A notion of "fundamentalism" in economics suggests that an object or individual may be arbitrarily well represented or "summarized" more precisely as the number of characteristics by which it is analyzed increases indefinitely.[2] This is intuitively appealing since, in the limit, one could include all the attributes that fully identify and distinguish an entity. For example, this notion is implicit and central to concepts and implementation of such techniques as hedonic regressions in hedonic pricing and demand analysis. In hedonic regression, a computer, for instance, is but a collection of its parts, which are sold in markets and generally experience technical improvement over time. This way a "true" price for computers is derived from the prices of its components. In prac-tice, only a finite number of characteristics can be measured. Assuming all agree to the adequacy of a necessarily finite number of attributes, the important task becomes one of assessing the similarity of two or more objects characterized in multiple dimensions. This is a daunting task, subject to many pitfalls and assumptions. Once it is understood that measurements are typically realizations of a number of random variables (e.g., the statis-tical measurement of a series of average measurements), the task of assessment of "equal-ity" or similarity can be assessed through multivariate statistical distributions and testing. It will be seen that formal testing is both necessary and challenging for scientific imple-mentation and to provide reliable and probative evidence. Two products or objects may be quite similar in some aspects but quite different in others. In rare cases, similarity in a few dimensions may be sufficient evidence if the allegations have been successfully addressed to those few characteristics.

DR. M'S METHODOLOGY

Dr. M presented a set of physical measurements on three different characteristics of a sample of mallets to measure his concept of "similarity." These three characteristics were:

1. Face width
2. Front-to-back length
3. Alignment lines

By way of explanation, the face width of a mallet is the distance across the part of the mallet that is perpendicular to the line of swing and actually strikes the ball.

The front-to-back length of a mallet is the distance from the face of the mallet to the back and of the mallet, parallel to the line of swing.[3] Alignment lines are physical or colored markings, usually parallel along the line of swing, which help the croquet player to align the hit properly.

Dr. M's concept of similarity is based on the probability that a randomly drawn mallet's characteristics would be "close" to those of the allegedly infringed mallet. If the estimated probability is negligibly small, the plaintiff would argue that a competing mallet with "similar" characteristics is adjudged to be an infringing mallet.

Dr. M made at least two critical assumptions about these three mallet characteristics: (1) These characteristics each follow a known distribution, and the relevant distribution is the normal (or "bell curve") distribution across his sample of mallets; and (2) these three characteristics are independent of one another. As we will discuss, both of these assumptions, while expedient, are inappropriate and unsupported. Dr. M used sample statistics from these measurements across his sample of mallets to compute what he referred to as a test of the probability that the two mallets at issue, the Cramer Mallet and the Duff Mallet, would demonstrate "similarity" with regard to these characteristics. Specifically, Dr. M computed the probability that a randomly selected mallet would exhibit measurements for these three characteristics within a small interval around the corresponding measurements for the Duff Mallet.

Before further detail is given that will help in practical refutations of this approach, it is helpful to note a fundamental conceptual problem with Dr. M's "metric." Unlike the number of balls in a box, the measurement of the face width of a mallet is continuous, that is, it could have infinitely many values from the shortest mallet to the longest mallet. In statistics, for all such continuously distributed measurements (including normal variables), the probability of the selection of any single value in the distribution is zero. It is only intervals over which there is a probability. However, by extension, the probability that a particular measurement would fall into an arbitrarily small interval can be made to be arbitrarily small, by simply shrinking the measurement interval. Thus, Dr. M's metric is tautological under his own assumptions: A priori, no two mallets would have a significant probability of having very "close" measurements, in any dimension/attribute.

Dr. M's calculations were presented in his expert report, and are reproduced here. Table 1 presents measurements of the three mallet characteristics selected by Dr. M to examine for the two mallets at issue in this matter.

Table 1: Duff Mallet and Cramer Mallet Measurements

	Face Width	Length	Alignment Lines
Duff Mallet	3.4017	3.296	1.882 ± 0.1125
Cramer Mallet	3.4153	3.373	1.8415

Table 2: Face Widths		Table 3: Front-to-Back Length		Table 4: Alignment Lines	
Mean	4.1761	Mean	2.0891	Mean	1.1400
Variance	0.22	Variance	0.20	Variance	0.82
Standard Deviation	0.47	Standard Deviation	0.44	Standard Deviation	0.91
Skew	0.40	Skew	0.50	Skew	0.92
Kurtosis	2.39	Kurtosis	-0.47	Kurtosis	0.002

(continues)

Table 1: Duff Mallet and Cramer Mallet Measurements *(Continued)*

Table 2: Face Widths		Table 3: Front-to-Back Length		Table 4: Alignment Lines	
P = Probability (of)		P = Probability (of)		P = Probability (of)	
P(<3.401)	0.04834	P(<3.25)	0.994572	P(<1.7695)	0.995472
P(<3.416)	0.05166	P(<3.40)	0.998397	P(<1.9945)	0.998397
P(3.401 ≤ W ≤ 3.416)	0.00331	P(3.25 ≤ W ≤ 3.40)	0.002924	P(1.7695 ≤ W ≤ 1.9945)	0.07074

Tables 2, 3, and 4 present summary statistical measures on the three characteristics for the sample of mallets chosen by Dr. M for his analysis.[4] Each table presents the mean and the variance (a measure of the dispersion of the data around the mean) for each characteristic. In addition, the skew (a measure of excess length in either tail of the distribution) and kurtosis (a measure of the heaviness of the tails) are also provided.

The last row in Tables 2 to 4 provides the probability calculations alluded to earlier. These figures purport to show the probability that a randomly selected mallet would have measurements of the characteristic in question within the particular interval Dr. M selected. It is important to note that Dr. M's choice of interval length is completely ad hoc. Dr. M offers no explanation or justification of how the selection of these particular intervals was derived.

In the hypothetical distribution shown in Exhibit 13.1, the probability that some measured quantity x falls between 40 and 60 is given by the shaded area. In practice, it is easier to calculate the probability that x is less than 60 and the probability that x is less than 40, and then subtract the latter from the former. Using the figures given in Tables 2 to 4, Dr. M calculates what he refers to as the probability that a randomly selected mallet would exhibit measurements for all three characteristics that fall within the selected intervals as:

Pr{Randomly selected mallet has a Face Width x where $3.401 \leq x \leq 3.416$} =
$$(0.04834 - 0.05166) = 0.00331$$

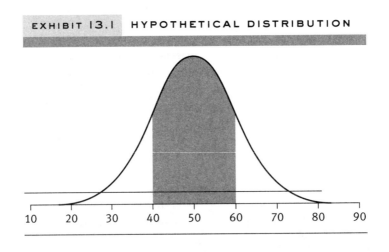

EXHIBIT 13.1   HYPOTHETICAL DISTRIBUTION

Pr{Randomly selected mallet has a Front-to-Back Length y where $3.25 \leq y \leq 3.40$} =
$$(0.994572 - 0.998397) = 0.002924$$
Pr{Randomly selected mallet has alignment lines z where $1.7695 \leq z \leq 1.9945$} =
$$(0.995472 - 0.998397) = 0.070744$$
Pr{All three are true} = $0.00331 \cdot 0.002924 \cdot 0.0707 = 6.85 \cdot 10^{-7}$, or one chance in 1.46 million

The crux of Dr. M's argument is that he believes that this result, based on his assumptions, provides sufficient evidence for one to reasonably conclude that the two mallets at issue could not be so "similar" by chance alone and that indeed the Cramer mallet must therefore infringe on the Duff mallet.

Note that these authors do not maintain that the use of elementary probability theory is inappropriate here. Elementary applied statistics, when used properly, can make a powerful impression on the triers of fact in a patent matter. But Dr. M's report is not properly grounded in the correct statistical fundamentals, and thus much of the work in his report is rendered speculative.

GENERAL SIMILARITY AMONG MALLETS

Dr. M states explicitly in his report that he is attempting to rebut the notion that all mallets are relatively similar. To demonstrate in a simple way why Dr. M's methodology does not allow one (even in principle) to conclude that mallets cannot be similar by chance alone or to draw any meaningful statistical inference whatsoever from the data on his ad hoc choice of mallet characteristics, we utilized the data reported in the appendices to Dr. M's report. Those tables present the individual measurements of the three characteristics selected by Dr. M across the entire sample of mallets. Dr. M measures the face width for a sample of 172 mallets, the front-to-back length for a sample of 23 mallets, and the alignment lines for a sample of 13 mallets. This, unfortunately, leaves a sample of only 8 mallets (in addition to the Duff Mallet and the Cramer Mallet) for which Dr. M provides all three measurements.

While it is a flawed methodology, for illustrative purposes only we performed the same analysis as Dr. M except that instead of measuring the similarity between the two mallets at issue, we applied Dr. M's approach to two other mallets in the sample. Following the methodology implicit in Dr. M's analysis, we selected intervals based on the relative differences between the two mallets we selected for analysis. With regard to the face width, we calculate the probability that these two mallets would both fall into the interval between 3.6030 and 3.3845 as $P = 0.064789$. With regard to front-to-back length, we calculate the probability that these two mallets would both fall into the interval between 2.1655 and 2.2110 as $P = 0.039792$. With regard to alignment lines, we calculate the probability that these two mallets would both fall into the interval between 0.3405 and 0.3030 as $P = 0.010979$. Using these figures, Dr. M's approach indicates that the probability that a randomly selected mallet would exhibit measurements for all three characteristics that fall within the selected intervals as:

$$\text{Pr}\{\text{All three are true}\} = 0.064789 \cdot 0.039792 \cdot 0.010979 = 2.83 \cdot 10^{-5},$$

or one chance in 35,330

This exercise shows how vacuous Dr. M's analysis is as an indication of statistical evidence of theft of intellectual property. That the two mallets we just examined should show such "unlikely similarity" in a sample of only eight mallets provides strong evidence that many mallets are exceedingly similar with regard to the characteristics identified by Dr. M.

Another point can be made with reference to examination of the three characteristics separately. Again, using the underlying assumptions of Dr. M's methodologies and based on the measurement of face width, it should be *extremely unlikely* that any two mallets would have the exact same measurement for face width. The basis for Dr. M's underlying assumption and methodology is questionable, given that croquet has been played since the 1400s and while technology has changed, we have seen no evidence, nor has Dr. M offered any, that mallets' face widths have changed significantly.[5] Dr. M is assuming that no two mallets should be the same in the categories he has chosen and that mallets that are "not copied" should not have similar measurements in the categories he has chosen. In effect, Dr. M is assuming his own conclusion; that is, he assumes that in order for the dimensions of any two mallets to be "close," one must have been copied from the other or it is a very rare statistical event to have occurred by chance.

But in the sample of 172 mallets for which Dr. M measured face width, there are five pairs of mallets with precisely the same face width, measured to 1/10,000th of an inch. In addition there is one group of three mallets with exactly the same face width. Thus, regardless of the measurements for the other two characteristics (which Dr. M provides for only 8 mallets), the fact that two mallets have the exact same face width means that the probability of arriving at these similarities by chance approaches zero. Once again, this conclusion is predicated on Dr. M's underlying maintained hypothesis that if any two mallets have "similar" measurements for a given attribute, it must be due to copying or be due to a very rare statistical event occurring. If Dr. M's approach is a statistically sound one, it should be *infinitely unlikely* that any two mallets would have the exact same measurement for face width. Using his data, we have just demonstrated that is not the case.

The data demonstrate conclusively that many mallets exhibit similar measurements for these characteristics, which were chosen by the plaintiffs' own expert. The test of "sameness" upon which Dr. M's entire report relies is in fact common to numerous mallets in the sample he provides. Thus, we find Dr. M's approach completely devoid of probative value in this matter.

STATISTICAL TESTS

As further evidence of the general similarity among many mallets with no insidious motives, we used the data in Tables 1 to 4 of Dr. M's report to examine the profile of the

EXHIBIT 13.2   DISTRIBUTION OF MALLETS ACCORDING TO FACE
WIDTHS

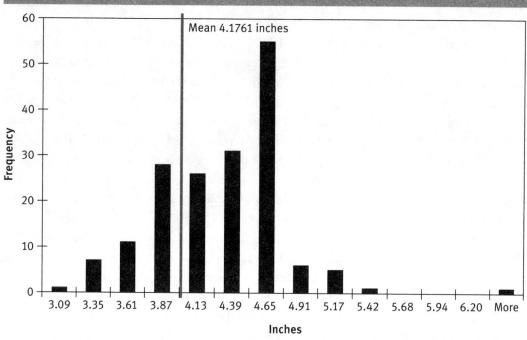

"average" or "representative" mallet according to each of the three characteristics he chose for his analysis. For example, beginning with face width, the average mallet has a face width of 4.1761 inches. Exhibit 13.2 graphs the distribution of face widths around the mean of 4.1761 inches.

We then used the data provided by Dr. M to calculate some basic statistical ratios, or t-tests. The purpose of these tests is to determine whether the measured differences across mallets for these various elements are more likely due to chance or rather represent meaningful differences from a statistical perspective. These tests demonstrate clearly that neither the Duff Mallet nor the Cramer Mallet differs from the "average" or "representative" mallet to any customary degree of statistical significance. These t-statistics are obtained from first taking the difference between the face width of the Cramer Mallet (3.4153 inches, or that of Duff Mallet, 3.4017 inches) and the "average" of the distribution, 4.1761 inches, and then dividing this difference by the standard deviation of .47 found in Table 2. Both of these t-statistics are less than 1.96, the cutoff for significance at the 95 percent level. Thus, the Cramer Mallet and the Duff Mallet are statistically no different from the "average" mallet. As a result, there is no valid statistical reason to assert that their similarity is probative here. Using the raw data on face widths, we then calculated that out of the 172 mallets for which Dr. M measured face width, only 9 are statistically distinct from the average mallet at the 95 percent confidence level. Furthermore, we calculate that 91 mallets are statistically similar to the Cramer Mallet and 93 mallets are statistically similar to the Duff Mallet. In other words, *virtually all* mallets in this sample are statistically indifferent from the average mallet based on face width and in most cases are not statistically different from either the Cramer Mallet or the Duff Mallet.[6]

We then analyzed the data on front-to-back length for each mallet. Analysis of the data in Table 3 demonstrates that while both the Cramer and Duff mallets are statistically different from the "average" mallet length using similar *t*-statistics to those computed earlier, the data also demonstrate that several other mallets are of statistically similar length to the Cramer Mallet and the Duff Mallet. To demonstrate this, we computed a *t*-statistic based on the difference between the Cramer Mallet (3.3730 inches, or the Duff Mallet, 3.2960 inches) and the remaining mallets in the appendix for which Dr. M measured the front-to-back length. In four cases, the value of this *t*-statistic is less than 1.96, meaning that the length of these mallets is statistically indistinguishable from the Cramer Mallet and the Duff Mallet.

The analysis of Table 4 and the underlying data indicate that, again, there is no statistically significant difference between Cramer and the "average" mallet based on this attribute, the characteristic Alignment Lines. The relevant *t*-statistic here is the difference between either the Cramer Mallet measurement (1.8415 or the Duff Mallet measurement, 1.882) and the mean (1.1400), divided by the standard deviation of 0.91. These *t*-statistics are far less than 1.96. Furthermore, the data demonstrate that only one mallet is statistically different from the average mallet and that no mallet is statistically different from either the Cramer Mallet or the Duff Mallet. In other words, virtually all other mallets in this sample are not statistically different from the average mallet, the Cramer Mallet, or the Duff Mallet based on this characteristic. We must reiterate that all of these conclusions are based on giving a "similarity test" interpretation to a simple statistical exercise, which we do not believe is appropriate in the first place.

NONINDEPENDENCE OF MALLET CHARACTERISTICS

Dr. M's probability calculations are also flawed because they rely crucially on the assumption of independence, that is, the idea that each of the three attributes chosen by Dr. M is unrelated to the other attributes for any given mallet. But these measurements are not in fact independent from one another; they are interrelated as part of the overall design parameters that govern modern mallet design. In fact, suppose the U.S. Croquet Association rules for mallets and irons states: "When the club head is in its normal address position, the dimensions of the head must be such that the distance from the heel to the toe is larger than the distance from the face to the back."[7] In other words, it must be the case that the face width is greater than the front-to-back length. Thus, as a matter of hypothetical USCA rules, these two measurements are not independent. As such, the multiplication of three already artificially small probability numbers is incorrect as a threshold matter and compounds the prior errors. Indeed, given a large enough number of attributes or characteristics to compare and small enough intervals over which to measure differences, *every mallet will appear unique.* Consequently, the findings of these small probabilities of falling within small intervals is meaningless, and can be arbitrarily reproduced for numerous other pairs of mallets in the expert's own data set as shown earlier.

The correct approach would be to have a joint test of equality of the selected attributes, based on the joint distribution of those attributes. There are several methods available for estimating such distributions, the chief among them being the nonparametric kernel methods, requiring very large samples (not available here, or generally). Alternatively, approximate asymptotic methods (e.g., the Kolmogorov-Smirnov metric[8] or maximum likelihood techniques) can be used to fit parametric distributions and/or to test the fit of the data to any distribution. The latter also will generally require large samples for reliability. Mechanically, however, such approximations can be implemented, and are indeed the most common, albeit implicit, justification for applications of statistics in law and many other fields. For instance, central limit theorems can be invoked that suggest, for large samples, the joint distribution of the measured attributes around some desired value (true values, means, averages, "other objects") is approximately normal. Once this is accepted, a number of multivariate test statistics are available for testing equality of two vectors (of attributes). The most commonly used is a chi-squared statistic, which is merely a generalization of the *t*-statistics we reported, but taking into account the dependence between the attributes. This would be an example of a joint test of the hypothesis of "similarity" in several dimensions.

To be more specific, the distances between pairs of corresponding characteristics are measured and arranged in a vector W, which would have an approximate normal distribution. Given the known normal distribution, it is possible to estimate the variance (covariance matrix) of this vector of measurements. Under the hypothesis that objects are equal, the computed value of the statistic:

$$Q = W'[Cov(W)]^{-1'}W$$

is then compared with the significance level of a chi-squared distribution with appropriate degrees of freedom. If Q is larger than the critical level, the hypothesis of "similarity" or equality is rejected at a desired level of statistical confidence. One says that similarity is not supported to a degree of statistical confidence (e.g., 95 percent).

An alternative, sequential application of single dimension tests, such as *t*-tests, can be considered but require care and sophistication in controlling for test "size" (e.g., the Bonferroni method). This latter alternative falls under the topic of multiple comparisons and testing and would be difficult to justify in situations like the present case, where various attributes do not have any natural order or logical nesting. It is also possible that in some applications, one may wish to test whether one object's attributes are all larger (or smaller) than another object's. Such ranking tests, or tests of inequality restrictions, are available, for instance by using chi-bar-squared tests or extended Kolmogorov-Smirnov tests.[9]

PRESENTATION OF STATISTICAL EVIDENCE

Besides the usual hurdles in preparing a statistical analysis, the adversarial process of litigation raises further issues that the expert must address:

- *Absence of measures of statistical confidence*

    Dr. M's probability computations are not accompanied by statistical indications of significance and thus lack statistical validity. This is important in legal applications because not only the results but in particular *the reliability* of those results dictate the admissibility and weight offered to statistical testimony. Dr. M failed to indicate how the mallets were measured, which obviously is the starting point for all of his analysis and potentially the most critical. Errors in this first step will render his entire analysis speculative. Because of Dr. M's failure to provide standard errors for his estimates, he in fact offers "statistical-sounding" assertions that are not actually based on reliable statistics.

- *Data reliability issues*

    In particular with regard to litigation, it is important that all data relied on by the expert are clearly described. Apparently Dr. M was provided access to many mallets. There is no mention of how these mallets were selected or if the selection was random. What was eventually revealed is that all of the mallets were provided by the plaintiff, the owner of the intellectual property in question (i.e., the inventor of the Duff Mallet). These mallets were assembled by the plaintiff and kept in a shack in his backyard long before the initiation of the litigation in question. One might speculate that the plaintiff selected these mallets because he liked them, and thus that his own mallet design is likely to be closer to these mallets than a true random sample. In any case the mallets are not likely to be a random sample in any meaningful sense. That in and of itself is a major issue when calculating statistical significance, as the simple mean and variance calculations are invalid without random sampling.

- *Assumptions regarding the distribution of the data*

    As is obvious from Exhibit 13.1, the distribution of face widths for this sample of mallets is hardly normal. Even the expert's own computations of skew and kurtosis are different from those of the normal distribution (for which the correct theoretical values are 0 and 3, respectively).[10] Furthermore, the expert report does not provide any of the standard tests for normality extant in the statistical literature and text. Indeed, the report is totally silent as to the method of estimation of the data distributions, and therefore the method of estimating the probabilities that are the centerpiece of the unsupported conclusions of similarity between mallet measurements. Failing this, Dr. M could have relied on nonparametric tests, that is, tests that make no specific assumption about the distribution in the underlying data.

- *Ad hoc choice of mallet attributes*

    In any statistical analysis, it is important that the expert clearly state the rationale for the choice of attributes to be measured as well as the sample population and any sampling plans utilized. Ad hoc choices may suffer from biases that render the results of any statistical analysis meaningless. Dr. M offers no arguments or evidence to support the decision to characterize mallets with the particular attributes/measurements that he chose to analyze. There is no statistical or industry evidence provided. In particular, a bit of basic research on croquet club design indicates that these parameters are important to the performance of a mallet:

- o Materials of construction
- o Shaft axis location
- o Shaft entry point
- o Type of insertion
- o Center of gravity measurements
- o Face-to-back width

None of these attributes is measured in the expert report of Dr. M, nor does he discuss what characteristics might be appropriate or why.

On the surface, we seem to have been presented with a conundrum. On one hand, statistics can be manipulated to show the apparent "uniqueness" of every mallet. On the other hand, statistical analysis is capable of demonstrating that most mallets are extremely similar as a general matter. In that sense, this case study certainly demonstrates that statistics can be a powerful tool, here in rebuttal. As for the original affirmative decision to use statistics in this case, there may be no general agreement about which mallet characteristics are actually important to the function of the mallet or against what type of metric any measure of "sameness" should reasonably be compared. As in many applications, it may simply be the case that applied statistics cannot resolve the question per se, but does provide information that will have to be weighed by the fact finder in conjunction with other forms of evidence to ultimately decide the liability question here.

NOTES

1. *Cf., e.g.,* Cressie and Read (1984).
2. Kolm (1977).
3. On many mallets, particularly older models, this distance is quite small, being only the width of the mallet head. On newer models, particularly those with alignment lines, this distance can be several inches.
4. Although, as we discuss later, the samples for the three characteristics are not the same.
5. Anecdotally, we understand that most croquet mallet face widths are approximately the same as the diameter of the hoop, or about 4.5 inches.
6. Note that implicit in this calculation is Dr. M's assumption that the underlying distribution is normal. But as we discuss later in detail, because certain values produced by this distribution do not match those of the normal distribution, this assertion is dubious. As such, the significance values for the normal or t-density are conservatively high here.

7. USCA "Rules of Croquet"; hypothetically, of course. There are, however, rules like this in golf.

8. Hogg and Craig (1987).

9. *See* Maasoumi (1998) for a review.

10. The skew measures the amount of asymmetry in a normal distribution; the kurtosis measures excess weight in the tails of the distribution.

References

Cressie, N., and T. R. C. Read. "Multinomial Goodness-of-Fit Tests," *Journal of the Royal Statistical Society Series* 46, no. 3 (1984): 440–464.

Hogg, Robert V., and Allen T. Craig. *Introduction to Mathematical Statistics,* 5th ed. (Prentice Hall, New York, 1987).

Kolm, S. C. "Multi-dimensional Egalitarianism," *Quarterly Journal of Economics* 91 (1977): 1–13.

Maasoumi, Esfandiar. *Companion to Econometric Theory,* ed. Badi Baltagi (London: Basil Blackwell, 1998).

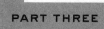

PART THREE

Economics of Copyright, Trademark, and Trade Secret Damages

CHAPTER 14

Using Statistics in Copyright Cases

DANIEL MILLIMET
SMU

MICHAEL NIESWIADOMY
University of North Texas

DANIEL SLOTTJE
SMU and FTI Consulting, Inc.

This chapter describes the general concepts of hypothesis tests and how they can be used to determine the impact of an important explanatory variable in an actual copyright infringement case. We show that rigorous econometric techniques can be used in intellectual property rights cases to assist the judge or jury in determining the level, if any, of damages to award.

INTRODUCTION

In many intellectual property rights cases, a plaintiff alleges that some infringement or other action (X) has negatively impacted plaintiff's profits (Y). To determine the economic validity of the claim, it is necessary to determine the economic factors (possibly including the alleged action) that influence the plaintiff's profits. One way to do this is a process that involves econometrically estimating the impact of various factors on the plaintiff's profits and then testing for the statistical significance of each factor.[1]

ECONOMIC MODELS

One way to assess the impact of a set of factors on a firm's profits is to specify a model of a firm's profits. Such a model is typically based on economic theory. For example, suppose that a firm's profits can be expressed by this equation:

$$Profit\ (Y_i) = \beta_0 + \beta_1 P_{Yi} + \beta_2 P_{Xi} + \beta_3 I_i + \beta_4 A_i \tag{14.1}$$

where $i = 1, \ldots, n$.

In equation (14.1), *Profit* (Y_i) stands for the profits earned by firm *i* from the sale of product *Y*. A variable on the left-hand side of an equation such as (14.1) is called the dependent variable. The variables on the right-hand side of the equation are called the independent (or explanatory) variables. In our example, P_Y stands for the price of *Y*, P_X stands for the price of a related product (which may be a substitute or complement for product *Y*), *I* stands for per-capita income of the consumer, and *A* stands for advertising expenditures for product *Y*.[2] Other factors could be considered, but we will assume that the factors listed are the most important. In reality, the set of important factors will always be case specific. β_0 is called the intercept, β_1 is called the coefficient on P_Y, β_2 is the coefficient on P_X, β_3 is the coefficient on income, and β_4 is the coefficient on advertising. A coefficient on an explanatory variable indicates the expected amount that a given profit level will change when the explanatory variable changes one unit, holding all other explanatory variables constant. For example, if β_1 equals -1.7, then profit will decrease 1.7 (e.g., 1.7 thousands of dollars) when P_Y increases one unit (e.g., \$1).

DETERMINISTIC VERSUS STOCHASTIC MODELS

The profit function in equation (14.1) is called a deterministic relationship because it is assumed that the quantity demanded of the product in question can be determined precisely (without error) if the values of the explanatory variables (e.g., P_Y, P_X, *I*, and *A*) are given. Unfortunately, there is no way to know the exact relationship between a dependent variable and a potential set of explanatory variables. There will always be some unknown factors that could potentially affect the demand for the product, or there may be isolated accounting errors in a firm's profits. Any changes in unobserved factors will have small random effects on this relationship. When random effects are present, the relationship is known as a stochastic relationship. For each value of an independent variable, there is a distribution of random values of the dependent variable. To indicate that the profit equation has a stochastic relation, we add a disturbance term (ε_i) to equation (14.1), which yields equation (14.2):

$$\text{Profits } (Y_i) = \beta_0 + \beta_1 P_{Yi} + \beta_2 P_{Xi} + \beta_3 I_i + \beta_4 A_i + \varepsilon_i \qquad (14.2)$$

where $i = 1,\ldots,n$.

Equation (2) states that observation *i* of the Profit function can be described as being affected by the values of the independent variables and a random error term that is called ε_i. An error term is included because there are a myriad of factors that can have very small impacts on the dependent variable. These other factors individually may push profits up or down slightly, but as a whole they act as a random error term. To fully specify the model in equation (14.2), we must describe the (assumed) characteristics of the error term. The assumptions of what is known as the classical linear regression model (CLRM) are (1) ε_i is normally distributed, the expected value of ε_i equals zero, (3) the variance of ε_i is a constant, σ^2, (4) the covariance between ε_i and ε_j equals zero for all i not equal to j, and (5) the independent variables are nonstochastic (i.e., are uncorrelated with ε_i). Much of econometric modeling involves testing the validity of these assumptions for a particular data set and making the appropriate adjustments if needed.[3]

Equation (14.1) is referred to as the population regression line. Equation (14.2) is the population regression line augmented by a random error term. To keep the notation simple, we will write equation (14.2) as

$$Y_i = \alpha + \beta X_i + \varepsilon_i \tag{14.3}$$

X usually represents a matrix (simply a rectangular array of numbers) of values of the independent variables, with each column containing the n values for a given independent variable (such as income), β is a vector of coefficients, and α is a scalar. For pedagogical purposes, however, we will assume that there is only one independent variable at this time (thus, β is also a scalar). The coefficients (α and β) are referred to as parameters. α is referred to as the constant term or the Y-intercept, as it represents the expected value that Y takes when X is zero. β is referred to as the slope. Exhibit 14.1 illustrates how values of Y are distributed around the population regression line, where $E(Y)$ denotes the expected value of Y (i.e., the value of Y if ε equals zero).

Since the population parameters are unknown, we must estimate the values of these parameters, which yields a sample regression line. The sample regression line is written as:

$$\hat{Y} = \hat{\alpha} + \hat{\beta} X \tag{14.4}$$

where a "^" over a parameter corresponds to its estimated value.

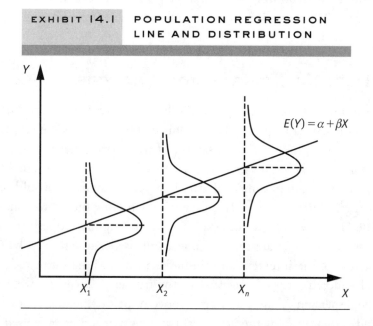

EXHIBIT 14.1   POPULATION REGRESSION LINE AND DISTRIBUTION

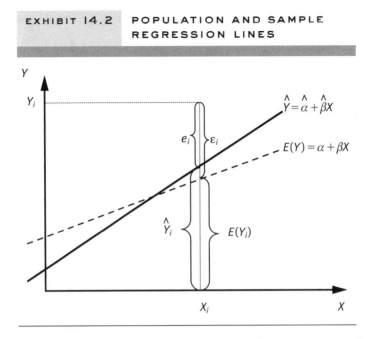

EXHIBIT 14.2   POPULATION AND SAMPLE REGRESSION LINES

For a specific value of Y_i, equation (14.4) is written as

$$Y_i = \hat{\alpha} + \hat{\beta} X_i + \hat{e}_i = \hat{Y}_i + \hat{e}_i \tag{14.5}$$

where the last term is referred to as the residual, which is an estimate of the true error term.

This residual term is extremely important in determining the line that fits the data best and in conducting hypothesis tests. Exhibit 14.2 illustrates the difference between the population and sample regression lines, as well as the difference between the true error term and the residual.

LINE OF BEST FIT: REGRESSION ANALYSIS

The most common method of using the residuals in determining the line of best fit is referred to as ordinary least squares (OLS). This method chooses the line that minimizes the sum of the squared residuals for the sample of data that we have obtained. It is important to understand that the results that we derive are based on the particular sample of data that was available. If another sample of data had been drawn, we would have calculated different estimates. Thus, we must rely on statistical sampling theory to conduct our hypothesis tests. The OLS method has important statistical sampling properties, namely that the estimators of the parameters are the best linear unbiased estimators.[4] The OLS formulas provide estimators of the intercept and the slope, as well as the estimated standard error. The estimated standard error is a measure of the true error term. In other words, it is an estimate of the dispersion of the data points above or below the line; it corresponds to the estimated standard deviation of the error term, ε. The standard error is used (among other things) to calculate the standard errors of the estimated intercept and slope. Knowledge of the standard error of the slope is essential to determining how reliable the estimate of the slope is. This reliability is used to determine the statistical significance of the variable.

To determine if an independent variable has a statistically significant impact on the dependent variable, it is important to recognize that we do not know the true value of the independent variable's coefficient, but we do have an estimate. For most purposes, we are interested in determining if the true (but unknown) coefficient on the explanatory variable is different from zero. For example, we might want to test if an alleged patent infringement by Firm A reduced the profits of Firm B. We would expect the sign of the coefficient to be negative, but we must determine if the estimated coefficient is far enough away from zero to give us enough confidence to assert that the sign of the true coefficient is negative. Since we only have an estimate of the impact (which is measured with some error), we must conduct a hypothesis test to determine if the true coefficient is statistically different from zero. If the results of the hypothesis test indicate that we can be reasonably certain that the true coefficient is not equal to zero, then we say that the coefficient is statistically significant.

FUNDAMENTALS OF HYPOTHESIS TESTING

There are five basic steps in a hypothesis test. First, we must describe the null hypothesis. Usually in the null hypothesis we assume that the true parameter is equal to zero, namely:

$$H_0 : \beta_1 = 0. \tag{14.6}$$

Assuming the parameter has a value of zero is akin to assuming that the explanatory variable in question has no effect on the dependent variable (recalling equation (14.1)). This null hypothesis is sometimes referred to as a straw man. If this straw man is still standing after the test, then we say that we "fail to reject" the null hypothesis. Note that we do not conclude that the null hypothesis is true; rather, the data simply do not provide sufficient evidence to reject it. If we can knock the straw man over (i.e., we "reject" the null hypothesis), however, we conclude that the null hypothesis is false. A hypothesis test is somewhat akin to deciding the fate of a person in a criminal trial. In a trial the null hypothesis states that the person is "not guilty" until proven so. "Not guilty" may either imply that the person did not commit the crime or simply that there was insufficient evidence to conclude that the person did commit the crime. Only if we have overwhelming evidence (such as beyond a reasonable doubt in a criminal trial) would we reject our null hypothesis of no impact (and thus conclude that a person is indeed guilty of the crime). Thus, in our statistical models, failing to reject the null hypothesis means we do not have sufficient empirical evidence to conclude that the explanatory variable has a statistical effect on the dependant variable.

In the second step we describe the alternative hypothesis. Usually we say that the alternative is that the true parameter is not zero and write it as:

$$H_A : \beta_1 \neq 0. \tag{14.7}$$

In the third step, we need to construct a test to allow us to discern between these alternative hypotheses, so we calculate a test statistic involving our estimated coefficient. Since our estimated coefficient is based on a sample of data, we need to know the statistical properties of the distribution of the estimator. Before describing the test statistic that is used in testing the significance of an explanatory variable in a regression model, we will describe the basic nature of a hypothesis test for a simple example.

Suppose we want to test the assertion that the average weight of a person in Gotham City is 200 pounds. This assertion (200 pounds) is referred to as the null hypothesis and would be written as

$$H_0 : \mu_0 = 200 \tag{14.8}$$

where μ_0 = true mean of the population of Gotham City.

To test this null hypothesis, we collect a random sample of 25 persons and calculate their average (i.e., mean) weight. Suppose the mean weight for our sample is 180. Some persons in our sample weighed over 200 pounds, but the sample average is less than 200 pounds. Thus, our estimate, $\hat{\mu}$, of the unknown parameter, μ, equals 180. How strongly do we believe in the null hypothesis (i.e., the mean weight in the population is 200 pounds)? Is it possible that the mean weight in Gotham City really is 200 pounds and that by some small chance our sample happened to pick mainly lightweight persons? Yes, it is possible, but the question is how likely of a scenario this represents. Relying on our intuition, most of us might reject the null hypothesis, albeit recognizing that there is a small chance that we are doing so erroneously.

In general, we can be more precise in our hypothesis testing if we know something about the distribution of people's weights. If the distribution of weight in the population follows, say, a normal distribution (the famous "bell-shaped" curve), and we know the standard deviation of the distribution (a measure of how dispersed our data are), we can determine precisely what the probability is that we are erroneously rejecting the null hypothesis. For example, for a variable that is normally distributed, the probability of a sample mean being within plus or minus two standard deviations of the population mean is approximately 95 percent. Suppose that we know that the population standard error is 20 pounds.[5] It can be shown that the standard deviation of the sample mean is 4 pounds ($20/\sqrt{25}$).[6] Then 95 percent of the time the mean weight of a random sample of size 25 will be in the interval ranging from two standard deviations below the mean (192 pounds) to two standard deviations above the mean (208 pounds), if the true mean is 200 pounds. Since our sample mean weight (180 pounds) does not lie in the interval of 192 to 208, we are more than 95 percent confident that the mean weight of the population is not 200 pounds; or, equivalently, there is less than a 5 percent chance that the true mean weight is 200, but that we could randomly sample 25 people and obtain a sample estimate of 180 pounds.

The interval from 192 to 208 is known as a confidence interval and is one method of testing our hypothesis. The confidence interval contains all possible values of the sample mean such that we are incurring more than a 5 percent chance of erroneously rejecting the null hypothesis if we decide to reject the null hypothesis. Stated differently, if the sample mean lies outside the confidence interval and we reject the null hypothesis, then we know that there is less than a 5 percent chance we are doing so incorrectly. Unfortunately, the problem that we have described only occurs in an ideal setting. Usually we do not know the standard error of the population. We describe the solution to this problem in the context of a *t*-statistic in the next paragraph.

An equivalent method of testing the null hypothesis (and one that is more often reported in studies) involves calculating a test statistic and comparing it to a predetermined critical value. Usually we use a test statistic referred to as a standard normal. For a sample mean coming from a normal distribution, we use the test statistic for a standard normal,

$$\frac{(\overline{X} - \mu_0)\,\sqrt{n}}{\sigma} \sim N(0,1) \tag{14.9}$$

where

μ_0 = mean of the population
n = sample size
σ = population standard error

However, we have a problem implementing this hypothesis test; the population standard error σ is not known. To know σ for certain, we would need to collect data on every person in the city, for example, all 1,000,000 persons in Gotham City, which would be prohibitively costly. We collected a sample of 25 persons to save costs, but we recognize that we only have information coming from a sample, not the entire population. This implies that we do not know the population standard error. However, we can rely on the sample for an estimate of the standard error. It can be shown that an unbiased estimator of σ, called "s," can be calculated as

$$s = \left(\frac{\sum_i (X_i - \overline{X})^2}{n - 1} \right)^{0.5} \tag{14.10}$$

When s is substituted for σ in equation (14.8), the statistic is now distributed as a *t*-distribution rather than a normal distribution. For this example, the *t*-distribution is written as

$$\frac{(\overline{X} - \mu_0)\sqrt{n}}{s} \sim t_{n-1} \tag{14.11}$$

The n−1 subscript is called the degrees of freedom. The shape of the distribution depends on the number of degrees of freedom (i.e., on the sample size). The *t*-distribution is symmetric and shaped like the normal distribution, but it has more weight in the tails; that is, it has more probability mass in the far right and far left hand sides of the distribution. As the sample size grows larger, the *t*-distribution converges to the shape of a normal distribution.

HYPOTHESIS TESTING IN A REGRESSION MODEL

Now that we have described a t-statistic in general, we can explain how a t-statistic is used in testing the significance of a potential explanatory variable in a regression model such as an estimated demand equation. For a simple regression model (with only one explanatory variable (X)), the estimated standard error of the model is given by the formula:

$$s = \left(\frac{\sum_i (Y_i - \overline{Y})^2 - \hat{\beta} \sum_i (X_i - \overline{X})(Y_i - \overline{Y})}{n-2} \right)^{0.5} \tag{14.12}$$

The estimated standard error of the model is needed to calculate the estimated standard error of the estimated coefficient $(\hat{\beta})$ according to this formula:

$$S_{\hat{\beta}} = \left(\frac{s^2}{\sum_i (X_i - \overline{X})^2} \right)^{0.5} \tag{14.13}$$

It can be shown that the ratio of the estimated coefficient (minus its mean) to its estimated standard error has a t-distribution, with $n-2$ degrees of freedom, as given by the following formula

$$\left(\frac{\hat{\beta} - \beta}{S_{\hat{\beta}}} \right) \sim t_{n-2} \tag{14.14}$$

As stated earlier, in most hypothesis tests we are interested in knowing if the regression coefficient is statistically different from zero. This implies that our null hypothesis is that β is zero or that the variable has no effect on the dependent variable. Thus, the t-statistic simplifies as the ratio of the estimated coefficient to its standard error. Assume that the estimated standard error of the coefficient is 2.2 and the estimated coefficient is 4.1. Then our calculated t-statistic is 1.86 ($= 4.1/2.2$). Most statistical software packages provide the estimated coefficients, the estimated standard errors of the coefficient, and the t-values in their printouts. Now we are prepared to perform a test of statistical significance.

In the fourth step, we determine the critical value of the t-statistic, based on the probability of the Type I error that we are willing to accept. A Type I error is the probability of falsely rejecting a true null hypothesis. A Type II error is the probability of failing to reject a false null hypothesis. A Type I error is similar to the error in convicting an innocent person. A Type II error is similar to allowing a guilty person to go free. Usually statisticians choose a 5 percent or 10 percent probability of Type I error. In some cases, the costs of making a Type I and Type II error are known. If this is the case, the optimal Type I and Type II error terms can be solved for to minimize the total cost of making a mistake. In many cases there are no particular values of the costs to use, so the usual practice is to use 5 percent or 10 percent Type I error rates.[7] Let us start by allowing for the possibility of a 10 percent Type I error. In our simple example, we have 23 degrees of freedom

$(n-2) = 25 - 2$. The "2" in this formula is due to estimating 2 parameters, α and β. The value of a t-statistic with 23 degrees of freedom has 5 percent of its mass to the right of 1.714 and 5 percent of its mass to the left of -1.714. This is referred to as a two-tailed test because we are concerned about values that are either too large or too small.[8]

In the fifth, and final, step we compare the calculated t-statistic to the critical value of the t-statistic. If the calculated value of the t-statistic is greater (in absolute value) than the critical value, we reject the null hypothesis that the variable has zero impact and conclude that the variable is a statistically significant variable. If the calculated value of the t-statistic is less (in absolute value) than the critical value, we fail to reject the null hypothesis that the variable has zero impact and conclude that the variable is *not* a statistically significant variable. In our simple example, the critical values (for a two-tailed 10 percent error) are 1.714 and -1.714. These critical values are indicated in Exhibit 14.3 for a t-distribution with 23 degrees of freedom. Our calculated t-statistic is 1.86, which is greater than 1.714. Thus, we would reject the null hypothesis that the true coefficient is zero. (In statistics we say that we reject the null hypothesis if our calculated statistic lies in the tails.) In layman's terms, we conclude that the explanatory variable has a statistically significant impact on the dependent variable. Since we used a 10 percent two-tailed error rate, we would say that we are 90 percent confident that the variable is statistically significant. If we choose to use a 5 percent two-tailed error rate, the critical values are 2.069 and -2.069. Since our calculated t-statistic does not exceed 2.069, we would conclude that we are not 95 percent confident that the variable is statistically significant. Our confidence level lies between 90 percent and 95 percent. The exact confidence level is 92.4 percent. This figure is usually

EXHIBIT 14.3   *t*-DISTRIBUTION (23 DEGREES OF FREEDOM)

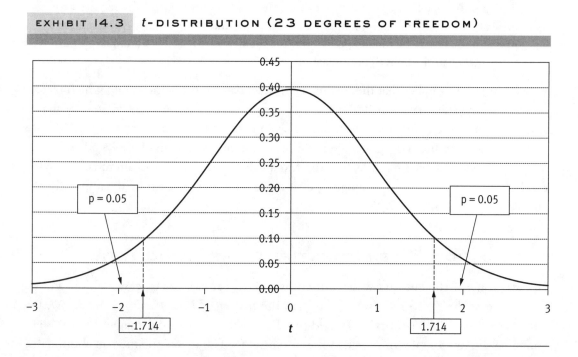

provided in most statistical packages. It can also be calculated in spreadsheet packages such as Excel.

In multiple regression models (which include several independent variables), the formulas for the estimated standard error of the estimated coefficients are different,[9] but the calculation of the t-statistics is the same. The procedure for testing the significance of an explanatory variable is also the same. We will now describe hypothesis testing in a multiple regression model using an actual case study involving copyrights.

HYPOTHESIS TESTING IN A COPYRIGHT DAMAGES CASE

This example is based on a copyrights damages case study published by Basmann and Slottje (2003), in a matter where Slottje served as the expert. The case involved the use of a logo by a professional sports franchise. The name of the franchise has been fictionalized to protect the identity of the parties. A logo is a symbol that identifies a team. Much of the globe has been exposed to some very high profile logos on sportswear, such as the little red bull from the National Basketball Association's Chicago Bulls or the blue and white star of the National Football League's Dallas Cowboys.

This issue has significant statistical ramifications because Title 17 of the United States Code Section 504(b) forms the grounds for damages awarded by the court for the infringement of a copyright and states:

> The copyright owner is entitled to recover . . . any profits of the infringer that are attributable to the infringement and are not taken into account in computing actual damages. In establishing the infringer's profits, the copyright owner is required to present proof only of the infringer's gross revenue, and the infringer is required to prove his or her deductible expenses and the elements of profit attributable to factors other than the copyrighted work.

Section 504(b) implies that the infringer (or defendant) must demonstrate which factors beside the copyright have affected sales of the product in litigation. This view of damages as delineated by the courts provides a natural avenue for applying econometric methods to statistically determine damages. Determining the contribution of the alleged infringed logo on the sales of merchandise, holding fixed other determinants of merchandise sales, can be achieved by using a multiple regression methodology that explicitly adjusts for the alleged infringement.

CASE STUDY: *PETER PLAINTIFF V. THE YAZOO YETI*

In 2001, one of the authors was retained by a professional sports team, which will be referred to as the Yazoo Yeti, Inc. ("Yeti"), in the matter of *Peter Plaintiff v. Yazoo Yeti, Inc.* Mr. Peter Plaintiff ("Plaintiff") claimed that he suffered financial damages due to use of a logo by the Yeti for sales of merchandise in the 1990s. The logo contained an abominable

snowman flying through the air, shooting a ball ("logo"). The plaintiff alleged that he created the logo that the Yeti appropriated. In the trial in the United States in U.S. Federal
Court (patent cases in the United States are always in federal court), the Plaintiff won on
the liability issue. Subsequently, the defense counsel for the Yeti requested that one of the
authors analyze the economic issues surrounding claims for monetary damages. To determine the portion of the profits that were solely attributable to the logo, other variables
that affect sales of Yeti merchandise (e.g., sweatshirts, shorts, ball caps, pennants, etc.) must
be considered. In order to isolate the relative contribution of the logo, as well as other factors, on Yeti merchandise sales, the expert formulated and estimated an econometric model.

It is likely that sports fans purchase Yeti merchandise for a variety of reasons such as their
affection for the team, affection for the players on the team, the team's winning tradition,
the team's lengthy tenure in the city, and so on. It is also conceivable that fans purchased
team merchandise simply because they like the logo. The expert used econometric models
to test these hypotheses. We now describe the models.

The authors estimated the effect of a logo change on franchise merchandise sold using
this estimating equation:

$$\ln(y_{it}) = \alpha_i + \lambda_t + L_{it}\delta + X_{it}\beta + \varepsilon_{it} \tag{14.15}$$

where

y_{it} = value of the merchandise sold by franchise i in year t

α_i = franchise-specific intercepts

λ_t = year-specific effects

L_{it} = a binary variable taking a value of unity if a franchise changed its logo from
the previous year, zero otherwise

X_{it} = a vector of franchise attributes, such as attendance at games, unemployment in
a given area, wins by the team, and so on

The authors estimated a specification of equation (14.15) that restricts $\alpha_i = \alpha$ for all i.[10]
Equation (14.15), in its simplest form, assumes that ε_{it} is independent and identically distributed across observations; it is the classical linear regression model discussed earlier.
Next, the authors maintained the assumption of a constant intercept across franchises, but
allowed the error term to follow what is known as an AR(1) process. An AR(1) process
assumes a variable is correlated with its immediate past period value. This state is said to
be autocorrelated. Since the data in the Basmann and Slottje (2003) study were cross-section data over time, autocorrelation might be present. This is estimated by feasible generalized least squares (FGLS). Feasible GLS corrects for both cross-section heteroskedasticity
(meaning unlike variances) and contemporaneous correlation.[11] The third specification
allowed each franchise to have a unique intercept and estimated (14.15) with fixed effects
methods; the error terms are again assumed to be identical and independent. The α_is are
allowed to vary across teams and capture the effects of all time invariant, team-specific
unobservables (such as market size and fan support) that affect sales revenue. Since these

are unobservable, the model was "first-differenced" to examine the change in sales revenue from one year to the next. First-differencing subtracts last period values from the current period values of the variables.

The data set is a panel (data on the same set of firms over time) containing information on the 31 franchises in Yeti's league during the period 1991 to 2000. Over 300 observations were available. The authors relied on previous theoretical and empirical research on demand for team merchandise[12] to determine the explanatory variables to include in the model: previous won/loss record, winning the league championship game in year t, playing in the league championship game in year t, binary variables for being a new franchise or relocating from a different city, and the seating capacity of the team's home stadium.

The authors also controlled for the socioeconomic characteristics of each franchise's home market: city population, per-capita income, and the local unemployment rate. Exhibit 14.4 reports the summary statistics of the variables contained in the economic models, for teams that had switched their logos in the previous years and for those teams that had not.

EXHIBIT 14.4   SUMMARY STATISTICS, 1991–2000

Variable	Logo Changers		Logo Nonchangers	
	Mean	Standard Deviation	Mean	Standard Deviation
Merchandise Sold (Millions US$)	273.43	112.75	218.17	117.04
Tickets Sold (100,000s)	0.53	0.07	0.48	0.12
Franchise Age (Years)	43.14	15.45	40.38	21.70
New Team (1 = Yes)	0.00	0.00	0.02	0.13
Relocated Team (1 = Yes)	0.00	0.00	0.01	0.08
Wins (Per Season)	9.93	2.84	7.90	2.95
Losses (Per Season)	6.07	2.84	8.09	2.95
Big Cup Champ (1 = Yes)	0.07	0.27	0.03	0.17
Big Cup Loser (1 = Yes)	0.21	0.43	0.02	0.15
Stadium Capacity (10,000s)	6.97	0.66	6.62	1.51
Population (Millions)	6.44	6.32	4.73	4.82
Per Capita Income (10,000s US$)	2.99	0.50	2.67	0.48
Unemployment Rate	4.16	1.55	5.03	1.90

EXHIBIT 14.5   PARAMETRIC ESTIMATES OF THE LOGO EFFECT

Independent Variable[a]	OLS (1)	GLS-AR(1) (2)	OLS-FE (3)	OLS-FE-AR(1) (4)
Logo Change	0.31	0.00	−0.04	0.10
(1 = Yes)	(0.28)	(0.01)	(0.18)	(0.13)
Franchise Effects	No	No	Yes	Yes
Year Effects	No	Yes	Yes	Yes
Joint Significance of Year Effects	$F(8,244) = 1.05$ ($p = 0.40$)	$x^2(8) = 20.63$ ($p = 0.01$)	$F(7,215) = 2.48$ ($p = 0.02$)	$F(6,186) = 2.34$ ($p = 0.03$)

[a] Each specification also includes controls for: franchise age, number of wins, whether the team won the league championship, whether the team lost in the league championship, arena capacity, total ticket sales, and the population, unemployment rate, and mean per capita income of the franchise's home metropolitan area. Number in parentheses is the standard error. "Yes" means the variable is statistically significant at the 5 percent level. "No" means the variable in question is not statistically significant at the 5 percent level. The number in parentheses under the F-statistic is the probability that the variables are jointly significant at the 5 percent level.

Exhibit 14.5 presents a summary of the empirical results for the models discussed and generalized in equation (14.15). Since the main focus of the model is on the effect of the logo change, the coefficients of the other explanatory variables are not shown. However, the authors did test the joint impact of the other explanatory variables. They determined that team wins in the previous year, the team's participation in the Big Cup in the previous year, the team winning the Big Cup, and ticket sales do have a statistically significant (at the 95 percent level) and positive impact on sales.[13] They also found that there were significant differences from year to year in merchandise sales for all teams.[14]

The franchise and year-effect variables were included in the economic models to control for these important effects and to be able to isolate the impact of the logo change. Now we will discuss how the null hypothesis of the effect of the logo change was tested using a t-test. We will use the OLS results to illustrate this; the t-tests for the other specifications (e.g., GLS-AR(1)) are done similarly. The estimated coefficient is 0.31. The standard error of the estimated coefficient is 0.28. Using equation (14), we obtain a t-statistic of $1.11 = (0.31/0.28)$. Using a t-table for 244 degrees of freedom (found in most statistics and econometrics books[15]), we find that there is a 14 percent chance of the t-statistic being larger than 1.11 and a 14 percent chance of the t-statistic being smaller than -1.11. Thus, the two-tailed probability of a Type I error is 28 percent.[16] Since 28 percent is much larger than the 10 percent probability of Type I error that most researchers use, we would say that we fail to reject the null hypothesis that the coefficient on the logo change is significantly different from zero.

Interestingly, the plaintiff's expert tried to argue that the appropriate test was a one-tailed test. He argued that the p-value was only 0.14. However, his reasoning was incorrect. Since a logo change can have either a positive or negative (suppose that the logo was detested by the public) impact on sales, a two-tailed test is appropriate (a one-sided test corresponds to an alternative hypothesis of $H_A: \beta > 0$). Moreover, even using a one-tailed test, the probability associated with the hypothesis that the true coefficient on the logo change variable is not zero is less than 90 percent, which is the lower bound used to determine statistical significance by the majority of, if not all, econometricians. The empirical results summarized in Exhibit 14.5 also indicate under the other various estimation procedures that logos do not have a statistically significant impact at either the 90 or 95 percent confidence level, under the null hypothesis that the coefficient is zero.

The conclusion the author drew in his expert report was

> Examining the results, in particular the impact of a logo change on sales revenue, shows that conditional on the other control variables in the model, a logo change has no statistically significant effect on sales revenue in Model (1). Thus, once we control for the success of the team, its division (any division can be randomly picked as the benchmark by which the other divisions are measured), its team colors, the team's age and history (i.e., new or recently relocated), stadium capacity and attendance, and the year, whether or not a franchise altered its logo from the preceding year has no influence on its merchandise sales revenue in the next year.

CONCLUSION

This chapter has described the general logic of hypothesis tests and how they can be used to determine the impact of an important explanatory variable in an actual copyright infringement case. We have shown that rigorous econometric techniques can be used in intellectual property rights cases to assist the judge or jury in determining the level, if any, of damages to award. In order to conduct a hypothesis test on the impact of a logo change, the authors formulated a model of the possible explanatory factors (including the logo) that are expected to impact sales of team merchandise. After estimating an econometric model, the authors conducted a hypothesis test on the null hypothesis that the logo change had zero effect. This null hypothesis could not be rejected at a reasonable p-value (5 percent or 10 percent). The two-tailed p-value was 0.28. This implies that the probability of falsely rejecting the null hypothesis of zero impact (of logo change) is 28 percent. Thus, we do not have sufficient evidence to conclude that the logo change had any statistically meaningful impact on merchandise sales. This method of testing the potential impact of events or variables has applications to other areas of intellectual property as well, such as patents and trademarks.

NOTES

1. Econometrics is a subdiscipline of economics that applies statistical techniques to analyze relationships among economic variables.
2. Two goods are substitutes if an increase (decrease) in the price of good X causes the demand for good Y to increase (decrease). Orange juice and apple juice are examples of substitute consumption goods. Two goods are complements if an increase (decrease) in the price of good X causes the demand for good Y to decrease (increase). Cars and gasoline are examples of complementary goods

3. *See* Kmenta (1986) for a discussion of these issues.

4. "Best" means the estimator has the smallest variance. "Unbiased" means that the expected value of the estimator is equal to the true value. *See* Kmenta (1986) for a discussion of these issues and for the formulas for estimators of intercept and the slopes.

5. The standard error (sometimes called standard deviation) of a random variable is equal to the square root of its variance. The variance of a variable (X) is defined as $\sigma^2 = E(X - \mu_0)^2$, where "$E$" is the notation for "expected value."

6. If a random variable is distributed normally with a mean of μ and a standard deviation of σ, then the mean of the variable is distributed normally with a mean of μ and a standard deviation of $\sigma/\sqrt{n}$. *See* Kmenta (1986).

7. *See* Kmenta (1986) for a particular example of costs of these errors.

8. For a discussion of one-tailed and two-tailed tests, *see* Kmenta (1986) for details.

9. *See* Kmenta (1986) for the formulas. Matrix formulas are used when several variables are involved.

10. This section is somewhat technical. However, our main emphasis is to describe the hypothesis tests that were conducted after these technical models were estimated. The interested reader can consult Wooldridge (2001) for details.

11. *See* Gujarati (2003, p. 483) for a discussion of this procedure.

12. *See, e.g.,* Buchanan and Slottje (1995).

13. This is shown in the second row of Exhibit 14.5 labeled "Franchise Effects." The joint F-test uses as a null hypothesis that all of the coefficients of the variables involved in the test (e.g., the franchise specific variables) are each equal to zero. This hypothesis was rejected in two of the four specifications. *See* Gujarati (2003) for a detailed description of a joint F-test.

14. This is shown in the third and fourth row of Exhibit 14.5. The joint F-test uses as a null hypothesis that all of the coefficients of the variables involved in the test (e.g., the yearly dummy variables) are each equal to zero. This hypothesis was rejected in three of the four specifications. *See* Gujarati (2003) for a detailed description of a joint F-test.

15. The significance of the t-statistic can also be calculated easily in Microsoft Excel.

16. The probability of a Type I error is often referred to as a p-value. In this case the two-tailed p-value is 0.28.

References

Basmann, R. L., and D. J. Slottje. "Copyright Damages and Statistics," *International Statistical Review* 71, no. 3 (2003): 557–564.

Buchanan, M., and D. Slottje. *Pay and Performance in the NBA* (Greenwich, CT: JAI Press, 1995).

Gujarati, D. *Basic Econometrics* (New York: McGraw-Hill, 2003).

Kmenta, J. *Elements of Econometrics.* New York: Macmillian, 1986).

Wooldridge, J. M. *Econometric Analysis of Cross Section and Panel Data* (Cambridge, MA: MIT Press, 2001).

CHAPTER 15

Quantification of Damages in Trademark Cases

BLAKE INGLISH
FTI Consulting, Inc.

This chapter presents a comprehensive discussion of how damages are quantified in trademark cases. A basic understanding of the relevant statutes, case law, and economic theories is essential in any effort to appropriately quantify damages in trademark disputes.

INTRODUCTION

In a time of increasing reliance on intellectual property (IP), trademarks have become a key component in the successful strategy of many businesses. Trademark applications filed with the United States Patent and Trademark Office (USPTO) have nearly doubled in the past 10 years.[1] Today, many companies engage in litigation to actively defend their trademarks and protect their name, reputation, market position, and profitability. Every year between 1995 and 2004, there were more cases filed in U.S. District Courts related to trademark rights than patents or copyrights.[2] A basic understanding of trademarks and relevant damages considerations can be of tremendous benefit to companies that rely on these forms of IP to identify their products or services as well as to the firms that assist them in resolving trademark disputes.

GENERAL TRADEMARK INFORMATION

General Definition

According to the USPTO, a trademark is a word, phrase, symbol or design, or a combination of words, phrases, symbols, or designs, that identifies and distinguishes the source of the goods of one party from those of others.[3] The Lanham Act refers to trademarks as any word, name, symbol, or device, or any combination thereof (1) used by a person, or (2) which a person has a bona fide intention to use in commerce and applies to register on the principal register established to identify and distinguish his or her goods, including a unique product, from those manufactured or sold by others and to indicate the source of the goods, even if that source is unknown.[4]

The purpose of a trademark is "to guarantee a product's genuineness. In effect, the trademark is the commercial substitute for one's signature."[5]

Inclusive Definitions

The term *trademark* is inclusive of several other terms.

Trade Name   A trade name differs from a trademark insofar as it distinguishes a company, partnership, or business whereas a trademark differentiates a product. In short, a trade name is "the name under which a business operates."[6] IBM is an example of a trade name.

Service Mark   A service mark is the same as a trademark, except that it identifies and distinguishes the source of a service rather than a product.[7] The same protection is afforded for service marks as for trademarks under the Lanham Act.[8] United Airlines is an example of a service mark.

Trade Dress   Trade dress refers to "the overall appearance and image in the marketplace of a product or a commercial enterprise," which may include a product's packaging and labeling or an enterprise's design and decor.[9] Courts have defined trade dress as involving "the total image of a product, and may include features such as size, shape, color or color combinations, texture, graphics, or even particular sales techniques."[10] It "encompasses the design and appearance of the product together with all the elements making up the overall image that serves to identify the product presented to the consumer."[11] An example of trade dress is the shape of a Coca-Cola bottle.

Collective and Certification Marks   The Lanham Act also covers collective and certification marks, including indications of regional origin, within its scope.[12] A certification mark serves to "certify regional or other origin, material, mode of manufacture, quality, accuracy, or other characteristics of such person's goods or services or that the work or labor on the goods or services was performed by members of a union or other organization."[13] An example of a certification mark is the Good Housekeeping Seal of Approval.[14] A collective mark is used by or is intended to be used by members of a cooperative, an association or other collective group of organization, including marks indicating membership in a union, an association or other organization.[15] For instance, "CPA" is a collective mark used to distinguish those members of the American Institute of Certified Public Accountants who have met certain requirements to practice accounting.

Distinctiveness

Trademarks can have different levels of distinctiveness, including fanciful, arbitrary, suggestive, descriptive, and generic.

A *fanciful* trademark is a made-up or coined word designed for the sole purpose of serving as a trademark (e.g., Xerox, Exxon and Kodak). Fanciful trademarks are inherently distinctive and are thus provided trademark protection.[16]

Slightly less strong than fanciful marks are *arbitrary* marks, which may be a common or existing word used as a mark for goods or services for which it does not describe or have a direct or established relationship (e.g., Apple/Sun—computer products, Baby Ruth—candy).[17]

Suggestive trademarks are weaker types of marks but are still generally protectable without proof of secondary meaning. These types of trademarks might indirectly suggest, rather than describe, a characteristic, attribute, or benefit of the trademarked product; the consumer would then draw a conclusion about the nature of the product using his or her imagination (e.g., Microsoft—software for microcomputers, Netscape—Internet software).[18]

Descriptive marks, which are typically not protectable, describe a quality, characteristic, or purpose of the trademarked product (e.g., Raisin Bran— cereal with raisins). It is possible, however, for descriptive marks to become entitled to trademark protection if it can be demonstrated that the mark has acquired distinctiveness and secondary meaning.[19]

Generic terms cannot constitute trademarks. These trademarks are merely "associated with or known as a particular category of goods or services to which it relates, thereby ceasing to function as an indicator of origin."[20] A term can either be generic from the outset or become generic usually through improper use over a long period of time (e.g., Aspirin and Cellophane).[21] Other trademarks that have risked similar fates include Xerox and Kleenex.

Registration

Process When registering a trademark, an application must include a clear drawing of the mark as well as a listing of the goods or services to which the mark will be associated.[22] In this way, a listing of the goods and services may result in the avoidance of potential future disputes by allowing the USPTO and the public to identify similar marks that may refer to like goods or services. After registration, this listing may be refined or limited to a smaller set of goods or services, but may not be expanded to include additional goods or services.[23] After an application is submitted to the USPTO, an examination is performed by an attorney.[24]

Usage Registration through the USPTO is not necessarily required to establish ownership of or claim rights to a particular trademark. While all that is required is "legitimate use of the mark,"[25] there are benefits to completing the registration process. Such benefits include the registered trademark's ability to serve as a public announcement of the use of such a trademark as well as to potentially enhance its product's position in relation to foreign goods and markets.[26] If the trademark is not already being used prior to submission of the application (current use of the mark in commerce), the applicant must have a bona fide intention to use the trademark as identified on the application and must begin its use prior to being granted registration from the USPTO.[27] As a result, an applicant cannot obtain a trademark registration merely to preclude someone else from using that mark.[28]

The rights to a registered trademark may last as long as the trademark continues to be used and as long as the requirement for the trademark owner to file an "Affidavit of continuing use" is met.[29]

TRADEMARK INFRINGEMENT LITIGATION

The primary body of law regarding trademarks, found in Section 15 of the United States Code, is influenced by the Lanham Act. Enacted in 1946, the Lanham Act has since undergone revisions and updates to make it relevant to the issues surrounding the current uses of trademarks. The goal of trademark law is to prevent deception and customer confusion and to protect property interests in trademarks.[30]

Concepts Unique to Trademark Infringement

Likelihood of Confusion   During the attorney's trademark registration process examination, a search is performed for conflicting, pending, or registered trademarks. The factors in evaluating this "likelihood of confusion" include: (1) the similarity of the marks and (2) the commercial relationship between the goods and/or services listed in the application.[31] In reviewing the trademarks, the USPTO can register similar marks if it is found that "confusion, mistake, or deception is not likely to result for the continued use by more than one person of the same or similar marks under conditions and limitations as to the mode or place of use of the marks or the goods on or in connection with which such marks are used."[32]

Eight factors have been analyzed in assessing the "likelihood of confusion" associated with multiple trademarks:

1. The similarity in the overall impression created by the two marks (including the marks' look, phonetic similarities, and underlying meanings)
2. The similarities of the goods and services involved (including an examination of the marketing channels for the goods)
3. The strength of the plaintiff's mark
4. Any evidence of actual confusion by consumers
5. The intent of the defendant in adopting its mark
6. The physical proximity of the goods in the retail marketplace
7. The degree of care likely to be exercised by the consumer
8. The likelihood of expansion of the product lines.[33]

Courts have opined that "a plaintiff who seeks money damages under the Lanham Act Section 43(a) must include evidence of actual customer confusion, while a plaintiff seeking injunctive relief under that statute need only show a likelihood of confusion."[34]

Secondary Meaning   A trademark has "secondary meaning" when it becomes uniquely associated with a specific source through continued use.[35] A trademark must either be inherently distinctive in that it is "unusual in the context of its use, and therefore memorable,"[36] or have secondary meaning in order to be protected by trademark law. Infringement is demonstrated when a trademark is deemed to be inherently distinctive or to have secondary meaning and also is shown to have likelihood of confusion.[37] When trying to determine whether a given term has acquired secondary meaning, courts will often look to circumstantial evidence such as (1) the amount and manner of advertising; (2) the volume of sales; (3) the length and manner of the term's use; and (4) the results of consumer surveys.[38]

Dilution   "Dilution differs from normal trademark infringement in that there is no need to prove a likelihood of confusion to protect a mark. Instead, all that is required is that use of a 'famous' mark by a third party causes the dilution of the 'distinctive quality' of the mark."[39] Examples of trademarks that may be considered famous include Pepsi, Ford, and Sony. The Federal Trademark Dilution Act of 1995 lists several factors that may assist the court in determining whether a trademark is "famous," including:

1. The degree of inherent or acquired distinctiveness of the mark
2. The duration and extent of use of the mark in connection with the goods or services with which the mark is used
3. The duration and extent of advertising and publicity of the mark
4. The geographical extent of the trading area in which the mark is used
5. The channels of trade for the goods or services with which the mark is used
6. The degree of recognition of the mark in the trading areas and channels of trade used by the marks' owner and the person against whom the injunction is sought
7. The nature and extent of use of the same or similar marks by third parties
8. Whether the mark was registered under the act of March 3, 1881, or the act of February 20, 1905, or on the principal register[40]

Further, whether actual dilution has occurred may be evaluated using three different means:

1. "Proof of an actual loss of revenues"
2. "The skillfully constructed consumer survey"
3. "Relevant contextual factors such as the extent of the junior mark's exposure, the similarity of the marks, [and] the firmness of the senior mark's hold"[41]

It has been recognized that the plaintiff's trademark need not be nationally famous for dilution to occur; it is enough for a mark to be strong in a particular geographical or product area.

False Advertising

While the Lanham Act primarily pertains to trademarks, the issue of false advertising is also included in its scope. False advertising is defined as the misrepresentation of "the nature, characteristics, qualities, or geographic origin of his or her or another person's goods, services, or commercial activities" in commercial advertising or promotion.[42]

Nonmonetary Remedies

Injunction   While various forms of damages may be sought in trademark-related claims, oftentimes the more immediate remedy sought is a temporary or permanent injunction. In addition, in cases where the infringer is found to be an "innocent infringer" or "innocent violator," the remedy available is an injunction.[43] In trademark law, "a finding that a trademark has been infringed does not necessarily require that an accounting be ordered where an injunction will satisfy the equities of the case."[44]

Seizure and/or Destruction   The court may decide that a product containing the alleged infringing or counterfeit trademark be seized as a remedy to stop the sale or distribution of the product.[45] The court may also order the destruction of the infringing products.[46]

CALCULATING TRADEMARK DAMAGES

In regards to damages available for infringement of a trademark, the Lanham Act dictates that "the registrant shall not be entitled to recover profits or damages unless the acts have been committed with knowledge that such imitation is intended to be used to cause confusion, or to cause mistake, or to deceive."[47]

Unlike the role of the *Panduit* test or *Georgia-Pacific* factors in patent infringement matters, case law may not have set a strong and clear precedent for the calculation of damages related to trademark infringement. However, guidance is provided through certain cases. In addition, some of the general concepts of damages calculations from other types of IP or commercial damages disputes are useful for their relevance to the realm of trademark infringement damages.

Types of Damages

The Lanham Act provides for the recovery of (1) defendant's profits, (2) any damages sustained by the plaintiff, and (3) the costs of the action.[48] Several measures of damages may fall into these categories: the plaintiff's lost profits, the defendant's profits, the plaintiff's actual business damages, the attorney's fees, or some combination thereof. In analyzing potential damages, it is imperative that the various elements of damages do not overlap. For instance, if making claims for both plaintiff's lost profits and defendant's profits, one would need to exclude the sales achieved by the defendant related to the lost profits claim when calculating the additional sales that the defendant benefited from for the defendant's profits claim.

Plaintiff's Lost Profits   Plaintiff's lost profits can be calculated using the traditional three-column approach in which "would have been" profits less actual profits equals lost profits. In addition, the determination of lost profits usually involves measuring lost sales and adjusting for incremental costs.

Lost Sales   Quantification of lost sales may be calculated using a variety of methodologies, including trend analysis, projections based on contemporaneous documents, and a market share approach. The precise method to choose and rely on may vary based on the level of documentation as well as the specific facts and circumstances of the case.

- *Trend analysis.* One method of estimating lost sales is to analyze the trend in sales. If sufficient data exists to plot the sales over time prior to the introduction of the infringing product, it can be compared to the sales occurring after the introduction of the infringing product. By estimating what the continued trend would have been based on historical sales, the difference between the "would have been" sales and the actual sales is the lost sales resulting from the infringing product. The projections must be "grounded in reality" and linked to the infringer's actions or the estimates may be rejected.[49]

- *Actual versus contemporaneous projections.* Documentation detailing sales projections that were prepared prior to the introduction of the infringing products can be useful in estimating lost sales. The ability of similar documents to accurately forecast sales projections can lend credibility for their use in litigation. Using such documentation, the future projections compared to the actual results can function as an estimate of potential lost sales.

- *Market share.* For situations other than a two-player market in which one party's lost sale (the plaintiff) is the other party's gained sale (the defendant), an analysis of the relevant market may be particularly helpful in evaluating the market dynamics and determining an approximation of the sales that would have been achieved by the plaintiff in a "but for" multiple-player market. For example, courts have used a market share approach in which the plaintiff's lost sales were estimated by evaluating the plaintiff's market share in a hypothetical market where the defendant would not have existed.[50]

Incremental Costs   The plaintiff must deduct costs that it would have incurred if it had achieved the sales discussed previously. Some costs, such as costs of goods sold or some equivalent measure, may be fairly straightforward to identify. Other costs may require more detailed analysis and discussions with knowledgeable company personnel in order to assess the relevant costs and their fixed or variable nature. An underlying issue to consider when evaluating costs is capacity. For instance, did the company have sufficient capacity to produce and sell the product, or would it have had to build another plant or hire additional salespeople?

In a case where the plaintiff did not make a profit on its sales of the product at issue, lost profits were calculated using the contribution to overhead that each unit's sale contributed.[51]

Damage Period   The damage period may be calculated in several ways, depending on the specific facts and circumstances for any given case. The beginning of the damage period will likely occur on the initial sale of or marketing efforts related to the infringing product. The conclusion of the damage period may be any number of points in time, such as the time at which an injunction was enforced (past), the time of trial if the infringer continues its sales of the infringing product (present), or some time into the future if it can be proven that the infringer's acts have impacted the plaintiff's future sales (future).

Prejudgment Interest   Prejudgment interest may be awarded at the discretion of the court.

Defendant's Profits   Defendant's profits are awarded under different rationales including unjust enrichment, deterrence, and compensation.[52] In one case, the court found that if the defendant's infringement is deliberate and willful, an accounting of the defendant's profits is appropriate under a theory of unjust enrichment.[53] The D.C. Appellate Court has held that it was not appropriate to award defendant's profits to the plaintiff when the plaintiff had not proven that the defendant had acted willfully or in bad faith.[54] However, a recent opinion in the Third Circuit has interpreted the Lanham Act such that willfulness is merely "a factor, not a prerequisite" in deciding whether the infringer's profits should be disgorged.[55] Direct competition between the two products is not necessary for defendant's profits to be awarded.[56]

Sales   The plaintiff shall be required to prove defendant's sales only.[57] When calculating the defendant's sales for a claim in which a plaintiff's lost profits claim has also been made, it is imperative to exclude the sales related to the lost profits claim in order to avoid double-counting. Some courts have allowed the plaintiff to recover profits even though the defendant lost money on the theory that the plaintiff should not be prejudiced by the defendant's inefficiency. In a situation in which the defendant had suffered losses during the damage period, the court "awarded the defendant 15 percent of the amount received from the sale" of the infringing product during the relevant time period.[58]

Relevant Costs and Apportionment   The defendant must prove all elements of cost or deduction claimed related to the defendant's sales that are proved by the plaintiff.[59] Similar to the analysis and calculation of costs related to a claim for plaintiff's lost profits, costs that were incurred in the course of the production and sale of the infringing product must be identified. Certain administrative expenses may be ruled an improper deduction if these expenses are not demonstrated to be variable costs.[60] In one case, a suggested proportionate share of overhead expenses was rejected as a cost deduction because the expenses did not increase variable to the infringing sales, or the defendant's sales of the infringing product were a very small part of their total overall sales.[61] The defendant may also attempt to prove that the sale of the infringing product resulted from additional factors other than the infringing feature—in this case, a trademark—and incorporate an estimate of the portion of sales that could be directly attributable to the infringing feature into their profits calculation. For example, a court attributed only 30 percent of a hotel's profits to the infringement and unfair competition by apportioning the profits based on the duration of stays and source of business.[62]

Other Types of Plaintiff's Damages   Elements of damage awards for which the courts have granted monetary relief include the cost of responsive or corrective advertising, the delay in widespread product rollout due to the infringement, and compensation related to the permanent distortion of the market, among others.[63]

Price Erosion   A portion of damages may result from price erosion. Price erosion may occur if the infringer sells the infringing product at a lower price in direct competition with the trademark owner's product. Not only may the trademark owner lose sales and subsequent profits due to the lower price (potentially claimable as lost profits), but prices may also need to be lowered in order to retain sales of the product. As a result, damages may be sought to compensate for the price erosion due to infringement.

Corrective Advertising   The plaintiff may be entitled to some measure of damages for actual amounts spent in corrective advertising responsive to the infringer's actions or some estimate thereof. One award for false advertising claims has been calculated as the amount spent by the defendant for false advertising multiplied by the percentage of geographical overlap between the two companies. In this particular case, the award was measured by the number of states in which the plaintiff operated compared to the number of states in which the defendant also operated and falsely advertised. This amount was then reduced by the Federal Trade Commission's guideline, which deemed 25 percent of the false advertising budget as an appropriate amount to spend on corrective advertising.[64]

Attorney's Fees   Attorney's fees may be awarded to the prevailing party in "exceptional cases."[65] Courts have interpreted this language as intending to allow the recovery of fees "in infringement cases where the acts of infringement can be characterized as 'malicious,' 'fraudulent,' 'deliberate,' or 'willful.'"[66] Another circuit has opined on the standard to award attorney's fees, stating that "willfulness short of bad faith or fraud will suffice when equitable considerations justify an award and the district court supportably finds the case exceptional."[67]

Other Damages Issues

Reasonable Royalty   Reasonable royalties are a form of damages that are typically associated with patent infringement disputes. However, this may also be an appropriate form of damages for trademark infringement. In certain circumstances, the monetary benefit to the infringer may be the royalty avoided during the sale of the infringing product. Therefore, the trademark owner may be entitled to these royalties. Furthermore, in at least one case, the measure of the plaintiff's lost profits has been found to be the royalties that were not paid to the plaintiff for the use of the trademark.[68] In reversing a district court's ruling on defendant's profits to be a percentage of sales that was deemed to be "a windfall to the plaintiff," the 7th Circuit Appellate Court suggested that a more appropriate remedy may be a reasonable royalty, which would be a more accurate reflection of the defendant's unjust enrichment.[69]

Counterfeit Mark   In disputes concerning the use of a counterfeit mark, the plaintiff may choose to seek statutory damages or actual damages and profits. Statutory damages would equal an amount ranging from $500 to $1 million per counterfeit mark per type of goods or services sold, depending on whether the use of a counterfeit mark was willful or not. Unless there is a finding of extenuating circumstances, the court would then treble profits or damages as well as award attorneys' fees for cases in which an infringer has been found to have intentionally used a counterfeit mark. In addition, the court has the discretion to award prejudgment interest.[70] If the plaintiff proves that the defendant acted willfully in the infringement, the court has concluded that a trebling of damages is required.[71]

Domain Name   In disputes involving the infringement of a domain name, the plaintiff may choose to seek actual damages and profits or statutory damages. Statutory damages would equal an amount ranging from $100 to $100,000 per domain name, as decided by the court.[72]

Damage for Dilution   The only remedy available for a "famous" mark is an injunction, unless it is found that the infringer had a willful intent to "trade on the owner's reputation or to cause the dilution of the famous mark." In that case, the trademark owner may be able to seek damages.[73]

International Considerations   The Madrid System, as established by the Madrid Agreement (1891) and Madrid Protocol (1989), allows for a single trademark registration that spans all participating countries, thereby making registration and protection of trademarks more simple and affordable.[74] As of September 2005, 78 countries were a party to the Madrid Agreement and/or Madrid Protocol.[75] In the United States, foreign nationals from countries that have participated in trademark conventions or treaties are entitled to the benefits outlined in the Lanham Act, including the remedies against unfair competition.[76]

CASE STUDY: CALCULATING DAMAGES FOR TRADEMARK INFRINGEMENT

For purposes of illustration, this hypothetical case study is provided to demonstrate some of the issues and methods to consider when quantifying damages in trademark infringement disputes. This simplified example is not inclusive of all damages theories or considerations, but merely highlights some approaches.

Summary of Case Assumptions

- Local Wheels has manufactured and sold over 200,000 high-end bicycles per period in Texas.

- In addition, Local Wheels had excess manufacturing and marketing capacity to handle an additional 50,000 units in bicycle sales each period.

- In an effort to expand, Local Wheels entered into a wholesale relationship with Big Cal, a California chain of stores, in period P1 and allowed Big Cal to sell its L2W brand of bicycles.

- Local Wheels provided marketing and advertising support in California to Big Cal from period P1 to period P8 to help stimulate demand for its L2W product.

- Since period P1, Big Cal has sold several brands of bicycles including a private-labeled bicycle named Big C.

- In period P4, Big Cal changed the name of its private-labeled bicycles from BIG C to L3W, adjusted the design and color of the bike to look similar to the Local Wheels brand, and started selling and advertising the L3W bicycles.

- As a result of a trademark lawsuit filed by Local Wheels, Big Cal received an injunction in period P6, which prevented it from marketing or selling products using the L3W brand. Big Cal immediately stopped selling the L3W brand and switched back to selling its original Big C bicycles. Due to contractual agreements, Local Wheels continued to sell the L2W bicycles to Big Cal even after the infringement.

- Local Wheels has historically sold all of its bicycles for $100 each.

- Local Wheels' historical per unit (bicycle) incremental costs are:

    Manufacturing: $ 55
    Shipping: $ 10
    Selling (Commission): $ 5

- Big Cal has historically sold all of its bicycles for $150 each.

- Big Cal's historical per unit (bicycle) incremental costs are:

    L2W: $100
    Big C / L3W: $ 80

Assuming the courts found that Big Cal infringed on the trademark "L2W" and that Local Wheels was entitled to damages resulting from Big Cal's actions, how should the damages be quantified?

Damages Calculation

Plaintiff's Lost Profits   In evaluating the lost profits suffered by Local Wheels, an analysis of the sales and relevant costs is performed, both for the actual and "would have been" scenarios.

Based on a review of the sales reported in Exhibits 15.1, it is apparent that from period P4 to P5 during the time of infringement, L2W unit sales dropped off by 67 percent. While this does provide some support for a causal relationship, it is important to consider

EXHIBIT 15.1   BIG CAL L2W BICYCLE SALES (IN UNITS)

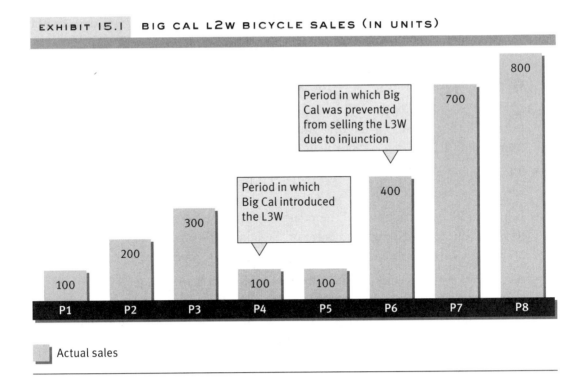

Actual sales

other factors, such as changes in marketing, advertising, consumer preferences, competing products, seasonality, and overall market size before reaching any conclusion. In addition, a well-crafted survey can be a relevant consideration when evaluating causation.

Another analysis that might provide additional support for causation would be to see if Big Cal's L2W per-unit profits of $50 ($150 selling price − $100 variable costs) are less than its private-label bicycle per unit profits of $70 ($150 selling price − $80 variable costs), thereby suggesting that Big Cal had economic incentive to shift demand from the L2W to its private-labeled bicycles.

Assumptions need to be made and supported regarding L2W "would have been" sales growth in order to quantify the potential lost sales. Absent the infringement, would the L2W sales have dropped off, remained constant, or increased? A review of the actual L2W sales immediately prior to infringement as well as immediately after the injunction indicates that the sales level would have likely continued to grow at a rate of 100 units per period. Based on this assumption, Local Wheels lost a total of 900 units in sales (see Exhibit 15.2).

Another potential consideration when determining the appropriate damages period is the timing and magnitude of both the infringer's marketing efforts and the infringing product sales. One or both factors may have directly impacted the sales of the infringed product. The fact that they both occurred at the same time in this case suggests that the damage period started in period P4.

EXHIBIT 15.2   BIG CAL L2W BICYCLE SALES AND LOSSES (IN UNITS)

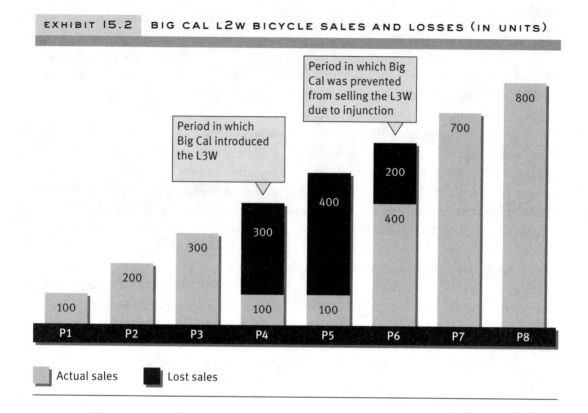

Sometimes it is important to consider the price elasticity of demand as well as the potential effects of an infringer's actions on a plaintiff's pricing strategy when calculating the total dollar value of lost sales. In this case, all of the bicycles sold by Big Cal are assumed to have sold for $150, which suggests these issues were not a factor.

Once the quantity of lost sales has been established, it is important to calculate the plaintiff's "would have been" incremental costs. The initial steps of this type of analysis usually begin with a review of financial documents to identify potentially relevant cost categories (e.g., manufacturing costs), followed by a more detailed analysis to determine the fixed versus variable nature of these costs. Based on the information provided, it appears that the per-unit incremental costs that Local Wheels would have incurred equaled $70 (manufacturing $55 + shipping $10 + selling $5). Even though these were the only reported historical variable costs, it is important to consider whether some of the costs that have historically been considered fixed would be incremental due to capacity constraints or other reasons. A quick comparison of the maximum potential lost unit sales quantified in this case of 900 bicycles to Local Wheels' available capacity of 50,000 units suggests that it was not capacity constrained.

Due to the infringement, Local Wheels lost sales totaling $90,000 (900 lost unit sales × $100 selling price) and would have incurred incremental costs totaling approximately $63,000 (900 lost unit sales × $70 incremental costs per unit) in making those sales. Based

on this calculation, the lost profits due to the infringement were $27,000 ($90,000 lost sales
− $63,000 incremental costs).

Defendant's Profits   The first step in a disgorgement claim is to determine the amount
of ill-gotten sales by the defendant. Based on a review of Exhibit 15.3, it appears that Big
Cal had infringing L3W sales totaling 1,100.

It is possible, however, that Big Cal's sales of the infringing products resulted from additional factors other than the trademark. Big Cal may be able to apportion some of its L3W
sales based on various information, including its historical sales of Big C bicycles (its pred-
ecessor private labeled bicycle), which experienced sales totaling 200 bicycles per period
immediately prior to and after the infringement. As seen on Exhibit 15.4, this would suggest that Big Cal's L3W sales attributable to the trademark infringement were limited to
a total of 700 units.

When seeking a disgorgement claim in addition to a lost profits claim, it is important
to quantify the overlapping sales and remove them from either the lost profits claim or the
disgorgement claim. In this case, Big Cal's incremental profit per bicycle totaling $50 ($150
selling price − $100 incremental costs) appears to be higher than Local Wheels' incre-
mental profits of $30 ($100 selling price − $70 incremental costs). In order to maximize
its potential damages award, Local Wheels would need to remove the 700 bicycles from
its lost profits claim above and disgorge the profits from Big Cal totaling $35,000 (700
units × $50 incremental profits per unit). As mentioned previously, the specific facts and
circumstances associated with any particular dispute must be taken into consideration in
order to determine the most appropriate measure of damages. For example, there are instances
in which a reasonable royalty may be the most appropriate form of damages.

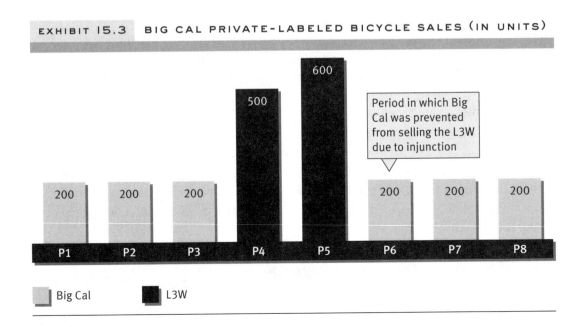

EXHIBIT 15.3   BIG CAL PRIVATE-LABELED BICYCLE SALES (IN UNITS)

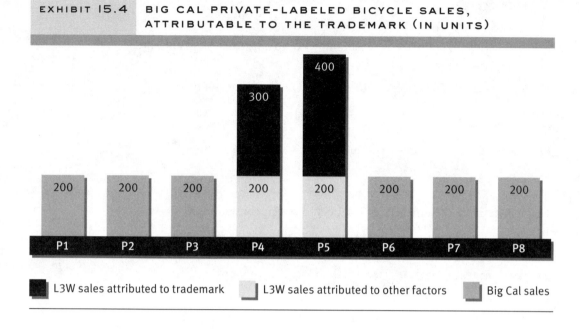

EXHIBIT 15.4   BIG CAL PRIVATE-LABELED BICYCLE SALES, ATTRIBUTABLE TO THE TRADEMARK (IN UNITS)

Legend: ■ L3W sales attributed to trademark   □ L3W sales attributed to other factors   ▨ Big Cal sales

CONCLUSION

The importance of trademarks in commerce and the protection of their rights continue to be critical factors in the success and growth of companies. A basic understanding of the relevant statutes, case law, and economic theories is essential in any effort to appropriately quantify damages in trademark disputes.

NOTES

1. www.uspto.gov/web/offices/com/annual/2004/060416_table16.html.
2. www.uscourts.gov/judicialfactsfigures/table2.02.pdf.
3. www.uspto.gov/web/offices/tac/doc/basic/trade_defin.htm.
4. 15 U.S.C. § 1127.
5. *Black's Law Dictionary,* 7th ed., Bryan A. Garner, editor in chief (St. Paul, MN: West Group, 1999).
6. *Id.*
7. www.uspto.gov/web/offices/tac/doc/basic/trade_defin.htm.
8. 15 U.S.C. § 1053.
9. *Black's Law Dictionary,* 7th ed. (St. Paul, MN: West Group, 1999), p. 1500.
10. *Two Pesos, Inc. v. Taco Cabana, Inc.,* 505 U.S. 763 (1992); *Roulo v. Russ Berrie & Co., Inc.,* 886 F.2d 931; 1989 U.S. App. LEXIS 15079; 12 U.S.P.Q.2D (BNA) 1423; Copy. L. Rep. (CCH) P26,478.
11. *Best Cellars, Inc. v. Wine Made Simple, Inc., LJG Wines, Inc.,* 320 F. Supp. 2d 60; 2003 U.S. Dist. LEXIS 3958.

12. 15 U.S.C. § 1054.

13. 15 U.S.C. § 1127.

14. International Trademark Association: www.inta.org/info/faqsD.html#8.

15. 15 U.S.C. § 1127.

16. www.inta.org/info/glossary; *Black's Law Dictionary,* pp. 1500–1501.

17. *Id.*

18. *Id.*

19. www.inta.org/info/glossary.html.

20. *Id.*

21. *Id.*

22. www.uspto.gov/web/offices/tac/doc/basic/appcontent.htm.

23. *Id.*

24. www.uspto.gov/web/offices/tac/doc/basic/afterapp.htm.

25. www.uspto.gov/web/offices/tac/doc/basic/register.htm.

26. *Id.*

27. 15 U.S.C. § 105.1.

28. www.uspto.gov/web/offices/tac/doc/basic/appcontent.htm.

29. 15 U.S.C. § 1058(b); www.uspto.gov/web/offices/tac/doc/basic/maintain.htm.

30. *Ameritech, Inc. v. American Information Technologies Corporation d/b/a Ameritech,* 811 F.2d 960, 1987 U.S. App. LEXIS 2243; 1 U.S.P.Q.2D (BNA) 1861.

31. www.uspto.gov/web/offices/tac/doc/basic/afterapp.htm.

32. 15 U.S.C. § 1052.

33. www.bitlaw.com/trademark/infringe.html: [re E.I. du Pont de Nemours & Co., 476 F.2d 1357, 177 USPQ 563 (CCPA 1973)].

34. *Best Cellars, Inc. v. Wine Made Simple, Inc., LJG Wines, Inc.,* 320 F. Supp. 2d 60; 2003 U.S. Dist. LEXIS 3958 in ref. to Resource Developers, 926 F.2d at 139–40.

35. *Two Pesos, Inc. v. Taco Cabana, Inc.,* 505 U.S. 763 (1992).

36. www.nolo.com.

37. *Two Pesos, Inc. v. Taco Cabana, Inc.,* 505 U.S. 763 (1992).

38. *Zatarain's, Inc. v. Oak Grove Smokehouse, Inc.,* 698 F.2d 786 (5th Cir. 1983).

39. www.bitlaw.com/trademark/dilution.html.

40. 15 U.S.C. § 1125(c).

41. *Ringling Bros.-Barnum & Bailey Combined Shows, Inc. v. Utah Division of Travel Development,* 170 F.3d 449; 1999 U.S. App. LEXIS 4179; 50 U.S.P.Q.2D (BNA) 1065.

42. 15 U.S.C. § 1125(a).

43. 15 U.S.C. § 1114(2).

44. *Champion Spark Plug Co. v. Sanders,* 331 U.S. 125; 67 S. Ct. 1136; 91 L. Ed. 1386; 1947 U.S. LEXIS 2997; 73 U.S.P.Q. (BNA) 133.

45. 15 U.S.C. § 1116.

46. 15 U.S.C. § 1118.

47. 15 U.S.C. § 1114(1).

48. 15 U.S.C. § 1117(a).

49. *Otis Clapp & Sons, Inc. v. Filmore Vitamin Co.*, 754 F.2d 738; 1985 U.S. App. LEXIS 28979; 225 U.S.P.Q. (BNA) 387.

50. *BASF Corp. v. Old World Trading Co., Inc.*, 41 F.3d 1081; 1994 U.S. App. LEXIS 32677; 1994-2 Trade Cas. (CCH) P70,790.

51. *Id.*

52. *Roulo v. Russ Berrie & Co., Inc.*, 886 F.2d 931; 1989 U.S. App. LEXIS 15079; 12 U.S.P.Q.2D (BNA) 1423; Copy. L. Rep. (CCH) P26,478.

53. *Babbitt Electronic, Inc. v. Dynascan Corp.*, 38 F.3d 1161; 1994 U.S. App. LEXIS 33188; 33 U.S.P.Q.2D (BNA) 1001; 8 Fla. L. Weekly Fed. C 817.

54. *Alpo Petfoods, Inc. v. Ralston-Purina Co.*, 302 U.S. App. D.C. 259; 997 F.2d 949; 1993 U.S. App. LEXIS 17605; 27 U.S.P.Q.2D (BNA) 1455; 1993-2 Trade Cas. (CCH) P70,462.

55. Banjo Buddies, Inc. v. Renosky, 3rd App. 03-2038/2107.

56. *Tamko Roofing Products, Inc. v. Ideal Roofing Company, Ltd.*, 282 F.3d 23; 2002 U.S. App. LEXIS 3578; 61 U.S.P.Q.2D (BNA) 1865.

57. 15 U.S.C. § 1117(a).

58. *Otis Clapp & Sons, Inc. v. Filmore Vitamin Co.*, 754 F.2d 738; 1985 U.S. App. LEXIS 28979; 225. U.S.P.Q. (BNA) 387.

59. 15 U.S.C. § 1117(a).

60. *Roulo v. Russ Berrie & Co., Inc.*, 886 F.2d 931; 1989 U.S. App. LEXIS 15079; 12 U.S.P.Q.2D (BNA) 1423; Copy. L. Rep. (CCH) P26,478.

61. *Playboy Enterprises, Inc. v. P.K. Sorren Export Co.*, 546 F. Supp. 987; 1982 U.S. Dist. LEXIS 15712; 218 U.S.P.Q. (BNA) 795.

62. *Holiday Inns, Inc. vs. Airport Holiday Corporation*, 493 F. Supp. 1025; 1980 U.S. Dist. LEXIS 12613; 212 U.S.P.Q. (BNA) 208.

63. *Alpo Petfoods, Inc. v. Ralston-Purina Co.*, 302 U.S. App. D.C. 259; 997 F.2d 949; 1993 U.S. App. LEXIS 17605; 27 U.S.P.Q.2D (BNA) 1455; 1993-2 Trade Cas. (CCH) P70,462.

64. *Big O Tire Dealers, Inc. v. The Goodyear Tire & Rubber Co.*, 561 F.2d 1365; 1977 U.S. App. LEXIS 11703; 195 U.S.P.Q. (BNA) 417.

65. 15 U.S.C. § 1117(a).

66. *Roulo v. Russ Berrie & Co., Inc.*, 886 F.2d 931; 1989 U.S. App. LEXIS 15079; 12 U.S.P.Q.2D (BNA) 1423; Copy. L. Rep. (CCH) P26,478.

67. *Tamko Roofing Products, Inc. v. Ideal Roofing Company, Ltd.*, 282 F.3d 23; 2002 U.S. App. LEXIS 3578; 61 U.S.P.Q.2D (BNA) 1865.

68. *Babbitt Electronic, Inc. v. Dynascan Corp.*, 38 F.3d 1161; 1994 U.S. App. LEXIS 33188; 33 U.S.P.Q.2D (BNA) 1001; 8 Fla. L. Weekly Fed. C 817.

69. *Sands, Taylor & Wood Co. v. Quaker Oats Co.*, 978 F.2d 947; 1992 U.S. App. LEXIS 20674; 24 U.S.P.Q.2D (BNA) 1001.

70. 15 U.S.C. § 1117(b).

71. *Babbitt Electronic, Inc. v. Dynascan Corp.*, 38 F.3d 1161; 1994 U.S. App. LEXIS 33188; 33 U.S.P.Q.2D (BNA) 1001; 8 Fla. L. Weekly Fed. C 817.

72. 15 U.S.C. § 1117(d).

73. 15 U.S.C. § 1125.

74. International Trademark Association: www.inta.org/madrid.

75. World Intellectual Property Organization: www.wipo.int/treaties/en/documents/pdf/g-mdrd-m.pdf.

76. 15 U.S.C. § 1126.

CHAPTER 16

Economic Damage Quantification in Trademark Matters

Jeffrey A. Dubin
Visiting Professor of Economics
University of California, Santa Barbara
Co-Founder and Partner
Pacific Economics Group, Pasadena, California

One approach to splitting the profits between owners and users of a trademark is the "25 percent rule" attributed to Goldscheider (Goldscheider and Marshall 1980). This rule of thumb states that typically one-quarter to one-third of the profit should be apportioned to the licensor for the use of the trademarked product. Regardless of the validity of the rule, there is no question that the rule is commonly cited and applied in the licensing community. The purpose of this chapter is to develop an econometric estimate of the trademark fraction based on an economic analysis of trademark value. Trademark fractions determined for five products using econometric demand analysis show considerable variation and are generally much larger than the 25 percent rule would suggest.

INTRODUCTION

Brand names and trademarks have long been recognized to confer value to their owners. Meanwhile, a hodge-podge of methods for determining these values exists, and often they appear to have no clear economic foundation or support.[1] (One such method, the income method, forecasts the future profit stream arising from the sales of a given branded product and then allocates a fraction of this profit stream to the brand. If a licensor and licensee are involved, the fraction of future profit attributable to the brand should be the basis for the royalty payment that the licensee would pay the licensor for use of the brand. One approach to splitting the profits between owners and users of a trademark (or in determining a reasonable transfer price for a firm with international operations) is the "25 percent rule." This rule of thumb states that typically one-quarter to one-third of the profit should be apportioned to the licensor for the use of the trademarked product.

The 25 percent rule and is sometimes known as the Goldscheider rule or Goldscheider fraction, or simply the trademark fraction.[2] Some empirical support for the rule comes from analyzing actual transactions and comparing these to estimated operating profits. Other justifications for the rule appear to be weak.[3] One justification is that 25 percent is what numerous others have agreed to and "that's just how it is." Another explanation is that 25 percent of the work to get a product to market is in the idea, and the remainder is due to the going concern of the business that will actually sell the product. Yet another explanation is that a buyer/user will require a three times return on costs before making the investment and commitment in a new project. Regardless of the validity of the rule, as a practical matter there is no question that it is commonly cited and applied in the licensing community. The purpose of this chapter is to develop an alternative estimate of the trademark fraction based on an economic fundamentals analysis of trademark value.

Specifically, I consider the economic value for five trademarks of the Carnation Company circa 1985—Coffee-mate, Carnation Evaporated Milk, Carnation Instant Breakfast, Mighty Dog (dog food), and Fancy Feast (cat food). These five brands were among Carnation's best-known brands; each has a relatively large market share, and each commands a price premium relative to its unbranded competitors. For this group of brands, there was both sufficient data to estimate product demand reliably and enough variety among the products to illustrate the nature and range of trademark values. The tools of demand analysis are used to quantify these characteristics and to calculate the trademark's economic value. I estimate trademark fractions with systematic variation across products and in overall magnitude relative to the one-quarter to one-third rules of thumb.

In brief, there are two basic components to the economic analysis of trademark value. First, historical sales data on branded products and their competitors are used to estimate respective demand functions. The demand function can be used, with knowledge of production costs, to determine the profitability of a product under alternative pricing strategies. The demand function summarizes all relevant information about the market for a product, such as special population segments that purchase a particular product, seasonal variations in purchases, levels of advertising spent, and characteristics of similar products in the same market. The second component of the economic analysis is a method for calculating the value of a brand trademark from the demand functions for the brand and its competitors. From an economic perspective, the value of a brand trademark to a producer is the difference between the profits that it would earn operating with the trademark and the profits it would earn operating without that trademark.

A formula giving the appropriate split of total profit between the trademark and non-trademark components is derived in Section III. The fraction of total profits attributable to the trademark, that is the "trademark fraction," is shown to depend on the market shares of the trademark brand versus that of the unbranded product (private label and generic goods) and their respective price elasticities.[4] In general, the greater the price elasticity of the branded good relative to the price elasticity of competing unbranded goods, the lower the fraction of profit which should be allocated to the brand trademark.

Basis for the Demand Approach

The economic value of a brand or trademark reflects a manufacturer's ability to command a higher selling price and/or market share for the branded good than it would attain for an essentially identical unbranded good. Uncertainty about the quality of, or lack of familiarity with, unbranded alternatives makes many consumers reluctant to purchase such products even when they sell at a considerable discount to branded goods. This has two consequences, which will be demonstrated mathematically later.

1. Because consumers prefer the branded good to its unbranded competitors, the branded good can be sold at a higher price than the unbranded good.

2. Despite the price premium, the producer of the branded good is usually able to sell larger quantities than the unbranded producer.

The combination of price premium and increased market share determines the relative profitability of branded and unbranded goods. From an economic perspective, the appropriate value for a trademark relates to the loss in profit that would ensue if the branded producer were denied use of the trademark. The purpose of econometric demand analysis is to estimate what price the producer of a branded good would charge if forced to sell the identical good without the brand label, and what quantity it would be able to sell at that price. If these prices and quantities can be estimated with sufficient accuracy, it is possible to determine the value to the holder of the brand trademark, as a portion of profit or sales.

The econometric method is based on two assumptions:

1. Consumers would perceive that unbranded goods produced by the branded producer were identical to other private-label goods. Quality differences in many goods are often in the eye of the beholder. To the extent that quality or technological differences exist or are perceived, the value of these is reflected in the econometric method, because any such differences are incorporated in consumer demand.

2. A branded producer's unit costs are the same whether it produces branded or unbranded goods. If the branded product is, in fact, superior to private-label alternatives, then the branded producer may be able to lower its costs by producing goods equivalent to those currently sold under private label. However, the branded producer may possess technological advantages that allow it to produce superior products at little or no additional cost, so that it could eventually reestablish its brand advantage over private-label products.

In summary, econometric demand analysis can be used to estimate the hypothetical profits of a branded producer selling without its brand trademark. Using this method, the value of the trademark (expressed as a percentage of sales) due to the holder is equal to the difference between its actual (with the brand) economic profits and its hypothetical (without the brand) economic profits, divided by total actual sales revenue.

DEMAND ANALYSIS AND BRAND PROFITABILITY

Generally, the holder of a brand trademark has a monopoly with respect to the differentiated demand for its branded product, although the existence of close substitutes—other branded and unbranded goods—constrains its ability to set prices. The maximum profit earned by the branded producer represents price (set to maximize profits) in excess of cost at a volume determined by the demand function. The profit, in this case, is $\pi = Q(P - C)$, that is, the quantity sold (Q) multiplied by the per-unit profit $(P - C)$. However, the value of a brand trademark in contributing to operating profits generally will be less than the total operating profits from selling the branded good. The reason for this is that even without use of the brand trademark, the producer would still be expected to earn some economic profit. The profit earned by the branded producer while selling unbranded goods is given by $\pi' = Q'(P' - C)$, that is, the quantity sold (Q') multiplied by its per-unit profit $(P' - C)$.

The economic value of the brand trademark is the difference between what the producer can earn selling the branded product (π) versus what the producer could earn without the trademark (π'). This difference may be expressed as:

$$V = \pi - \pi' = Q(P - P') + (Q - Q')(P' - C)$$

The first component, $Q(P - P')$, is the per-unit price premium associated with the brand, $(P - P')$, multiplied by sales quantity, (Q), of the branded good. In effect, this first component equals the total value of the price premium for the brand. The second component, $(Q - Q')(P' - C)$, represents the increase in sales volume attributable to the brand trademark, $(Q - Q')$ times per unit profits of the unbranded producer, $(P' - C)$. The second component therefore represents the value of increased market share. Using Lerner's rule, it follows that for the brand producer:

$$\frac{P - C}{P} = \frac{1}{\varepsilon} \tag{16.1}$$

where ε = differentiated demand price elasticity in brand market.

As noted, if the branded producer were to switch to production of unbranded goods, it would no longer be a monopolist. The branded producer, because of the scale of its production, would still have market power in the unbranded market, but competition with other unbranded producers would tend to reduce its markup rate $(P' - C)/P'$. Under Cournot oligopoly, the markup rate for an oligopolist (producing an unbranded product) is:

$$\frac{P' - C}{P'} = \frac{S'}{\varepsilon'} \tag{16.2}$$

where

S' = branded firm's quantity share in the unbranded market

ε' = price elasticity of demand in the unbranded market.

The economic value of the trademark (R), determined as a percentage of sales, equals

$$R = \frac{V}{PQ} = \frac{Q(P-C)}{PQ}\left[1 - \frac{Q'(P'-C)}{Q(P-C)}\right] \tag{16.3}$$

which represents the per-period value of the trademark divided by the per-period total sales revenue. As can been seen from the structure of equation (16.3), the value R is the product of two factors. The first factor, $Q(P-C)/PQ$, is the economic operating margin (total economic profits divided by total revenues). The second factor:

$$G = 1 - \frac{Q'(P'-C)}{Q(P-C)} \tag{16.4}$$

$$= 1 - \frac{P'Q'S'/\varepsilon'}{PQ/\varepsilon} = 1 - S'\frac{\alpha'_0 T'P'\varepsilon}{\alpha_0 TP\varepsilon'}$$

is the proportion of economic profits realized due to the brand or trademark (i.e., the "trademark fraction"), where $\alpha_0 = Q/T$ and $\alpha'_0 = Q'/T'$ are the branded producer's shares of total industry unit sales (including other branded goods as well as unbranded goods) before and after its switch to unbranded production, and T and T' are total industry unit sales before and after the switch.[5] Since:

$$\frac{P'}{P} = \frac{C/P}{C/P'} = \frac{1 - \frac{1}{\varepsilon}}{1 - \frac{S'}{\varepsilon'}}. \tag{16.5}$$

we obtain:

$$G = 1 - S'\frac{\alpha'_0}{\alpha_0}\frac{T'}{T}\frac{\varepsilon - 1}{\varepsilon' - S'}. \tag{16.6}$$

The analysis is completed by making a few assumptions about aggregate market response to the elimination of a brand. The first assumption is that total industry sales are unaffected by a brand elimination, that is, $T' = T$. Next, I make some assumptions about how relative market shares change in response to elimination of a brand. In Dubin (1998) the market share model for branded and unbranded goods was assumed to be multinomial logit (MNL). Specifically, that study assumed that when a specific branded alternative was eliminated, a proportional increase in the market share of the remaining branded and unbranded goods would occur.[6]

Let α_1 denote the market share of unbranded alternatives. Then the MNL assumption implies that α_1 increases to $\alpha'_1 = \alpha_1/(1 - \alpha_0)$ after brand zero is eliminated. Let S denote brand zero's quantity market share of its own sales and of unbranded sales prior to the hypothetical loss of the trademark (i.e., $S = \alpha_0/(\alpha_0 + \alpha_1)$). I assume that the branded producer will continue to capture this relative market share after brand loss so that $S' = S$ where S' denotes the relative market share after brand expiration. Under these assumptions, brand zero's market share changes from α_0 to $\alpha'_0 = S'\alpha'_1 = S\alpha'_1$. Since $(1 - S)/S = \alpha_1/\alpha_0$, we have:

$$\frac{\alpha'_0}{\alpha_0} = \frac{S\alpha'_1}{\alpha_1}\frac{\alpha_1}{\alpha_0} = (1 - S)\frac{\alpha'_1}{\alpha_1}.$$

and under MNL:

$$\frac{\alpha'_0}{\alpha_0} = \frac{(1 - S)}{1 - \alpha_0}.$$

Finally:

$$G = 1 - S\left(\frac{\alpha'_0}{\alpha_0}\right)\left(\frac{\varepsilon - 1}{\varepsilon' - S}\right)$$

$$= 1 - \frac{S(1 - S)}{1 - \alpha_0}\left(\frac{\varepsilon - 1}{\varepsilon' - S}\right). \tag{16.7}$$

DATA DESCRIPTION

This section describes the data used in the demand analysis presented in the next section. Three categories of variables are used in the demand analysis: sales data, macroeconomic and demographic indicators, and product specific variables. Data on sales (quantity sold and average selling price) are drawn from two different sources, the "Nielsen Research Report to Carnation Company Inc." (Nielsen Research 1979–1984) and the "SAMI Basic/ Special Report" (Selling Area Marketing, Inc. 1979–1984), found in Carnation's marketing files. The use of Nielson and SAMI data for elasticity determination is similar to elasticity measurement based on store-level scanner data. My analysis controls for demographic factors in the demand analysis and computes product-level rather than store-level elasticities. A variety of different sources are consulted for variables anticipated to affect the demand of particular products.

Nielsen Reports

The primary source for data on selling prices and quantities is a series of surveys conducted by the A. C. Nielsen Company. Nielsen uses a national probability sample of 1,050 stores in the continental United States to calculate its estimates. The data are obtained bimonthly through in-store audits. During each store visit, Nielsen personnel count all products on the shelf, in displays, and in the back room or storage area. Sales volume is computed as the sum of purchases from warehouses, brokers, or other distributors over a two–month period (as shown on invoices), less the increase in inventory from the previous visit. Shelf prices are recorded as the retail price after adjustment for any promotional pricing that may have been in effect on the day of the visit. Data are reported on total pounds or cases sold, retail price, percent of volume sold with retail advertising support (local advertising, special prices, ad coupons, and displays), total inventory quantities, and total store sales for those selling the particular product or brand (called "all commodity volume" or ACV).

SAMI Reports

An alternative source of sales data for some of the products are reports on warehouse withdrawals compiled by the Strategic Areas Marketing, Inc. (SAMI) service (a division of Time-Life until the late 1980s, but subsequently sold to Information Resources, Inc.). SAMI reports average shelf price and case volume every four weeks for 54 market areas. The SAMI data are not based on a probability sample. Instead, SAMI personnel collect data on withdrawals made by individual retail stores from participating food distributor warehouses in each of the 54 markets. The data cover approximately 80 percent of the total ACV in each market, so that any bias introduced by the lack of full coverage is expected to be small.

Socioeconomic Data

A number of demographic variables are anticipated to affect demand. To account for these effects, as well as shifts in consumer demand caused by unemployment and population growth, area demographic and economic indicators are collected from various editions of the *State and Metropolitan Area Data Book* (U.S. Department of Commerce, Bureau of the Census 1982, 1986, 1991). These variables include: total population, percent of population of Hispanic origin, and per-capita personal income. The variables are collected for each metropolitan statistical area (MSA) for the period 1979 through 1984 on an annual basis, although not every year is available. (Missing data are interpolated.) Data are then matched to either Nielsen or SAMI regions as appropriate.

Leading National Advertisers Data

Leading National Advertisers (LNA) tracks multimedia advertising expenditures across the United States in six major media: consumer magazines, newspaper supplements, network television, spot television, network radio, and outdoor billboards. LNA publishes quarterly breakdowns of spending in these media by brand and company in its "LNA Multi-Media Report Service" (Leading National Advertisers 1979–1984). LNA includes only companies that spend over $25,000 in all six media combined. Bimonthly expenditures are interpolated from the quarterly totals.

CPI Data

Prices in this study are deflated using a monthly consumer price index (CPI) for four census regions, published by the U.S. Department of Commerce, Bureau of Labor Statistics (1979–1984).

ANALYSIS

To estimate an economic value for the trademarks at issue, I rely on the brand price elasticity and the price elasticities for the unbranded competitors. The demand elasticities used to calculate the trademark fraction are estimated using retail price data. A complete presentation of the econometric analysis for each of the five products is presented in Dubin (1998). Here I illustrate the methodology for the coffee creamer demand model.

The demand models for coffee creamer were estimated for 16-ounce size products. The basic demand equation relates the logarithm of the bimonthly sales of creamer to the logarithms of the real price per pound for the creamer in question and to the logarithms of the real prices of substitute creamers.[7] The demand equation also allows for trend and seasonality in the consumption pattern as well as for regional effects. Finally, the demand equation specifies that creamer sales are potentially influenced by the level of real income per capita, the frequency of coffee consumption (measured in coffee cups consumed per day per capita), the total volume of all sales in the region (all commodity volume), real advertising of branded creamers, and retail support, including in-aisle displays, in-ad coupons, or special pricing.

The demand function has the log-linear form:

$$\log Q_{bsrt} = \alpha + \log P_{bsrt}\beta_1 + \log P'_{bsrt}\beta_2 + X_{bsrt}\gamma + \varepsilon_{bsrt}$$

where

Q_{bsrt} = bimonthly quantity of creamer sold by brand b
    in size category s, in region r, in period t.

The price of the creamer is P_{bsrt} and denotes the average selling price for the brand b, in size s, sold in region r, at time period t.

The price vector P'_{bsrt} captures the prices of substitute brands and sizes in the same period and region. The explanatory factors X_{bsrt} depend on the brand, size in question, location, and time period. The vector X_{bsrt} includes seasonal effects, time trend, advertising, real income per capita, cups per day per capita, special promotions, and so on. The own-price elasticity—that is, the price elasticity of quantity-demanded of a particular brand with respect to its own price, holding all other prices fixed—is:

$$e = \frac{\partial \log Q_{bsrt}}{\partial \log P_{bsrt}} = \frac{P_{bsrt}}{Q_{bsrt}} \times \frac{\partial Q_{bsrt}}{\partial P_{bsrt}} = \beta_1$$

The price elasticities of quantity-demanded of a particular brand with respect to the prices of substitute goods are similarly the coefficients β_2.

Exhibit 16.1 summarizes the dependent and explanatory variables for the coffee creamer demand models.

The model for coffee creamer estimates the demand for 16-ounce creamer as a function of the prices of 16-ounce creamers and the prices of 22-ounce creamers. Exhibit 16.2

| EXHIBIT 16.1 | VARIABLE DEFINITIONS FOR COFFEE CREAMER MODEL |

Variable	Definition
lscm16	logarithm of sales of 16-ounce Coffee-mate, pound basis
lscr16	logarithm of sales of 16-ounce Cremora, pound basis
lspl16	logarithm of sales of 16-ounce Private Label, pound basis
lpcm16	logarithm of price of 16-ounce Coffee-mate
lpcr16	logarithm of price of 16-ounce Cremora
lppl16	logarithm of price of 16-ounce Private Label
lpcm22	logarithm of price of 22-ounce Coffee-mate
lpcr22	logarithm of price of 22-ounce Cremora
lppl22	logarithm of price of 22-ounce Private Label
trend	linear time trend
seas1	December–January period
seas2	February–March period
seas3	April–May period
seas4	June–July period
seas5	August–September period
lrinc	logarithm of real personal income
lcpd	logarithm of cups of coffee consumed per day
lacv16	logarithm of all commodity volume
rscmdis	retail support displays Coffee-mate
rscmiac	retail support in-ad coupons Coffee-mate
rscmsp	retail support special prices Coffee-mate
rscrdis	retail support displays Cremora
rscriac	retail support in-ad coupons Cremora
rscrsp	retail support special prices Cremora
rspldis	retail support displays Private Label
rspliac	retail support in-ad coupons Private Label
rsplsp	retail support special prices Private Label
ladcar	logarithm of real advertising expenditure for Coffee-mate (LNA derived)
ladcrm	logarithm of real advertising expenditure for Cremora (LNA derived)

shows the regression results for the 16-ounce models. (Coefficients significant at the 95% significance level are marked in red).

The demand for Coffee-mate 16-ounce dry creamer depends significantly on relative prices. As the price of 16-ounce Coffee-mate creamer rises, consumers are predicted to purchase less 16-ounce Coffee-mate creamer. The other price effects show that 16-ounce Private Label and 22-ounce Coffee-mate creamer are economic substitutes for Coffee-mate 16-ounce creamer. The pattern of seasonal effects reveals that significantly more 16-ounce Coffee-mate creamer is purchased in the February–March bimonth as compared with the June–July and August–September periods. Additionally, the summer periods show generally lower demand than either the fall or winter periods. These results are consistent with a commodity that is consumed with coffee, where the seasonality of coffee consumption leads to the seasonality of creamer consumption.

EXHIBIT 16.2	ESTIMATED COFFEE CREAMER DEMAND MODELS		
	CM #1 LSCM 16	CM #2 LSCR 16	CM #3 LSPL 16
trend	−0.024	0.028	−0.064
lpcm 16	−2.006	−0.023	0.145
lpcr16	0.220	−1.491	0.236
lppl16	0.359	0.123	−1.441
lpcm22	0.918	0.254	0.605
lpcr22	−0.058	−0.160	−0.066
lppl22	0.232	0.255	0.675
seas1	0.020	−0.278	−0.330
seas2	0.166	−0.109	−0.173
seas3	−0.007	0.000	−0.105
seas4	−0.154	0.244	−0.036
seas5	−0.166	0.059	0.025
lrinc	0.118	0.935	0.169
lcpd	0.419	2.562	1.939
lacv16	0.139	0.070	0.176
racmdis	−0.003	—	—
rscmiac	0.007	—	—
rscmsp	0.003	—	—
rscrdis	—	−0.003	—
rscriac	—	−0.001	—
rscrsp	—	0.005	—
rspldis	—	—	0.001
rspliac	—	—	−.002
rsplsp	—	—	−0.001
ladcar	0.001	0.037	0.016
ladcrm	0.020	−0.045	0.002
R-Squared	0.892	0.894	0.823
Number of Observations	404	404	404
Standard Error of the Regression	0.179	0.280	0.247

The real per-capita income and coffee consumption per day variables were not always statistically significant from zero. However, all commodity volume was highly significant, indicating that areas with larger markets will also sell more creamer. The retail support variables indicate that of the three forms—displays, in-ad coupons, or special prices—only in-ad coupons and special prices have a significant impact on the demand for 16-ounce Coffee-mate product. The presence of each of these leads to higher sales. Finally, the LNA advertising variables suggest that advertising for Coffee-mate did not significantly increase the demand for Coffee-mate. The regression model provides an excellent fit to the historic pattern of sales, as 82 to 89 percent of the variation in demand was explained by the models.

ESTIMATED TRADEMARK FRACTIONS AND CONCLUSIONS

To calculate the trademark fraction (the percentage of profits attributable to the trademark), I use elasticity values from the branded and private label estimated demand models. These elasticities are summarized in Exhibit 16.3.[8]

In order to calculate the trademark value as a percentage of revenues using the formulas derived in earlier, it is necessary to calculate economic operating margins. Accounting operating margins do not include a charge for a "normal" rate of return on plant, equipment, and other assets that have alternative uses. As a result, I have utilized the identifiable fixed assets for each division of the Carnation Company, plus an allocation of the general corporate assets, times a rate of return for alternative uses of capital, to obtain an economic operating margin. These figures are listed in Exhibit 16.4.

For example, with Coffee-mate 16-ounce creamer, in 1984 the fixed assets associated with the Instant Division of the Carnation Company as a percent of sales were 29.1 percent (combining fixed and general assets). I assume a weighted average cost of capital of 13.0 percent, which leads to an offset in the accounting operating margin of 3.8 percent. The results for the trademark fractions are given in Exhibit 16.5.

For example, selecting the numbers for Coffee-mate 16-ounce creamer gives us:

α_0 = market share of the branded commodity = 51.3%

α_1 = market share of the private-label commodity = 28.2%

| EXHIBIT 16.3 | SUMMARY OF MARKET SHARES AND PRICE ELASTICITIES |

	Coffee-mate 16 oz. Creamer	Carnation Evaporated Milk	Carnation Instant Breakfast 6-packet	Mighty Dog Dog Food	Fancy Feast Cat Food
Market share of the branded commodity	51.3%	30.8%	80.3%	5.9%	3.9%
Market share of the private-label commodity	28.2%	47.8%	17.6%	2.2%	8.7%
Elasticity of the branded commodity	2.01	2.03	1.47	2.42	4.27
Elasticity of the private-label commodity	1.44	1.22	1.74	2.25	1.61

EXHIBIT 16.4   SUMMARY OF CAPITAL CHARGE CALCULATION

	Coffee-mate 16 oz. Creamer	Carnation Evaporated Milk	Carnation Instant Breakfast 6-packet	Mighty Dog Dog Food	Fancy Feast Cat Food
Fixed assets (as a percentage of sales)	25.8%	11.8%	25.8%	11.3%	11.3%
General corporate assets (as a percentage of sales)	3.3%	3.3%	3.3%	3.3%	3.3%
Resulting total assets (as a percentage of sales)	29.1%	15.1%	29.1%	14.6%	14.6%
Weighted average cost of capital	13.0%	13.0%	13.0%	13.0%	13.0%
Margin attributable to return on fixed assets (as a percentage of sales)	3.8%	2.0%	3.8%	1.9%	1.9%

ε = elasticity of the branded commodity = 2.01

ε' = elasticity of the private-label commodity = 1.44.

Using these numbers results in:

$$S = \frac{\alpha_0}{\alpha_0 + \alpha_1} = \frac{0.513}{0.513 + 0.282} = 0.645$$

Applying this result to equation (16.7) results in:

$$G = 1 - \frac{S(1-S)}{1-\alpha_0} \frac{\varepsilon - 1}{\varepsilon' - S)} = 1 - \frac{0.645(1-0.645)}{1-0.513} \frac{2.01-1}{1.44-0.645}$$

$$= 1 - 0.470 \times 1.270 = 0.403$$

This value of 40.3 percent corresponds to the value listed in Exhibit 16.5 under "Coffee-mate 16-oz. Creamer" for its trademark fraction percentage of economic profit. The trademark fraction is then multiplied by the economic operating margin in order to arrive at a royalty rate.

As can be seen from Exhibit 16.5, the economic value of the trademark, expressed as a percentage of revenues, ranges from 1.3 percent for evaporated milk to 26.4 percent for Carnation Instant Breakfast. The percentage value for Coffee-mate, Mighty Dog, and Fancy Feast are 17.5 percent, 18.5 percent, and 11 percent, respectively. These royalty rates are consistent with expectations. The most unique and differentiated products have higher royalty rates, while the least differentiated products (such as evaporated milk) have the lowest

EXHIBIT 16.5   SUMMARY OF TRADEMARK FRACTION CALCULATIONS

	Coffee-mate 16 oz. Creamer	Carnation Evaporated Milk	Carnation Instant Breakfast 6-packet	Mighty Dog Dog Food	Fancy Feast Cat Food
Accounting operating margin (as a percentage of sales)	39.8%	5.2%	46.5%	25.0%	26.9%
Rate of return on fixed assets (as a percentage of sales)	3.8%	3.0%	3.8%	1.9%	1.9%
Economic operating margin (as a percentage of sales)	36.0%	2.2%	42.7%	23.1%	25.0%
Trademark fraction percentage of economic profit	40.3%	57.2%	61.8%	80.3%	43.8%
Percentage of revenues	14.5%	1.3%	26.4%	18.5%	11.0%

royalty rates. The trademark fractions just determined show considerable variation and are generally much larger than those touted in typical profit-split rules of thumb. Of course, practitioners of the profit-split methodology reasonably argue that the one-quarter to one-third allocation is only a starting point for an exact calculation in any given situation with discretion left to the analyst. This analysis casts doubt on the usefulness of the Goldscheider rule while providing an alternative based on economic and econometric analysis.

NOTES

1. *See, e.g.,* Reilly and Schweihs (1998) or Smith (1997).
2. The 25 percent rule is reviewed in Goldscheider, Jarosz, and Mulhern (2002) and Lee (1992). It is called the Goldscheider fraction in Goldscheider and Marshall (1980) and the trademark fraction in Dubin (1998).
3. *See, e.g.,* Razgaitis (2003).
4. Generics, while different from private-label commodities in packaging and marketing, account for less than 1 percent of total food sales. In my analysis I do not distinguish between private-label and generic commodities.
5. As discussed in Dubin (1998), equation (16.4) embodies five useful observations:
   1. The greater the price difference between the branded and unbranded products (i.e., the lower the ratio of P' to P), the higher is G.
   2. The greater the difference between the branded producer's market shares before and after the switch to unbranded production, the higher is G.

3. The greater the branded producer's prospective share of unbranded production (i.e., the higher S'), the lower is G.

4. The greater the drop in total industry unit sales resulting from the switch to nonbranded production, the higher is G.

5. The more elastic branded demand is to unbranded demand (i.e., the higher the ratio of ε to ε'), the lower is G. It is also important to note that equation (16.4) shows that merely comparing elasticities in the branded and unbranded markets may not be revealing of relative profits to the producer without also considering market share in the unbranded market.

6. The multionomial logit assumption is relaxed in Dubin (2004).

7. Data on powdered non-dairy coffee creamer sales are taken from Nielsen research reports (described above), covering the time period from December 1978–January 1979 to October–November 1984. The analysis is limited to sixteen and twenty-two ounce sizes of Coffeemate, Cremora, and Private Label creamer. Sales are reported in thousands of pounds. Retail support is measured by the percentage of sales involving displays of the product, coupons, or special prices. Coffee consumption is derived from two sources of data: Nielsen research reports (1979–1984) and the "United States of America Coffee Drinking Study—Winter 1987," published by the International Coffee Organization (1987). The Nielsen report has the same format as described above. The Coffee Drinking Study is conducted annually. It is based on telephone interviews with approximately seventy-five hundred persons aged ten and over and representative of the population in the continental U.S.

8. A complete discussion of the five products appears in Dubin (1998).

REFERENCES

Dubin, Jeffrey A. *Studies in Consumer Demand—Econometric Methods Applied to Market Data* (Boston: Kluwer Academic Publishers, 1998).

Dubin, Jeffrey A. "Valuing Intangible Assets with a Nested Logit Market Share Model," forthcoming, *Journal of Econometrics.*

Goldscheider, Robert, and James T. Marshall. "The Art of Licensing—From the Consultant's Point of View" 2, *The Law and Business of Licensing* (1980): 645.

Goldscheider, Robert, John Jarosz, and Carla Mulhern. "Use of The 25 Per Cent Rule in Valuing IP," *Les Nouvelles Journal of the Licensing Executives Society* 37, no. 4 (December 2002): 123–133.

Lee, William. "Determining Reasonable Royalty Rates," *Les Nouvelles Journal of the Licensing Executives Society* 27, no. 3 (September 1992): 24.

Leading National Advertisers, "LNA Multi-Media Report Service" 1979–1984, www.census.gov.

Nielsen Research, "Nielsen Research Report to Carnation Company Inc." 1979–1984, www.census.gov.

Razagaitis, Richard. *Valuation and Pricing of Technology-Based Intellectual Property* (Hoboken, NJ: John Wiley & Sons, 2003).

Reilly, Robert F., and Robert P. Schweihs. *Valuing Intangible Assets.* (New York: McGraw-Hill, 1998).

Strategic Areas Marketing, Inc., "SAMI Basic/Special Report," 1979–1984, www.census.gov.

Smith, Gordon. *Trademark Valuation* (New York: John Wiley & Sons, 1997).

State and Metropolitan Area Data Book (Washington, DC: U.S. Department of Commerce, Bureau of the Census 1982, 1986, 1991).

U.S. Department of Commerce, Bureau of Labor Statistics (1979–1984).

CHAPTER 17

Evaluation of Damages Claims in a Trade Secrets Case

ROBIN C. SICKLES
Rice University and LECG, LLC, Houston, Texas

ASHOK AYYAR
Rice University, Houston, Texas

We study a case *AAA. v. BBB* handled by the first author, in which trade secret information was allegedly misappropriated. Reviewing the case record brought to light problems in the prepared damages claim. By flagging these issues in practicum, this chapter should serve as a guide to intellectual property damages claims. We begin the study with a strategy and method for building a sound damages model and then annotate the study's findings with our analysis.

INTRODUCTION

Intellectual property (IP) misappropriation scenarios require an economic valuation of the IP asset to assess damages. It is an emerging challenge to the many players in the IP arena. The Uniform Trade Secrets Act of 1985 denotes a trade secret as:

> information, including a formula, pattern, compilation, program device, method, technique, or process, that: (i) derives independent economic value, actual or potential, from not being generally known to, and not being readily ascertainable by proper means by, other person who can obtain economic value from its disclosure or use, and (ii) is the subject of efforts that are reasonable under the circumstances to maintain its secrecy.

Texas, the jurisdiction of this case, does not observe the Uniform Trade Secret Act. There, trade secret violations are not treated as property issues but as breaches of confidential relationships when applicable. Since the seminal case *Hyde Corp v. Huffines,* Texas courts consider the relationship between defendant and plaintiff before they conclude that an injunction is suitable.[1]

No matter the jurisdiction, however, a trade secret is unique from other intellectual properties because injunctive relief may not serve as redress, as once the secret leaks to the industry at large, by definition, it is of no value. If the infringement is limited to one party and the information has not leaked to the market, calculating economic damages involves re-creating a "but for" world in which infringement did not occur and then comparing that state to the one after infringement.[2] The precedent for damage assessment in a trade secret or patent situation is ergo comparable.

The harbinger decision in IP infringement was *Panduit v. Stahlin*. To obtain damages, the court in *Panduit* ruled that the IP owner must prove: "(1) demand for the patented product, (2) absence of acceptable non-infringing substitutes, (3) his manufacturing and marketing capability to exploit the demand, and (4) the amount of the profit he would have made."[3]

Courts often employ a two-supplier test for prong (2), where an IP owner must show: "1) the relevant market contains only two suppliers, 2) its own manufacturing and marketing capability to make the sales that were diverted to the infringer, and 3) the amount of profit he would have made from these diverted sales."[4] In a two-supplier market, it is a small leap of faith to assume the owner would have made the infringer's sales. Precedent does not fully bolster the two-supplier test, as cases since *Panduit* have permitted recovery in situations where many substitutes have existed, making test (2) even more lax. The definition of a substitute itself is left to the vagaries of the legal system, but typically when an acceptable substitute is available, lost profits from price erosion cannot be recovered, only lost profits from lost sales.[5]

The challenge to field experts, then, is demonstrating points (1) and (4). From point (1), experts must show that the patented feature or cachet of the unpatented product directly satisfies consumer demand. Point (4) insists the plaintiff should be able to quantify, to a reasonable degree, the potential demand for the product. In the case study, consultants and marketing experts for the plaintiff attempted to demonstrate demand for the product by their expectation of future market potential.

Case Background: *AAA Technologies v. BBB, Inc.*

The first author investigated the statistical reliability of alleged trade secret damages suffered by plaintiff fictitiously referred to as AAA Technologies. AAA contracted defendant fictitiously referred to as BBB, Inc. to help develop its product line and form strategic alliances as necessary. AAA sued on grounds of misappropriation of its trade secrets, a range of biotechnology and biomaterial products yet to be developed or patented, with a number of potential applications. For all intents and purposes these inchoate products and information regarding them were proprietary, confidential, and thus regarded as trade secrets until patented. Being preproduction, no actual sales had been made, and so experts were summoned to project the future value of the trade secrets.

AAA retained a consulting firm, fictitiously referred to as BEST Consulting, LLC (BESTCO) to do this very task and devise a damage claim against BBB, expounded in the BESTCO supplemental report to damages model in *AAA v. BBB*. BESTCO generated the damage claim using net present value calculations to determine AAA's loss, arriving at a figure in the millions of dollars.

DAMAGES CALCULATIONS

There are five main measures of damages in trade secret cases.

1. The value of the trade secrets to the plaintiff at the time they were first misappropriated if they have been destroyed; otherwise their diminution.

2. The plaintiff's lost profits as a result of lost sales.

3. The price erosion of the plaintiff's products caused by the defendant's unlawful competition, called price erosion with causality.

4. The defendant's unjust enrichment, expressed by the value of the trade secrets to the defendant at the time of taking, but also considering

   I. Plaintiff is entitled to disgorgement of defendant's profits.

   II. Profits from sales made possible by product development or collateral sales connected to the misappropriation.

   III. Research and development costs avoided by defendant.

5. A royalty on gross sales that the defendant would hypothetically pay to legally license the use of the trade secrets. The royalty payment should restore the plaintiff's lost profits.

Method (1) includes valuation of the trade secrets considering factors such as cost of acquisition and market valuation. Naturally, the brick-and-mortar asset valuation techniques of yesteryear do not apply so neatly to the IP world. To determine the loss, methods (2) to (4) are choice. Lost profits are simply lost revenues due to loss of sales, minus marginal costs of production saved. Price erosion is a by-product of entry of an additional competitor in a particular market; generally the added competition lowers the market-clearing price—given a relatively low elasticity of demand. The immediate result is depressed profitability as the lower price squeezes profit margins for the IP owners. Unjust enrichment is the benefit to the defendant if he or she is able to exploit the trade secret.

In this particular case, the misappropriation occurred before there were any physical sales by either party. Therefore, the grounds outlined in methods (2) to (4) were not applicable. In many cases, the plaintiff is entitled to research and development expenses saved by the infringing party; however, since BBB worked in conjunction with AAA to develop its product line, (4). III did not apply either. BESTCO compiled its damage claim by method (5), a reasonable royalty payment on potential sales.[6] Experts re-created the "but for" world, evaluating market penetration, product business cycle, and price markups from patent monopoly, to determine the value of potential sales, and, thereafter, a reasonable royalty on those sales.

BESTCO valued AAA sales potential with a discounted future cash flow model as in equation (17.1).

$$\frac{FCF \times p}{(1 + r)^t} \tag{17.1}$$

where

FCF = future cash flow from sales

r = cash flow discount rate, also known as the weighted average cost of capital

t = period of time from now

p = probability of the cash flow, an adjustment for uncertainty

Developing the cash flow discount rate r begins with a U.S. treasury bond maturing on or near the valuation date. A risk premium is then added to compensate for the difference between average market returns in the stock market (a proxy for the market is the Standard & Poor's 500 Index) and the safe treasury bonds. Using the asset's Sharpe Beta measure, the weighted average cost of capital is established. Finally, a premium is added for the extra risk associated with the small size of AAA, relative to the size of comparable public companies in the industry.[7] Exhibit 17.1 presents a summary of the discount rate methodology.

The probability of the future cash flow is implicitly tied to the probability of winning a lawsuit to defend the trade secret, because unless the trade secret is defensible in court, it is not an asset to the company.[8] Trade secrets by nature are valuable only because the owner has them *and* outsiders do not. BESTCO also adjusted the present value calculations for uncertainty, utilizing a flat success rate based on historical data for parallel products. The uncertainty arose primarily from the crucible known as the Food and Drug Administration (FDA) approval process and is the proxy for p, the probability of the cash flow.

BESTCO identified sales potential from the applicable market segment, assuming growth of market size and subsequent income stream from 2003 to 2023 (the life of the trade secret cum patent), accounting for terminal value of the product also. Reasonable royalties are a

EXHIBIT 17.1 SAMPLE CALCULATION OF DISCOUNT RATE

Discount Rate		
Risk-free rate	3.71	10-year treasury bond
Market return	11.4	Expected 10-year market return of S&P 500
Risk premium	7.69	Market return — risk-free rate
Asset beta	1.1	Average of 16 small biotech company asset betas
Cost of capital	12.2	WACC calculation
Small cap premium	2.0	Risk premium for small-cap companies
Ra Discount Rate	**14.2**	**Calculation**

ad valorem percentage of all expected sales derived from the trade secret, discounted in present value terms, adjusted for uncertainty.

$$\text{Royalty payments} = \frac{[(\text{Expected sales}) \times (\text{risk adjustment}) \times (\text{royalty \%})]}{(1+r)^t} \quad (17.2)$$

where

expected sales = [(# of consumers of product$_a$) × (product$_a$ penetration) × (AAA market share) × (price)]

risk adjustment = probability of the cash flow, p

royalty % = a flat slice of all projected sales leveraging the value of the trade secret

BESTCO's royalty rate mimicked a hypothetically negotiated licensing fee. In determining a reasonable royalty rate post hoc, courts have relied on the precedent of *Georgia Pacific v. US Plywood Champion Papers* (1970). The royalty should serve as redress for lost profits, not lost sales. (The owner cannot recover revenues in full because he has not incurred the corresponding expenses.) As such, while the royalty base is gross sales, the intent of the royalty is to compensate for lost profits.

Panduit called for more severe than licensing royalty payments in instances of infringement, otherwise "the infringer would be in a 'heads-I-win, tails-you-lose' position," where the infringer would have nothing to lose and everything to gain if he could count on paying only the normal, routine royalty a licensee might pay.[9] That said, the royalty as defined by *Georgia Pacific* promised the infringer a residual profit after the royalty payment. Balancing these two forces, courts ruled to protect intellectual property, as *Panduit* put it, because the "right to exclude others is the essence of the human right called 'property.'"[10] Most of all, *Panduit* carved out a place for today's practitioners in IP valuation, authorizing "the use of experts in determining a reasonable royalty. However, the reliance on [expert witness] Scofield's testimony was clearly erroneous."[11] Interestingly, this factor is the sine qua non in the examination of the case in this chapter. Interviews with experts were the source of estimates on penetration of the particular product, market share, and market size. Market growth was projected using research; price, royalty percentage, risk, and discount rate were gleaned from analogs and competitor data. In sum, AAA's expectation of sales, discounted into present value in equation (17.2), was almost entirely contingent on quality testimony from experts.

SUMMARY OF OPINIONS

Based on the study of the confidential record produced in connection with this litigation, a summary of opinions was set forth by the first author for BBB.

- The BESTCO damages claim was highly dependent on the design, implementation, and interpretation of pro forma interview responses.

- The results derived from the BESTCO interviews are spurious for at least these reasons:
  - Flawed survey design
  - Flawed survey implementation
  - Flawed interpretation of survey results
- The uncertainty imputed to the success of the products was incomplete and imprecise.
- The BESTCO royalty rate did not take the *Georgia-Pacific* factors into consideration.
- Because the BESTCO record, including survey results, royalty rate, and uncertainty, were unreliable, the BESTCO damage claim is equally unreliable and should be set aside.

A discussion of the basis for these opinions is expounded in the balance of this chapter, which can be used as a template for analyzing pitfalls in similar trade secret and patent infringement cases.

Reliance on Interview Questions

The BESTCO damages claim was highly dependent on the design, implementation, and interpretation of interviews performed by BESTCO. The BESTCO damages model populated key inputs, such as market growth rates, expected penetration rates, and prices, among others, with data culled from various interviews conducted by BESTCO employees. These inputs drove the damages claim in the BESTCO model; if only one or two inputs changed, the model results swung drastically. For example, 50 percent of Product A damages calculated by BESTCO on behalf of AAA were based on three responses to one question. If a randomly chosen sample of respondents were asked questions that were accurate, statistical theory proposes the mean of the sample has a distribution that is close to a normal distribution (the classic bell curve) when the sample size gets large. What *large* means, definitively, depends in part on how normal the underlying data are as well as on how truly random the sample is. As a shorthand heuristic, the Central Limit Theorem holds the normal approximation is true with at least 30 observations chosen randomly from a distribution that is identical for each observation. A sample of 30 allows the plus/minus two standard deviation rule (two sigma) to take hold for evaluating uncertainty. For a standard normal curve, plus/minus one standard deviation around the sample mean will contain the true population mean (e.g., average penetration rate) 68 percent of the time. Plus or minus two standard deviations contains the true population mean 95 percent of the time. If 30 respondents are used, then the sample mean and variance estimates hold water in estimating the true population mean. By using as few as three responses, well shy of what could reasonably be viewed as an acceptable number of responses (e.g., a minimum of 30), BESTCO's estimation system lacked stability enough to buttress the cogency of their model. Practitioners must adhere to the guideline of 30 (remember Mark Twain's bitter repartee: "Lies, damned lies, and statistics").

Note that interviews in and of themselves were appropriate; indeed, probative expert testimony from special masters often provide the crux of an IP court's opinion. It was the manner in which BESTCO conducted the interviews that discredited their testimony and estimate. Therefore, to the extent that the BESTCO interviews were biased, inaccurate, and/or statistically unreliable, the model results were also biased, inaccurate, and/or unreliable. Practitioners must take caution in gathering unbiased and robust data in market research, as expert testimony will undoubtedly be called into question. Expect a motion to strike expert testimony, a power granted to the court by the *Daubert* rule.[12]

SPURIOUS AND UNRELIABLE INTERVIEW RESULTS

Flawed Survey Design

BESTCO employed a survey design flawed in at least three ways. First, the survey incorporated biased product descriptions, rendering the responses insignificant. AAA had yet to bring any of said products to bear and moreover had failed to develop prototypes. While legal proceedings with inchoate ideas are not necessarily faux pas, it became exceedingly unlikely that experts could make an objective and nonspeculative estimation of the potential market for the pie-in-the-sky products described in the questionnaire.

BESTCO used product descriptions created by AAA personnel, without seeking an objective, purely third-party description of the products' merits. AAA personnel had the obvious incentive to manipulate these product descriptions to their liking and thus bias the survey results. An e-mail from an AAA executive to BESTCO suggested that such doctoring actually occurred when concocting the product profile used for the cosmetics interviews. After reviewing the profile prepared by BESTCO, which was based on information gleaned from AAA employees, the AAA executive said:

> I am not really happy with most of this. I am attaching a couple of "Confidential" documents that I have prepared for our current efforts to enter the <-> arena. These don't look much like yours, but you should be able to use them to fix yours some. When this is done, perhaps I can help you polish it.

Considering that the survey respondents were not provided with tangible product prototypes that they could see, touch, and/or smell, and that no such prototypes even existed to verify AAA's product descriptions, this type of manipulation rendered the product descriptions biased. The interview data can be trusted, therefore, only to the extent that the product description is trustworthy.

Second, BESTCO's method of locating respondents was biased. The basic tenet of probability sampling is that a sample will be representative of the population from which it is selected, if all members of the population have an equal chance of being selected in the sample. Probability theory allows researchers to estimate the accuracy of a sample when probability sampling is used. Probability sampling avoids conscious or unconscious biases in the selection of subjects and the recording of information from those subjects. Without probability sampling there is no statistical authenticity. By faxing potential respondents and offering "honorariums" to participants, BESTCO ensured a nonrandom sample that contained a clear self-selection bias. Only individuals who valued the "honorariums" more than their time would respond. Finding willing participants gratis may seem onerous, but it is a safeguard against the self-selection bias.

Finally, BESTCO did not labor to judge if those interviewed were suitably qualified to resolve the questions posed to them. BESTCO assumed the select few respondents possessed knowledge on legion subjects, ranging from market expansion possibilities, growth rates of a number of nonintegrated market segments, peak market penetration rates, years to peak market penetration, price premiums that could be charged and the percentage of market penetration corresponding to various price premiums, and average material costs from the manufacturers. In example, an expert subspecialist physician was presumed to wield expertise to opine on the market for and other matters related to an altogether distinct subspecialty. Such assumptions were in direct conflict with BESTCO's own published materials.

> Primary research with input from key purchase decision-makers for the products . . . provides the best estimate of likely market share.

AAA's aspired to secure partnerships and strategic alliances with manufacturers or distributors who had the full wherewithal to bring their experimental products to market. It would be members of this demographic who could pinpoint likely market share and royalty rates. BESTCO neglected to interview a single potential business partner, even excluding partners previously approached by AAA to ascertain how those companies would value the trade secrets (in terms of market penetration, staying power, etc.) or what kind of royalty arrangement they would negotiate. Some key purchasers and decision makers not interviewed include end users, product salespeople, venture capitalists, insurance company buyers, and hospital purchasing agents, among others. In populating a sample of experts, practitioners should consider an exhaustive list of all the players in marketing the product, beginning with a consultant's method known in industry parlance as Porter's Five Forces.

Based on the factors, BESTCO's survey design was flawed, which resulted in spurious and unreliable interview data.

Flawed Survey Implementation

BESTCO missed the mark in its sampling procedure. The implementation of the survey was flawed for at least three reasons.

1. The survey proffered leading questions, which further biased the interview results. For example, BESTCO posed this question to respondents in the cosmetics interviews:

    > We have seen the following estimates for the 5-year growth of these segments:
    >
    > Product A—15%

Product B—1%

Product C—0%

Do you agree with these figures? Why/why not?

Rather than allowing the interviewee to provide an unbiased opinion, the question goaded the interview toward BESTCO's baseline perception of growth rates. Similar leading questions were echoed in the other interview segments. Biases were accordingly embedded in the interview results. Just as leading questions are frowned on in court, they are also problematic in obtaining objective data.

2. BESTCO did not endeavor to calibrate the accuracy or quality of the interview responses by asking "sleeper" questions—questions with verifiable answers—either fictitious information about which the respondent is asked his or her opinion or actual information about which the respondent should know. For example, rather than asking the "leading" question just mentioned, BESTCO should have asked the respondents where the segment growth rates have been historically and then compared those answers to its own baseline results. Such questions would have helped to gauge the quality and reliability of the answers provided by the respondents.

3. The BESTCO interviews were applied in an inconsistent format, with equally inconsistent questions. More specifically, some interviewees were only asked a single question or a small subset of the questions that were posed to other respondents within the same interview segment. BESTCO provided no basis or rationale for implementing its survey in such an inconsistent manner.

Based on at least these three points, BESTCO's survey implementation was flawed and, accordingly, the interview results were spurious and unreliable.

Flawed Interpretation and Use of Survey Results

BESTCO's interpretation of the survey results was flawed for a number of reasons. As previously discussed, the BESTCO survey design and survey implementation were flawed; any output derived from flawed inputs is imperfect and discredits BESTCO's interpretation. BESTCO also did not subject its survey results to any statistical or mathematical testing in establishing the standard error associated with its model results. When building its damages model, BESTCO often used the calculated median of the survey responses (or, arbitrarily, and/or without explanation, the mean) as inputs for key model components, implying that calculated medians (and means) were unequivocally true of the entire population of possible respondents. At times, the number of responses relied on when making such assumptions was as small as two. Had BESTCO published the standard deviations of the responses, the wide variation in means and medians would have been glaringly obvious and instantly cast the efficacy of the model in doubt. BESTCO did not deign to test the efficacy of its interview sample, represented by the statistical significance, and framed this issue quite fittingly itself:

> We very rarely conduct statistical analysis of the results of interviews because our
> clients do not find significant benefit in it and because we rarely conduct the hun-
> dreds of interviews required to make statistical analysis useful.

While BESTCO contended that hundreds of interviews were the threshold for statistical analysis, the company did not meet it nor even one that any expert would recommend
as a practical matter—a minimum of 30 interviews for building a numerically credible
damages model.

Similarly, BESTCO erred by not testing the sample statistics for potential bias. Among
other things, biases can be due to nonrandom selective responses by survey recipients and
by inaccurate product descriptions by survey writers. The former source of bias can be
examined by a careful and intensive follow-up of the characteristics and responses of those
who initially declined to respond. Rather than complete the task, BESTCO expediently
maintained that bias does not exist in its survey because interviewees (sometimes as few
as three) provided a wide range of responses to survey questions. BESTCO conceded:

> We did not perceive any systematic bias in the respondents themselves nor in their
> responses. This is borne out by the range of responses we received on specific ques-
> tions, all of which we incorporated in our analysis.

Not only does a wide range of survey responses fail to eliminate the possibility of a
biased survey sample, but it also reduces the reliability of the calculated means and medians for the model. The three responses used in the claim could well have been outliers; more
concern for the statistical significance of output was in order. Practitioners should reexam-
ine the significance and the meaning of output before marrying themselves to the sample.

Finally, when incorporating the survey results into the damages model, BESTCO
employed an ex parte methodology. BESTCO selectively integrated interview results in
its damages model and determined when to rely solely on interview results and when to
augment interview results with additional BESTCO analyses, without providing any basis
for these decisions. This suggests that some interview respondents were deemed, for some
reason, more reliable than others, and that some interview responses needed additional support from BESTCO. For example, the interviews with Mr. Smith and Mr. Jones, who have
nearly 70 years' worth of combined experience in the cosmetics industry, were excluded
from BESTCO's model. From all appearances, there was no rationale for such exclusions.

Based on at least these points, BESTCO's interpretation and use of the survey results
was flawed.

UNCERTAINTY IN THE MODEL

The probability that the trade secret was of economic value to AAA—that is, the probability that the intellectual property was commercially viable—depended greatly on FDA
approval. AAA's IP biotechnology portfolio would be scrutinized to the letter by the FDA
before allowing its products to reach the market.

BESTCO accounted for this uncertainty in the model in (17.2), expecting the probability of a successful FDA approval as either 27 percent or 60 percent, depending on the product. As an early-stage biotech start-up company, in an industry already marked by the mercurial and lengthy FDA approval process, the success of AAA's technologies was dubious and the IP portfolio speculative. After all, even biotech juggernauts regularly struggle with the approval process, making their products real hit-or-miss phenomena.

BESTCO procured such high success rates by using analog success rates, comparing medical devices against all pharmaceutical products. Professionals should observe that this practice would draw guaranteed criticism, as drugs are a far cry from medical devices like the ones AAA hoped to market. Both are experimental and speculative but have obvious dissimilarities that make the comparison toothless and immaterial. Regardless of BESTCO's specific methodology, convincing experts and judges alike that an early-stage biotech company has a 60 percent chance of striking gold is a tall order. Any entrepreneur can attest to a much lower expected probability of success in launching a new business, let alone the chance of success for a speculative, "revolutionary" biotech venture. Most professionals understand the challenge and likelihood of a revolution in the biotech world and understand the resources it takes to exploit a discovery. It is unreasonable to any professional, not just a statistician, that a business opportunity should appear with 60 percent odds of explosive growth and success. A more reasonable alternative for BESTCO in projecting the probability of success would have been a comparison to similar-size companies in the same industry. Again, interviews with industry-savvy professionals, such as venture capitalists, would have served BESTCO well in this regard.

AAA's IP portfolio leveraged a common biotechnology, essentially applied in a number of addressable markets. All of the products effectively shared a common, systematic risk—a negative halo effect. One product's failure would spell doom for the rest, provided the defect was intrinsic to the patented biomaterial. The negative halo effect means the probability of success for one AAA product was not statistically independent of the probability of other related products.

Furthermore, once the FDA rejected a claim, AAA would have to reengineer the process or possibly reinvent the product entirely. Even if the revamped biomaterial could pass the FDA's crucible, the dynamics of the market may have changed demand entirely, possibly to the point of obsolescence. The longer the approval process, the more uncertainty accrues. The probability of a second success is extremely dependent on time to approval. Market demand can change rapidly and force firms to alter or abandon their core businesses. If AAA staked the entire business on the approval of one biomaterial and its spin-offs, the correlation between success rates and the risk of the market both present substantial uncertainties to be carefully weighed, all the while noting the dependence of the probabilities. There were more dimensions of complexity to AAA's risk profile, marked by multiple outcome states with a dependent probability assigned to each. Since BESTCO's cursory risk assessment failed to address these pertinent issues in calculating uncertainty, the damages claim inaccurately portrayed the risk factor in the valuation of the trade secrets. In a speculative industry like biotech, bombastic claims like AAA's simply will not withstand a more thorough analysis.

ROYALTY RATES

Generally, reasonable royalties are used when the plaintiff has not incurred lost profits and unjust enrichment cannot be determined. In the words of Judge Learned Hand:

> The whole notion of a reasonable royalty is a device in aid of justice, by which that which is really incalculable shall be approximated, rather than that the patentee, who has suffered an indubitable wrong, shall be dismissed with empty hands.[13]

The rule of law in reasonable royalty originated from *Georgia-Pacific,* and the idea is to simulate a willing buyer negotiating a reasonable licensing fee from a willing seller, in an arm's-length discussion. In hammering out a deal, parties will size up these business forces, presented in Exhibit 17.2, adapted for the case at hand.

Factors 1, 2, and 15 from the exhibit are the starting points for determining an initial royalty rate. The remaining factors guide the initial rate toward a final one. Because BESTCO failed to evaluate the *Georgia-Pacific* factors, its reasonable royalty claims were unsubstantiated. The verdict in the analysis here was ten factors pressing downward and only three upward, for a net effect pushing the royalty rate significantly downward.

EXHIBIT 17.2   *GEORGIA-PACIFIC V. US PLYWOOD*: 15 FACTORS TO DETERMINE A REASONABLE ROYALTY RATE

Factors	Directional Pressure	Justification
1. The royalties[a] received by the patentee for the licensing of the patent in-suit, proving or tending to prove an established royalty	Downward	No damages awarded in defense of the IP hitherto. If the IP had been upheld by a past royalty, AAA had a stronger case for collecting royalties in the present action.
2. The rates paid by the licensee for the use of other patents comparable to the patent in-suit	Not applicable	Like #1, a comparable transaction is a benchmark for commencing this analysis.
3. The nature and scope of the license, as exclusive or nonexclusive; or as restricted or nonrestricted in terms of territory or with respect to whom the manufactured product may be sold	Upward	Exclusive agreements have a natural tendency toward higher licensing fees.
4. The licensor's established policy and marketing program to maintain the patent monopoly by not licensing others to use the invention or by granting licenses under special conditions designed to preserve that monopoly	Downward	AAA was a business organized around invention and IP. Its business model was to license all products, scattering its patent monopoly.

| EXHIBIT 17.2 | *GEORGIA-PACIFIC V. US PLYWOOD*: 15 FACTORS TO DETERMINE A REASONABLE ROYALTY RATE (CONTINUED) |

Factors	Directional Pressure	Justification
5. The commercial relationship between the licensor and licensee, such as whether they are competitors in the same territory in the same line of business or whether they are inventor and promoter	Downward	Inventor and promoter match the AAA and BBB relationship perfectly. They penned a continual agreement, lowering ongoing transaction costs. Their codependent relationship would lead to lower royalties in a licensing agreement.
6. The effect of selling the patented specialty in promoting sales of other products of the licensee; the existing value of the invention to the licensor as a generator of sales of nonpatented items; and the extent of such derivative or convoyed sales	Not applicable	BBB is not a for-profit commercial entity.
7. The duration of the patent and the term of the license	Upward	Early in its life cycle, the product could be licensed for years to come.
8. The established profitability of the product made under the patent; its commercial success and its current popularity	Downward	Contact with potential business partners suggested less than stellar success in the stars for AAA.
9. The utility and advantages of the patent properly over the old modes or devices, if any that had been used for working out similar results	Downward	As a litmus test of commercial potential, AAA did not command attention, venture capital funding, or any other licensing agreements.
10. The nature of the patented invention; the character of the commercial embodiment of it as owned and produced by the licensor; and the benefits to those who have used the invention	Downward	No benefits of the invention to date, realized or unrealized.
11. The extent to which the infringer has made use of the invention and any evidence probative of the value of that use	Downward	BBB did not harness the invention at all. A zero value of use declines the rate slightly.
12. The portion of the profit or of the selling price that may be customary in the particular business or in comparable businesses to allow for the use of the invention of analogous inventions	Upward	Biotech products can be very profitable, fetching high price premiums.
13. The portion of the realizable profit that should be credited to the invention as distinguished from nonpatented elements, the manufacturing process, business risks, or significant features or improvements added by the infringer	Downward	AAA seemed content to license all downstream functions to BBB and then other parties. AAA would not be able to capture much of the product's markup from manufacturing and the like; that would be reserved for their business partners.

(continues)

EXHIBIT 17.2	GEORGIA-PACIFIC V. US PLYWOOD: 15 FACTORS TO DETERMINE A REASONABLE ROYALTY RATE (CONTINUED)

Factors	Directional Pressure	Justification
14. The opinion testimony of qualified experts	Downward	Some experts pointed up, others down. Considering that the testimony was botched, this factor should dip the rate marginally.
15. The amount that a licensor (such as the patentee) and a licensee (such as the infringer) would have agreed on at the time the infringement began if both had been reasonably and voluntarily trying to reach an agreement; that is, the amount that a prudent licensee—who desired, as a business proposition, to obtain a license to manufacture and sell a particular article embodying the patented invention—would have been willing to pay as a royalty and yet be able to make a reasonable profit and which amount would have been acceptable by a prudent patentee who was willing to grant a license	Downward	AAA had too little bargaining power to reach a licensing fee in its favor. The products' development hinged too much on BBB's knowledge, research facilities, and efforts.

Source: Georgia-Pacific v. US Plywood-Champion Papers, 1970.

Not to be ignored is the interest on the royalty itself. Substantial time can elapse since the original infringement and even since the commencement of the legal action. If the court is awarding damages based on methods (2) to (4), the plaintiff receives interest on the sum since the date of last infringement as well as court costs.

CONCLUSION

From the outset, attorneys must differentiate their two responsibilities: (1) arguing for/against the existence and infringement of the IP asset and (2) reaching a damage figure appropriate to the case. Typically, law firms subcontract the second function to economic consultants, accountants, and other experts.

BESTCO, one such consultant, developed a damages model with inputs derived from poorly designed, bias-laden surveys that were improperly applied to a small number of nonrandom respondents and, subsequently, misinterpreted. Reliable probability sampling, which permits estimates of sampling errors, is predicated on properly designed and conducted surveys. In this case, BESTCO's misuse of probability sampling generated unreliable results, due to the poorly designed and conducted surveys. The uncertainties were incorrectly identified and imprecisely assigned. The royalty rate was grossly out of line. Consequently, the resulting claim was deemed statistically unreliable and should be disregarded.

Estimating damages in this case should have been approached in a different manner. The survey should have included many more respondents, ideally experts more qualified to pass judgment on matters such as market penetration and existing market conditions. Neutral product descriptions or, better yet, prototypes would be necessary for an expert to make an informed assessment of the product's marketability and mass production feasibility.

AAA collecting damages at all was debatable. Prongs (2) and (3) from *Panduit* must evince production capabilities and the absence of substitutes, both of which AAA failed. Prong (1) requires palpable demand, and AAA did little to corroborate its unilateral claim with industry backing or business partner testimony. Asserting the existence of a trade secret is another legal burden AAA did not bear. IP owners must prove their proprietary information has existence, ownership, access, and notice, before the information is protected as a trade secret.[14] Plaintiffs must identify the exact trade secret information allegedly swindled. (Note this is not an issue in patent cases, where patents are clearly delineated when filed.) The plaintiff must also show causation; the defendant must be the primary cause of the diminution of the trade secret. With these and other legal mandates left unsatisfied, AAA may not have been eligible to recoup damages at all, let alone collect a reduced claim based on this study.

NOTES

1. Hewitt and Nayef (2004).
2. Halligan and Weyand (2005), pg. 4.
3. *Panduit v. Stahlin Bros. Fibre Works, Inc.*, 1978.
4. *State Industries, Inc. v. Mor-Flo Industries, Inc.*, 1989.
5. See III for further detail.
6. Newmann and Gering (2004).
7. A complete review of discount rates and valuations can be found in Pratt, Reilly, Schweis (2000).
8. Halligan and Weyand (2005).
9. *Panduit v. Stahlin*, 1978.
10. Ibid.
11. Ibid.
12. *Daubert et al. v. Merrell Dow Pharmaceuticals* (1995).
13. *Cincinnati Car Co. v. New York Rapid Transit Corp.*, 1933.
14. Halligan and Weyand (2005).

REFERENCES

Brodie, Kane, and A. J. Marcus. *Investments,* 6th ed. (New York: McGraw-Hill/Irwin, 2004).

Cincinnati Car Co. v. New York Rapid Transit Corp., 66 F.2d 592, 595 (2d Cir. 1933).

William Daubert, et al. v. Merrell Dow Pharmaceuticals, 43 F.3d 1311; U.S. App. 1995.

Georgia-Pacific Co. v. U.S. Plywood-Champion Papers Inc., 318 F. Supp. 1116; 1970 U.S. Dist. LEXIS 11541; 166 U.S.P.Q. (BNA) 235.

Halligan, Mark, and R. F. Weyand. "The Economic Valuation of Trade Secret Assets," *The Computer and Internet Lawyer* 22, no.7 (2005).

Hewitt, Lester, and Romi Nayef. "Trade Secret Update," HIPLA/University of Houston 19th Annual Institute on Intellectual Property Law, 2004.

Moore, McCabe. *Introduction to the Practice of Statistics,* 4th ed. (New York: W. H. Freeman Publishing, 2002).

Newmann, Glenn, and R. Gering. "Damages Aren't Always Patently Obvious," *Journal of Accountancy* 198, no. 5 (2004).

Panduit Corp. v. Stahlin Bros. Fibre Works, Inc., 575 F.2d 1152, 197 U.S.P.Q 726 (6th Circ. 1978).

Pratt, Reilly, and R. P. Schweis. *Valuing a Business: The Analysis and Appraisal of Closely Held Companies,* 4th ed. (New York: McGraw-Hill, 2000).

State Industries, Inc. v. Mor-Flo Industries, Inc., 883 F.2d 1573, 12 USPQ 2D 1026 (CAFC 1989).

Uniform Trade Secrets Act, drafted by the National Conference of Commissioners on Uniform State Laws (1985).

CHAPTER 18

A Primer on Trademarks and Trademark Valuation[1]

MICHAELYN CORBETT
LECG, LLC

MOHAN RAO
LECG, LLC

DAVID TEECE
LECG, LLC

A trademark is a distinctive word, phrase, name, or symbol that is used in commerce to indicate the source of a good or service and to distinguish it from the goods or services of others. Although trademarks have existed for centuries, they have become of great importance in recent years. In fact, it is hard to imagine key elements of today's global commerce proceeding without trademark protection. Sought-after products around the globe have widely recognized trademarks: Coca-Cola, McDonald's, Sony, Disney, Microsoft, and Apple, to name just a few. Like patents, trademarks can constitute a significant portion of a firm's asset value and, therefore, need to be strategically developed and protected. As recognition of their increasing importance in commerce, damage awards in trademark infringement litigation have reached tens of millions of dollars, with some awards exceeding $100 million. In this chapter, we provide a primer on trademarks and trademark valuation. We discuss the economic principles of licensing and describe some of the commonly used approaches to trademark valuation, particularly in the context of licensing trademarks.

WHAT IS A TRADEMARK?

A trademark is a distinctive word, phrase, name, or symbol that is used in commerce to indicate the source of a good or service and to distinguish it from the goods or services of others. In addition, domain names on the Internet are also subject to trademark laws.[2] Some examples of trademarks include Rolex for timepieces, the Pillsbury doughboy symbol for baked goods, and the "Got milk?" slogan of America's milk processors.

What Constitutes an Acceptable Trademark?

To be protectable, trademarks must be inherently distinctive or possess "secondary meaning" (i.e., the public associates a particular symbol with a single entity). Furthermore, the trademark must be nonfunctional. Commonly used words for objects, such as *belt, glass,* or *chair,* generally cannot be registered as trademarks. For instance, a company cannot register the trademark "apple" to describe a product of fruit that grows on a tree because that merely describes what it is. However, a company might be able to register the trademark "Apple" to identify a particular brand of computer product because it is not descriptive in that context at all. Instead it is a highly arbitrary identifier and subject to trademark protection. Geographic names and surnames are generally off limits to trademark protection. In addition, trademarks cannot be lewd or immoral. However, the criteria for trademark registration can be a challenge to understand. While companies and individuals cannot simply register ownership of common words or phrases, they can turn a *distinctive* combination of words into a trademark. For example, the Wheaties cereal (owned by General Mills) is associated with the well-recognized trademarked slogan "The Breakfast of Champions."

A trademark is likely to fall under one of three categories:[3]

1. *Coined words (or "fanciful" words)* are invented words without any real meaning in any language (e.g., Prozac or Lexus). Coined words often have the advantage of being easy to protect, as they are more likely to be considered distinct. The downside is that some coined words may be more difficult for consumers to remember. They are neither descriptive of the products they represent nor easy to associate with other things more familiar to a consumer.

2. *Arbitrary marks* are trademarks that consist of words that have a real meaning in a given language. The meaning of such words, however, has no relation to the product itself or to any of its qualities (e.g., Dove for soap or Polo for clothing). While the level and ease of protection is generally high for arbitrary marks, as with coined words, greater effort may be required to create a direct association between the mark and the product in consumers' minds.

3. *Suggestive marks* are marks that hint at one or some of the attributes of a particular product. For example, the trademark Coppertone attempts to characterize the results of using a particular suntan lotion, intending to capture one of the most appealing aspects of such products (i.e., a deep, dark tan). Another example is the trademark "Lucent" used by Lucent Technologies to associate "clear" with telecommunication products. The appeal of suggestive marks lies in their ability to act as an advertising mechanism to create a direct association in the mind of consumers between the trademark, certain desired qualities, and the product. The perceived risk of suggestive

marks, however, is that they may be considered not sufficiently distinctive to meet the criteria for trademark protection.

Different Types of Trademarks

There are four types of trademarks:

1. *Service marks.* A service mark is a type of trademark that identifies and distinguishes the source of a service rather than a product. Examples of service marks include Kinko's for photocopying services and FedEx for express delivery.

2. *Collective marks.* Collective marks are used in indicating membership in a group or an association where only members of the group or organization can use the collective mark. Examples of collective marks include the AFL-CIO, Rotary International, or the CPA designation to indicate members of the Society of Certified Public Accountants.

3. *Certification marks.* Certification marks are used in certifying the quality, regional origin, or other origin of a product or service. A certification mark certifies that a product or service meets a certain standard of quality or is of a regional origin. An owner's function is to exercise control over use of the mark by others, ensuring that their products and services meet specified quality standards. Incidentally, use of a certification mark by others may not be refused as long as the required standard compliance is met.[4] Examples of certification marks include wine from the Champagne region of France, the Good Housekeeping Seal of Approval, and the Certified Vegan symbol on food products administered by Vegan Action.

4. *Trade dress.* In addition to a label, logo, or other identifying symbol, a product may come to be known by its distinctive packaging or manner of presentation. *Trade dress* refers to the way in which a product—or place of business—is "dressed up" to go to market. Examples of trade dress include the yellow packaging of Kodak film, the Golden Arches of a McDonald's restaurant, and the distinctive red label on a Campbell's Soup can. The particular style and ambience of a retail outlet can also, in some circumstances, constitute trade dress. Exhibit 18.1 presents examples of the different types of trademarks.

A Trademark Is Not the Same as a Trade Name or Brand

Trademarks are closely related to trade names and brands. A trade name is used to identify a company or a business and serves as the name of the company or a business. In contrast, a trademark or service mark is used to identify the source of the products or services that the company or business sells or provides. In practice, however, the distinctions between trademarks and trade names and the laws that govern them are not always clear. For instance, only trademarks can be registered in the federal or state trademark registries. Trade names are registered at the state level, often with the secretary of state. Trademarks are

EXHIBIT 18.1	TYPES OF TRADEMARKS
Service Marks	Burger King Blockbuster Roto Rooter
Collective Marks	AAA (American Automobile Association) Realtor CFE (Certified Fraud Examiner)
Certification Marks	Harris Tweeds (a special weave from a specific area in Scotland) Stilton cheese (a product from the Stilton locale in England) Star-K Kosher
Trade Dress	Coca-Cola bottle Distinctive decor of Two Pesos Mexican restaurant Red border of *Time* magazine cover

afforded a higher level of protection than trade names. For instance, a trademark holder may face a legal challenge if the trademark is not inherently distinctive; the trade name holder bears no burden to prove the distinctive nature of the underlying name. Moreover, while both concern themselves with "similarity," trade name law is less concerned with confusion of marks and more with deception and the resulting harm to business reputation.[5] For instance, Philip Morris, a company name, is a trade name whereas Marlboro is a trademark for a specific brand of cigarettes from Philip Morris.

Brands and trademarks also are closely linked, although there are subtle distinctions between the two concepts. A brand can be loosely thought of as an accumulation of assets that may or may not include trademarks. For instance, the McDonald's "brand" includes trademarks such as Big Mac, the Golden Arches symbol, and the Ronald McDonald name and logo. In contrast, Linoleum is also a brand; however, there is no longer a trademark associated with the "linoleum" product. The close relationship among trademarks, trade names, and brands means that it can often be difficult to separate the incremental financial contributions by each of these intangible assets for valuation purposes.

A Trademark Is Not the Same as Goodwill

An enterprise typically contains a portfolio of intangible assets, which may include various forms of intellectual property. For many years the bundle of intangible assets was simply referred to as *goodwill*. Trademarks were often simply considered goodwill or patronage—the ability to attract and retain customers who will recommend the business to others. As valuation experts have begun to focus on intangibles, efforts have been made to break down the "black box" known as goodwill and identify and analyze the individual components of a firm's intangible assets. Thus, for the purpose of trademark valuation, it is now well recognized that it is no longer necessary to fall back on the use of the term *goodwill*.

Why Do We Care about Trademarks and Why Are They Needed?

Trademarks serve a variety of economic and business purposes. The traditional rationale for trademark protection is to allow an enterprise's customers to distinguish its products or services from those of its competitors. In that regard, a trademark is in some ways the "face" of a business. Thus, a fundamental principle underlying trademarks is protection of the reputation of particular products or services from "copycat" producers that could confuse consumers regarding which product or service they are purchasing. Alternatively, actual competitors may begin to mimic certain characteristics of a successful trademark in ways that could lead to consumer confusion. For example, in 1991, Merriam-Webster, one of the market leaders in college dictionaries, sued a competitor, Random House, after the latter changed the name of its dictionary from *RH College Dictionary* to *Random House Webster's College Dictionary*.[6] In addition, Random House adopted a trade dress similar to *Merriam-Webster's Ninth New Collegiate Dictionary*. Among the similarities between the two competing works were the bright red dust jackets, the use of the generic word *Webster's* in combination with the descriptive term *College* or *Collegiate* on the cover, and the name *Webster's* in large white vertical letters on the spines. An important question in this litigation was to determine the likelihood of customer confusion due to Random House's new dress cover on its dictionaries.

Second, a successful trademark is seen as a mark of quality assurance. A customer who is pleased with the quality of a product or service will continue to associate high quality with that trademark. Overtime, a consistently high-quality product is likely to result in a trademark with a strong reputation, which, in turn, could translate into significant value for the owner. For example, Cadillac is often associated with class and luxury while Toyota is frequently associated with dependability.

Third, trademarks provide a mechanism by which to protect an owner's investment in advertising and promotion. Firms often spend significant resources in advertising and promoting their trademarked products. General Motors, for instance, spent almost $4 billion on advertising in 2004. By comparison, the U.S. government spent over $1.2 billion on advertising in the same year. These investments, however, may not generate rewards until many years into the future. Without trademark protection, owners might not invest in developing distinctive and widely recognized brands and trademarks, to the detriment of consumers. Consequently, trademarks are important from a commercial perspective and should be properly viewed as business assets.

Exhibit 18.2 lists the 10 leading national advertisers as measured by 2004 advertisement spending.

In its annual special report, *BusinessWeek* magazine presents the world's most valuable brands as determined by Interbrand Corporation. Interbrand values brand assets based on discounted future earnings. As discussed earlier, brand value reflects, in part, the intellectual property assets, including trademarks, of the owner. Without endorsing its methodology, Exhibit 18.3 presents Interbrand's list of the 10 most valuable brands in 2005.[7]

EXHIBIT 18.2   10 LEADING NATIONAL ADVERTISERS BY 2004 ADVERTISING SPENDING

Rank	Advertiser	Advertising Expenditures (in billions US$)
1	General Motors	4.0
2	Procter & Gamble	4.0
3	Time Warner	3.3
4	Pfizer	3.0
5	SBC Communications	2.7
6	DaimlerChrysler	2.5
7	Ford Motor	2.5
8	Walt Disney	2.2
9	Verizon Communications	2.2
10	Johnson & Johnson	2.2

Source: *Advertising Age*, June 27, 2005, p. 6.

How Does One Obtain a Trademark?

There are a number of ways in which trademark status can be obtained. In the United States, individual state statutes govern the registration and protection of state trademarks and service marks. Registration of state trademarks is typically accomplished through the secretary of state. There also are federal trademarks for goods and services in interstate commerce, governed by federal law at 15 U.S.C. § 1125 (the Lanham Act). Federal trademarks are registered through the U.S. Patent and Trademark Office (USPTO). Finally, rights in trademarks and service marks may arise solely from use, even without state or federal registration. These are common law rights.[8]

EXHIBIT 18.3   10 MOST VALUABLE BRANDS OF 2005

Rank	Advertiser
1	Coca-Cola
2	Microsoft
3	IBM
4	GE
5	Intel
6	Nokia
7	Disney
8	McDonald's
9	Toyota
10	Marlboro

Source: *BusinessWeek*, August 1, 2005, pp. 90–94.

At the global level, trademarks are covered by a number of multilateral treaties and agreements such as the Paris Convention, the Madrid Agreement, the Trade Related Intellectual Property Rights (TRIPS) agreement, the Trademark Law Treaty, the Nice Agreement, and the Vienna Agreement.[9]

Currently, registration of a trademark is effective for 10 years, but registration can be renewed indefinitely so long as the mark continues to be in active use and has not become generic. Unlike patents, active trademarks can last in perpetuity.

How Are Trademarks Protected and How Can They Be Damaged?

The Trademark Act of 1946 (also known as the Lanham Act) is the U.S. law governing trademarks and is administered by the USPTO. It protects products and services that have trademarks from use that is "likely to cause confusion, or to cause mistake, or to deceive."[10] The Lanham Act was amended in 1988 with the passage of the Trademark Law Revision Act (TLRA). The TLRA remedied the problem by which a business or individual seeking to register a trademark in the United States must be using the mark in interstate commerce before applying for registration, a practice not required in most other countries. The TLRA gave all applicants the choice of applying to register marks on the basis of preapplication use in commerce or on the basis of a bona fide intention to use the mark in future commerce (intent-to-use).[11] The TLRA also contained provisions to help deal with the high volume of inactive, but registered, trademarks, including a reduction in the renewal period from 20 to 10 years.

In January 1996, the Federal Trademark Dilution Act (FTDA) was signed in the United States, providing owners of famous trademarks with a federal cause of action against those that lessen the distinctiveness of such marks by the use of the same or similar trademarks on similar or dissimilar products or services. Thus, the antidilution statutes can apply even if it were unlikely that customers would confuse the source of the goods or services with those sold by the owner of the famous mark. The antidilution laws essentially protect trademarks from two forms of injury: blurring and tarnishment.[12]

Blurring occurs when the distinctiveness of a famous mark is lessened through overuse by others in different contexts, thereby reducing its value even though a consumer may not be confused as to the source of the goods. For instance, a ball point pen manufacturer using a mark similar to "Rolls-Royce" on its products may serve to diminish the mental association made between "Rolls-Royce" and the line of goods it is normally associated with—ultra-luxury cars. Therefore, the strength of Rolls-Royce's trademark could be weakened if the public now associates the mark with a different source or a "lesser" product.

Tarnishment damages the goodwill or reputation of the mark by associating it with an inferior product or showing it in a distasteful light. Tarnishment occurs when a party uses a famous mark in association with unwholesome or defective goods or services, particularly when the unauthorized use involves illegal activity or crude behavior. For example, if an X-rated movie portrays actresses in Chicago Bears' cheerleading uniforms, the Chicago Bears' reputation could be tarnished. Tarnishment may also occur when an individual attempts to parody a famous trademark in a derogatory fashion.

The right to exclude others from using a trademark is not absolute, however. Rather, trademark owners only have the right to protect their goodwill by prohibiting others from misrepresenting the marks in commerce or otherwise using the marks in a damaging manner to the trademark holder. A trademark owner's ability to stop others from using its trademark, or a confusingly similar one, depends on such factors as whether:

- The trademark is being used on competing goods or services (goods or services compete if the sale of one is likely to affect the sale of the other)
- Consumers would likely be confused by the dual use of the trademark
- The trademark is being used in the same vicinity or is being used on related goods (such as goods that will likely be noticed by the same customers, even if they do not compete with each other)

Improper use of a trademark, or allowing others to use a trademark improperly, can result in the trademark becoming generic and open to use by others in the public domain. Once a trademark ceases to distinguish products or services as produced from a single source, the trademark's legal protection may be compromised. Examples of products that have become generic terms in the United States but were once protectable trademarks include "aspirin," "nylon," and "corn flakes." In fact, herein lies a dilemma for trademark owners: A widely recognized trademark reflects success in getting consumers to associate a specific product with that trademark or brand. However, using the trademark to describe a class of products (such as Kleenex for tissues) puts the trademark at risk. Thus, trademark owners have a strong incentive to vigilantly guard the use of their trademarks. Gordon Smith cites the rather imaginative efforts by Xerox Corporation to protect its trademark from becoming generic through advertising campaigns in the media that plead: "When you use 'Xerox' the way you use 'aspirin,' we get a headache."[13]

The rights to a trademark can also be lost through abandonment if its use is discontinued with an intent not to resume. The basic premise is that trademark law only protects marks that are being actively used and parties are not entitled to "warehouse" potentially useful marks. For instance, in a prominent case, a federal court in New York found that the Los Angeles Dodgers had abandoned rights to the Brooklyn Dodgers trademark.[14] In a more dramatic example, Procter & Gamble (P&G) allowed the trademark on its White Cloud toilet paper to lapse in 1994 when its attention was focused on the more expensive Charmin brand toilet paper. The White Cloud trademark was promptly picked up by a private entrepreneur and sold to Wal-Mart. Wal-Mart, in turn, started using the White Cloud trademark in competition with P&G's Charmin. As P&G executive Tom Muccio later commented: "The beauty about White Cloud for Wal-Mart was that we had built that Mercedes image and they brought it in at Chevy prices."[15]

Trademarks and the Internet

The emergence of the Internet and its unprecedented expansion led to new complications for the ownership and protection of trademarks. While trademarks are used in a variety of ways on the Internet, mirroring their use in non-Internet commerce, a primary area of concern was related to domain name registration.[16] A private company, Network Solutions Incorporated (NSI), began registering domain names in the United States under an exclusive contract with the National Science Foundation in 1993.[17] Names were registered on a first-come, first-served basis with no checking of trademark status or violations. In fact, NSI took the position that it was not responsible for trademark disputes, which it expected would be resolved between the parties through normal legal channels.

However, there are several significant problems associated with the Internet and trademarks. A trademark such as "Apple" can be famous in a number of different lines of commerce. For instance, it is the trademark of Apple Computer but also of Apple Records, the Apple Club, the Apple Bank, Fiona Apple, and the American Professional Partnership for Lithuanian Education (APPLE), to name just a few. The obvious question is who should have right to the domain name www.apple.com? There is no easy way to map a similar trademark associated with different lines of commerce with a single domain name reflecting that trademark. This technical limitation led to a second problem known as cyber-squatting.

Cybersquatting is the registering, selling, or using of a domain name with the intent of profiting from the goodwill of someone else's trademark. For a while, the practice was rampant.[18] Early disputes related to trademarks used as domain names were typically settled privately or through arbitration and often involved the payment of "ransom" to obtain the domain name. One of the first disputes resolved through arbitration involved the Princeton Review Management Corporation and Stanley H. Kaplan Educational Center, Ltd., two well-known test preparation firms and fierce competitors. Princeton Review registered the domain name kaplan.com. Potential customers visiting kaplan.com would be welcomed to the Princeton Review. Web users would be asked to contribute to a list of complaints against Kaplan, evidently for the purpose of taunting and belittling Kaplan.[19] Kaplan sued Princeton Review for trademark infringement and eventually gained rights to the kaplan.com domain name. Under the provisions of the 1999 Anti-cybersquatting Consumer Protection Act (ACPA), a victim of cybersquatting in the United States can now sue or fight a cybersquatter using an international arbitration system.[20]

How Are Trademarks Valued?

Trademarks are typically valued for one of three purposes: (1) in the context of a licensing transaction or acquisition, including as part of a business acquisition; (2) for regulatory compliance, such as in transfer pricing; and (3) in the context of litigation. The economic principles behind the valuation remain essentially the same in each context. Next we discuss some of the commonly used valuation approaches, particularly in the context of trademark licensing.

Principles of Licensing

A license represents a transfer of certain rights to an asset from the licensor to the licensee. A licensing transaction occurs because both the licensor and the licensee expect future economic benefits from the transfer of rights. There are typically two primary channels for a trademark owner to exploit its intellectual property: (1) direct exploitation and (2) indirect exploitation. Direct exploitation allows the owner to retain the full bundle of intellectual property rights to an asset but also requires that the owner have the necessary resources to fully exploit the asset. For example, a regional manufacturer may be unable to meet the challenges of realizing expanded commercialization of its trademarked product. A university might have valuable trademarks that could be exploited by developing logo apparel, but it does not have the capability or the desire to get into apparel manufacturing. Faced with this issue, an alternative channel for an owner to exploit its property without putting additional capital at risk is to license it, that is, indirect exploitation. But licensing the technology may also come with risks. For example, the licensor faces the risk that the licensee may not adequately market a product or may not be able to fulfill its financial obligations to the licensor. Therefore, from a licensor's perspective, the decision to exploit the technology on its own or through licensing requires a careful assessment of the relative expected benefits and expected costs associated with each option.

A potential licensee would be willing to license a technology if it generates *incremental* economic benefits over alternative business opportunities available to the licensee. For instance, an apparel manufacturer might license a trademark if it allows the manufacturer to enter a new market, serve a larger market, or earn a higher return on investment. Like the licensor, the licensee also faces a number of risks associated with the licensing transaction. First and foremost, the licensee undertakes the risk of deploying capital to manufacture, distribute, and sell the licensed products. While the licensee's capital investment and fixed costs may be known, the success of the licensed product is not guaranteed. For instance, changes in the state of the economy or in industry circumstances might make the business model unsustainable.

In a licensing situation, a trademark holder (the licensor) effectively "rents" certain rights to the trademarked property to another party (the licensee). The rental payment in return for an agreed upon use of the intellectual property is referred to as a licensing or royalty payment. Generally, the licensor will not rent out all rights to a trademark but rather set out specific rights of use for the licensee. Some elements of the rights include the term of use, geographic territory, termination provisions, and trademark quality control. In addition, a trademark license may be bundled in a licensing agreement with other rights to intellectual property.

Royalty payments are generally determined through negotiation between the licensor and licensee and, as such, should represent a market-based outcome. The negotiated fee and royalty rate should reflect a *fair market value* for the asset to be transferred and should make both the licensor and the licensee better off. Fair market value is commonly defined as the amount at which an asset would change hands between a willing licensor and a willing licensee, neither being under any compulsion to buy or sell and both having reasonable knowledge of the facts.

Division of the economic benefits of an asset between a licensor and a licensee often entails a valuation analysis. There are three widely used approaches to valuing intellectual property, including trademarks: the *cost approach, market approach,* and *income approach*.[21] We consider each of these approaches next.

Cost Approach

The cost approach values assets based on the cost to create and develop the assets. The premise behind the cost approach is that no party involved in an arm's-length transaction would be willing to pay more to use the property than the cost to replace the property. In the context of patents, for instance, a potential licensee would not pay more to license a patent than the cost to design around the technology contributed by that patent. An alternative to designing around the technology would be to purchase the technology. Accordingly, a potential licensee would not pay more to license the technology than it would have to pay to purchase or create the technology.

Unlike patents, it may not be feasible to "design around" famous trademarks, that is, create comparable trademarks in any meaningful way. For instance, one cannot easily build characters comparable to Mickey Mouse, Elmo, or Dora by incurring the same costs as those required to build these trademarks. But the cost approach may be of value when the assets under consideration involve less famous trademarks where it is possible to develop comparable trademarks.

One possible starting point in applying the cost approach may be to collect information to estimate the cost to "rebuild" the trademark. This is often done by calculating the present value of the past costs incurred to build a comparable trademark. Examples of expenditures that might go into creating a trademark include concept development, trademark searches, consumer testing, package or logo design, and advertising and promotional campaigns.

In addition to the difficulty in "designing around" a famous trademark, the cost approach can have serious additional limitations. The backward-looking nature of the cost approach does not fully measure the economic benefit that may be derived from the trademark. For instance, two trademarks that cost approximately the same to create may have very different income streams associated with them. Nonetheless, the cost approach may still be useful in instances where a comparable trademark can be created and where the costs for such creation are known or can be estimated.

Market Approach

The market approach references a market with comparable transactions to determine the fair market value of an asset. The degree of reliance on comparable transactions depends on an assessment of the transactions to determine if they are sufficiently similar to provide an indication of the fair market value for the assets in question. Factors to consider include the nature of the assets being transferred, the industry and products involved, agreement terms, and other factors that may affect the agreed-on compensation.

The market approach is often helpful in determining the running royalty rates in specific licensing transactions based on similar transactions in the marketplace. As an example, suppose that you are an executive in the licensing department of a university and are considering a potential transaction with an apparel manufacturer to produce university logo apparel under license.[22] One approach would be to look for comparable transactions between other similarly situated universities and evaluate their licensing terms. Exhibit 18.4 presents publicly available data on comparable licensing terms for a selected sample of universities. From the table, one can determine that the average comparable royalty rates range from a low of 7.5 percent for Harvard University to a high of 15 percent for the University of Oregon. These royalty rates for comparable transactions provide both the licensor (the university) and the licensee (the apparel manufacturer) information of the "market" for university trademarks. The university can pick a rate in this range after further refining the set of comparables and use that rate as a basis for its much broader licensing program.

While the market approach can be extremely useful in valuing intellectual property for licensing purposes, finding comparable transactions can be tricky. First, by its very nature, intellectual property is somewhat unique. Any market approach analysis will likely require reasonable adjustments. Second, the details of many licensing transactions involving trademarks are not publicly available. However, the market approach can be quite useful in valuing trademarks in instances where such information is available and comparable transactions can be found.

| EXHIBIT 18.4 | MARKET APPROACH—SELECTED UNIVERSITY TRADEMARKS |

Licensor	Low Rate (%)	High Rate (%)	Summary of Terms
University of Oregon	8.0	15.0	Limited nonexclusive right to use selected university marks on licensed articles for a percent of net sales; guaranteed minimum royalty payment of $1,000 for apparel and $500 for other products
University of Arkansas	8.0	10.0	Limited nonexclusive right to use selected university marks on licensed articles for a percent of the wholesale cost; annual advance royalty guarantee of $200
Michigan State University	8.0	8.0	Limited nonexclusive right to use selected university marks on licensed articles for a percent of net sales, unspecified advance royalty fee required
Harvard University	7.5	7.5	Limited nonexclusive right to use selected university marks on licensed articles for a percent of the net sales price; annual advance royalty guarantee of $1,000

Source: Office of Trademark Management, University of Oregon; University of Arkansas, Business Affairs; University Licensing Programs, Michigan State University; Office for Technology and Trademark Licensing, Harvard University.

Income Approach

The income approach is a method used to value intellectual property assets based on the present value of the future income stream generated by an asset. There are three major inputs to the income approach: (1) expected future cash flows from the asset; (2) economic life of the asset; and (3) business risk associated with the realization of the cash flow stream. The key goal is to estimate the present value of incremental profits generated by the asset over its economic life, taking into account the risk associated with generating those profits. Once the present value of the incremental profits is determined, these profits are split in some manner between the licensor and licensee, typically in the form of a royalty.

Returning to the example we used earlier while discussing the market approach, consider how the university and the apparel manufacturer might negotiate the terms of a licensing transaction under the income approach. Exhibit 18.5 presents data on potential sales by the apparel manufacturer. Suppose that the terms of a potential license to produce logo apparel is for four years. The apparel manufacturer can produce either the licensed logo apparel or its own "house brand" apparel (its next best alternative). The logo apparel is likely to command a price premium over the house brand apparel (e.g., say, $18.20 for the logo apparel versus $14 per unit for the house brand). Furthermore, the logo apparel is likely to result in greater sales as well. The exhibit provides data on unit sales, prices, sales revenue, and costs to the apparel manufacturer under each option.

Based on the data in Exhibit 18.5, we can calculate the *incremental* profits attributable to the university trademark for each year. Incremental profits are simply the additional profits generated by the logo apparel versus the house brand. Since these profits are estimated for future years, we need to adjust for the time value of money. In addition, there is some risk associated with the revenue streams for future years, so we need to discount those future cash flows as well. A discount rate is usually used to account for both the time value of money and the risk associated with cash flows. For the purposes of our example, we use a discount rate of 10 percent. Using the discount rate, we calculate the net present value (NPV) of sales and NPV of the incremental profits. The NPV of incremental profits as a percent of the NPV of sales provides the *maximum* royalty (21 percent in this case) that a potential licensee would be willing to pay to license the trademark. In all likelihood, however, a licensee would expect to pay something less than the expected NPV, so as not to remit all of its expected profits to the licensor. Thus, in actual licensing transactions, the licensor and licensee would negotiate within this range of 0 to 21 percent. Alternatively, the licensee could seek to evaluate whether the incremental profit *after* paying a royalty to the licensor provides sufficient return to justify licensing. Thus in the current example, even if the university sets a royalty rate of 10 percent to license its logo, the licensee would earn 11 percent in incremental profit. The licensee must decide whether this option makes sense in light of other opportunities it might have.

CONCLUSION

A trademark can be defined as a distinctive word, phrase, name, or symbol that is used in commerce to indicate the source of a good or service and to distinguish it from the goods

EXHIBIT 18.5	DISCOUNTED CASH FLOW MODEL

Sales of University Logo Apparel

	2006	2007	2008	2009
Unit Sales	6,710	6,820	6,963	7,095
Price per Unit	$18.20	$18.20	$18.20	$18.20
Sales Revenue	$122,122	$124,124	$126,727	$129,129
Costs per Unit	$9.80	$9.80	$9.80	$9.80
Total Costs	$65,758	$66,836	$68,237	$69,531
Operating Profits (A)	$56,364	$57,288	$58,489	$59,598

Sales of House Brand Apparel

	2006	2007	2008	2009
Unit Sales	6,100	6,200	6,330	6,450
Price per Unit	$14.00	$14.00	$14.00	$14.00
Sales Revenue	$85,400	$86,800	$88,620	$90,300
Costs per Unit	$9.00	$9.00	$9.00	$9.00
Total Costs	$54,900	$55,800	$56,970	$58,050
Operating Profits (B)	$30,500	$31,000	$31,650	$32,250
Incremental Profit Attributable to Trademark (A − B):	$25,864	$26,288	$26,839	$27,348
NPV of Sales:	$116,439	$107,589	$99,859	$92,502
NPV of Incremental Profit:	$24,660	$22,786	$21,149	$19,591
NPV of Incremental Profits as Percent of NPV of Sales:	21%			

or services of others. Trademarks serve important business and economic purposes and are often valuable business assets whose worth merits protection. A trademark's worth may be evaluated for a number of purposes, including in the context of licensing, acquisition, regulation, or litigation. The three most common valuation techniques for trademarks are the income approach, the market approach, and the cost approach. While the income and market approaches are generally the most appropriate in the context of valuing trademarks, use of any one of the techniques may depend on the information available and the particular circumstances of the valuation.

NOTES

1. The opinions expressed in this chapter are those of the authors. The information contained in this chapter does not constitute legal advice, and you should consult with your own legal counsel regarding trademark and other intellectual property law.

2. Lechter (2002), p. 152.

3. *See, e.g.,* Smith and Parr (2005), p. 38.

4. Belson (1999), § 13.1–13.2.

5. For a discussion of trade names in the State of Florida, *see* Beckman (2003).

6. *Merriam-Webster, Inc. v. Random House, Inc.,* 35 F.3d 65 (2nd Cir. 1994).

7. It is not clear to us that Interbrand Corporation's methodology properly disaggregates all of the relevant intangibles.

8. Daniel (1999), §§ 15.2–15.3.

9. "International Treaties," International Trademark Association.

10. 15 U.S.C § 1114(1)(a), (1995).

11. Daniel (1999), §§ 15.2–15.3.

12. Small and McKay (2002), pp. 173–176.

13. Smith (1997), p. 49.

14. *Major League Baseball Properties, Inc. v. Sed Non Olet Denarius, Ltd.,* 817 F. Supp. 1103 (S.D.N.Y. 1993).

15. Ellison, Zimmerman, and Forelle (2005), p. A1.

16. A domain name is a computer "address" for a reserved site where one's presence located on a computer linked to the Internet can be found.

17. Meadows (1997), p. 6.

18. Small and McKay (2002), pp. 173–176.

19. Brunel (1996), Chapter 3.

20. The Internet Corporation for Assigned Names and Numbers (ICANN) was established in 1998 by the U.S. government to act as the new technical coordinating body for the Internet. ICANN was designed to alleviate many of the problems confronting NCI with respect to trademark disputes. *See, e.g.,* Girasa and Girasa (2002), pp. 224–225.

21. Smith and Parr (2000), pp. 163–173.

22. Trademark licensing and merchandising is big business for universities. University-related logo retail market was estimated at about $3 billion in 2003. *See* Zaslow (2003).

References

"National Advertisers Ranked 1 to 50." *Advertising Age,* June 27, 2005.

Belson, Jeffrey. "Certification Marks in the Competitive Commercial Environment." In *Intellectual Property in the Global Marketplace: Volume 1, Electronic Commerce, Valuation, and Protection,* ed. Melvin Simensky, Lanning G. Bryer, and Neil J. Wiklof, 2nd ed. (New York: John Wiley & Sons, 1999).

Brunel, André. "Trademark Protection for Internet Domain Names." In *The Internet and Business: A Lawyer's Guide to the Emerging Legal Issues* (Wakefield, MA : Computer Law Association, 1996).

Daniel, Al J. Jr. "Imperative Strategies for Protecting Intangible Assets: The U.S. Market." In *Intellectual Property in the Global Marketplace: Volume 1, Electronic Commerce, Valuation, and Protection,* ed. Melvin Simensky, Lanning G. Bryer, and Neil J. Wiklof, 2nd ed. (New York: John Wiley & Sons, 1999).

Ellison, Sarah, Ann Zimmerman, and Charles Forelle. "P&G's Gillette Edge: The Playbook It Honed at Wal-Mart." *Wall Street Journal Online,* January 31, 2005.

Girasa, Rosaria J., and Roy J. Girasa. *Cyberlaw: National and International Perspectives* (Upper Saddle River, NJ: Prentice Hall, 2002).

"The 100 Top Brands." *BusinessWeek,* August 1, 2005.

"International Treaties." International Trademark Association, updated April 2005.

Lechter, Michael A. "Copyright, Software, and Web Site Issues in the Internet World." In *The Licensing Best Practices: The LESI Guide to Strategic Issues and Contemporary Realities,* ed. Robert Goldscheider (Hoboken, NJ: John Wiley & Sons, 2002).

Meadows, Joan. "Comment: Trademark Protection for Trademarks Used as Internet Domain Names," *University of Cincinnati Law Review* 65, no. 1323 (Summer 1997).

Small, Thomas M., and Kenneth D. McKay. "Trademarks, Trade Names, and Trade Dress." In *The Licensing Best Practices: The LESI Guide to Strategic Issues and Contemporary Realities,* ed. Robert Goldscheider (Hoboken, NJ: John Wiley & Sons, 2002).

Smith, Gordon V. *Trademark Valuation* (New York: John Wiley & Sons, 1997).

Smith, Gordon V., and Russell L. Parr. *Intellectual Property: Valuation, Exploitation, and Infringement Damages* (Hoboken, NJ: John Wiley & Sons, 2005).

Smith, Gordon V., and Russell L. Parr. *Valuation of Intellectual Property and Intangible Assets,* 3rd ed. (Hoboken, NJ: John Wiley & Sons, 2000).

Zaslow, Jeffrey. "Sports Fans Snap Up Souvenirs of Winners Beating Losers: Mascots Boiled or Grilled?" *Wall Street Journal,* November 12, 2003.

Index